Educational Policies and Practices of English-Speaking Refugee
Resettlement Countries

Transnational Migration and Education

Series Editors

Shibao Guo (*University of Calgary, Canada*)
Yan Guo (*University of Calgary, Canada*)

Editorial Board

Ali Abdi (*University of British Columbia, Canada*)
Mary V. Alfred (*Texas A&M University, USA*)
Vanessa de Oliveira Andreotti (*University of British Columbia, Canada*)
Gulbahar H. Beckett (*Iowa State University, USA*)
Yiping Chen (*Jinan University, China*)
Fred Dervin (*University of Helsinki, Finland*)
Allan Luke (*Queensland University of Technology, Australia*)
Linda Morrice (*University of Sussex, UK*)
Susan L. Robertson (*University of Cambridge, UK*)
Hongxia Shan (*University of British Columbia , Canada*)
Annette Sprung (*University of Graz, Austria*)

VOLUME 5

The titles published in this series are listed at *brill.com/tmae*

Educational Policies and Practices of English-Speaking Refugee Resettlement Countries

Edited by

Jody L. McBrien

BRILL
SENSE

LEIDEN | BOSTON

All chapters in this book have undergone peer review.

The Library of Congress Cataloging-in-Publication Data is available online at http://catalog.loc.gov

Typeface for the Latin, Greek, and Cyrillic scripts: "Brill". See and download: brill.com/brill-typeface.

ISSN 2542-9779
ISBN 978-90-04-40188-4 (paperback)
ISBN 978-90-04-40186-0 (hardback)
ISBN 978-90-04-40189-1 (e-book)

Copyright 2019 by Koninklijke Brill NV, Leiden, The Netherlands.
Koninklijke Brill NV incorporates the imprints Brill, Brill Hes & De Graaf, Brill Nijhoff, Brill Rodopi, Brill Sense, Hotei Publishing, mentis Verlag, Verlag Ferdinand Schöningh and Wilhelm Fink Verlag.
All rights reserved. No part of this publication may be reproduced, translated, stored in a retrieval system, or transmitted in any form or by any means, electronic, mechanical, photocopying, recording or otherwise, without prior written permission from the publisher.
Authorization to photocopy items for internal or personal use is granted by Koninklijke Brill NV provided that the appropriate fees are paid directly to The Copyright Clearance Center, 222 Rosewood Drive, Suite 910, Danvers, MA 01923, USA. Fees are subject to change.

This book is printed on acid-free paper and produced in a sustainable manner.

*To all refugees and to all who support their efforts
to rebuild their lives through education*

∴

Let us claim children as 'zones of peace.' In this way, humankind will finally declare that childhood is inviolate and that all children must be spared the pernicious effects of armed conflict. Let us take this opportunity to recapture our instinct to nourish and protect children. Let us transform our moral outrage into concrete action. Our children have a right to peace.

GRACA MACHEL, *Report to the UN Secretary-General on the impact of armed conflict on children*, August 26, 1996

Contents

Preface IX
Acknowledgements XI
List of Figures and Tables XII
Notes on Contributors XIII

Introduction 1
    Jody L. McBrien

PART 1
Australasia

1 Stop Labeling Me as Traumatised or as Mentally Unwell – I am a Resilient Survivor: A Discussion of the Pathologising Effects of Trauma Labelling for Former Refugees in Contrast to a Strengths-based Settlement Programme Model 17
    Maria Hayward

2 Education of Resettled Refugees in Christchurch, New Zealand 42
    Zhiyan Basharati and Lucia Dore

3 Refugee Student Transitions into Mainstream Australian Schooling: A Case Study Examining the Impact of Policies and Practices on Students' Everyday Realities 57
    Amanda Hiorth

4 Systemic Policy Barriers to Meaningful Participation of Students from Refugee and Asylum Seeking Backgrounds in Australian Higher Education: Neoliberal Settlement and Language Policies and (Deliberate?) Challenges for Meaningful Participation 88
    Caroline Lenette, Sally Baker and Asher Hirsch

PART 2
North America

5 Community Initiatives to Support Refugee Youth: A Canadian Perspective 113
    Jan Stewart

6 In the Era of Bans and Walls: The Integration of Education and
   Immigration Policy and the Success of Refugee Students 131
        *Asih Asikin-Garmager, Duhita Mahatmya, Leslie Ann Locke
        and Ain A. Grooms*

7 Utilising Digital Storytelling as a Way to Understand the Complexities of
   the Haitian Refugee Transmigration Experience 156
        Elizabeth Paulsen Tonogbanua

8 Expanding Educational Access to Create Self-Sufficiency: The
   Post-Secondary Educational Experiences of Resettled Refugees
   in Florida 177
        Tara Ross, Jody L. McBrien and Briana Byers

PART 3
Europe

9 Refugee Children and Young People in Ireland: Policies and Practices 199
        Merike Darmody and Samantha Arnold

10 Smoothing the Bumpy Road? An Examination of Some Targeted Initiatives
    for the Education of Refugee and Minority Ethnic Children and Young
    People in Ireland 220
        Rory Mc Daid

11 An Underclass of 'the Underclass'? Critically Assessing the Position of
    Children and Young Refugees in the UK Educational System during a Time
    of Austerity 240
        Helen Murphy

12 Schooling Displaced Syrian Students in Glasgow: Agents of Inclusion 267
        Melanie Baak

Conclusion 293
        Jody L. McBrien

Index 297

Preface

The idea for this book came to me soon after I'd spent eight months in New Zealand as an Ian Axford Fellow in Public Policy, working with the Ministry of Business, Innovation, and Employment (MBIE) and Ministry of Education (MOE) to analyse the country's new strategy for resettling refugees. I discovered many practices that I found far superior to my own country's policies (the US). I also became acquainted with Australia's practices, which I found more similar to those of the United States.

Given that the United States, Australia, and Canada, primarily English-speaking countries, resettle the largest number of refugees annually (even now, despite drastic US reductions in 2018), it seemed important to provide a volume of research that would allow scholars, policymakers, and those working with refugees to compare policies and practices for educating resettled refugees in these countries. As I have mentioned in some of my previous publications, education frequently falls at the end of the queue when it comes to resettlement, as agencies concentrate on the more immediate needs of housing and employment so that resettled families can begin to pay for their own life necessities. Education typically falls to school systems and individual teachers, most of whom receive little to no training on the journeys of refugees, nor on their needs and their capabilities.

Major educational challenges include the struggle to teach English to refugee populations with highly diverse backgrounds. They range from students with no prior school experiences to those who attended excellent schools prior to the collapse of their country's security, such as the case of Syria. Other important aspects for successful schooling include culturally appropriate psychosocial support, a sense of belonging, and filling in the gaps of content knowledge.

The chapters in this volume provide important information about what is working and on-going issues regarding the challenges in the English-speaking resettlement countries in Australasia (New Zealand and Australia), North America (Canada and the United States), and Europe (England, Scotland, and Ireland). By bringing together chapter authors who are experts in these countries' policies and practices, we hope to provide useful cross-cultural knowledge to those tasked with the critical job of educating refugees who long to rebuild lives from the ashes of tragedies.

As I write this preface, popular rhetoric throughout the world has moved from support to fear and angry rejection of refugees and asylum seekers by numerous political leaders and the general public. Such sentiments make the work of resettlement and acculturation that much more difficult for refugees and those who educate and otherwise support them. Yet, it is education, and not the immediate needs of housing and employment, that can provide long-term benefits, not only to the refugees themselves, but also to the nations into which they resettle. Positive support through education can provide resettled students with the ability to achieve professional careers, which will benefit communities and the national economy. Ultimately, it can provide those resettled with a commitment to their new nations.

On a personal note, I began my work with refugee resettlement and education shortly after the attack on the Twin Towers in New York City when I was a doctoral student at Emory University. Just a few miles from Emory was Clarkston, Georgia – a town that has been called 'the most diverse square mile in America.' It is the largest hub of resettlement in the south eastern United States aside from Miami, which primarily resettles Cuban and Haitian refugees and asylum seekers. I spent three years volunteering as an after-school tutor and working as a summer camp counsellor at an independent resettlement centre in Clarkston, where I met the adolescent girls who became participants in my dissertation study. Seventeen years later, I remain in touch with four of them. They are remarkable young women. Two have bachelor's degrees, and two have master's degrees. All became US citizens. They have successful careers in education, medicine, and architecture. One has taught in the United States, Cote d'Ivoire, the Czech Republic, and South Korea. Another was a research assistant at the Centre for Disease Control (CDC) and Vanderbilt University. Three are happily married. Their lives included a great deal of anguish, and they confronted (and continue to confront) prejudice and discrimination. However, because they also encountered generous teachers and agency support, they have ultimately triumphed in their new situations.

Refugees are not merely victims of terrible circumstances. They are highly resilient and capable individuals looking for the chance to contribute and grateful for safety. When welcomed, they become loyal residents of the nations that offer them refuge. The authors of this book offer their work as ways to improve the policies and practices of supporting these newcomers through education.

Acknowledgements

First, I offer my gratitude to the chapter authors of this book. I appreciate their research, their work and commitment to the ideals of the book. And I am grateful for their patience. As I have found in calling for chapters and editing the book, an edited book takes great commitment and time. Life happens. Authors fall ill; family members require support. Changes occur at authors' institutions that cause them to reprioritise their time. Inevitably, the time line for publication changes. All authors have been gracious to recognise these ebbs and flows in production.

Additionally, I would like to thank our publisher, Brill Sense, for supporting the production of our book. Special thanks to Evelien van der Veer, Marti Huetink, Jolanda Karada, and Shibao Guo for their initial help and support.

I am grateful to my institution, the University of South Florida, Sarasota-Manatee, for the numerous ways in which it has supported my work with resettled refugees over many years.

Finally, I thank my family for understanding the often-solitary life of an academic. Creating research publications adds up to many hundreds of hours in one's office with the need for quiet and privacy. My extroverted husband remains highly understanding of this process.

Figures and Tables

Figures

1.1 Strengths-based refugee-centred model.   27

3.1 Moo Dar Eh's future dream to become a piano teacher.   67

3.2 Moo Dar Eh feels mixed emotions at her upcoming transition.   70

3.3 Moo Dar Eh recalls her first weeks of high school.   72

3.4 Moo Dar Eh on the right with her friend at high school, six months post transition.   75

3.5 The three phases of transition.   77

5.1 Bioecological model.   118

6.1 The number of refugee arrivals in Iowa, 2006–2017.   137

6.2 SCSD student enrolment trends, 2006–2017.   140

9.1 Overview of trends of asylum seekers and refugees in Ireland, 2010–2015 (Office of the Refugee Applications Commissioner [now International Protection Office]; Reception and Integration Agency; Eurostat; Office of the Promotion of Migrant Integration; Tusla. Note: 2012 and 2015 based on December monthly report – no annual report available on website).   206

9.2 Age of minor residents in Direct Provision, 2016 (Reception and Integration Agency, 2016).   207

9.3 Separated children referred into State care, 2010–2016 (Social Work Team for Separated Children, 2017).   208

9.4 Type of language support provision.   211

Tables

3.1 The processes of transition.   68

3.2 A de-identified replica of Moo Dar Eh's two-week rotation timetable.   71

6.1 Demographic characteristics of Iowa and SCSD (2016–2017).   135

6.2 Top 5 largest groups resettled in Iowa, 2006–2017.   136

11.1 Synopsis of benefits of the UK Refugee Council SMILE Programme for child refugees and young people.   244

11.2 School and community recommendations from the Citizen's Panel (IEF & NICIE, 2010).   248

11.3 Laws pertaining to child refugee status in the UK (UK Home Office, 2017).   254

Notes on Contributors

Samantha Arnold
is an Adjunct Assistant Professor of Law at Trinity College Dublin. Samantha holds a Ph.D. from the School of Law, Trinity College Dublin and an LL.M. in European Refugee Law awarded by University College Cork. Her research interests include refugee and immigration law and policy and children's rights law.

Asih Asikin-Garmager
is a post-doctoral research scholar in the Centre for Evaluation and Assessment at the University of Iowa. She received her Ph.D. in Educational Policy and Leadership Studies from the University of Iowa. Her professional interests include program evaluation, including assessments of English Language Learning (ELL) program evaluation.

Melanie Baak
is a Research Fellow in the School of Education at the University of South Australia and the convenor of the Migration and Refugee Research Network (MARRNet). In 2017 she was an Australian Government Endeavour Research Fellow in the School of Education at the University of Glasgow. Her research and teaching interests broadly cover areas of equity and inclusion, particularly in schools, with a focus on refugee education and resettlement

Sally Baker
is a Lecturer in the School of Social Sciences and the education 'focal point' for the Forced Migration Research Network at The University of New South Wales. Sally's teaching and research interests centre on language, literacies, transition, and equity in higher education, particularly with regards to culturally and linguistically diverse students, and refugee students in particular. Sally's recent co-written book, *Refugees in Higher Education: Debate, Discourse, and Practice*, is published with Emerald.

Zhiyan Basharati
is a former Kurdish refugee who came to New Zealand 17 years ago as part of the New Zealand refugee quota system. She completed a Doctor of Philosophy in Forensic Psychology at the University of Canterbury. Zhiyan is the Spokesperson & Health Coordinator for Canterbury Refugee Resettlement & Resource Centre (CRRRC). She has served in the community under a number of roles, including Founder & Advisor of the New Zealand National Refugee Youth Council (NZNRYC, National Youth NGO); Strengthening Refugee Voices (SRV)

National Advisory Group – Ministry of Business, Innovation and Employment (MBIE); Vice-Chair of Multicultural Strategy Working Party for Christchurch City Council (CCC); Member of Culturally and Linguistically Diverse Services Advisory Committee (CALD) for Specialist Mental Health Services (SMHS) at Hillmorton Hospital Canterbury District Health Board (CDHB); and Chairperson of Consumer Council for CDHB.

Briana Byers

is a graduate student at the University of South Florida. She is currently a full-time Academic Advisor at the University of South Florida. Her research interests include retention and persistence of at-risk undergraduate student populations including refugees.

Merike Darmody

is a Research Officer at the Economic and Social Research Institute and an Assistant Professor at Trinity College Dublin, Republic of Ireland. While working mainly in the area of education, she is also interested in broader issues of the relationship between the individual and society. Much of her recent work has focussed on diversity and migration in education.

Lucia Dore

has been a financial journalist/editor in the UK and Middle East as well as in Asia/Pacific. She was head of a news wire service in the Middle East and has produced a documentary on refugees, entitled *Stepping Up: NZ's Response to the Refugee Crisis*. Previously, she was an economist at the New Zealand Treasury.

Ain A. Grooms

is an Assistant Professor in the Educational Policy and Leadership Studies Department at the University of Iowa, USA. Her research focuses on access to educational opportunity, and uses the intersection of race, class, and place to examine the impact of historical and contemporary policies on the achievement of students of colour. Dr. Grooms previously served as an educational policy analyst in Atlanta, a college advisor at a youth development organization in East Harlem, New York City, and a founding administrator of a college preparatory charter high school in Boston. She received her Ph.D. in Education Administration and Policy from the University of Georgia.

Maria Hayward

is a senior lecturer at The Auckland University of Technology, New Zealand. She leads the education team at the Mangere Refugee Centre. She has worked in the field of refugee education for over 20 years. Her research involves the education of newly arrived refugees, resettlement issues, and refugee education.

Amanda Hiorth
is a language educator at the University of Melbourne Graduate School of Education. She has with keen interests in second language learning theory, plurilingualism, and humanist language teaching approaches. Amanda's work focuses on highlighting issues of social equity and improving educational experiences and outcomes for refugee-background students in the Australian mainstream education system.

Asher Hirsch
is a Senior Policy Officer at the Refugee Council of Australia, the national umbrella body for refugees and the organisations and individuals who support them. His work involves research, policy development, and advocacy on national issues impacting refugee communities and people seeking asylum. Asher is also completing a Ph.D. at Monash University in refugee and human rights law.

Caroline Lenette
is Senior Lecturer in the School of Social Sciences, University of New South Wales, Sydney, Australia. She is the arts-based research 'focal point' of the interdisciplinary Forced Migration Research Network. Over the past ten years, Caroline has used arts-based methods in social-justice focused research in collaboration with co-researchers with lived experiences as refugees and asylum seekers. Together, they have explored stories of wellbeing and settlement, especially from women's perspectives. Caroline's research explores how storytelling can influence decision-makers towards meaningful change, and the ethical considerations of collaborative, arts-based research. Her book, *Sanctuary: Arts-based Methods in Refugee Research,* will be published with Springer in 2019.

Leslie Ann Locke
is an assistant professor of Educational Policy and Leadership Studies at the University of Iowa. She received her Ph.D. from Texas A&M University in 2011. Her research interests include leadership for social justice, schooling for students from marginalised groups, equity-oriented education policy, and qualitative methodologies.

Duhita Mahatmya
received her B.Sc. in Psychology from Drake University and her M.Sc. and Ph.D. in Human Development and Family Studies from Iowa State University. She

is currently an Assistant Research Scientist in the College of Education at the University of Iowa. Her research examines how family, school, and community environments shape academic and social-emotional development from early childhood to young adulthood.

Jody McBrien

is a Professor at the University of South Florida, teaching courses in human migration, international human rights, and comparative and international education. She has conducted research on all three aspects of what the UN labels 'durable solutions' for refugees (voluntary repatriation, local integration, and resettlement) in the US, Canada, Ghana, Uganda, New Zealand, Australia, Japan, and Greece. She was an Ian Axford Fellow in Public Policy in 2014 and a Visiting Professor/Researcher at Soka University, Tokyo, in 2017. She was recently awarded a Fulbright Specialist Award.

Rory Mc Daid

is a lecturer in Sociology of Education and Research Methods in Marino Institute of Education, Dublin, Ireland. He is assistant co-ordinator of Lóchrann, the centre for intercultural education at MIE. Dr Mc Daid is a Visiting Research Fellow at the Cultures, Academic Values and Education research centre in the School of Education, Trinity College, Dublin. His research interests include the experiences of immigrant children and teachers in schools and education for refugee and asylum seeking children and young people.

Helen Murphy

is a critical social psychologist working at the University of East London and has been writing and producing research papers on the psychological health and wellbeing of individuals, groups and communities. Originally from Northern Ireland, Helen is now part and parcel of the great London metropolis and has seen her country and homeland change in the face of Brexit and austerity in the UK since 2008. The chapter is positioned within this socio-economic context.

Tara Ross

has a background in politics and policy with an emphasis on research of vulnerable populations. Her master's degree is in International Affairs from Ohio University, where she studied Latin American politics and spent several years researching social programs in Nicaragua after the war. Her Ph.D. is in Educational Leadership from Keiser University where she studied higher education for resettled refugees. Dr. Ross is an experienced leader in higher education, having worked in a variety of university settings for 18 years. She has provided operational support for non-governmental organizations working with refugees in Africa, Asia, and the Middle East.

Jan Stewart

is Deputy Provost and Associate Vice-President, Academic at The University of Winnipeg and Acting Executive Director of The Global College. Jan was the lead investigator of a three-year national research program funded by SSHRC, CERIC, and Mitacs to examine promising practices for supporting refugee and newcomer youth. She is the lead investigator of a provincially-funded research program exploring the mental health needs and challenges for refugee youth and a SSHRC funded study on the settlement, education and psychosocial needs of Syrian refugees in Canada. Jan recently completed the Harvard Medical School Certificate in Global Mental Health: Trauma and Recovery.

Elizabeth Paulsen Tonogbanua

received her doctorate in education from the University of Massachusetts Boston's Urban Education, Leadership, and Policy Studies' program. Her dissertation, *Transmigration Experiences of Newcomers in the Context of an English-only Education: Sense-making by Former Newcomer ELLs*, won the Alumni Award for Dissertation Research from the Department of Leadership in Education in 2015. She also earned a Post-MA from New York University's Multicultural Multilingual Studies program in Teaching English to Speakers of Other Languages.

Introduction

Jody L. McBrien

The year 2019 is a fortuitous time to publish a book about education for refugees resettled to English-language nations. Record numbers of refugees since 2014 have been the subject of international political debates, with ardent supporters and opponents in host Western countries as well as political agreements to send refugees back to countries with poor economic means, such as Turkey and Greece (Amnesty International, 2017; BBC, 2017; Bluemel, 2017; Karakoulaki, 2018). Although refugees are being politicised and frequently maligned as people seeking better economic opportunities or even people aligned with terrorist organisations, the stories of the majority – families fleeing from life-threatening situations in their homelands –receive insufficient attention or are problematically expressed, as responses to their stories are often met with angry nativist sentiments and beliefs that resettled refugees will create an environment of chaos (Ghani, 2018; Woolsey, 2018). Some governmental reactions have created situations of profound mental health disorders, such as increasing youth despair and suicidal attempts on the island of Nauru, a primary site for those seeking asylum in Australia (Amin & Kwai, 2018).

Historically, English-speaking countries have provided the most opportunities to permanently resettle refugees who have not been able to either return to their home countries or begin new lives in the countries to which they originally fled. The United States had long been a front-runner, especially since the Refugee Act of 1980. Between the signing of that act and prior to the 2016 presidential election, the United States resettled an average of 75,000 refugees annually. The Trump administration has reduced the annual intake to an all-time low. According to Pew Research, the United States decreased resettlement more than any other country in 2017 (Connor & Krogstad, 2018). The 2018 ceiling was placed at 45,00, but only 24,000 refugees were actually admitted. The 2019 ceiling is even lower, at 30,000. Ireland and Great Britain have always had relatively low entry numbers, and Great Britain does not assure full resettlement, as it retains the right to deport refugees. Australia's policies, particularly regarding asylum seekers, have been stringent; and human rights groups have asserted that the policies rank high in human rights violations (Human Rights Watch, 2018; The Guardian, 2018). Canadian levels in 2017 were below its numbers between 2000–2015 by about 100 (Canadian Council for Refugees, 2017). However, in 2018, for the first time, Canada surpassed the United States in numbers resettled, at 28,000 (Markusoff, 2019). New Zealand

© KONINKLIJKE BRILL NV, LEIDEN, 2019 | DOI: 10.1163/9789004401891_014

announced an increase in its resettlement programme from 750 to 1,000 in 2019 and 1,500 in 2020 (Global Legal Monitor, 2016).

Given the high levels of worldwide refugees, a growing number of scholars have examined ways in which to help refugees resettle and acculturate into other nations when they are unable to return to their homelands. To date, the UNHCR has determined three durable situations for refugees. The first and preferred solution involves voluntary repatriation, a return to one's homeland. Most refugees fitting within the UN definition of a refugee flee because they must, not because they want to. As a result, they are only able to return to their homeland if the country reaches a re-stabilised government and other political conditions that would render the refugees free from harm. The second solution is local integration, in which refugees can establish themselves as residents in the country to which they first fled. These countries must be willing to grant the refugees access to a livelihood, housing, permanent residence, and education.

The third, and least likely solution is third country resettlement. Currently, less than 1% of the world's 68.5 million refugees receive this opportunity. The number of resettlement countries has grown, from 14 in 2005 to 37 in 2016 (UNHCR, 2016). Still, the need far exceeds the opportunities.

Regarding countries that do offer resettlement most prioritise adult needs, as the adults will be responsible for taking care of their children. Thus, essentials such as housing, food, health, and employment upend concerns for appropriate educational supports for refugee children. Many refugee organisations hand over the responsibility for the children to school districts once they have helped to enrol them. Unfortunately, neither most schools nor university teacher training programmes offer instruction regarding the special needs of refugee children. This lack often results in problematic interactions between the refugee children, their teachers, and their peers. In my own research observations, I have witnessed a refugee student overwhelmed by a routine fire drill (given no prior notice, the student was traumatised by what reminded her of war blasts), a Bosnian refugee girl told by a guidance counsellor to aim for vocational training (she has since won numerous academic awards, received a master's degree, and taught in three countries), and a Muslim student failed by a physical education teacher for not wearing the gym uniform of shorts and a short-sleeved shirt. She received a four-year scholarship to a women's college, interned at the Centre for Disease Control (CDC), received a medical master's degree, worked as a researcher at Vanderbilt University, and is currently an adjunct faculty member at a university in North Carolina.

The examples I provide above are, sadly, exceptions. Poor teacher training can result in tragic life outcomes for resettled refugee students. The documentary *Rain in a Dry Land* (Makepeace, 2006) depicts a highly enthusiastic refugee boy who wants to enter the medical profession. Lack of support from his

INTRODUCTION

US teachers causes him to drop out of high school. Much research indicates significant challenges faced by resettled refugee students who receive insufficient guidance and support (Anders & Lester, 2015; Bonet, 2018).

Aside from psychological challenges, the primary need of both refugees and other immigrants is that of learning English. In the United States, only Florida and California require teacher candidates to be certified in teaching English to speakers of other languages, and that only because law suits were brought against the states. Most countries do not have requirements for teachers to know how to help students whose first languages are not the language of the country in which they live. Given that many refugee and other immigrant children state that their language teachers are the ones who they connect with the most, it is problematic that most teachers cannot make such connections.

This volume examines educational opportunities and challenges in each of the English-speaking countries of resettlement. It is divided into geographical regions – Australasia, North America, and Europe. Interestingly, these designations do not necessarily indicate regional similarities for supporting refugee education. For example, there are considerable differences between Australia and New Zealand's efforts to resettle refugees; and Australia's policies may be more similar to those of the United States. Authors of each chapter have considered country policies and attempts to support refugee children as well as challenges presented by political and educational frameworks. This book offers voices of both new and established scholars' contributions based on their work in the field.

Part 1: Australasia

Maria Hayward describes the need for a strength-based rather than a pathologising perspective. She illustrates problems associated with some therapy and medical approaches; among them, passive responses in which former refugees come to see themselves as victims. In the review of past research, she points out that refugees themselves want help that allows them to return to normal living conditions. Such approaches focus on language acquisition and stable employment and housing.

Hayward sees educational spaces as places to create a positive approach. As the Director of Education at the Mangere Refugee Resettlement Centre in New Zealand, Hayward focuses teacher training on the resilience of refugees to survive traumatic events rather than as needy victims. Through this approach, she stated that 'staff preferred to identify and describe refugee-background learners (RBLS) as survivors rather than victims, as strengthened rather than damaged by their life experiences, as empowered individuals as opposed to passive respondents or victims, and, importantly, as assets to the new community.' In her role as director, Hayward takes a constructivist approach building from learners' prior knowledge and skills. She also views self-directed activities, problem solving, and choices of the students as important elements of acculturation.

The environment and curriculum at the Mangere Centre has been carefully constructed to offer numerous supports and safety. For instance, cultures and languages of the former refugees appear on wall displays and in materials. Instructors hold meetings in which they can reflect on situations and ways to handle them in supportive and welcoming ways. Physical safety is examined, and all staff are trained to understand that newcomers may be unfamiliar with some Western appliances and procedures. They are also trained to recognise potential stressors such as sudden loud noises or shouting. Predictable routines contribute to providing a sense of stability.

Zhiyan Basharati and Lucia Dore conducted research on the Hagley College Homework and Support Centre in Christchurch, New Zealand. Similar to Hayward, their mixed methods research found that the education centre provides positive qualities, such as resilience, life-saving skills, and hope. The authors also note the importance of English language learning, as included in the New Zealand Resettlement Strategy (2013), for resettled refugees to obtain higher wage jobs and tertiary education.

Basharati and Dore reflect on how much of the literature concentrates on trauma, loss, and marginalisation. Their study cites government documents that recognise the importance of education to overcome and move beyond such tragedies. The majority of students utilising the Hagley College Homework and Support Centre found it helpful for their studies, passage of standardised New Zealand tests, and movement into higher education. However, there were also comments about a lack of access to teachers and computers. Although the centre is helpful, it is not sufficient in meeting the students' needs.

Amanda Hiorth's research investigates Karen refugee-background adolescents and educational transitioning from English language schools (ELS) to mainstream education in Australia. Her ethnographic study examines Victoria's policies to recognise and provide for multicultural, multilingual students (while also noting their 'disadvantages'). Hiorth notes that time provided at English language schools is insufficient for catching up in academic English proficiency. Additionally, refugee background students are frequently conflated within categories including other English language learners; thus, specific needs and teacher training about refugees are inadequate.

Hiorth describes research that calls for more comprehensive services that would include school and national cultural lessons, parent involvement, teacher training, and transitional support. She recognises the notion of care

INTRODUCTION

as a critically responsive pedagogy. She points to Cummins' (2000) framework of relations in power theory caring and collaborative work between students and teachers. Problems included transitional processes that happened 'to' refugees, not 'with' them. Social aspects of transition (care) are important in the resettlement of refugees: 'Human connection is at the heart of learning.' Stakeholders seemed unaware of this important aspect, as there is a general lack of knowledge about various steps in transition. Hiorth suggests increased information to policy makers and increased funding to provide more time in ELS and bridging programs as two examples.

Caroline Lenette, Sally Baker, and Asher Hirsch describe systemic policy barriers to refugees and asylum-seeking students seeking higher education in Australia. The authors describe substantial differences in support between refugees designated as 'Offshore' and those seeking asylum ('Onshore' policies). The discrepancies between categories of refugees and asylum-seeking youth are seen as resulting in 'years of missed opportunities particularly for younger generations.'

The researchers note that only 1% of refugees have access to higher education, in comparison to 34% of students worldwide. This results in a major untapped potential of the world's youth. They find that inadequate language learning support is a major factor that disrupts refugees' and asylum seekers' ability to access higher education, particularly for those requesting asylum through the Onshore policy.

As is the case in the United States, so there are territorial differences in English language services in Australia, with areas having high concentrations of English language learners having more services than ELLs in rural areas. The researchers also note the problem of neoliberal policies that have narrowed the opportunities for newcomers to receive advanced language learning, resulting in fewer opportunities for skilled jobs and high wages.

Part 2: North America

Jan Stewart begins with the world statistics about numbers of children affected by refugee and resettlement experiences. She notes that teachers frequently describe their lack of preparation to assist these children, as it is not part of their teacher preparation or professional development training. These comments are reflected in other chapters regarding the lack of teacher preparation for teaching refugee and asylum-seeking children. Stewart suggests a critical need to create holistic support of community, family, and school systems as well as partnerships with community organizations and settlement services. She notes the need for resettlement communities and schools to recognise cultural diversity and ways in which 'expectations and methods of serving their populations may not be culturally appropriate for populations when considered in the context of diversity.'

Stewart utilises Bronfenbrenner's (1979) Bioecological Systems Theory to inform her research, which involves interactions between various levels of relationships in the child's life. Her study focuses on qualitative data from resettlement workers in Manitoba and their perceptions of best practices to support refugee students. This robust research includes interviews with over 300 participants: staff at service provider organizations, community members, teachers, students, school administrators, and school consultants. Results were used to develop youth advisory councils, professional development and training for teachers, a comprehensive support guide, and a conference for in-service teachers.

Stewart's research indicates a need for teachers to work with parents and to familiarise themselves with community support services. It suggests the importance of classroom welcoming. Extracurricular activities were found to increase positive adjustment. As such, there is a need for transportation and funding. Additionally, there is a need for mentors to refugee students regarding further education and career internships as well as career development programs. Stewart adds the importance of creating networks between refugees and Canadian-born neighbours.

Asih Asikin-Garmager, Duhita Mahatmya, Leslie Ann Locke, and Ain A. Grooms's study examines challenges to refugee children resettled in the US Midwestern state of Iowa. They found that the goals of the No Child Left Behind legislation (NCLB) for English Language Learners (ELLs) were not met. Additionally, there were problems assessing ELL groups. Self-contained 2-year classrooms faced problems of refugees not achieving acquisition of academic English. This is not surprising, given Cummin's (1979) research on the time it takes to become fluent in academic English (typically, 5–7 years). The researchers' study indicates the challenges of receiving sufficient funding in areas that are small and rural. They also note a problem that is common throughout the United States: the problem of requiring immigrant and refugee children to take standardised state tests a year after arrival.

Asikin et al. describe a history of refugee welcoming in Iowa and advocacy of ELL programmes for workforce development and students. The large meatpacking industry in the state has long been a draw to migrants who do not have advanced employment skills. In 2008, however, one of the largest US Immigration and Customs Enforcement (ICE) raids occurred in the city studied by the researchers, with nearly 400 arrested. The raid reduced the town's population by 20% and included the arrest of 18 juveniles. Post-raid

INTRODUCTION

problems included an increase in school absenteeism by students of Hispanic background due to fear and trauma.

The researchers found a need to address students' psychosocial needs. School administration and teachers recommended that communities and parents need to become important partners. Some schools hired second-language community people as translators. They also met with diverse community partners (such as Somalis). These changes supported teachers to learn about diverse cultures, religions, and languages. The researchers reflect on the role of schools to help their communities accept the diversity of newcomers.

Elizabeth Paulsen Tonogbanua's study explores 'how Haitian refugee English Language Learners (ELLs) in Boston Public Schools (BPS) made sense of their transmigration experiences through a digital storytelling project.' She created a digital storytelling project with Haitian newcomer students to capture their reflections about their adaptation and adjustment to the BPS academic environment.

Boston Public Schools statistics indicate a population of nearly 56,000 students: 42% Hispanic, 35% Black, 14% White, 9% Asian, and < 1% other. Students whose first language is not English represent 71 different languages. Most have been taught in an English-only setting since 2002. There is no district-wide policy to provide schools with information on how to welcome newcomers into their schools.

In her study of Haitian 'refugees' in the Boston Public School district, Tonogbanua states, 'If schools are to support the education of refugee students, they must take seriously their capacity to socialise, acculturate, accommodate, integrate, involve and care.' Her study extends the definition of refugees to include those who must move due to environmental damage. Though not a part of the 1951 Convention or 1967 Protocol, many experts are calling for an expansion of the definition (Berg, 2011; Brennan, 2003; McBrien, 2016; Millbank, 2000; Rohl, 2005).

Tonogbanua cites a challenge against Boston Public Schools, which indicated that it 'failed to properly identify and adequately serve thousands of ELLs as required by the Equal Education Opportunities Act of 1974 and Title VI of the Civil Rights Act of 1964' (as cited in Zehr, 2010). In order for ELLs to be successful in the United States, as maintained by the Justice Department and the Office for Civil Rights, they need ESL classes at the beginner and intermediate levels, and embedded ESL strategies used in instruction for advanced-level ELLs. Both federal agencies are working with the BPS to ensure that all ELLs have access to ESL classes. To meet this need, ESL-licensed teachers have been hired, and general educators within BPS have been offered trainings to ensure that their instructional strategies adhere to current best practices. Problematic practices resulted from Massachusetts embracing factually inaccurate 'English-only' policies based on the Unz campaign in California against bilingual education.

These resulted in many ELL students being placed into Special Education, suspended, retained, or choosing to drop out.

Tonogbanua states that the 2010 Haitian earthquake victims were resettled at a better time in Massachusetts's educational practices for supporting ELLs, in spite of on-going restrictive teaching policies. For example, many relocated into neighbourhoods with large populations of Haitians, providing psychosocial support. However, there remained multiple levels of discrimination. She cited examples of discrimination by African-Americans (Haitians are considered 'Black'), who did not accept these students; and by Haitians who had been in the United States longer and identified as Americans. Tonogbanua recommended needs for multiple levels of social integration support, including health and adolescent supports.

Tara Ross, Jody McBrien, and Briana Byers examine the challenges of higher education for refugees in the United States; specifically, in the state of Florida. Overall, they recognise that US refugee policies emphasise employment over education. This policy leads to a practice in which resettled refugees do not have adequate time to learn enough English to apply for well-paying jobs. Many of the refugees had prominent positions in their home countries, in fields such as education and medicine. Obstacles they face include re-certification in their fields, varying quality of English classes, and the ability to take such courses, due to US policy on self-sufficiency and the cost of childcare needed for parents taking such courses. The expectation by higher education institutions that applicants will produce proof of secondary school diplomas also discourages refugees from entering universities, as they frequently are not able to provide such paperwork. Finally, the cost of attending US institutions of higher learning is frequently prohibitive for resettled refugees.

In their qualitative study, the researchers found that participants believed in the power of education to provide a sense of belonging in their new country. They recognised a need for cultural adaptation to succeed. And they saw higher education as an opportunity to understand the diversity of cultures in the United States. When asked about important improvements that would facilitate educational success, participants suggested scaffolded learning, additional support so that they could learn English and national culture, improvements in the re-certification process, and support for building social networks to gain cultural capital.

Part 3: Europe

Merike Darmody and Samantha Arnold explore the unique history of Ireland's movement from a country of emigration to one of economic prosperity,

INTRODUCTION

causing it to be a country of immigration. They explain that by 2016, 'non-Irish nationals living in the country had reached 11 per cent' (CSO, 2017). They describe categories of refugees, which have different possibilities for resettlement:

1. Programme refugees resettled through UNHCR can gain free tertiary education after 3 years in country
2. Asylum-seeking 'Convention refugees' may come to be reunited with their families or arrive with their families to seek asylum. While they wait for their claims to be processed, they can access free primary and secondary education, but would have to pay for tertiary, typically at international rates. Many eventually receive a status of programme refugees and can receive free tertiary education; however, their years in Direct Provision do not count.
3. Unaccompanied minors. Those from Calais have Programme refugee status; most who are unaccompanied are prioritised in the asylum application process.

The authors acknowledge the need to recognise not only the children's vulnerabilities, but also their agency. They state that people in each of these categories have particular needs that may be overlooked in the largely 'mainstream' approach to education in Ireland. As examples, programme refugees may have had protracted stays in camps, with the result that their educational opportunities have been disadvantaged. Research on asylum-seeking children in Direct Provision indicates that this situation is detrimental to children's growth and development. Unaccompanied children are often not encouraged to apply for refugee status until they near the age of 18, making them more vulnerable to aging out of state protection (and losing the opportunity for free tertiary education). This, in spite of evidence that separated children are highly likely to succeed if given access. The fact that no national data are collected on separated children in Ireland, as 'The numbers of refugees and asylum seekers in Ireland are very small compared to the wider non-Irish population/demographic,' exacerbates their challenges, as their needs vary from other migrants due to their experiences with war, torture, and other violence.

Unfortunately, the Intercultural Education Strategy that worked towards inclusion and integration was disbanded as a result of austerity measures in recent years. Approaches to ELL strategies vary by schools and the numbers of ELL children in the schools. There are no specific governmental policies on supporting parent involvement of migrant/refugee children, so this is mainly dependent on individual schools. Teachers noted that parental lack of English contributed to low involvement.

Rory Mc Daid explores the challenges of refugee children living in Direct Provision in Ireland. He describes families' lack of choice (e.g., for the kinds of food that they eat, inadequate space and ability to invite other children to where they live, inadequate money for children's extracurricular activities, and lack of work for parents to provide role models for their children).

Mc Daid's work examines the challenge of a highly centralized Irish administration of primary and secondary schools, as it is largely supervised by religious organisations. In contrast, the Council of Europe recommends the ability of local education authorities (LEAs) to recognise what they need for their individual areas. He offers a comparison with a LEA model in England.

The primary purpose of this chapter is to provide an evaluation of the Migrant Access Programme in Dublin for 13–18 year-olds, incorporating numerous educational activities and geared towards supporting English language learning. Similar to New Zealand's English Language Learning Progressions, the framework concentrates on core competencies of speaking, reading, writing, and listening. Support is also provided to teachers.

Since 2008, the Integrate Ireland Language and Training (IILT) organisation has been closed due to lack of funding After that date, there have been no country-wide strategies to train teachers. This has resulted in additional disruption for adolescent migrants who must accelerate language skills for more advanced subject understanding, and who may have experienced long periods of disrupted education. Sheltered instruction can provide needed support.

Mc Daid also investigates a second project, the Schools' Cultural Mediation Programme, which concentrates on parental involvement. This programme developed a panel of 35 translators addressing 35 languages in the northern district of Dublin. The translators assisted with parent/teacher meetings, eliminating the need for children to take this role.

Helen Murphy's chapter argues that recent responses to refugees and asylum-seekers have been stringent in the UK. Most asylum cases are denied. However, a 2015 Vulnerable Persons Relocation (VPR) scheme was created to help resettle as many as 20,000 Syrians. The VPR scheme provides 'full refugee status for 5 years with full access to employment rights and access to public welfare funds.'

Refugee student experiences in the UK include the 'lack of availability of school places for refugee children and young people, transition issues in Year 11, and the reluctance of schools to take in pupils in the middle of term time' (Brownlees & Finch, 2010). Murphy argues that refugee children are viewed through their label rather than as children in need of education. She examines the Supporting and Mentoring in Learning and Education (SMILE) project set up by the UK Refugee Council and funded by the UK Department

INTRODUCTION

for Education in 2008 in Greater London, Yorkshire, and the Midlands. SMILE staff recognise 'the intensity of support that is needed for child refugees and young people in the education system to allow them to thrive and flourish.' However, many areas in the UK do not have this kind of program. UK studies elucidate the growing number of immigrant populations in recent years who need supportive programming. Murphy notes that there are other successful, though isolated programmes, such as the Belfast integrated school 'Citizens' Panel' in Northern Ireland, which gives voice to students at the school.

Murphy cites Morrice's (2009) study, which concludes that 'once refugees enter the UK higher education system, they are not treated as a special group of students with differing needs and are, therefore, not tracked, making their experiences and journey more difficult and complex.' Family support is noted as a need for integration and for unaccompanied asylum-seeking children (UK Department of Education and the Home Office, 2018). Unfortunately, various policies and laws that require safeguards and welfare for asylum-seeking children can cause them to feel frightened and criminal.

Increased child poverty in the UK since 2013 indicates that children and youth 'will be particularly vulnerable as a group to fare worst in this [current] context of austerity.' Numerous suggestions are offered to increase the opportunities for refugee children and youth.

Melanie Baak examines Syrian refugees relocated to Glasgow, Scotland. She notes the need to recognise actions of 'agents of inclusion' to replicate positive methods of support. Scotland's deliberate choice to support refugees and asylum seekers and strategies have resulted in positive responses of Scottish persons regarding resettlement, as compared to the UK in general and Europe as a whole.

Baak focuses on inclusive research that includes those with disabilities. She includes Australian literature and practice for comparative perspectives. Her research sees researchers as change agents through their ability to challenge systemic inequality. Baak argues for the need for multiple actors to facilitate inclusion – school leaders, teachers, staff, students, and families. Her qualitative work includes interviews with educational staff and Syrian parents. As is common with other studies in this book, she found challenges based on refugees' lack of English language knowledge and teachers' lack of training on working with refugee students.

As recommendations to facilitate improvement, Baak suggests an increase in teachers' home visits to create a better understanding of refugee families' cultures and needs and to create trust. She finds that these visits strengthen feelings of inclusion in refugee families – 'Oh, someone cares.' Baak notes an example of a teacher recognising the academic ability of a Syrian boy and wonders why more teachers do not recognise such talent or work harder to support the talents of refugee students. She recognises the additional burden placed on English as an Additional Language (EAL) teachers in Scotland (much the same as on English language teachers in other countries). She also explains that when a teacher chooses to learn some basic phrases in a language which is the first language for some of her students, such as Arabic, she models the language learning process, offers connection, and allows these students to be the experts in her language acquisition. Beyond the teaching staff, Baak indicates that including EAL staff in the enrolment process creates a more welcoming practice, as do small, everyday practices that create a welcoming school climate.

∴

In brief, themes echoed across continents and between new and accomplished researchers, indicate similar needs for particular practices in order to support resettled refugees to reach their full potential and to successfully integrate into their countries of resettlement. They need time to adequately learn both the language and the culture of their new nations. They need cultural and social support to appropriately navigate the structures of their countries of resettlement. Students need a network that includes not only themselves, but also advocates within their schools, ways to create friendships with local students, and networks that include their parents. Resettled refugees need policies that allow for them to make their own decisions about housing and other life provisions. Teachers require training to understand ways in which to support refugee students. Policy makers must examine policies that work against best practices of resettlement. Refugee resettlement should never be about improving a resettlement county's economic situation. It is, rather, a humanitarian response. However, when countries create educational and social policies that truly benefit refugees, the ultimate outcome is an overall increase in the host country's economic gains.

It is within this framework that we present our research on educational policies and practices in the six primarily English-speaking countries of refugee resettlement.

References

Amin, M., & Kwai, I. (2018, November 5). The Nauru experience: Zero tolerance immigration and suicidal children. *The New York Times.* Retrieved from https://www.nytimes.com/2018/11/05/world/australia/nauru-island-asylum-refugees-children-suicide.html?emc=edit_th_181108&nl=todaysheadlines&nl id=280623001108

INTRODUCTION

Amnesty International. (2017, September 22). *Greece: Court decisions pave way for first forcible returns of asylum-seekers under EU-Turkey deal.* Retrieved from https://www.amnesty.org/en/latest/news/2017/09/greece-court-decisions-pave-way-for-first-forcible-returns-of-asylum-seekers-under-eu-turkey-deal/

Anders, A. D., & Lester, J. N. (2015). Navigating authoritarian power in the United States: Families with refugee status and allegorical representation. *Cultural Studies/Critical Methodologies, 15*(3), 169–179.

BBC News. (2017). *Germany to resume sending migrants back to Greece.* Retrieved from https://www.bbc.com/news/world-europe-40850938

Berg, C. (2011, October 18). Why cling to an outdated refugee convention? *The Drum.* Retrieved from http://abc.net.au/news/2011-10-19/berg-why-are-we-clinging-to-an-outdated-refugee-convention/3577538

Bluemel, J. (Producer). (2018, January 23). Exodus: The journey continues. *PBS: Frontline.* Retrieved from https://www.pbs.org/wgbh/frontline/film/exodus-the-journey-continues/

Bonet, S. W. (2018). "So where are the promises of this America? Where is the democracy and where are the human rights?": Refugee youth, citizenship education, and exclusion from public schooling. *Curriculum Inquiry, 48*(1), 53–69.

Brennan, F. (2003). *Tampering with asylum: A universal humanitarian problem.* St. Lucia: University of Queensland Press.

Bronfenbrenner, U. (1979). *The ecology of human development: Experiments by nature and design.* Cambridge, MA: Harvard University Press.

Brownlees, L., & Finch, N. (2010). *Levelling the playing field: A UNICEF UK report into provision of services to unaccompanied or separated migrant children in three local authority areas in England.* UNICEF. Retrieved from http://lastradainternational.org/lsidocs/1012_levelling-playing-field_original.pdf

Canadian Council for Refugees. (2017). *2017 Immigration levels – comments.* Retrieved from http://ccrweb.ca/en/2017-immigration-levels-comments

Central Statistics Office (CSO). (2017). *Profile 7: Migration and diversity.* Retrieved from http://www.cso.ie

Connor, P., & Krogstad, P. M. (2018, July 5). For the first time, US resettled fewer refugees than the rest of the world. *Pew Research Center.* Retrieved from http://www.pewresearch.org/fact-tank/2018/07/05/for-the-first-time-u-s-resettles-fewer-refugees-than-the-rest-of-the-world/

Cummins, J. (1979). Cognitive/academic language proficiency, linguistic interdependence, the optimum age question and some other matters. *Working Papers on Bilingualism, 19*, 121–129.

Cummins, J. (2000). *Language, power and pedagogy: Bilingual children in the crossfire.* Clevedon: Multilingual Matters Ltd.

Ghani, F. (2018, August 13). How Islamophobia is driving anti-refugee sentiment in Korea. *Aljazeera.* Retrieved from https://www.aljazeera.com/indepth/features/islamophobia-driving-anti-refugee-sentiment-korea-180813062317079.html

Global Legal Monitor. (2016, June 15). *New Zealand: Annual refugee quota increased.* Retrieved from http://www.loc.gov/law/foreign-news/article/new-zealand-annual-refugee-quota-increased/

Human Rights Watch. (2018). *Australia: Events of 2017.* Retrieved from https://www.hrw.org/world-report/2018/country-chapters/australia

Karakoulaki, M. (2018, April 11). EU-Turkey deal: The burden on refugees in Greece. *Open Migration.* Retrieved from https://openmigration.org/en/analyses/eu-turkey-deal-the-burden-on-refugees-in-greece/

Makepeace, A. (2006). Rain in a dry land. *PBS POV.* Retrieved from https://www.youtube.com/watch?v=uZXaOY_7cIU

Markusoff, J. (2019, January 23). Canada now brings in more refugees than the U.S. *Macleans.* Retrieved from https://www.macleans.ca/news/canada/refugee-resettlement-canada/

McBrien, J. L. (2016). Refugees and asylum seekers. In A. Peterson, R. Hattam, M. Zembylas, & J. Arthur (Eds.), *The Palgrave international handbook of education for citizenship and social justice* (pp. 143–162). London: Palgrave MacMillan.

Millbank, A. (2000). *The problem with the 1951 Refugee convention, Parliament of Australia.* Research paper 5 2000-01. Retrieved from http://www.aph.gov.au/About_Parliament/Parliamentary_Departments/Parliamentary_Library/pubs/rp/rp0001/01RP05

Morrice, L. (2009). Journeys into higher education: The case of refugees in the UK. *Teaching in Higher Education, 14*(6), 661–672. Retrieved from https://doi.org/10.1080/13562510903315282

Rohl, K. (2005). *Fleeing violence and poverty: Non-refoulement obligations under the European Convention of Human Rights* (UNNHCR Working Paper No. 11). Retrieved from http://www.uhhcr.org/41f8ef4f2.pdf

The Guardian. (2018, March 2). *Scathing UN migration report mars Australia's first week on human rights council.* Retrieved from https://www.theguardian.com/australia-news/2018/mar/02/scathing-un-migration-report-not-ideal-start-to-australias-human-rights-council-tenure

UK Department of Education and the Home Office. (2018). *National transfer scheme protocol for unaccompanied asylum seeking children.* Retrieved from https://assets.publishing.service.gov.uk/government/uploads/system/uploads/attachment_data/file/750913/NTS-Protocol-Final-October-2018.pdf

UNHCR. (2016). *Information on refugee resettlement.* Retrieved from http://www.unhcr.org/en-us/information-on-unhcr-resettlement.html

Woolsey, B. (2018, January 20). German city bans new refugees as anti-migrant mood increases. *The Telegraph.* Retrieved from https://www.telegraph.co.uk/news/2018/01/20/german-city-bans-new-refugees-anti-migrant-mood-increases/

Zehr, M. A. (2010). Boston settles with federal officials in ELL probe. *Education Week, 30*(7), 10.

PART 1

Australasia

CHAPTER 1

Stop Labeling Me as Traumatised or as Mentally Unwell – I am a Resilient Survivor

A Discussion of the Pathologising Effects of Trauma Labelling for Former Refugees in Contrast to a Strengths-based Settlement Programme Model

Maria Hayward

Introduction

Sequelae of the refugee experience are typically listed as trauma, deprivation, loss, and post-traumatic stress. However, individuals have also overcome difficult circumstances; and in recent years, former refugees, service practitioners and academics have begun decrying the over-use of deficit terms and designations such as 'trauma' and 'Post-Traumatic Stress Disorder (PTSD).' This chapter firstly examines the academic literature that critiques these constructs and then presents alternative, strengths-based approaches for supporting refugee settlement and integration. Interventions which see refugees in asset rather than in deficit terms are discussed as is an innovative, strengths-focussed education programme employed by teaching staff at New Zealand's national refugee reception centre. The pedagogical model underpinning this programme includes elements designed to ensure newly-arrived refugee participants feel welcome, safe, empowered and self-confident, and that they are provided with the opportunity to develop trusting relationships, to plan for a new future, and to develop a range of settlement skills and competencies. These elements arguably have therapeutic qualities and could constitute an effective and appropriate pedagogic model for mitigating trauma effects for former refugees.

New Zealand is a signatory to the United Nations Convention on Refugees (1951) and is one of fewer than twenty nations internationally which have pledged to an annual refugee quota programme. As part of this commitment, 1,000 refugees are currently welcomed in groups of approximately 170 individuals per intake, to begin new lives in this country. Ethnic or national origins of recent arrivals to New Zealand include Syrian, Burmese, Columbian and Bhutanese, as well as smaller groups from Sri Lanka, Afghanistan, Central Africa and other Middle Eastern countries. All new-arrivals reside for six weeks at a reception centre in Auckland where they undergo physical and mental health screening whilst also attending an on-site education programme.

© KONINKLIJKE BRILL NV, LEIDEN, 2019 | DOI: 10.1163/9789004401891_001

This programme comprises language and settlement classes delivered by the Auckland University of Technology (AUT) Refugee Education Centre (REC). The latter section of this chapter describes a settlement education model (with particular reference to its piloted version at the REC), which, in counterpoint to the deficit (trauma-based) paradigms, derives its methodology from strenghts- and rights-based, ecological and post critical theories.

The chapter begins with a synopsis of the origin of Post-Traumatic Stress Disorder (PTSD) and refers to new research, which claims that a PTSD diagnosis can undermine positive progress and agency (personal control) for former refugees. Academic literature is cited which establishes grounds for alternative environments for healing opportunities and it is proposed that a well-designed education programme could possibly be one such environment. Arguably professionals often use the label 'traumatised' indiscriminately, and its overuse in refugee settlement contexts can reinforce deficit framing (Hughes & Pupavac, 2005; Marlowe, 2010; Rodriguez, 2015).

The relevance of trauma treatment for former refugees certainly is not denied, though some studies have found the Western models of treatment to be ineffective (Geltman, Augustyn, Barnett, Klass, & Groves, 2000; Munroe-Blum, Boyle, Offord, & Kates, 1989). This chapter suggests that non-pathologising therapeutic interventions in more 'normal' environments can achieve positive outcomes and may even be more accessible and undoubtedly less stigmatising for refugee-background individuals. To this end, an examination of alternative approaches is presented which focuses on resilience and acknowledgement of skills and strengths rather than on a pathological diagnosis (such as PTSD). Following this is a detailed description of the New Zealand (NZ) model and the key principles that comprise the strengths-based praxis at the Centre. The REC programmes, policies, and practices were developed using a refugee-centred focus underpinned by a set of values and guiding principles including an authentic welcome, respect, trust, rights, positive relationships, safety, inclusion, power-sharing, capacity-building, creativity, and compassion.

The template for this programme model intentionally excludes the words 'trauma' or 'mental health' in its descriptors; nevertheless, an understanding (by teachers) of typical refugee experiences and the co-related effects are critical to its refugee-centred design. The World Health Organisation (WHO) definition of mental health is 'a state of well-being in which every individual realizes his or her own potential, can cope with the normal stresses of life, can work productively and fruitfully, and is able to make a contribution to her or his community.' This chapter describes, in detail and with applied examples, the components of the REC programme, and it discusses how each feature provides therapeutic effects to aid good mental health, whilst concurrently

STOP LABELING ME AS TRAUMATISED

developing literacy and/or English language skills in conjunction with key settlement education.

The Trauma Debate

A discussion about the implications of a diagnosis of trauma or Post-Traumatic Stress Disorder (PTSD) is important for understanding the underpinnings of the aforementioned education model. PTSD was first given disease status by the American Psychiatric Association (1980) as a consequence of the lobbying movement in support of Vietnam War veterans. Since then a range of assumptions has been made about individuals affected by war trauma and as a result, a significant tranche of international funding has been dedicated to programmes in 'basic trauma alleviation' for survivors of war (Summerfield, 1999, p. 1451). Derek Summerfield, who has published prodigiously on trauma and the alleviation of its effects, claims that there is no 'working definition' of the word 'trauma' and the various definitions that do exist are 'indiscriminate and expansive,' so that almost all refugees find they have been given a PTSD diagnosis (Summerfield, 1999, p. 1459).

Following the clinical assessments, there is a tendency to tabulate findings, which naturally indicate high mental health needs among refugee communities, and this is what has provided a basis for claims for financial resources (Summerfield, 1999; Watters, 2001). More recent studies continue to show that mental illness rates among resettled refugees are higher than the general population (Mitschke, Praetorius, Kelly, Small, & Kim, 2017; Yanni, Naoum, Odeh, Han, Coleman, & Burke, 2013). However, placing a diagnosis of a psychological illness or a label of PTSD on a former refugee can be said to pathologise the person (Kerbage & Marranconi, 2017; Kim & Kim, 2014; Summerfield, 1999), and this is frequently accompanied by the conviction that either therapy treatment or medicalisation is needed (Pupavac, 2001, 2004; Summerfield, 2004). Furthermore, Marlowe (2018) and Pupavac (2004) both argue that the 'trauma' label has been politicised and can situate former refugees as victims and potential burdens on society because they are 'damaged … diseased, deviant, destitute and deserving' (Marlowe, p. 67). The latter association ('deserving') is often crucial for obtaining protection from the United Nations High Commission for Refugees (UNHCR) or entry into refugee camps, but in resettlement the negative framing can unfortunately provide excuses for negative stereotyping and prejudice and for governments wishing to reduce the number of settling refugees.

Summerfield has been joined by a growing cluster of academics who also question whether the best chance of recovery from trauma for refugees really is to cast them as victims and to have their resilience, resourcefulness, and rage ignored or minimalized (Bracken, Giller, & Summerfield, 1995; Thabet & Vostanis, 2000). Stubbs and Soroya (1996) contend that therapists benefit from this reductionist approach as it creates clients for their services. Indeed, Watters even claims that psychologists 'talk up numbers' in order to increase funding for their counselling services (2001, p. 1710). Pupavac holds a similarly sceptical stance and asserts that 'the mere description of a given community or population having experienced conflict is sufficient for international agencies to deem them to be suffering from post-traumatic stress disorder (PTSD) and in need of psycho-social assistance' (2001, p. 362). She cautions that 'a coercive rehabilitative aspect' can follow this determination, and this is in contradiction to the notion that self-determination and personal agency are generally considered pivotal to recovery (Pupavac, 2001, p. 361), especially when the client has previously lost power and autonomy. Such a diagnosis and subsequent treatment not only place the client in a role as 'victim', but also does not acknowledge the client's wishes or agency regarding the recovery process (Marlowe, 2010, 2018). The British Red Cross (RC) noted in their report on the Kosovo situation that: 'If one matches the needs expressed by refugees, host families and RC staff ... with what a PS (psycho-social) programme could provide, there is a relatively modest role for a PS programme' (1999). These studies and reports should, at the very least, convey a cautionary message regarding PTSD and other trauma diagnoses and treatments for resettling refugees.

In many countries, including New Zealand (cf. Immigration New Zealand website), newly arrived refugees undergo initial needs assessments to determine appropriate levels of support. The mental health assessments seek to establish whether the individual is psychologically unwell, and/or whether they have a 'disorder' (PTSD). Clinicians then tend to steer refugees towards counselling or medical 'cures' as they seek to fit the concerning symptoms into health parameters.

But former refugees themselves can feel stigmatised by this identification. Kerbage and Marranconi (2017) claim that their struggle becomes 'reduced to a list of symptoms out of their context' (p. 209). Watters confirms that former refugees generally do not perceive themselves as mentally unwell, but instead as suffering 'from (the effects of) ... social, political and economic circumstances' (2001, p. 1716), which diminish when the contexts change or merely over the course of time. Nevertheless, the assumption continues to be made in many countries that stress or distress need firstly to be measured, and then relieved with clinical therapy, possibly with medication as well.

In order to avoid the pathologising diagnoses, Watters' (2001) rather radically recommends that these needs assessments be administered not by medical and mental health staff, but by 'generic workers who do not exclusively inhabit realms of social or health care' (p. 1716). Perhaps teachers could even be included in this cohort of generic workers. Additionally, Watters suggests that intervention options in the first instance include practical activities such as help with welfare benefits, accommodation, health care etc, possibly also education and training. Other scholars further comment that 'clinic-based mental health services (for refugees) ... are not culturally well-matured to the world views of those they are intended to serve' (Miller & Rasco, 2004, p. 32) because psychotherapy and psychopharmacology stem from northern Europe and reflect 'western' thinking which lessens their effectiveness with former refugees (Bracken, Giller, & Summerfield, 1995; Lustig et al., 2004). Miller and Rasco posit that, 'it is simply outside of the scope of clinic-based mental health services to address these (displacement-related) stressors (in refugees) effectively' (p. 32).

Although formal mental health intervention (such as counselling therapy) is undeniably important for some individuals, the above findings and opinions in concert suggest that more emphasis should be placed on alternative solutions and, in particular, what refugees themselves declare that they need. Psychological or mental health issues are seldom stated by refugees as a major settlement stressor and this has been documented in various studies (Colic-Peisker & Tilbury, 2003; Marlowe, 2010; Muecke, 1992).

In a keynote address at the AUT Refugee Conference in 2003, Adam Awad, chairperson of the New Zealand National Refugee Network, reflected the perspective of many former refugees when he implored professionals to cease treating refugees as if they were mentally ill and suggested they should instead adopt more empowering stratagems that might provide support in 'building our confidence (so) we can deal with our own mental health issues in this new environment' (Awad, in Abbott & Nayar, 2011, p. 47). 'What we need,' he added, 'is for our supporters to listen carefully to us'; nevertheless, 'the mental health system in New Zealand we find ... to use a Māori term ... mess(es) with our mana.'[1] He added a further dimension when he opined: 'As we get stronger we discover, as have women, Māori, Pacific and others before us, that our "helpers" don't want us to stand on our own feet. They want to keep helping us' (Awad in Abbott & Nayar, 2011, p. 47).

Karpman (2014) labelled this type of co-dependent behaviour the 'Drama Triangle.' The triangle is created, he said, when the 'rescuer' and 'victim' interact in such a way that the victim is given permission to fail and therefore remains dependent on the rescuer. The potential reward derived for the rescuer is that they can ignore their own anxiety and issues. That is, their primary motivation is avoidance of their own problems, but this becomes disguised as concern for the victim's needs. The victims have their needs met because the rescuer appears to be taking care of them. Unfortunately, however, the individuals are not rescued at all, because they do not gain autonomy or the ability to move beyond their trauma.

Agger and Mimica (1996) also discuss dependency in therapeutic work and say that even a diagnosis such as PTSD can result in individuals remaining dependent (on medication or clinical therapy) and/or continuing to be victims. In order to avoid this, they prefer to describe 'symptoms of trauma' rather than using a disorder label and advise that services should do likewise and aim to not only alleviate the symptoms but also to build strength and enablement. The dependent victim outcome was indeed one of the reasons that some studies have found clinical psychological services for refugee survivors to be of limited value (Bisson & Deahl, 1994; Rose, Bisson, Churchill, & Wessely, 2002; Watters & Ingleby, 2004). Other studies describe the medicalisation process as disempowering for refugees (Fassin & Retchaman, 2009; Malkki, 1996).

Colic-Peisker and Tilbury (2003) conducted an interesting study, which corroborated the dependency triangle and the inconsequential effect of formal therapy for some individuals. They looked at the effects on settlement of two different 'healing' approaches: the medical/mental health versus inclusion (living and participating in the community without medical or therapeutic intervention) models. More than 200 people of various ethnicities were involved in the study. After a detailed analysis of data, the researchers categorised participants either as 'achievers and consumers', or as 'endurers and victims.' Their typology found that the health model, with its over-emphasis on trauma, created a tendency towards learned helplessness. One man, for example, after years of unemployment sought counselling, which he described as not really helping him but that it simply 'gave him something to do' (p. 77). This participant, when offered the opportunity to work, expressed he did not perceive himself capable of doing so. Another participant (p. 80) saw his 'mental health problem' as a reason *not* to seek work or join language classes, but instead to qualify for welfare payments and get public housing sooner. Some participants in the study 'made it clear that they used counselling services expecting that this would provide them with practical help' such as finding employment or helping with family reunion applications (p. 82). The authors of this study concluded that a medical or pathological approach contributed towards a 'passive' response in which former refugees felt and behaved like victims. However, where emphasis was placed on environmental factors such as being part of a welcoming community, or having suitable housing, as well as engagement in meaningful life experiences such as education or employment, respondents saw themselves as 'achievers or consumers.' The authors postulated that it might be more worthwhile to consider how programmes that offer skills enhancement to aid future employment prospects could more positively aid the resettlement and recovery process.

Colic-Peisker and Tilbury join a growing number of academics who maintain that conventional mental health treatments do not foster resilience and autonomy, and they favour approaches and services that do not pathologise or victimise former refugees (Marlowe, 2018; Miller & Rasco, 2004; Pupavac, 2004; Rousseau, Drapeau, Lacroix, Bagilishya, & Heusch, 2005; Summerfield, 1999, 2001, 2004, 2005; Watters, 2001). The point at issue, then, is what *is* seen as helpful for former refugees. Refugees stress (as did Awad, 2011) the importance of developing their 'own resources, conceptualised through their human and social capital' (Colic-Peisker & Tilbury, 2003, pp. 61–62). Social capital, which includes language skills and knowledge of social norms, is, of course, a pre-requisite for community engagement as well as for gaining sustainable employment. A major New Zealand study also identified the predominate preoccupation of former refugees was for language acquisition, employment and stable housing (Dunstan, Dibley, & Shorland, 2004).

Emerging research indicates that normalisation[2] and engaging in regular daily life, is a key factor in the healing process. Two decades ago, Summerfield (1995, 2001) was already demonstrating from studies that most refugees went on to function effectively in their new environment, despite a traumatic past. Similar findings are apparent in more recent studies. For example, Thabet and Vostanis (2000) established that within a year of settlement in a safe environment, the prevalence of PTSD in their sample dropped from over 40% to less than 10%, with no intervention whatsoever. They concluded, therefore, that symptoms of distress diminish with the passing of time and the normalisation of the environment. Likewise, at a forum in 2011 on migrant mental health in Auckland, New Zealand, guest speaker Doctor Kannan Subramaniam described how 90% of the people who experienced the 2004 tsunami in Sri Lanka stated that they had recovered within six months with no intervention whatsoever, leaving only about 10% in need of psychological support (also reported in the paper by Hollifield et al., 2008).

Colic-Peisker and Tilbury (2003) claim that 'normal' programmes may be more important than psychological intervention and Rousseau and Guzder (2008) suggest that strengths-based educational programmes and activities could be a more satisfactory alternative to mental health programmes. Indeed, Mollica (2004), who has written prolifically on refugee trauma treatment, has stated that programmes emphasising resilience and community may, in fact, be more suitable for refugee-background clients than Western-style (one-one-one) counselling. Thus, the wishes of former refugees and of a cluster of academics concur. But if education programmes are to have a healing framework, the question of how this can be achieved should also be investigated. For many refugees who choose not to access clinical therapy, a classroom could become an important place where healing can occur (Matthews, 2008; Jalbert, in Paul, 1986). Educational environments may be well placed to provide preventive therapy to refugee learners in that teachers are

> typically given the most esteem and trust by refugees among the service-providing professionals in the resettlement program; they spend by far the most time in face-to-face contact with refugees during their earliest days here; they are responsible for the group setting that often becomes a most welcome part of a refugee's early acculturation experiences – the classroom; and they provide refugees with what many experts consider to be the most important of all social survival tools – the skill to communicate. (Jalbert, in Paul, 1986)

Education Programmes

Education programmes can certainly provide normality and routine for former refugees, while simultaneously imparting the pre-requisites for social engagement, employment, or further study. Well-designed programmes can also incorporate activities that reinstate confidence, power, trust, positive relationships, and safety (all of which are elements of loss in the typical refugee journey). They have the capacity to either reduce or prevent the accumulation of stress for former refugees, thereby affording an opportunity for recovery from trauma. Educational environments can also add to stress and anxiety levels if they are poorly constructed or delivered. The onus, therefore, is on educators to ensure they do no further harm and carefully design programmes and create environments that are welcoming, safe and affirming (as well as productive). These environments can also be healing. A child soldier survivor and internationally acclaimed writer, Ishmael Beah, expressed the sentiment at Morehouse College, Atlanta USA, in October 2014: 'What I most needed (following my arrival in the USA), was a normal day. I needed to make new friends and acquire new memories' (Beah, 2014). He added that receiving counselling by a stranger for one hour at a time was culturally meaningless and unhelpful to him. The new memories derived from his school experiences, he said, soon replaced his old, bad memories. Creating a space for new, trusting relationships to develop and positive memories to accrue is something that is easily achieved by educationalists in the formal learning environment. Nothing would seem more normal and natural than a day at school or in a tertiary institution. Miller and Rasco (2004) contend that good community education programmes provide a 'different sort of mental health work' (p. 32). Pipher talks similarly about education and its potential therapeutic effects. She says:

> Teachers may not deal with trauma directly, but they are part of the healing process. They give their students order and predictability. After the chaos and confusion of their lives, order, ritual and predictability are part of this reassurance (of safety). (Pipher, 2002, p. 115)

This chapter, therefore, now presents a model for a strengths-based, refugee-centred education programme which is accompanied by examples of how key elements are implemented at the Refugee Education Centre in Auckland (REC), New Zealand. The REC teaching team resolved to incorporate into programmes their learning from findings and recommendations in academic literature regarding effective strategies for assisting settlement and recovery. Their aim was to ensure that the entire learning environment became an ecological 'source of social support for its members' (Miller & Rasco, 2004, p. 37). Thus, the pedagogic and andragogic approaches were designed not only to develop language, literacy and other skills, but also to acknowledge and build on strengths and to reinstate rights, hope, trust, safety, self-esteem, and power. Each of these components were to be situated within a welcoming, inclusive and supportive environment.

The initial task, therefore, in contemplating the design of a refugee-centred settlement programme was for teaching staff to critically reflect on the prevailing discourse used in relation to refugees. Staff was made aware of the ways that language can determine how people and situations are framed and this, in turn, affects decisions that impact on learner responses and outputs. The discourse about refugees is typically dominated by an abundance of deficit terms, including trauma, PTSD, deprivation, suffering, poor health, vulnerability, anxiety, damage, loss and so on. By concentrating only on the deficit aspect of the refugee experience, professionals could neglect consideration of holistic and positive qualities (Matthews, 2008; Rodriguez, 2015). Miller and Rasco (2004) reiterate that the 'refugee problem' is one of context which relates to a particular situation only, and most former refugees have lived normal and fulfilling lives before their sudden and brutal displacement. They have drawn on strength, faith, hope, tenacity and a myriad of other skills and stratagems in order to survive difficult circumstances (Marlowe, 2010).

Teachers at the REC, therefore, in consonance with these understandings, sought to employ the language of survival, resilience, and capability in their thinking, planning, designing, and delivery of programmes. Specifically, staff preferred to identify and describe refugee-background learners (RBLS) as survivors rather than victims, as strengthened rather than damaged by their life experiences, as empowered individuals as opposed to passive respondents or victims, and, importantly, as assets to the new community. Teachers' own perceptions were, therefore, formed by the knowledge that their learners arrived with skills and knowledge and, importantly, had shown remarkable resilience in surviving traumatic events (Marlowe, 2010; Matthews, 2008; Pupavac, 2002; Watters & Ingleby, 2004). Recognition of resilience and capacity was seen be the critical first step for building on strengths.

The strengths-based methodology adopted by teachers at the REC incorporates a constructivist approach (Brooks & Brooks, 2001), which elicits learner prior knowledge or expertise, and new learning is built on this. Centre staff also looked at how a communal environment could be actively engineered where the notions of welcome, inclusion, and trust were amplified. In this milieu, friendships could develop and be nurtured which, in turn, might provide a model of the social support needed to aid the recovery process (Cassity & Gow, 2005). The opportunity for feedback and for individuals to express what they themselves wanted or needed to learn was also incorporated into the pedagogy.

Accordingly, the REC 'refugee-centred' approach was one that was predominantly consumer- (or student-) led, and not provider-led. Teachers identified the aspects that distinguish the refugee background from that of migrants or other learners and they educed from this what might be needed to mitigate the consequences of the RBL prior circumstances. The features of the educational template that follows were deemed to conform to a refugee-centred pedagogy. This new paradigm is presented, explained, and corroborated with examples of its implementation in the authentic setting of the Auckland Refugee Education Centre.

The REC model (Figure 1.1) includes clusters of components considered crucial for effective teaching and support of refugee-background learners, and these have become the values that underpin all decisions at the Centre.

The REC sought to be a place where normal life replaces chaos and disruption, where learning and purpose replace boredom, where there is sharing of power and not a diminution of personal control and rights; it also sought to be a place of welcome and new friendships and not of alienation or exclusion, a place of affirmation and not of denigration or maltreatment. In keeping with the model, it was determined that the culture at the Centre be infused with behaviours of respect and compassion. It was noted that the compassion should not be represented as pity (as cautioned by Rodriguez, 2015).

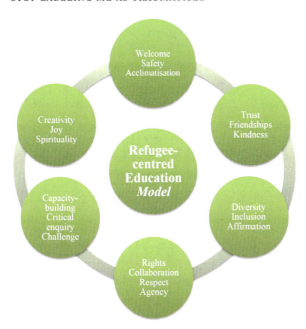

FIGURE 1.1   Strengths-based refugee-centred model

To mitigate this tendency, teaching staff, engaged in critical reflective practice (Freire, 1990) about how their behaviour was enacted.

The Centre was also to be a place of learning, challenge, joy, and creative activity. Staff employed ecological principles (Bronfenbrenner, 1992) derived from their knowledge of the backgrounds and experiences of former refugees as well as of settlement challenges. As this Centre is a residential site, staff have easily been able to work with families and other professionals when issues of concern arose. Quality teaching and assessment strategies were incorporated into the teaching methodology as was a whole-school approach (Matthews, 2008), with policies and structural practices aligned to the refugee-centred elements from the model in Figure 1.1.

An authentic welcome is a primary consideration in a programme whose participants have been forced to flee home countries and were not welcomed (given legal status) in the countries they had fled to. 'Welcoming environments create a sense of self-worth, security and belonging that enables students to form new relationships and make friends', stated Matthews (2008, p. 40). Individual teachers at the REC determined how they would each convey a genuine message of welcome in their own classrooms, but all incorporated a common intent which could be summarised as: *You are welcome, you have a right to free and quality education, to respect and trust; this is your place as well as ours, and you deserve a clean, safe, and pleasant learning environment. You belong here and have a right to receive the best we can give.*

Welcoming each group with warmth, smiles, home language greetings, and clear explanations about the programmes was seen to assist with enabling new arrivals to not only feel part of the new place, but also to feel empowered (in control) within it. Teachers articulated a welcome verbally and also in behaviours as well as in the physical appearance of their classrooms. The furnishings and resources of the refugee-centred classroom reflect what is valued – a warm reception, but more pertinently, it is the participants (and what they bring with them) who are seen to be valued in the classroom spaces. Wherever possible, therefore, at the REC, the range of home countries, languages and cultures were represented in pictures and realia around the room.

A place of learning also needs to be safe and inclusive. Furniture can be arranged in welcoming ways that equalise the teacher and learners and allow friendships to form and groups to work comfortably together. The REC purchased a range of modern chairs, soft cubes, couches and different-shaped tables for each of its rooms. The variety of seating, which could be seen to reflect diverse cultures and backgrounds, also offers choices and freedom for frequent re-arrangements. Additionally, the rooms at the REC were warm or air-conditioned to temperatures that are comfortable for learners (usually warmer than normal for this country). Representations of this country's cultures – especially the first (NZ Māori) culture were also displayed in almost every room. The latter aspect was deemed important, as New Zealand, like many other nations, was a colonised country with an insalubrious history of subjugation and denigration of indigenous people.

Discussion about the New Zealand Treaty of Waitangi[3] and its modern-day fiscal and land settlements for past wrongdoings was seen to provide a launching pad for critical enquiry about imperialistic behaviours and human rights, and is frequently a conversation that stimulates active engagement from the newly arrived cohort. Indeed, Luke (2018) claims, 'New Zealand is a remarkable exception (amongst Commonwealth countries), where all educational and language policy and intervention is responsible to address Indigenous language and cultural rights' (p. 232). The Treaty has enshrined those rights in law and the bicultural context provides a robust model for multiculturalism.

A feature of the education programme at the REC, which stems directly from knowledge about the refugee experience, is the assurance of a sense of safety for its participants. Most former refugees have lived in environments that were physically, emotionally, and intellectually unsafe. A genuine feeling of safety is a critical early step in recovery. Ensuring the physical environment is safe requires monitoring and auditing processes, which are conducted regularly at the Centre. These audits ensure that children and adults who encounter, for the first time, features such as steps, lifts, door or window locks, perhaps also electricity and modern plumbing, do not incur unnecessary injury.

In terms of the more ethereal definitions of safety, emotional and intellectual wellbeing require more thought and also for teachers to have understood the nature and likely consequential effects of the refugee journey. The majority of RBLs have lost not only material and non-material possessions, but also everyday rights such as the right to express opinions and experience joy, creativity, and other normal educational and life occurrences. The reinstatement of these opportunities in a safe environment is not only healing; it also substantially boosts self-esteem and wellbeing in individuals. Through affirmative and proactive behaviours, the memories of losses and traumatic experiences of RBLS can be replaced with new more positive memories and emotions.

Learning institutions are the ideal forum for this provision, and teachers at the REC intentionally adopted pedagogic methodologies which were interactive, inclusive, and, wherever possible, also fun. In order that all activities are emotionally safe, however, it is important for teachers to be aware of trauma triggers and professional boundaries. Almost anything can be a trigger for an RBL and it is impossible to predict what these might be for an individual, but a teacher who is attuned to noticing student reactions can ensure they are supported in these events. Examples of trauma triggers could be: a sudden loud noise, fire alarms, a smell (e.g smoke), a pictorial reminder of any aspect of a traumatic past event and even a question about family. In terms of teacher response (to a trauma-triggered reaction), sometimes merely a comment that the surprise has been noticed, is sufficient. This could be followed by a calm explanation of the trigger event (e.g: 'I'm sorry about that loud noise which may have startled some of you. I put too many objects on this shelf which obviously caused it to collapse'). Wherever possible, teachers at the REC provide prior warning of fire drills or material, which could potentially trigger a painful memory. Importantly, however, teachers are cautioned not to overstep professional boundaries by attempting to counsel RBLs about their past experiences, but to refer to specialists when trauma or concerning behaviour is observed. Howard (2018) suggests that educators should be 'trauma-aware'; that is, they should understand the behavioural consequences of complex (more than one instance) trauma and engage in proactive and reactive practices (such as those mentioned in this chapter) that will support neural repair. She suggests that, if there is a 'significant behavioural event', teachers should provide 'time and support for the dissipation of stress hormones and the settling of the sympathetic nervous system response' (p. 11). However, a learner who seems continuously distracted, angry or depressed, or a learner who reveals traumatic material in the classroom and who is also obviously distressed may need referral to a refugee-counselling expert.

Safety in the learning environment also includes intellectual safety, whereby opportunities for freedom of thought and expression are provided. Safety occurs when every individual knows that he/she has the right to freely discover and express opinions, ideas, thoughts, concerns, questions, and complaints. In (such) an intellectually safe environment, the teacher ensures every utterance is affirmed and that disparaging or denigrating comments towards others are not sanctioned. The teacher must also be prepared for comments which are discordant with his/her own viewpoints and take care not to wince when this occurs, but instead to listen and affirm, and encourage debate, critical enquiry, and reflection. A learner may, for example, contribute a comment that is misogynistic, racist or homophobic and if the teacher sensitively deconstructs the derivation of opinions, she or he may be able to uncover the fear that lies below the utterance, or alternatively, a deeply held religious belief. Socratic questioning is a useful pedagogic device for encouraging reflection and deep thinking (Hayward & U-Mackay, 2013). The teacher can also gently remind all learners of the law of the new country and possibly also discuss how a particular law came into being (for example, as a result of lengthy debate, research, opinion-canvassing, and clearer understanding of human rights).

A further aspect of the refugee experience is its unpredictability, lack of routine, and the inability to plan for the future. When there has been instability in the past, the restoration of structured regularity is important, whilst disruption to routines poses a further risk factor for refugees (Ahearn & Athey, 1991). In accord with this perspective, Wachs (1979) asserts that explicit structures and predictable events provide environmental stability and normalisation for refugees. Teachers at the New Zealand refugee reception Centre in Auckland resolved to make routines more explicit by displaying a daily plan to enable learners to regain a sense of control over their day.

Teachers also ensured that routines were maintained, or where there was to be a change, an advance explanation was given. The structure and regularity of a classroom programme also provides a distracting focus for individuals who wish to suspend haunting memories of the past and instead to accumulate 'new memories' (Beah, 2014). REC staff deemed that when occasions are particularly enjoyable, creative, and filled with *aroha*[4] (love and compassion), they will eventually predominate in memory banks. In the interim, they may simply provide welcome distractions. Many former refugees at the REC comment on the joy of being able to laugh, joke, and relax again in the on-arrival school at Mangere. Humour and laughter are a form of therapy (Tippens, 2017) and indeed can be heard throughout the day in every classroom at the REC.

Perhaps the most important aspect of a programme for newcomers is acquisition of (English) language, as this is undeniably the key prerequisite for gaining control or agency in the new social environment in New Zealand. Language is also the medium for developing new friendships and networks within the welcoming society, without which former refugees are more vulnerable to mental health problems (Watters, 2001). This promotion of wellbeing, through the development of relationships and agency has been described as a form of therapy known as 'primary prevention' (Albee & Kimberly, 1993; Williams & Berry, 1991). When positive relationships form in the new social context, personal confidence and a sense of belonging are strengthened.

But language classes can provide more than just a useful social and empowerment skill. Cohon, Lucey, Paul, and LeMarbre Penning (1986) suggest that a range of activities should be integrated into language classrooms that can be healing for RBLS. These might include collaborative group work, creative pursuits, mindfulness (focussing on the moment), problem-solving activities, possibly even anger management and interrelationship skill development. The language and settlement classes at the REC incorporate as many as possible of the aforementioned stratagems, which are seen to provide stress alleviation whilst concurrently cultivating useful integration skills.

Another typical component of the REC language programmes, which also has the potential to provide solace for individuals, is that of structured interaction and information-sharing exercises. Language practice can include opportunities for learners to share with others about themselves, their skills, interests, knowledge, experiences (perhaps as a new migrant), and backgrounds; for example, talking, writing or showcasing special items (Darvin & Norton, 2014). This type of group interaction not only strengthens identity, but also further contributes towards the development of sustaining friendships within the classroom. Emotional safety for RBLS can be maintained during these activities by offering choices about the content or scope of input and also by ensuring teachers are well informed and trained to be alert for trauma triggers.

Language programmes at the REC also include aesthetic activities such as music, creative writing, dance, art, and cooking (and sharing) food. Creative activities embedded in language programmes can provide opportunities for free and safe expression (Cassity & Gow, 2005). These endeavours 'support the transformation of past and present adversity through creativity' (Rousseau & Guzder, 2008, p. 546; Tolfree, 1996). Many academics describe how art or aesthetics education can further augment construction of identity in a new social environment (Danev, 1998; Eldebour, Baker, & Charlesworth, 1997; Howard, 1991; Nylund, Legrand, & Holtsberg, 1999; Schaefer & Drews, 2011; Torbert,

1990). At the REC, RBLS might draw or creatively describe events from their past; but equally, they might submit positive, joyful depictions from either their past or from their current situation. Importantly, the art or craft sessions represent a type of intermission in the intense language acquisition classes and provide students with a space to relax and consolidate. Interestingly, during this time they appear to more willingly take risks in their English conversation with teachers and with peers.

Opportunities for genuine learner input in programme design and structure is another important aspect of the refugee-centred approach developed at the REC. The elicitation of settlement concerns from newcomers can be a springboard for introducing and developing conflict-resolution and problem-solving skills. These skills can be fostered through critical thinking and questioning processes, which are integral to all mainstream education institutions and curricula in New Zealand. The facilitated discussions that occur at the REC allow opinions, questions, and concerns to be articulated; and this is followed by opportunities for analysis, critique, and, as appropriate, discussion about cultural negotiation. The process has the potential to not only affirm diversity, but also to demonstrate how societies can contain variance yet still function successfully.

With the assistance of interpreters, learners at the Centre are guided as a group in tasks that invite comparing, contrasting, and occasionally interrogating cultural practices, mores, and beliefs – including those of the new society. Teaching staff support and encourage negotiation and intercultural competency skills. This setting enables RBLs to make their own decisions regarding the retention of cultural norms and expectations or the negotiation of pathways and compromises for living in a new socio-cultural context. Critical thinking is closely linked to the concept of agency[5] as it stimulates individual thought and problem-solving capacity (Pennycook, 2001).

Restoring personal power or agency should arguably be a priority in all refugee programmes. Consequences of cumulative losses for individuals from refugee-backgrounds are frequently a strong sense of powerlessness accompanied by heightened levels of dependence and vulnerability (Van Tilburg, Vingerhoets, & Van Heck, 1996). If teachers are aware of ways that power can be shared, perhaps some of the sequelae of the past abuses can be ameliorated through the restoration of agency for learners.

At the REC individuals are taught about their rights under the Human Rights' legislation, but importantly are also invited to partake, wherever possible, in choices and decision-making regarding a range of classroom activities and topics. Decisions may include selection of topics and tasks as well as input into agreements about rules, prayer times, seating arrangements, class trips, and so on. Additionally, and of more significance, when issues arise, learners are encouraged to share ideas for possible solutions. An example may be cultural misunderstandings amongst ethnic groups or an adult conflict following a playground spat amongst children, or, as occurred recently, a complaint because some residents were singing and dancing in the evening during Ramadan (when others wished to quietly contemplate or pray). The latter was resolved quite simply. Muslim students were invited to share with others about the purpose and solemnity of Ramadan. The preference for a quiet environment before dusk when many people were at prayer was mentioned, and the other groups volunteered to either not sing during this time or to move to the far corner of the site beyond the audibility zone of the buildings. This type of problem-solving process supports the enhancement of agency, collaboration, and autonomy. It also provides an authentic experience of power-sharing by enabling former refugees to make their own decisions about negotiating cultural (and other) differences and not have these imposed on them.

Furthermore, the Resettlement Programme (orientation to New Zealand) at the REC was designed to allow classes to extend or reduce time on topics depending on the interest level of participants, and teachers willingly incorporated additional topics for discussion or research when students expressed interest or concerns about particular issues. When individuals are encouraged to partake in this type of self-initiated education, they are empowered through being able to take control not only of their own learning, but also of their new lives in the welcoming country (Hayward, 2007). This occurs more readily in an environment that permits learners to further investigate what they want to know (Brooks & Brooks, 2001). In recent intakes, for example, groups at the REC have requested further sessions on parenting without violence, whilst others have shown interest in voting or in employment opportunities in their designated settlement cities. These requests have been met within the flexible timetable. Many students have asked for more time to discuss New Zealand cultural practices. In some cases, learners have been able to research information themselves on iPads or computers which are available for student use in all classrooms.

Learners at the REC also engage in a range of co-operative activities which can have positive and powerful outcomes for participants. The more traditional (teacher at the front of the classroom) model tends to emphasise learners as 'individuals' – but many refugees prefer community-oriented formations (Englund, 1998; Miller & Rasco, 2004). The practice of group activity is a culturally appropriate and educative intervention, which reflects the collectivist backgrounds of a significant number of former refugees. Adam Awad (New Zealand chairperson of the National Refugee Network) commented that 'it is like we are one body and can only function effectively when all our parts and all our processes work properly' (NZ Herald, 2010). Co-operative, collaborative activities at the REC include pursuits such as group discussions and solution-seeking (mentioned above), preparation of a shared meal, group posters, presentations or other project work, craft sessions, games, and a multifarious range of classroom and learning activities involving more than one individual. Group activities not only provide fun; they are also empowering in that they place the 'marginalised ... in the position of subject' (Freire, 1970). Moreover, they can build on and showcase existing skills and are valuable for cultivating new relationships and friendship communities. This is in keeping with the constructivist underpinnings of the programme.

There is a further communal and indeed, quite spiritual feature of REC programme which is seen to contribute towards the informal process of healing for former refugees. This sits within the topic called *Taha Māori*, which incorporates the perspectives, values, and customs of New Zealand's first people and culture. The programme includes participation in a traditional Māori welcoming ritual or *powhiri*,[6] which is a ceremonial process during which guests are invited to speak publicly in response to welcoming speeches from the hosts (*tangata whenua*[7]). The inclusive roles in this ceremony create a very potent acknowledgement of equity for the newcomers with members of the host community. Refugee representative speakers frequently recount a synopsis of their journey and background during the speeches. in hearing these stories, the *tangata whenua* feel humility and empathy.

The refugee-background speakers feel validated, and they express their gratitude and keenness to contribute to this welcoming society. The powhiri provides an authentic welcome and affords clear links to the new community. Preparation for this ritual by AUT staff includes information and discussion about key concepts and values of New Zealand's indigenous culture. Several Māori concepts emphasise spirituality, and many refugees are from countries which place a high value on religious or spiritual explanations or responses (Miller & Rasco, 2004; Tippens, 2017). Rousseau and Guzder state that 'spirituality often occupies an important place in healing' and may provide 'tools' for mourning, for making sense of the world, and for fostering resiliency (2008, p. 541). The presenters of the Taha Māori session at Auckland's reception centre are themselves of Māori background and they share personal stories and songs and facilitate discussions with passion and emotion. Participants are invited to share and compare diverse cultural practices and beliefs. Topics such as transcendent connection with the land or with deceased ancestors, farewelling the dead (*tangi*), or genealogy (*whakapapa*) are frequently discussed at length in classes, and many groups strongly identify with the Māori rites, values, and perspectives. Parallels are also seen with concepts of community and family (*iwi* or *whanau*), and with rituals for naming, healing, social living (collectivist values), and the importance of sharing food (*kai*). Finally, the Māori concept of *aroha* (compassion) underpins not only this component, but indeed all activity at the Centre.

New Zealand government officials and the frequent international delegations that visit the REC have commented on the patently confident and relaxed demeanour of the RBLs. Teaching staff contends this is not random. Every aspect of the environment, the methodology, and the programmes are carefully considered and supported wherever possible by scholarly research as well as through processes of critical self-reflection. Programmes are *managed by well-informed and trained staff with the aim that dignity, self-respect, confidence, and personal power or agency are restored for all learners*. When students feel happy and safe, they also achieve better educational outcomes.

Conclusions

This chapter began with a discussion about the controversial elements of the Post-Traumatic Stress Disorder diagnosis and outlined research findings indicating the effect of this diagnosis on individuals of refugee backgrounds. The academic articles cited suggest that, for many, there may be negligible diminution of trauma symptoms as a result of a clinical diagnosis of PTSD, therapy, or medication. Indeed, the diagnosis itself would appear to be unwanted by some and could even be detrimental in terms of client (refugee) perception of their own ability to recover and develop independence in the new environment. Although it is acknowledged that there is definitely benefit for some individuals in therapeutic trauma management, this chapter proposes that community and language programmes can also provide healing for the high numbers of former refugees who do not seek formal psychological therapy. English or settlement classes, it is suggested, can be enhanced so that alongside developing useful skills and strategies for successful resettlement and integration into a new community, RBLs can contribute to the reinstatement of normalcy, agency, and rights for individuals, as well as engendering trusting relationships within a nurturing social environment.

The chapter has described essential components of these programmes as including a strengths-based teaching methodology that is affirming, collaborative, and couched within an inclusive, semi-structured environment that encourages individual input as well as a questioning approach and group problem-solving component. The programme, it is stressed, should emphasise the principles of welcome, respect, safety, sharing, and constructivist capacity-building. Finally, creativity and spiritualism are also identified as important features of the approach described.

The pedagogic template (Figure 1.1) outlined in this chapter does not ignore the refugee journey and its impact on the psyche and conduct of individuals. The prior environment defines this group of individuals and suggests the new environment can re-define them – not as mentally unwell – but as resilient survivors with talents, skills, and strengths. Therefore, the emphasis in this model is on capability and resilience rather than on the deficits of trauma or mental ill health. Above all, this approach seeks to allow former refugees whose prior lives had been disrupted by abnormal events, to begin to recover through the provision of a normal, healthy social (albeit bespoke) learning environment.

The measure of the success of such a 'healing' programme, Colic-Peisker and Tilbury (2003) suggest, is how refugees say they feel. This parallels the World Health Organisation definition of mental health quoted earlier in this chapter ('the extent to which people are happy, have a sense that they are fairly well in control of their lives and feel that they are valued, productive members of society'). In light of this, two recommendations are made: the first is that further research be undertaken with refugee participants to determine what they consider to be most helpful in their journey towards recovery, personal well-being, integration, and self-sufficiency. The second recommendation is that programmes for former refugees include elements such as those described in this chapter which are inclusive and collaborative, and which develop self-esteem and build on strengths and existing skills rather than seek to ascertain damage or deficit. Finally, it is hoped that citation of 'trauma' in relation to former refugees ceases to dominate academic literature and on-arrival services and that terms which focus more on assets or strengths, gain greater emphasis.

Notes

1   A NZ Māori (language) term referring to power, influence, status, spiritual power, charisma.
2   Returning to living in a normal state or condition (Merriam-Webster).
3   A Treaty signed in 1840 by New Zealand Māori chiefs and the British Crown with agreement about sovereignty and sharing resources.
4   NZ Māori.
5   'The capacity for willed (voluntary) action' (Scott & Marshall, 2005, p. 9).
6   NZ Māori: welcome (ceremony).
7   Literally: 'people of the land.'

References

Abbott, M., & Nayar, S. (Eds.). (2011). *Looking back moving forward: Refugee health and wellbeing in Aotearoa New Zealand* (pp. 42–47). Auckland: AUT Media.

Agger, I., & Mimica, J. (1996). *Psycho-social assistance to victims of war in Bosnia-Herzegovina and Croatia: An evaluation.* Brussels: ECHO.

Ahearn, F. L., & Athey, J. L. (Eds.). (1991). *Refugee children: Theory, research, and service* (Vol. 16). Baltimore, MD: Johns Hopkins University Press.

Albee, G. W., & Kimberly, D. R. (1993). An overview of primary prevention. *Journal of Counseling & Development, 72*(2), 115–123.

American Psychiatric Association. (1980). *Diagnostic and statistical manual of mental disorders* (3rd ed.). Washington, DC: American Psychiatric Association.

Awad, A. (2010, January 13). Refugees want to participate fully in NZ life. *New Zealand Herald.*

Awad, A. (2011). The voice of the community. In M. Abbott & S. Nayar (Eds.), *Looking back moving forward: Refugee health and wellbeing in Aotearoa New Zealand* (pp. 42–47). Auckland: AUT Media.

Beah, I. (2014, October 22). *UNICEF speaker series: 'Children not soldiers.'* Atlanta, Georgia: Morehouse University.

Bisson, J. I., & Deahl, M. P. (1994). Psychological debriefing and prevention of post-traumatic stress. *British Journal of Psychiatry, 165,* 717–720.

Bracken, P. J., Giller, J. E., & Summerfield, D. (1995). Psychological responses to war and atrocity: The limitations of current concepts. *Social Science and Medicine, 40,* 1073–1082.

British Red Cross. (1999). *Response to the international federation draft assessment of April 99.* London: British Red Cross.

Bronfenbrenner, U. (1992). *Ecological systems theory.* London: Jessica Kingsley Publishers.

Brooks, G., & Brooks, M. G. (2001). *The case for constructivist classrooms.* Upper Saddle River, NJ: Merrill Prentice-Hall.

Cassity, E., & Gow, G. (2005). Making up for lost time: The experiences of Southern Sudanese young refugees in high schools. *Youth Studies Australia, 24*(3), 51–55.

Cohon, J. D., Lucey, M., Paul, M., & LeMarbre Penning, J. (1986). *Preventive mental health in the ESL classroom: A handbook for teachers.* New York, NY: American Council for Nationalities Service.

Colic-Peisker, V., & Tilbury, F. (2003). 'Active' and 'passive' resettlement: The influence of support services and refugees' own resources on resettlement style. *International Migration, 41,* 61–91.

Danev, M. (1998). Library project 'step by step to recovery'. In D. Doktor (Ed.), *Art therapists, refugees and migrants: Reaching across borders.* London: Jessica Kingsley Publishers.

Darvin, R., & Norton, B. (2014). Transnational identity and migrant language learners: The promise of digital storytelling. *Education Matters: The Journal of Teaching and Learning, 2*(1), 55–66.

Dunstan, S., Dibley, R., & Shorland, P. (2004). *Refugee voices: A journey towards resettlement.* Social Policy, Research and Evaluation Conference, Department of Labour.

Eldebour, S., Baker, A. M., & Charlesworth, W. (1997). The impact of political violence and moral reasoning in children. *Child Abuse and Neglect, 21*, 1053–1066.

Englund, H. (1998). Death, trauma and ritual: Mozambican refugees in Malawi. *Social Science and Medicine, 46*, 1165–1174.

Fassin, D., & Rechtman, R. (2009). *The empire of trauma: An inquiry into the condition of victimhood* (R. Gomme, Trans.). Princeton, NJ: Princeton University Press.

Freire, P. (1970). *Pedagogy of the oppressed.* New York, NY: Herder & Herder.

Freire, P. (1990). A critical understanding of social work. *Journal of Progressive Human Services, 1*(1), 3–9.

Geltman, P. L., Augustyn, M., Barnett, E. D., Klass, P. E., & Groves, B. M. (2000). War trauma experience and behavioural screening of Bosnian refugee children resettled in Massachusetts. *Journal of Developmental and Behavioral Pediatrics, 21*(4), 255–261.

Hayward, M. (2007). *Applying post-critical approaches to refugee-centred education* (Unpublished MA thesis). AUT University, Auckland.

Hayward, M., & U-Mackey, A. (2013). Inclusiveness, power sharing and critical enquiry: Intercultural programme model for new settlers. *Intercultural Education, 24*(5), 430–441.

Hollifield, M., Hewage, C., Gunawardena, C. N., Kodituwakku, P., Bopagoda, K., & Weerarathnege, K. (2008). Symptoms and coping in Sri Lanka 20–21 months after the 2004 tsunami. *The British Journal of Psychiatry, 192*(1), 39–44.

Howard, G. S. (1991). Culture tales: A narrative approach to thinking, cross-cultural psychology, and psychotherapy. *American Psychologist, 46*, 187–197.

Howard, J. A. (2018). *A systemic framework for trauma-aware schooling in Queensland.* Brisbane: Queensland University of Technology.

Hughes, C., & Pupavac, V. (2005). Framing post-conflict societies: International pathologisation of Cambodia and the post-Yugoslav states. *Third World Quarterly, 26*(6), 873–889.

Immigration New Zealand website. (n.d.). https://www.immigration.govt.nz/about-us/what-we-do/our-strategies-and-projects/supporting-refugees-and-asylum-seekers/refugee-and-protection-unit/new-zealand-refugee-quota-programme

Karpman, S. (2014). *A game free life: The definitive book on the drama triangle and the compassion triangle by the originator and author.* San Francisco, CA: Drama Triangle Publications.

Kerbage, H., & Marranconi, F. (2017). Mental Health and Psychosocial Support Services (MHPSS) for Syrian refugees in Lebanon: Towards a public health approach beyond diagnostic categories. *European Scientific Journal, ESJ, 13*(10), 25.

Kim, I., & Kim, W. (2014). Post-resettlement challenges and mental health of Southeast Asian refugees in the United States. *Best Practices in Mental Health, 10*(2), 63–77.

Luke, A. (2018). *Critical literacy, schooling, and social justice: The selected works of Allan Luke*. New York, NY: Routledge.

Lustig, S. L., Kia-Keating, M., Knight, W. G., Geltman, P., Ellis, H., Kinzie, J. D., ... Saxe, G. N. (2004). Review of child and adolescent refugee mental health. *Journal of the American Academy of Child & Adolescent Psychiatry, 43*(1), 24–36.

Malkki, L. H. (1996). Speechless emissaries: Refugees, humanitarianism, and dehistori-cization. *Cultural Anthropology, 11*(3), 377–404.

Marlowe, J. M. (2010). Beyond the discourse of trauma: Shifting the focus on Sudanese refugees. *Journal of Refugee Studies, 23*(2), 183–198.

Marlowe, J. M. (2018). *Belonging and transnational refugee resettlement: Unsettling the everyday and the extraordinary*. New York, NY: Routledge.

Matthews, J. (2008). Schooling and settlement: Refugee education in Australia. *International Studies in Sociology of Education, 18*(1), 31–45.

Miller, K. E., & Rasco, L. M. (Eds.). (2004). *The mental health of refugees: Ecological approaches to healing and adaptation*. Mahwah, NJ: Taylor and Francis.

Mitschke, D. B., Praetorius, R. T., Kelly, D. R., Small, E., & Kim, Y. K. (2017). Listening to refugees: How traditional mental health interventions may miss the mark. *International Social Work, 60*(3), 588–600.

Mollica, R. F. (2004). Surviving torture. *New England Journal of Medicine, 351,* 5–7.

Muecke, M. A. (1992). New paradigms for refugee health problems. *Social Science and Medicine, 35,* 515–523.

Munroe-Blum, H., Boyle, M. H., Offord, D. R., & Kates, N. (1989). Immigrant children: Psychiatric disorder, school performance, and service utilization. *American Journal of Orthopsychiatry, 59*(4), 510–519.

Nylund, B. V., Legrand, J. C., & Holtsberg, P. (1999). The role of art in psychosocial care and protection for displaced children. *Forced Migration Review, 6,* 16–19.

Paul, M. (Ed.). (1986). *Preventative mental health in the ESL classroom: A handbook for teachers*. New York, NY: ACNS.

Pennycook, A. (2001). *Critical applied linguistics: A critical introduction*. New York, NY: Lawrence Erlbaum.

Pipher, M. B. (2002). *The middle of everywhere: The world's refugees come to our town*. Houghton, MI: Mifflin Harcourt.

Pupavac, V. (2001). Therapeutic governance: Psycho-social intervention and trauma risk management. *Disasters, 25,* 358–372.

Pupavac, V. (2002). Pathologizing populations and colonizing minds: International psychosocial programs in Kosovo. *Alternatives, 27,* 489–511.

Pupavac, V. (2004). War on the couch: The emotionology of the new international security paradigm. *European Journal of Social Theory, 7,* 149–170.

Rodriguez, S. (2015). The dangers of compassion: The positioning of refugee students in policy and education research and implications for teacher education. *Knowledge Cultures, 3*(2), 112–126.

Rose, S., Bisson, J., Churchill, R., & Wessely, S. (2002). Psychological debriefing for preventing Post Traumatic Stress Disorder (PTSD). *Cochrane Database Syst Rev, 2*(2).

Rousseau, C., Drapeau, A., Lacroix, L., Bagilishya, D., & Heusch, N. (2005). Evaluation of a classroom program of creative expression workshops for refugee and immigrant children. *Journal of Child Psychology and Psychiatry, 46*(2), 180–185.

Rousseau, C., & Guzder, J. (2008). School-based prevention programs for refugee children. *Child and Adolescent Psychiatric Clinics of North America, 17*, 533–549.

Schaefer, C. E., & Drewes, A. A. (2011). The therapeutic powers of play and play therapy. In C. E. Schaefer (Ed.), *Foundations of play therapy* (pp. 15–25). Hoboken, NJ: John Wiley & Sons.

Stubbs, P., & Soroya, B. (1996). War trauma, psycho-social projects and social development in Croatia. *Medicine, Conflict and Survival, 12*, 303–314.

Subramaniam, K. (2011). S19-04 psychological first aid following major disasters – The boxing day Tsunami, Sri Lanka, 2004. *Asian Journal of Psychiatry, 4*, S19.

Summerfield, D. (1999). A critique of seven assumptions behind psychological trauma programmes in war-affected areas. *Social Science and Medicine, 48*, 1449–1462.

Summerfield, D. (2001). The invention of post-traumatic stress disorder and the social usefulness of a psychiatric category. *BMJ: British Medical Journal, 322*(7278), 95–98.

Summerfield, D. (2004). 12 Cross-cultural perspectives on the medicalization of human suffering. In G. Rosen (Ed.), *Posttraumatic stress disorder: Issues and controversies* (pp. 233–246). Chichester: Willey.

Summerfield, D. (2005). My whole body is sick … my life is not good: A Rwandan Asylum seeker attends a psychiatric clinic in London. In D. Ingleby (Ed.), *International and cultural psychology series: Forced migration and mental health: Rethinking the care of refugees and displaced persons* (pp. 97–114). New York, NY: Springer.

Thabet, A. A., & Vostanis, P. (2000). Post traumatic stress disorder reactions in children of war: A longitudinal study. *Child Abuse and Neglect, 24*, 291–298.

Tippens, J. A. (2017). Urban Congolese refugees in Kenya: The contingencies of coping and resilience in a context marked by structural vulnerability. *Qualitative Health Research, 27*(7), 1090–1103.

Tolfree, D. (1996). *Restoring playfulness – Different approaches to assisting children who are psychologically affected by war or displacement.* Stockholm: Save the Children Sweden.

Torbert, M. (1990). *Follow me: A handbook of movement activities for children.* Englewood Cliffs, NJ: Prentice-Hall.

UNHCR. (1993). *The 1951 refugee convention.* Retrieved from http://www.unhcr.ch

Van Tilburg, M. A., Vingerhoets, A. J. J. M., & Van Heck, G. L. (1996). Homesickness: A review of the literature. *Psychological Medicine, 26*, 899–912.

Wachs, T. D. (1979). Proximal experience and early cognitive-intellectual development: The physical environment. *Merrill-Palmer Quarterly, 25*, 3–41.

Watters, C. (2001). Emerging paradigms in the mental health care of refugees. *Social Science and Medicine, 52*, 1709–1718.

Watters, C., & Ingleby, D. (2004). Locations of care: Meeting the mental health and social care needs of refugees in Europe. *International Journal of Law and Psychiatry, 27*, 549–570.

Williams, C. L., & Berry, J. W. (1991). Primary prevention of acculturative stress among refugees: Application of psychological theory and practice. *American Psychologist, 46*(6), 632.

World Health Organisation. (n.d.). https://www.who.int/features/factfiles/mental_health/en/

Yanni, E. A., Naoum, M., Odeh, N., Han, P., Coleman, M., & Burke, H. (2013). The health profile and chronic diseases comorbidities of US-bound Iraqi refugees screened by the International Organization for Migration in Jordan: 2007–2009. *Journal of Immigrant and Minority Health, 15*(1), 1–9.

CHAPTER 2

Education of Resettled Refugees in Christchurch, New Zealand

Zhiyan Basharati and Lucia Dore

Introduction

The United Nations High Commissioner for Refugees (UNHCR) report on refugee education states that some of the world's 31 million refugee children and adolescents under UNHCR's mandate who are of primary and secondary school-going age, between 5 and 17, have limited access to education (UNHCR, 2016). Some 3.5 million do not go to school at all (UNHCR, 2016). As stated in the report, refugees and those who have lost everything have an 'unquenchable thirst' and sheer desire to go out and rebuild their lives and communities (UNHCR, 2016, p. 7).

Providing education for refugees creates a protective and stable environment for young people when all around them seems to have descended into chaos (UNHCR, 2016). It imparts life-saving skills, promotes resilience and self-reliance, and helps to meet the psychological and social needs of children affected by conflict (UNHCR, 2016). In 2017, UNHCR submitted the files of over 75,100 refugees for consideration by resettlement countries (UNHCR, 2018). Resettlement States provide refugees with legal and physical protection, including access to civil, political, economic, social and cultural rights similar to those enjoyed by nationals (UNHCR, 2018).

New Zealand defines a quota refugee as someone who enters the country as part of the UNHCR quota system. A refugee, or his/her family, is typically interviewed in the country of origin, or near it, or in Asia. In New Zealand, the quota has been 750 since 1987 (Immigration New Zealand, n.d.) but in September 2018 the New Zealand Government agreed that the annual refugee quota will permanently increase to 1,500 in July 2020. New Zealand has a five-pronged strategy to its integration goals for refugee resettlement, determined by Immigration New Zealand (INZ). These goals are as follows: achieving self-sufficiency, ensuring health and well-being, living in good housing, participating in New Zealand life, and ensuring refugees have access to education (INZ, n.d., p. 3).

© KONINKLIJKE BRILL NV, LEIDEN, 2019 | DOI: 10.1163/9789004401891_002

Educational Strategies

The New Zealand Refugee Resettlement Strategy (RRS) (INZ, n.d.) was first established in 2012 to help refugees find work and improve their health and education outcomes. The overarching vision for the RRS is that refugees participate fully and 'are integrated socially and economically as soon as possible so that they are living independently, undertaking the same responsibilities and exercising the same rights as other New Zealanders and have a strong sense of belonging to their own community and to New Zealand' (INZ, n.d., p. 3). Under the auspices of Immigration New Zealand (INZ) the strategy is being implemented progressively and has been applied in the first instance to all quota refugees arriving in New Zealand from July 2013 (INZ, n.d.; UNHCR, 2014).

Education is the only goal that is measured against a target. In this case, the target is the proportion of refugee school leavers attaining the National Certificate of Educational Achievement (NCEA level 2) after five years or more in the New Zealand education system (INZ, n.d.). For example, 67% of refugee school leavers with five years in the New Zealand education system achieved NCEA Level 2 by 2014 (INZ, n.d., p. 7).

NCEAS are national qualifications for senior secondary school students, which set out levels of literacy and numeracy for Years 1 to 8. It replaced School Certificate, Sixth Form Certificate and Bursary and was introduced in 2002. Assessments and study projects form the greatest part of the accreditation. However, the failure to make a distinction between subjects – physical education is treated in the same way as physics, for example – has come into criticism by some students and teachers (Collins, 2018).

NCEAS are recognised by employers and are used as the benchmark for selection by universities and polytechnics. NCEAS are also readily accepted overseas, including by universities. When applying for employment, prospective employees can create a summary of their results from their record of Achievement (NZQA, n.d.). Because the New Zealand government has the NCEA as one of its targets, this indicates the government's high expectations for resettled refugee students. However, under the Labour-led government (the coalition government that took power in October 2017), NCEA will be abolished and schools will be free to choose their own ways of assessing children's progress. A new education target has not yet been put into the RRS (Moir, 2017).

In 2016/2017 the Ministry of Education (MoE) aimed to co-ordinate the implementation of the Language Assistance Services Project to address the barriers and gaps identified in the report on interpreter services and other language assistance services undertaken in 2015/2016 (INZ, n.d.). The Ministry has also begun to explore barriers to the provision of interpreter services and other language assistance to former refugees in New Zealand.

It has supported other initiatives for refugees such as homework programmes, information about schooling in multiple languages, bilingual tutors in schools, and an increase in funding for English language support for up to five years (Ministry of Education, 2015). However, in the 2009 Budget, Refugee Study Grants for tertiary education were disestablished for 2011 (Riggs, 2009).

Further literature on refugees shows that meaningful employment for all refugees, whether low- or high-skilled, is more likely if the goals of health and well-being and education/English language are given priority, at least in the first months throughout the initial year or two of resettlement (McBrien, 2014). Based on research conducted in New Zealand, the United States, and elsewhere, McBrien suggests a reprioritising of the categories (in the RRS), replacing work and participation by health and education as first priorities (McBrien, 2014). To critique the RRS, McBrien interviewed policymakers and other staff working at the MBIE and the MOE. She also interviewed NGO agency staff, teachers, and refugee background students from resettlement regions to learn their views about the new strategy and goals (McBrien, 2014).

The organization, Teachers of English to Speakers of other Languages Aotearoa New Zealand (TESOLANZ, 2003), concurs with McBrien's recommendations. Its report concludes that of all the factors that will assist with resettlement in New Zealand, proficiency in English is one of the most important. 'Few refugees can become full participants in New Zealand society without formal English education or skill upgrading' (TESOLANZ, 2003). Skill upgrading refers to the fact that refugees have to either retrain in New Zealand to meet professional requirements, or retrain to obtain a new skill entirely (TESOLANZ, 2003).

Research from UNHCR also suggests students from refugee-backgrounds are not accessing or completing tertiary study (UNHCR, 2018). One report concludes that this could be addressed through revised government education policy that includes refugee-background students as an equity group (O'Rourke, 2011). The report states, 'the strongest foundation for an effective program to provide equitable access to university education is including refugee-background students among those groups who receive equity consideration' (O'Rourke, 2011).

Another report gives a descriptive analysis of stakeholders' perspectives on significant changes in the refugee resettlement sector since 1987 (Gruner & Searle, 2011). Interviews were conducted from February to March 2010, in the main settlement locations of former refugees: Auckland, Hamilton, Wellington, and Christchurch. Twenty-two in depth interviews were conducted with 39 individuals. This included former refugees who work for government agencies and non-government organizations (NGOs). These views were supplemented with information from documentary sources over this period.

This study shows that the development of the education sector's responsiveness to the needs of refugee-background children and parents is key. Participants commented on the benefit of establishing specialist refugee education coordinators who understand the needs of refugees. Former refugees filled many of the positions within the MoE (Gruner & Searle, 2011). The Gruner and Searle study shows that the MoE can support initiatives included more formally in the resettlement strategy. The changes the resettlement strategy has undergone also suggest that the MoE is prepared to implement changes as new information about a programme comes in. This means that education programmes run by the MoE could be altered if deemed successful in meeting its target goals.

Literature on the refugee experience often focuses on trauma and loss, the marginalisation of refugees, and how this relates to education (Hamilton, Anderson, Mathieson, Loewen, & Moore, 2000). The New Zealand government, through its website 'Education Counts,' states: 'With extra initiatives and effective interventions that emphasise the critical learning, psychosocial and cultural needs of refugee students who have survived loss and cataclysmic events, it is possible for these students to transcend traumas and experience success within the school system' (Hamilton, Anderson, Frater-Mathieson, Loewen, & Moore, 2000). This highlights the fact the Government is aware of the many challenges refugees face, such as overcoming trauma and persecution.

Literature on Resettlement and Education

In carrying out this study we found that little research has been done in the realm of refugee education as it pertains to New Zealand. For this reason, we looked at how other countries and states have dealt with refugee education and considered what lessons New Zealand can learn from their experiences. In the article, 'Refugees and Education' (Waters & LeBlanc, 2005), although it discusses how the UN and the international relief agencies act as a 'pseudo-state' when it comes to educating refugees, the issues the refugee agencies face are much the same as those faced by sovereign states like New Zealand.

Waters and LeBlanc (2005) stated they there are three primary challenges to education for resettled refugees. The first challenge is identifying the needed curriculum and pedagogy. The second is that education is always embedded in political judgements. The third is 'that schooling is inherently embedded in broader issues of individual and economic development that for refugee populations are inherently unclear and often unimaginable' (Waters & LeBlanc, 2005).

The authors point out that 'education and training can contribute to the durable solution of "voluntary repatriation," through giving children the knowledge, skills and emotional stability to successfully re-enter the education system in their home country' (Waters & LeBlanc, 2005). An emphasis on literacy and numeracy are also important, as the article points out, the latter being very much the emphasis of our HHC study.

The conflict between state and non-state entities is continued by Buckner, Spencer, and Cha (2017). In their research, not only is the contradiction between government and unofficial government policy discussed, but so too is the importance of education for refugees, especially their integration into society. Buckner et al. (2017) suggest that a better starting place for understanding education policy implementation is to understand the often-competing sources of state and non-state authority that affect decision-making at the local level.

The importance of education is also highlighted in an article on Burundi, a country which experienced large-scale conflict-led emigration and substantial post-war refugee return, to explore differences in schooling outcomes between returnees (Fransen, Vargas-Silva, & Siegel, 2018). The study found that an additional year spent as a refugee while of schooling age is associated with a four to six percentage point increase in the likelihood of finishing primary school (Fransen, Vargas-Silva, & Siegel, 2018). Therefore, it is important to note that refugee children's experience of education is affected by insufficient support for learning the host-society language, isolation and exclusion (bullying, racism, difficulties making friends etc.). Some schools also provide special language units for refugee children in seeking to meet their needs, but recognise that such provisions limited opportunities for mixing with local children.

In the current study we examine how current educational programmes can help refugees and what support is needed. This chapter looks at educational outcomes for resettled refugees in New Zealand who have participated at the Multi-Ethnic Homework and Support Centre at Hagley College (HHC) located in the city of Christchurch. It will address the educational and employment outcomes of those students who attend, or have attended, HHC. This research is the first of its kind to look at the effectiveness of the HHC in terms of achieving educational outcomes and, ultimately, whether it helps students achieve their employment goals. The study also inquires how HHC can enhance New Zealand's RRS for education policies and if an education programme like HHC should be supported financially by Immigration New Zealand (INZ) under the New Zealand RRS.

Methods

This study adopts a mixed methods approach, using two surveys and qualitative research including observation and interviews. The research and methods were reviewed and accepted by the Hagley Homework Centre review board.

Setting

Hagley Homework Centre (HHC) is one of the refugee programmes run by Hagley College, a secondary school in Christchurch, New Zealand. HHC is open on Tuesday and Wednesday evenings from 5.00 pm to 7.30 pm. It is a place where refugee-background students, from years one to 13, can do their homework in a quiet space under supervision by qualified teachers.

The HHC was first started by members of the Somali community in 2000. They hired two rooms at Hagley College with qualified teachers, and financing came from the MoE. In 2005, there was an influx of refugees to Christchurch, and the refugee education coordinator at the MoE, with the support of the Canterbury Refugee Resettlement and Resource Centre (a regional NGO), wanted to make the programme accessible to all in the refugee community. The programme was eventually handed over to Hagley College to run and organise with the support of MoE.

Subjects

Part 1: High School Student Sample

The subjects for the study were a sample of 40 high school students who were attending HHC and aged between 13 and 25 years. The students were enrolled at various high schools across Christchurch. Sixty-five per cent were female (26 females) and 35% were male (14 males). Thirty-eight per cent of students who attended HHC came from Afghanistan; 30% from Somalia; 10% from Iraq; and 5% from Nepal, Bhutan and Iran. The remaining 3% were from Malaysia, India, and Japan. High school students who attended HHC had been living in New Zealand for a maximum of 17 years and minimum of 4 months, with an average of 6.13 years.

Students attended high school at different geographical locations at Christchurch. Students were enrolled in the following: 3% were year nine, 8% were year 10, 33% were in NCEA level one, 21% were in NCEA level two, and 18% were in NCEA level three. Also, 10% enrolled studied in ESOL (English for Students of Other Languages) programmes.

The resettled former refugee students came to live in New Zealand under the following categories: 61% came under the refugee family support category, 32% came under the refugee quota programme, and a remaining 8%described as other. Furthermore, 53% of high school students had received a primary level of education before residing in New Zealand, and 48% did not receive any previous education.

Part 2: Graduate Sample

The study comprised a sample of 30 graduate students aged between 18 and 35 years who attended HHC from the year 2000. Forty per cent of the graduate sample came from Afghanistan, and 30% from Kurdistan (or Northern Iraq). Ten per cent of graduates each came from Somalia and Bhutan; and 3% each came from Nepal, Egypt, and Indonesia. Most graduates had lived in New Zealand for 11.8 years, and the average time spent at HHC was four years. The students were later enrolled at tertiary education where they studied a range of subjects from a Diploma in Business Studies or a BA in Computer Science to a double degree in marketing and management or law and engineering. At Ara Institute of Canterbury (formerly The Christchurch Polytechnic Institute of Technology, that merged with Timaru-based Aoraki Polytechnic and became Ara Institute of Canterbury in 2016), former refugee students studied nursing, hospitality management, and architecture.

The graduates who attended HHC came to resettle in New Zealand under the following policies: 57% came under the refugee quota programme, 30% came under the refugee family support category, 7% were asylum seekers, and 7% were 'other.' Moreover, 50% of graduates had received a primary level of education before coming to New Zealand and 50% did not receive any previous education.

Measures

Part 1: High School Student-Attendees Questionnaire

The high school attendees' questionnaire comprised 26 questions and was designed in such a way that they were able to answer the questions simply and easily. They were asked how long they had spent at HHC, how often they attended classes, and how effective the classes were in moving them into higher education or enabling them to take up jobs.

Part 2: Graduate Questionnaire

The graduate questionnaire included 24 questions and was also designed to ensure that the graduates were able to answer the questions simply and easily. They were asked the length of time they had spent at HHC, how often they attended classes, and how effective the classes were in helping them prepare for tertiary education and obtaining their current positions.

Data Analysis

Quantitative Analysis

Our data includes both qualitative and quantitative methods. Descriptive statistics were used to characterise the overall sample from our quantitative analysis.

Qualitative Measures

Students who were attending, or had attended, HHC were interviewed. They were randomly picked, but only those who spoke English were chosen. Interpreters were not required. Interviews took 40 minutes, and they were transcribed and coded.

In addition, qualitative data were used to form conclusions to further validate the descriptive findings. The high school attendees' questionnaire included 26 questions, while the graduate questionnaire comprised 24 questions.

Results

Part 1: High School Students

The sample of high school students attended HHC for an average of four hours a week. Before entering NCEA or other higher levels of education, they had studied English (ESOL) for three years. Seventy-five per cent of respondents said that attendance at HHC was effective in helping them get to higher education, while 25% said that it did not help them achieve their study goals.

Our quantitative data revealed the following information. In terms of a future profession, 17% of respondents said they wanted to go into business, without being specific about what type of business. Thirteen per cent wanted to become accountants, 13% lawyers, and 3% social workers. Eight per cent of respondents said they wanted to become doctors, while 8% said they wanted a profession in information technology. Four per cent of respondents said they wanted to join the army, with 4% wanting to become game developers. Becoming an architect, a nurse, a software engineer, a dental hygienist or doing something in the construction industry were selected by 20% of respondents, or the equivalent of 4% for each category.

Qualitative interview questions focused on the importance of HHC achieving the students' academic goals. When students were asked in what ways the HHC helped them to achieve their goals, many said HHC provided a nice space to work, and that the teachers were helpful. One student stated, 'Of course almost everybody could achieve their study goals without HHC provided they are determined enough, but what HHC provides is a very good environment to study and receive help with studies.' Additionally, the HHC was viewed as a place to receive more help in language studies. One participant said, 'English as a second language is hard but with the HHC we can do it. I have passed all my exams with the help of HHC.'

The centre was also viewed as a space that increased motivation. One student said, 'For most of my life the only place I ever studied out of school was HHC. It's just a good place to study, which I find better than most places.' Other comments included, 'It helps us stay motivated,' and 'HHC helps to achieve higher grades.'

The majority of high school students found the HHC helpful, or even necessary to their success. One remarked, 'I couldn't live without the help of the Homework Centre.' Helpful aspects included both the environment and the access to individualised attention from teachers. As one student said, 'It does give me a nice space to do work as well as get help from teachers when I am stuck. As well as get more one-on-one help from teachers that I do not get in school.' Only one student interviewed thought that HHC did not provide help: 'I haven't attended HHC lately and it hasn't influenced my studies, which is a sign that I can achieve it without attending.'

The study asks how HHC enhances New Zealand's Refugee Resettlement Strategy (NZRRS) for education policies and if an education programme like the HHC should be supported financially by Immigration New Zealand under the NZRRS. The respondents overwhelmingly thought it should be included in the strategy and that it should be financed by the Immigration New Zealand for refugee resettlement.

Part 2: The Graduates

This part of the study was undertaken between July and November 2017 in Christchurch, New Zealand with a sample of 30 students aged between 18 and 35 years who attended HHC from 2000. The graduates were later enrolled at various courses at the University of Canterbury, Ara Institute of Canterbury, the University of Auckland, Otago University, and apprenticeship courses.

The graduates (former students) studied ESOL for a maximum of six years and a one-year minimum. The average number of years spent studying English to speakers of other languages (ESOL) was 2.59 years, and all of the students reached an NCEA level of understanding of English with an average of 3.10 years.

Graduates in the study attended university for a maximum of five years and for a minimum of one year. Many students had part-time, or even full-time, jobs while studying; the main occupations being sales assistants, sales consultants, and solicitors. This shows the extent to which these students are committed to completing their studies.

Among the graduates who participated in the survey, results indicated that the HHC was very important in providing them with additional support. They said it helped them achieve their NCEA goals, often with better grades than would have been the case without attending HHC. Of the graduates questioned, 47% said HHC helped them gain a merit in their NCEA and 30% stated HHC helped them to gain excellence. The remaining 23% said HHC had helped them gain their NCEA. The students spent on average 3.97 hours a week at HHC. English was the main subject in which students received tutoring at the HHC.

Themes that arose from qualitative measures among this group of students were similar to those of the younger students interviewed. Although several stated they would have managed without HHC, they also said that the centre greatly facilitated their understanding of required subjects. For instance, one student commented 'HHC made me understand my work I was given in school. It was hard for me to learn in class as the teachers would not fully explain how to do the work, but once I took it to HHC they made me understand the work.' This theme is also reflected in another graduate's comment: 'I would have achieved my schooling goals but not with good grades in some subjects.'

For some, the support offered at HHC was enough to help them pass courses and tests. This theme is expressed in the following quote,

> The Hagley Homework Centre helped with revision and having a place to concentrate with the appropriate help given. I saw many others who struggled with studying achieve their goals due to the addition of this help, and therefore the HHC helps with aiding students to achieve their goals.

Another stated, 'If I didn't attend HHC I wouldn't have understood any of my subjects.' And a third participant said, 'It helped me a lot throughout my schoolwork and especially with my exam.' These examples indicate that students managed to pass and move on to tertiary education thanks to the help they received.

However, other participants indicated that the support they received allowed them to not only pass, but also to exceed what they believe they could have achieved without the help of HHC. For instance, one student explained, 'I believe I could have achieved my school subjects but I would struggle to understand the content and may have struggled to endorse in excellence and merit.' Similarly, another participant stated, 'HHC helped me understand the work more to be able to get a higher grade.' One student believed that continuing at HHC as a family unit might have enabled her to achieve better results: 'Yes I attended HHC when I was young and if my parents still went there, I would have achieved better results in school.'

Another common theme was that of motivation. One participant stated,

> Need third party to help such as parents are supposed to help but they speak no English. Our peers had their English-speaking parents help them as that was their advantage. Thus HHC is good for refugee background. To help students answer questions they need third party help at home. Also HHC was a good motivation.

This quote also reflects the theme of increased motivation resulting from attending HHC, as does the following: 'Definitely would have been harder for me to gain the same level of understanding that all the other kids had, in saying that I could have done it all by myself but I probably would have struggled more so than I did now. Having HHC was more of a motivation.'

What Students Thought about HHC Resources

The participants were asked if HHC had enough resources, and 43% of respondents thought there were. However, 30% said there were not enough resources, while the remaining 27% were unsure. A lack of teachers, especially in subjects such as history, geography, and science, was a concern as was the need to queue up for help from teachers. To this point, one student stated, 'Sometimes there were no teachers to help me with subjects that were not their profession such as history and geography.' Students also suspected that there was a shortage of money to hire a sufficient number of teachers.

Comments about teacher shortages at HHC included both a simple shortage and a lack of culturally competent teachers. One student said, 'Access to teachers was difficult. We had no teachers for some subjects and we need teachers who work with refugees that are culturally competent.' Another student stated that 'there were more students' ratio compared to teachers, so sometimes we had to wait at least 40 minutes to an hour to receive help from experienced teachers with the subjects we were studying.' Beyond teachers, students commented on needs for technology and supplies. Participants remarked on the lack of computers and the need to queue up for them. Student conclusions about needs included the following: not enough teachers; too many students to have access to computers; not enough language teachers available; insufficient economic, media studies, arts, graphic design, and photography teachers.

Discussion

Most of the respondents to the survey said that HHC helped them achieve their goals to move onto higher education. Among the comments of the graduates who participated in the survey, they said that the HHC was very important in providing them with additional support. They said it helped them achieve their NCEA goals, often with better grades than would have been the case without attending HHC. Seventy-five per cent of high-school attendees said that attendance at HHC was effective in helping them get to higher education, while 25% said that it did not help them achieve their study goals.

Our analysis also shows that the refugees come from a variety of countries and that it took students an average of 3.10 years to reach their NCEA goal.

This research is important because it is the first research to look at the effectiveness of the HHC in terms of achieving educational outcomes and, ultimately, whether it helps students achieve their employment goals. The study asks how HHC enhances New Zealand's Refugee Resettlement Strategy for education policies and if an education programme like the HHC should be supported financially by Immigration New Zealand under the New Zealand Refugee Resettlement Strategy (NZRRS). The respondents overwhelmingly thought it should be included in the strategy and that it should be financed by the Immigration New Zealand under the NZRRS.

One of the aims of this chapter is to illustrate that HHC improves educational outcomes. The results from the survey show how this could be achieved and why teaching programmes like HHC should be included in New Zealand's Refugee Resettlement Strategy.

Attendance at HHC also indicated that an English-speaking refugee has a greater opportunity for success. Few refugees can become full participants in New Zealand society without formal English education or skill upgrading (TESOLANZ, 2003). Indeed, the findings from the HHC study show how important it is for a refugee-background person to be proficient in English and how it improves employment prospects.

Certainly, the HHC facilitates the learning of English, and many students have moved to higher education and have been successful in their chosen career. As Bloom, Donovan, and Udahemuka (2013) state, 'Education is seen by many people from refugee backgrounds as critical ... to obtain durable and on-going employment, access health services, and take part in the social and cultural life of their host country' (p. 36). The approach adopted by HHC, whereby refugee-background students help themselves, fits with the latest literature on refugees (Betts, Bloom, Kaplan, & Omata, 2016). In this way, rather than assuming that refugees are inevitably dependent, TESOLANZ (2003) states, 'We might help refugees to help themselves and in so doing simultaneously benefit host states.' Further, a programme such as the HHC allows students to improve their employment prospects, which, in turn, benefits society. For instance, this may result in an increased national tax benefit, as graduates gain better employment, or involvement in voluntary organizations.

Recommendations

Sixty-three per cent of graduates from HHC surveyed said that the institution was important in achieving an NCEA. Ninety-seven per cent of respondents said that HHC programme should be included as part of the resettlement policy for refugees. When asked the question: 'Should HHC become part of the policy of resettlement?' A repeated theme was the need for all refugees to be supported in their learning of English. As one student stated, the HHC could provide 'a chance for those who struggle to understand their studies but are determined to learn because they want to achieve their goals, but English maybe what is setting them back.' Another participant concluded that HHC (or similar centres that could be situated in resettlement areas around New Zealand) should be funded by the government because of the important services it offers to learn English,

> HHC should have the backing of the government because it helps include people who struggle to learn English and gives them the chance everyone else has; therefore, it should be a mandatory thing. Genuinely wouldn't be so confident in my English and University if it wasn't for HHC.

Another theme was broader, in recognising the need for educational support among all refugees, and not just those completing secondary school or planning to attend higher education institutions: 'It helps young and older people understand education and also shows that there is help and support out there and that they aren't alone.' This comment also alludes to the need for overall psychosocial support, and education as a means of supporting that need. Another theme was broader, in recognising the need for educational support among all refugees, and not just those completing secondary school or planning to attend higher education institutions.

After analysing the results from the research and reading current literature on education policies for refugees in New Zealand, we recommend an inclusive approach to education so that the needs of refugees are better understood and met. The positive results from HHC must be more widely communicated. Programmes such as the HHC should be included as part of the Refugee Resettlement Strategy. This means that such programmes should be rolled out across the country so that they are accessible to all refugees, UN quota refugees, and convention refugees (asylum seekers). Further, refugees should attend the classes at the Mangere Refugee Reception Centre and continue their extra-curricular education and training at HHC-like programmes. In terms of resources required to run the programme, these should be fully funded by the government. Refugee-background persons should be assessed individually, particularly in terms of English language skills and work readiness. The identification of career goals and the critical milestones of refugees are needed to ensure they are work ready and can achieve their career goals.

Conclusion

An overwhelming number of former refugees who graduated from a tertiary educational institution say that the learning platforms that are part of HHC should be included in New Zealand's resettlement strategy. Most refugees also say that HHC helped them achieve their goals, by supporting their goals and work habits. Most importantly, however, HHC provides a safe and tolerant environment where students can continue their studies. Therefore, they can share their views in a place where diversity is encouraged.

References

Betts, A., Bloom, L., Kaplan, J., & Omata, N. (2016). *Refugee economies: Forced displacement and development*. Oxford: Oxford University Press. Retrieved from https://www.rsc.ox.ac.uk/publications/refugee-economies-forceddisplacement-and-development

Bloom, A., Donovan, T., & Udahemuka, M. (2013). *Marking time experiences of successful asylum seekers in Aotearoa New Zealand*. A discussion document prepared by ChangeMakers Refugee Forum. Retrieved from https://crf.org.nz/sites/default/files/staff/Marking%20time%20%20Experiences%20of%20successful%20asylum%20seekers%20in%20Aotearoa%20NZ%20-%20FINAL%20--%20Dec%203.pdf

Buckner, E., Spencer, D., & Cha, J. (2017). Between policy and practice: The education of Syrian refugees in Lebanon. *Journal of Refugee Studies, 31*(4), 444–465.

Collins, S. (2018). NCEA debate: How can physics and tramping be valued equally? *NZ Herald*. Retrieved from https://www.nzherald.co.nz/nz/news/article.cfm?c_id=1&objectid=12004446

Fransen, S., Vargas-Silva, C., & Siegel, M. (2018). The impact of refugee experiences on education: Evidence from Burundi. *Journal of Development and Migration, 8*(1), 6.

Gruner, A., & Searle, W. (2011). *New Zealand's refugee sector: Perspectives and developments, 1987–2010*. A report from the Department of Labour (Unpublished). Retrieved from, http://www.mbie.govt.nz/publicationsresearch/research/migration/perspectives-and-developments.pdf

Hamilton, R. J., Anderson, A., Frater-Mathieson, K., Loewen, S., & Moore, D. W. (2000). *Interventions for refugee children in New Zealand schools: Models, methods, and best practice.* Report prepared for the Ministry of Education. Retrieved from http://thehub.superu.govt.nz/assets/documents/41424_interventions_0.pdf

Immigration New Zealand. (n.d.). *Refugee settlement, New Zealand resettlement strategy.* Retrieved from https://www.immigration.govt.nz/documents/refugees/refugeeresettlementstrategy.pdf

McBrien, L. J. (2014). *I ōreatetuātara ka patukiwaho: Competing priorities in the New Zealand refugee resettlement strategy.* Fulbright New Zealand. Retrieved from http://www.fulbright.org.nz/publications/2014-mcbrien/

Ministry of Education. (2015). *Ministry of Education support for refugee background students and their families in New Zealand schools.* Retrieved from https://niphmhr.aut.ac.nz/__data/assets/pdf_file/0011/11135/4.-Abdirizak-Abdi-Ministry-of-Education.pdf

Moir, J. (2017, December 14). Government announces complete shake-up of NCEA for 2018. *Stuff.* Retrieved from https://www.stuff.co.nz/national/education/99843984/government-announces-complete-shakeup-of-ncea-for-2018

National Qualifications Authority (NCQA). (n.d.). Retrieved from https://www.nzqa.govt.nz/ncea/understanding-ncea/

O'Rourke, D. (2011). Closing pathways: Refugee-background students and tertiary education. *Kōtuitui: New Zealand Journal of Social Sciences Online, 6*(1–2), 26–36. doi:10.1080/1177083X.2011.617759

Riggs, S. (2009). *Tertiary education and the 2009 budget.* Retrieved from http://teu.ac.nz/2009/06/tertiary-education-and-the-2009-budget/

TESOLANZ. (2003). *Refugees learning English.* Retrieved from http://www.tesolanz.org.nz/Site/Publications/Reports/Refugees_2003.aspx

UNHCR. (2014). *Resettlement handbook, country chapter: New Zealand.* Office of the United Nations High Commissioner for Refugees. Retrieved from http://www.unhcr.org/3c5e59d04.html

UNHCR. (2016). *Left behind: Refugee education in crisis.* Retrieved from http://www.unhcr.org/59b696f44.pdf

UNHCR. (2018). *Resettlement.* Retrieved from http://www.unhcr.org/resettlement.html

Waters, T., & LeBlanc, K. (2005). Refugees and education: Mass public schooling without a nation-state. *The University of Chicago Comparative Education Review, 49*(2), 129–147.

CHAPTER 3

Refugee Student Transitions into Mainstream Australian Schooling

A Case Study Examining the Impact of Policies and Practices on Students' Everyday Realities

Amanda Hiorth

Introduction

In Australia, tens of thousands of refugee applicants are accepted for permanent protection annually. In 2017 the government issued 27,626 offshore humanitarian visas with approximately one third of these being young people aged up to 18 years (Department of Immigration and Border Protection, 2017; United Nations High Commissioner for Refugees, 2017). Victoria is a diverse state with 172,336 students from language backgrounds other than English (LBOTE), and 13% of all Victorian students classified as English as an Additional Language (EAL) learners (Department of Education and Training, 2017c). Victoria also has the largest population of refugee-background (RB) young people in Australia, with over 9,000 RB students in public schools (State Government of Victoria, 2015).

While programs designed to support newcomers differ amongst states and territories, educational and language support in the form of English Language Schools (ELS) or centres accommodate learners before they enrol into mainstream schooling. In Victoria, newcomers are funded for an initial 20 weeks at an ELS. For RB learners who typically arrive with interrupted education backgrounds and limited literacy, an additional 20 weeks is often provided. Following this, students make the move into local mainstream schooling.

For RB students, life in a mainstream Australian school can be a strange and surprising experience. Students are required to learn a new language; acquire new values; compete with English-speaking peers who already have significant linguistic, cultural, and social advantages; and adjust to new ways of living in a very foreign environment (Miller, 1999). Students must also contend with adjusting to life in their new country of settlement (Centre for Multicultural Youth Issues, 2006) while managing the sometimes-turbulent period of adolescence (Victorian Foundation for Survivors of Torture, 2004). The move from the intimate and supportive environment of the ELS to the large

© KONINKLIJKE BRILL NV, LEIDEN, 2019 | DOI: 10.1163/9789004401891_003

bureaucratised institution of mainstream secondary school with less personal connections and high pressure learning environments has been found to trigger previous feelings of loss and trauma, to decrease feelings of self-worth, and increase anxiety (Refugee Education Partnership Project [REPP], 2007). Transition for RB learners can, therefore, be a disorienting experience, filled with discontinuities and challenges.

Links between the significance of transition and learners' future pathways into Australian society are often not made in educational or refugee-based literature; however, transition is a formative process in students' educational journeys. The inability of a society to enable its young people to reach their full potential through education can have serious social and economic ramifications (McBrien, Dooley, & Birman, 2017), particularly for RB young people for whom education is an essential part of resettlement and rehabilitation (Gifford, Correa-Velez, & Sampson, 2009; Hamilton & Moore, 2004; McBrien, 2005, 2009; Walsh, Este, Krieg, & Giurgiu, 2011). Schools play a vital role in stabilising the unsettled lives of RB young people, providing safe spaces for learning opportunities; facilitating intellectual and personal development; inducting learners into majority language, history, and culture; and, supporting socialization and acculturation into society (Gifford et al., 2009; Matthews, 2008; McBrien, 2005, 2014). These new skills have potential to build confidence for social and economic participation, to disrupt cycles of disadvantage (Commonwealth of Australia, 2009; Earnest, Housen, & Gilleatt, 2007; Gifford et al., 2009) and to enter into gainful employment (McBrien, 2014). Schools are training grounds for active citizenship (Refugee Education Partnership Project [REPP], 2007): a place where strong foundations for a successful future are laid. The impact of transition beyond education is, therefore, wide and far-reaching.

This chapter presents an ethnographic case study of newcomer Karen EAL students who made the move from ELS into mainstream high school in the state of Victoria, Australia. This study highlights daily realities of the transition journey common to many refugee students with experiences of interrupted education, limited literacy, beginning English language and literacy, personal disruption, and trauma throughout their lives.

Students' transitions to very new social, cultural, linguistic, and educational contexts are explored in this research, as well as the impact various policies and practices can have on students in transition. This investigation was undertaken to understand how to better support RB learners in transition, and was guided by the following research questions:

- What are the experiences of RB students as they transition into mainstream schooling?

– What educational policies and practices are in place for transitioning students?
– What is the impact on students in supporting or hindering students' transition?

Literature Review

What Is Transition?

Educational transition can be defined as a process of leaving one familiar location or level and moving into another unfamiliar or alternative location or level (Margetts, 2002). The process is characterized by tensions and uncertainties, and involves changes common to all students in a state of transition, including leaving old friends and making new ones, new modes of learning and development, strong emotional arousal, new identities and status, and trials of taking on expected behaviours or demands (Catholic Education Office, 2010; Department of Education and Early Childhood Development, 2009; Isakson & Jarvis, 1998; Margetts, 2002). Transition represents a new phase of life or milestone in the lives of students and families (Dockett & Perry, 2013), and is considered to be 'connected with … social[ly] regulated … developmental demands that require intensified and accelerated learning' (Kienig, 2013, p. 23).

Current Provisions for RB Learners in the Australian Education System

The Australian education system, as noted by Alikhan (2016), is 'ideally positioned to support refugee [background] students' educational, social and emotional needs' (p. 25), and Victorian state policy documents which provide guidelines on how to cater for these students have been cited as exemplary (Cummins, 2000). The Victorian government has published several documents recognising the diverse multicultural and multilingual array of students enrolled in Victorian schools, also acknowledging typically high levels of disadvantage amongst this cohort. The State Government of Victoria's (2008) social action plan, 'A Fairer Victoria,' is one policy document addressing disadvantage and promoting inclusion and participation for these diverse learners in schools and the wider society. The government pledged $1.2 million over four years for specialist EAL services built around a vocational curriculum for newcomer students. Although not specific to RB learners, the document does emphasise focused support at critical life transitions such as starting school and entering the workforce to ensure that disadvantage does not become entrenched.

Victoria's Department of Education and Training (DET) has also released policy documents including the Ministerial Statement Blueprint for Government Schools (Department of Education and Training, 2003). The document outlines a reform agenda for government schools to ensure that all students are provided high-quality education and genuine opportunities to succeed. One core strategy is recognizing and responding to diverse student needs. DETS website contains a substantial array of resources, guidelines, and advice for mainstream schools and teachers to cater for EAL learners, including 'Learning and Teaching Resources' (Department of Education and Training, 2016); 'Tools for Enhancing Assessment Literacy for Teachers of EAL' (Department of Education and Training, 2017a); 'Supporting EAL at transition to school' (Victorian Curriculum and Assessment Authority, 2016); and, the 'EAL Handbook' (Department of Education and Training, 2016). These documents and their guidelines are not prescriptive, nor focused specifically on RB learners in transition; however, school leaders and teachers can access ample resources through the Department's website to support learners in their move to mainstream schooling.

In spite of such provisions, there are still multiple issues for RB learners in the mainstream education system. Although the DET provides funding for newcomers via the New Arrivals Program and EAL Index Funding as identified in the Student Resource Package (Department of Education and Training, 2017b), this is not specific to RB learners in transition who require targeted support for a suite of complex needs. Time at the ELS is said to be wildly insufficient, given that it can take anywhere from five to ten years for learners with backgrounds of interrupted schooling and limitations in first language literacy to become proficient in academic registers of language necessary for mainstream school (Brown, Miller, & Mitchell, 2006; Collier, 1987; Cummins, 2007; Gibbons, 2006; Hammond, 2014). Lack of English fluency can contribute to feelings of insecurity, self-consciousness, increased levels of stress, lower self-esteem, and fear of being teased or alienated (Hyman, Vu, & Beiser, 2000; Matthews, 2008; Poppitt & Frey, 2007). Accessing education through barriers of limited linguistic understanding and literacy while adjusting to school can prove to be an immense challenge (Birman & Tran, 2017).

In a study about inclusive education for RB students in Queensland, students were rarely targeted with specific policies, instead, they were 'conflated with other categories such as EAL, or not mentioned at all' (Taylor & Sidhu, 2012, p. 32). The researchers also found that learning needs other than language were not attended to; resources were inadequate resulting in shortages of specialist teaching staff; and teachers were offered limited professional development to assist them in meeting the needs of RB students (Taylor et al.,

2012, also supported by Birman et al., 2017; Patel, Saudenmeyer, Wickham, Firmender, Fields, & Miller, 2017). These inadequacies, they claim, were a result of limitations in policy and provision, hampering teachers' and schools' capabilities to provide sufficient support and students' ability to access mainstream curriculum. Teachers in numerous studies report feeling unprepared, frustrated and challenged when catering to RB students and assisting them to achieve academically (Craighead & Ramanathan, 2007; Miller, 2009; Miller, Mitchell, & Brown, 2005; Refugee Education Partnership Project [REPP], 2007; Szente, Hoot, & Taylor, 2006; Weekes, Phelan, Macfarlane, Pinson, & Francis, 2011). Bodde (2011) calls for Australian schools to be properly funded and better equipped to provide effective teaching and support for RB learners in the huge gap between ELS and mainstream school (Hammond, 2014). Although provisions exist, learners in transition require far greater support.

Supporting RB Learners in Transition – What Works?
A number of studies are proposing viable solutions in recognizing the importance of transition and adjustment to schooling. The 'Good Starts' longitudinal project which tracked RB students over four years in their generalized resettlement to Australia recommends establishing bridging and transition programs to provide basic information about destination schools including culture, rules, expectations and enrolment procedures (Gifford, Correa-Velez, & Sampson, 2009). Other resettlement research projects suggest establishing transition models that offer comprehensive school inductions and supplementary assistance with mainstream classes; EAL support in curriculum areas; involving parents in schooling; and consistent support during transition such as assigning student buddies (Hamilton & Moore, 2004; Refugee Education Partnership Project [REPP], 2007). Hammond's (2014) work based in the New South Wales is the only study focusing specifically on RB learners in transition from ELS to high school. Hammond advocates to support learners by including stronger connections between ELS and high schools; providing on-going and targeted professional development for teachers; and specialized supports for RB learners.

Even without structural change, one solution offered in broader literature about supporting RB learners is to establish individual and caring relationships, getting to know students and responding to their needs. Teachers play a significant role in learners' school journeys, and caring is said to be one major pillar of culturally responsive pedagogies (Gay, 2000). Establishing respectful and caring relationships has been shown to promote healthy emotional and social development to empower minority students by legitimizing their voice and visibility, to empower identities, and to increase levels of engagement in school (Deiro, 2005; Gay, 2000; Henry, 2009; Kanu, 2008; Miller, 1999; Rutter & Jones, 1998). Caring relationships convey respect, restore dignity, have potential to foster resilience (Hamilton & Moore, 2004; Victorian Foundation for Survivors of Torture [VFST], 2004) and contribute towards a sense of belonging; important predictors for wellbeing among RB youth (Correa-Velez, Gifford, & Barnett, 2010). While such authors argue that caring relationships are merely principles of best practice teaching, the flipside is that this may place a heavy responsibility on the teaching profession, assuming a uniformity of perspective from teachers of RB students. Far more extensive research is therefore required to better understand learners' transition experiences, and to offer effective solutions to improve long-term education outcomes.

Theoretical Framework

The theoretical framework underpinning this research draws on Cummins' (2000, 2009) relations of power theory. Cummins' (2000) work explores structures of power extant in society – macro-interactions – and its impact on education systems and practices. The policies and practices of education systems and schools – micro-interactions – can be explained and understood within these frameworks of power and demonstrated in any number of ways, such as by pedagogical practice, student inclusion and teacher values.

Power relations and related practices within schools are never neutral and can determine student success or failure (Apple, 2014; Cummins, 1997). Cummins (2009) states that all practices within schools are either coercive – where dominant power structures subordinate minority groups, or collaborative – where power is co-created between dominant and minority groups. To explore and problematize these power relations is to uncover structures hidden within schools which impact on minority students. Cummins' theory offers effective ways to perceive, dissect and interpret the wider context of schooling, and to understand the ways collaborative and coercive practices facilitate or inhibit students in transition.

Cummins' work highlights the importance of relationships between educators and students in learning, drawing links to notions of caring relationships as one form of collaborative practice. Within teacher/student interactions a process of identity negotiation takes place, which, when affirming, has the potential to recognize learners' agency, resist devaluation, and respect basic human rights (Cummins, 1996). Affirming the identities of subordinated learners in the school community can, therefore, serve to challenge and transcend societal processes of subordination, thus enabling students to engage academically. Where such collaborative frameworks exist, power is co-created and shared amongst participants, resulting in empowerment that deepens students' sense of efficacy, and enables educators, students and communities to challenge the operation of coercive power structures (Cummins, 1997, 2000). The power relationship thus becomes an additive rather than subtractive one, ideal for a supportive environment for RB learners in transition.

Cummins' theory allows for a holistic and ecological view of an education system, exploring the embedded power relations at work within education structures. This framework enables a detailed examination of current policies and practices, and the impact these practices have in supporting or hindering learners' transitions into mainstream schooling.

Research Design

This research was part of a larger PhD project funded by a scholarship from the Australian government (see Hiorth, 2017; Hiorth & Molyneux, 2018; Molyneux & Hiorth, forthcoming). Conducted at the University of Melbourne, ethics approval was granted by both the University and the Victorian Department of Education. The broader study involved seven Karen adolescents, and ethnographic enquiry was chosen as it allowed myself as researcher to become immersed in students' lives throughout key moments of their transition journey. Utilizing ethnographic enquiry enabled trust and rapport to be built, and collection of rich and thick descriptions of students' transition experiences (Cohen, Manion, & Morrison, 2011; Denzin, 1999; Liamputtong, 2007; Punch, 2011).

Case study design provided an appropriate vehicle for in-depth analysis of the bounded system of transition, essential for understanding its context and students' everyday realities (Lincoln & Guba, 1990; Yin, 2008). The boundaries of this intrinsic case are the seven Karen RB students transitioning from ELS to mainstream schooling (Bell, 2005; Stake, 2005). No claim is made that this case represents other cases or can be generalized to other similar populations; rather, the purpose is to seek trends and themes, and to optimize understandings so that readers can draw their own conclusions (Stake, 2000). The aim of this project is to expand theoretical understandings about the nature of educational transition for RB students and to contribute to the growing pool of data in this field (Kervin, Vialle, Herrington, & Okely, 2006).

Methods

Methods used were common to the ethnographic approach and included data from interviews, observations, work samples, and pictures gathered over the one-year period of data collection (Hammersley, 2002; Yates, 2010). A total of 54 semi-structured interviews were conducted with students, their families, teachers at both the language school and respective high schools, and experts involved with either the Karen community or educational transition for refugee-background students. These interviews sought to reveal insights into the transition process from a range of stakeholder perspectives, and also served to build rapport and trust between myself as researcher, and the students and their families. Work samples were gathered from each of the students throughout transition to ascertain academic access to the school curriculum, and students were observed in class, at playtime and in their homes.

At times, it was necessary to step out of my role as researcher/observer and negotiate more active participation as advocate/supporter. This was done on a number of occasions when students showed signs of distress or requested assistance when navigating the extensive high school grounds, understanding homework tasks or more broadly questioning the Victorian education system. It therefore became incumbent upon me to keep detailed memos during the research in my role as researcher/advocate. This enabled me to reflexively explore the impact of my presence on students' experiences of transition and therefore to thoroughly investigate the phenomenon of transition itself.

One core source of data were eight pictures hand-drawn by each student based on key themes around transition such as their feelings on the first day at high school, and reflections on how they had settled in six months post transition. This task prompted students to reflect critically and reflexively upon various facets of their experiences and feelings during transition (Pink, 2004). Drawing provided students with an alternative mode to voice their experiences when the act of speaking or writing was challenging, and positioned students centrally as meaning makers and active agents in the process of research (Alerby, 2000; Pink, 2004; Punch, 2002; Wilkin & Liamputtong, 2010). Some of these pictures are featured in this chapter, and are used to impress upon the viewer the emotionality of students' lived transition experiences, further serving to offer a direct mode of communication between student and reader (Alerby, 2003; Einarsdottir, 2007). These carefully combined methods of data collection enable crystallization of the data (Richardson, 2000; Richardson & St. Pierre, 2005) and a sensitive yet systematic investigation into questions at the centre of this study.

Participants

A total of 41 participants were involved in this research project, at the heart of which were four girls and three boys aged between 12 and 18 years. All students were resettled in Metropolitan Melbourne as refugees on humanitarian visas within a year of this project commencing, and were due to exit the ELS at the same time. Karen learners, an ethnic minority group from Myanmar, were purposively chosen in order to develop deeper insights into one of the newest and expanding newcomer cohorts in Australia.

Consent for English-speaking adult participants was obtained after verbally explaining the project, providing a written plain language statement about the research and inviting participants to sign a consent form approved by the University's central ethics committee. For the Karen families, these processes were repeated using Karen translations of forms and assistance from a Karen interpreter to orally explain the research, answer questions and invite consent for both their own involvement and involvement of their child. Although all seven students were minors and only parental/guardian consent was required, it was extremely important that students' agency was respected by inviting their own consent to be involved in this project.

For one term I volunteered at the ELS, sitting in on classes together with the students, getting to know them and slowly building friendly and trusting relationships. With assistance of the school's Karen Multicultural Aide, I verbally explained the project in English and Karen to the students, upon which verbal consent, and then written consent with a Karen translated form was received. At all times during the research, I made sure to request permission to observe, interview or collect and use pictures from the each of the students, also reminding them that they were free to withdraw from the research at any time with no consequence. This process was done to ensure that students felt respected and fully informed in their ongoing involvement. All students provided on-going consented and no students chose to withdraw.

Moo Dar Eh

Moo Dar Eh (a pseudonym) was one of seven Karen students involved in this research. I have chosen to present Moo Dar Eh's singular, in-depth experience of transition, as this allows for the rich details and nuances of transition to emerge within the scope of a chapter. The reader is able to journey alongside Moo Dar Eh, thus grasping the nature of transition through her own lived reality. Moo Dar Eh's transition story was chosen as she was present for all stages of transition at the ELS and high school, unlike some of her peers. Furthermore, her journey from ELS to high school was representative of many commonly shared experiences of transition amongst other Karen learners (anecdotally) and other non-Karen RB learners (Gifford, Correa-Velez, & Sampson, 2009).

Moo Dar Eh was 12 at the time of this study and transitioned into high school Grade 7. She lived with her mother, father, grandmother and four younger sisters. Although of S'gaw Karen ethnicity, she was born and raised in Ban Mae Surin, a Karenni refugee camp on the Thai-Burma border. She attended the camp's Karenni primary school for five years, becoming literate in S'gaw Karen, Karenni and Burmese. Moo Dar Eh took care of her sisters and helped with the housework and cooking. Her parents, who had limited prior schooling, were unemployed and studied full time at the government funded Adult Migrant English Program. Moo Dar Eh was quiet, mature, obedient and introverted. In class at the ELS I observed her to be extremely quiet in the shadow of her Karen friends, at times barely audible. In break times with her girlfriends however, she was chatty, giggly and bubbly. It was not until a few months into data collection that Moo Dar Eh started to open up to me. Upon visits to her school she greeted me with warm hugs and shared her thoughts and feelings with candour and forthrightness. Moo Dar Eh had a lot to say when she felt comfortable, and appeared to enjoy the opportunity to be heard, acknowledged and valued. Her future dream was to become a piano teacher in spite of having never played the piano (Figure 3.1).

Results

This section describes the processes of transition in chronological order as they were observed. The data selected for inclusion in this section illustrate the central experiences of transition for Moo Dar Eh at each of the stages, and incorporate all modes of data collected over one year – four school terms. Transition was conducted by the ELS Transition Officer (TO) and processed as eight discrete stages beginning at the ELS and ending at high school (Table 3.1). Departmental policies, guidelines or school frameworks prescribed none of these stages: it was a process organically developed over years of transition practices at this particular ELS.

Stage 1: ELS Teacher Consultation

One term prior to transition the ELS TO met with Moo Dar Eh's homeroom teacher for an informal conversation about her language level and academic progress to better understand Moo Dar Eh and to form suitable recommendations for transition. Moo Dar Eh and her family were unaware of nor involved in this part of the process.

FIGURE 3.1   Moo Dar Eh's future dream to become a piano teacher

Stage 2: Student Consultation

Following teacher consultation, Moo Dar Eh was interviewed by the ELS TO to discuss her preferred pathway for transition. The ELS TO assumed students had already discussed transition with their families; however, Moo Dar Eh was unaware the consultation was to happen and had little idea about her options. The ELS TO suggested Howard Secondary College (a pseudonym) located in her neighbourhood, to which Moo Dar Eh agreed.

Moo Dar Eh's parents were relieved and grateful to the TO as they had little knowledge of the Victorian education system or pathways beyond the ELS. Her father was pleased with Howard Secondary College, as it was close enough to their home that Moo Dar Eh could walk there independently. He was confident in her abilities to succeed, believing that exiting the ELS meant she was now

TABLE 3.1   The processes of transition

Stages	Transition activity
Stage 1	ELS teacher consultation
Stage 2	Student consultation
Stage 3	Provisional enrolment
Stage 4	Formal enrolment
Stage 5	Transition day
Stage 6	Exit reports distributed
Stage 7	First day at high school
Stage 8	Follow-up visit

academically and linguistically ready for transition, yet unaware the reality was that 40 weeks of ELS funding had merely ended. He commented:

> I think that she improved a lot. She can understand more English and she can speak as well. The [ELS] teacher[s] teach her how to read, write, listen, write – everything. So I think maybe they prepare everything for the students to cope with the high school

Stage 3: Provisional Enrolment

Howard Secondary College was a public coeducational high school catering to Grades 7–12. It had 109 teachers and 1321 students of whom one third were LBOTE. Five per cent of the LBOTE students were Karen and of the four Multi-cultural Education Aides (MEA), two were Karen. Moo Dar Eh was placed into an EAL homeroom class, with which she attended all subjects.

The ELS TO contacted the school to register her provisional enrolment. Although public schools were obliged to accept students within Departmental zoning predicts, the ELS TO lamented that it was an uphill battle enrolling RB EAL students. Howard Secondary College's Assistant Principal perceived students to be a 'big hassle' and resented facing teachers who complained that 'they didn't know what to do with them in class.'

Stage 4: Formal Enrolment

Several weeks later Moo Dar Eh attended high school for the morning with her mother and the ELS to to complete official enrolment paperwork. The Assistant Principal spoke for 20 minutes about the College, providing Moo Dar Eh with a text-heavy information pack. Although there was a Karen MEA interpreting, the Assistant Principal spoke too quickly, overwhelming both Moo Dar Eh and her mother. The MEA and TO then assisted the family to fill out the forms.

Stage 5: Transition Day

Transition Day was conducted several weeks before exiting the ELS, and was an opportunity for Moo Dar Eh to attend an ordinary day at the College and orient herself to the new surroundings. Moo Dar Eh, her mother, and grandmother arrived early at reception. Moo Dar Eh commented that she felt scared and did not know what Transition Day meant, nor what it entailed. When I explained that she would spend the day at the school sitting in on classes and meeting teachers and students, she scrunched up her face and asked her mother for money to buy some lunch at the canteen.

Moo Dar Eh and her family met the school's EAL Director who asked her questions about her background, language level, and prior schooling experiences. Although the Director usually took students on a school tour and assigned a buddy for the day, time constraints meant this did not happen for Moo Dar. Walking to her first class she frowned and whispered loudly 'I don't want to go.' Several days after Moo Dar Eh told me she felt scared and found the classes to be exceptionally difficult in language and content. She had understood little and was particularly fearful of one teacher who 'talked very loudly.'

In an interview two days prior to leaving the ELS, Moo Dar Eh noted she was feeling incredibly nervous to start Grade 7, with little idea of what to expect in spite of 'Transition Day', commenting:

I feeling sad for saying friend goodbye and ... gonna [leave] this school.

In a picture capturing her feelings about transition (Figure 3.2), Moo Dar drew herself alone with her thoughts and imagining the journey ahead. Interpreting her picture in an interview, she emphasised how her facial expression illustrated conflicted emotions: her mouth a half smile, half frown. Although she noted that she felt happy about the prospect of 'learn many things' and 'have many friends,' she felt sad having to leave the ELS full of so many positive experiences. As the final bell rang at the ELS, I observed her running from the school in a hurry without so much as a goodbye to her teachers, classmates or friends.

Stage 6: Exit Reports Distributed

Prior to transition, Moo Dar Eh was sent home with her final ELS report. This was a thorough, five page document written by her homeroom teacher detailing her level and achievements in language, numeracy, social skills, and

FIGURE 3.2 Moo Dar Eh feels mixed emotions at her upcoming transition

learning behaviors. This report was also sent to Howard Secondary College's EAL Director in the assumption it would be distributed to her teachers. However, teachers interviewed for this study were surprised to hear of its existence. Moo Dar Eh and her family were not aware of this stage in transition.

Stage 7: First Day at High School

Moo Dar Eh began in the middle of the school year, at the start of term three when school routines and friendships were already established. The half

REFUGEE STUDENT TRANSITIONS INTO AUSTRALIAN SCHOOLING 71

TABLE 3.2   A de-identified replica of Moo Dar Eh's two-week rotation timetable

Monday – 1	Tuesday – 2	Wednesday – 3	Thursday – 4	Friday – 5
07F 7WODF2	07F 7SEDF2	07F 7MATF2	07F 7PEDF2	07F 7TEXF2
BC 11	WLC 8	ED 5	EO 9	MC 2
07F 7EALF2	07F 7MATF2	07F 7DRAF2	07F 7ARTF2	07F PEDF2
AH 9	ED 5	OZ 14	EE 8	EO 9
07F 7SCIF2	07F 7ITAF2	07F 7LITF2	07F 7NUMF2	07F 7MATF2
LQ 10	WW 14	EC 4	BU 16	ED5
07F 7SEDF2	07F 7WODF2	07F 7SCIF2	07F 7TEXF2	07F 7EALF2
WLC 8	BC 11	LQ 10	MC 2	AH 9

Monday – 6	Tuesday – 7	Wednesday – 8	Thursday – 9	Friday – 10
07F 7EALF2	07F 7LITF2	07F 7EALF2	07F 7SCIF2 LQ	07F 7EALF2
AH 9	EC 4	AH 9	10	AH 9
07F 7TEXF2	07F 7ARTF2	07F 7MATF2	07F 7DRAF2	07F 7NUMF2
MC 2	EE 8	ED 5	OZ 14	BU16
07F 7NUMF2	07F 7SEDF2	07F 7LITF2	07F 7ITAF2 WW	07F 7ITAF2
BU16	WLC8	EC 4	14	WW 14
07F 7SCIF2	07F 7MATF2	07F 7WODF2	07F 7SEDF2	07F 7PEDF2
LQ 10	ED 5	BC 11	WLC 8	EO 9

excitement Moo Dar Eh felt about starting high school quickly dissipated on her first day, and she commented that she felt 'only scared and sad' and 'not at all happy.' Moo Dar Eh was provided a complex timetable based on a two-week rotation (Table 3.2), which she was unable to make sense of. This meant she could not determine her classes or classrooms. Moo Dar Eh inevitably became lost on several occasions those first two weeks. Feeling distressed, she stated:

> I lost and I go to junior school the first day. The second day of school I go to office and I didn't know my class and I ask teacher to check Math and she [made] me go to Junior school and the teacher … she come and take [me].

Although the first day was considered to be the end of Moo Dar Eh's transition journey, I continued to collect data for two terms (six months) to track how

FIGURE 3.3   Moo Dar Eh recalls her first weeks of high school

she settled into life at Howard Secondary College. In the first few weeks Moo Dar Eh regularly stated she wanted to return to the ELS. In a picture drawn six months post transition recalling these initial weeks (Figure 3.3), Moo Dar Eh emphasised her fear, anxiety, and lack of positive emotions. The large school building loomed behind her as if a great unknown, not a pathway in sight to guide her. She drew herself as isolated and alone, without friends and an expression of nervous concern.

Friendships were a source of great concern for Moo Dar Eh, who commented she felt 'very scared [and] sad ... because I don't have a friend. I just sit like that and don't do anything.' The EAL Director had seated Moo Dar Eh with two Thai girls, expecting that they would welcome, support, and befriend her. Moo Dar Eh reluctantly joined the new friendship group with little other options, unable to communicate or feel comforted by the new culture. In an interview, Moo Dar Eh spoke about this difficult time:

Moo Dar Eh: I just walk with them [at lunchtime] and they're speaking Thai and I don't understand, but I just walk with them

Researcher: Ah, so you want to talk to them but you can't talk to them?

Moo Dar Eh: (Nods in agreement). And lunchtime when I walking with them they didn't eat rice and I bring rice and I can't eat. I want to share [all of our food together] with my friend [like we did at the language school], but when I first come [to high school] they didn't want to. So I just walk ... with them. I didn't eat lunch.

Researcher: Oh no. Did they eat something?

Moo Dar Eh: Yeah, they had their own food but they didn't share.

Academically, her first term was exceptionally challenging regarding the new language demands and complex class content. She appeared to understand little of what was going on around her, sitting quietly with pen in hand and looking around the room with a confused expression. At times she copied her peers or responded to teachers' questions with silence. Moo Dar Eh admitted to feeling bored in class. When disengaged, she lay her head on her desk or crossed her arms and slumped into her chair. Moo Dar Eh noted the large gap between the ELS and high school:

> It become so hard to do the work. The teachers talk too fast. When I go to class like I was just sit like that – I didn't do anything.

Stage 8: Follow-up Visit

The final stage of transition was for the ELS TO to visit Moo Dar Eh at high school one term following transition to conduct a follow-up survey about how she had settled in. Concerns would be fed back to the school's EAL Director and gathered data would feature in the ELS annual report. At the time of this research the ELS TO was unable to conduct this follow-up visit due to her heavy workload. Moo Dar Eh and her family were unaware of this stage of transition.

When I visited Moo Dar Eh two terms post transition, the anxiety I had previously observed dissipated, replaced by confidence in the familiarity of her daily routine. Although still unable to read her timetable, she had memorized classroom locations and teachers' faces, was able to navigate school grounds and arrived at class on time. In class, she was most engaged when teacher instructions were short, clear, and involved an achievable and well-scaffolded task. Textiles, woodwork and sports were her favourite subjects because they involved physical activity, reduced pressure on language and content, and she could rely on her strong skillset and creativity. She also loved art because her teacher was 'really nice and friendly.' Moo Dar Eh struggled to understand some classes, particularly when topics were disparate and limited in relevance to her daily life and prior experiences. For example, topics covered in Social Studies over one term included medieval punishment, Spokane Native American Indians, early river civilizations, and the pyramids of Egypt. She found homework challenging, often not understanding the task and unable to rely on family support.

Moo Dar Eh was enthusiastic to learn but internalized her academic failures, feeding into her decreasing confidence levels and perceived inevitable failure. When seeing her low score from her mathematics exam, she commented:

> I'm not good at study. I love Math, but I always fail Math. I don't know [why] – because I not study or something? I study, but when I do the test I will fail.

Moo Dar Eh's parents felt sorry they were unable to provide academic support, but believed her difficulties could be overcome if she just tried harder.

At the end of the school year, two terms post transition, Moo Dar Eh felt happier about life at Howard Secondary College. In a picture drawing herself at school (Figure 3.4), she featured herself and her new friend, smiling and standing together in school uniform. She had moved away from the Thai girls originally assigned by the EAL Director, and found another Karen girl with whom she had become very close. She attributed her new feelings of positivity about high school solely to this nourishing friendship. Once again I observed Moo Dar Eh to be her usual giggly and chatty self, comfortable and settled in her environment.

Discussion

This section of the chapter presents three key findings in response to the research questions. It explores Moo Dar Eh's experiences as representative of the case of the seven Karen students to better understand the phenomenon of transition from ELS to mainstream schooling, and discusses the impact various

FIGURE 3.4 Moo Dar Eh on the right with her friend at high school, six months post transition

education policies and practices had on the learners, as well as how these practices supported and/or hindered students' transition.

1. *Transition is a complex and non-linear process, which requires sustained and long-term support for learners*

Transition as implemented in the schools of this study was a linear succession of discrete stages lacking in formal, standardized processes and limited support. It was perceived to be a finite journey with a clear start and end point, where students were considered to have transitioned upon completion of their first day of high school. However, bridging the vast gaps between the ELS and mainstream school required ample time to prepare students and allay anxieties about how mainstream school 'works' and where they fit into the new system. Students aspired to find their place, to have their identity affirmed and to feel a sense of belonging in their new school communities. This was a far more difficult and long-term journey than any of the stakeholders had anticipated, and support was limited regarding physical and symbolic access to schools or implicit understandings about how to 'be' a student in an Australian school. Such a lack of collaborative practices (Cummins, 2000) meant that students were marginalized and disempowered in the mainstream school system.

Similar to findings of McBrien's (2009) study involving Southeast Asian refugee parents, families of the transitioning students were constrained in participating in schooling, in making informed decisions about transition and advocating for their children. This was due to their inexperience participating in formal schooling, their lack of confidence in understanding the Australian education system, and cultural perceptions of teachers as the educational experts of their children. Subsequently students and their families' voices, concerns, needs, and aspirations were rarely featured at the centre of transition. Instead, transition became a process that happened 'to' them, but not 'with' them; a process in which learners' agency was often ignored in the micro-interactions of everyday schooling (Cummins, 2009).

These coercive practices (Cummins, 2000) were unlikely constructed through ill intent, but the result of ignorance and systemic constraints such as limited supports for teachers, increased occupational expectations and excessive workloads (Centre for Multicultural Youth Issues [CMYI], 2006; Moll & Greenberg, 1990). Teachers, administrative staff and leadership teams were likely doing their best in an environment of ever-increasing demands, however these coercive relations of power ultimately resulted in marginalization and disempowerment for students, hindering transition.

In reality, everyday is transition day for vulnerable RB learners entering the mainstream school system. Transition requires reconceptualization in practice and policy regarding how it is perceived, defined, and enacted within schools. This study reveals transition to be a non-linear, recursive, long-term, and highly complex process. The timeline of when transition begins and ends is blurry, divergent, and unique to each student. Rather than discrete stages, it is more effective to prescribe 'phases' of transition, which encapsulate key junctures in the transition process and allow a more nuanced, iterative and individual approach. Acknowledging the lengthy nature of transition also enables sustained support for individual students across all phases. A new model representing these phases is presented in Figure 3.5.

The first phase Preparatory Transition occurs at the ELS and is a time of preparation for the move ahead – not only for students to become ready for school, but also for schools to become ready for students. This phase is marked by significant transition experiences such as enrolment and orientation to the

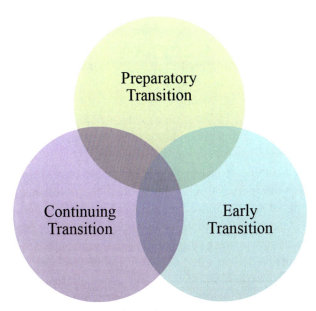

FIGURE 3.5   The three phases of transition

new school. The second phase Early Transition occurs during students' initial period at mainstream school. Although this phase cannot be rigidly set in time, the first days and weeks in the new setting is a critical time for students to find their bearings, begin acclimatizing, and for schools to make students feel welcome and included. The final phase is Continuing Transition and occurs at mainstream school. The pace and length of this phase is determined by individual students. It is a time where students oscillate back and forth, side to side, round and round, as they negotiate expectations of their new environment and find their place in the community. For some students this phase of transition may take months, and for others perhaps years. As captured in the diagram, all phases overlap and require sustained support throughout.

2. *Social aspects of transition are critical for RB learners, at the heart of which are caring relationships*

Social aspects of transition, while often overlooked by schools and teachers, held equal if not more importance for students than other aspects of schooling. Caring relationships impacted positively upon students' transition, deeply supporting the process. In the context of Cummins' (2000) relations of power theory this might be an unsurprising finding: one key factor of collaborative relations are positive interactions between teachers and students, where power is co-created and shared between dominant and minority groups. In fact, when students in this study were able to make trusted connections with teachers and subsequently access support, they felt safe, secure, and engaged in learning. My dual role as researcher/advocate also contributed to students' self-efficacy and confidence, as they reported feeling supported and encouraged to manage some of the challenges that arose in transition. As a result of these positive social interactions, students' sense of belonging to the whole-school community became stronger and their emerging identities as Australian students were enriched.

Human connection is at the heart of learning. Prior studies have emphasised how crucial positive interpersonal relationships can be for vulnerable EAL learners in accessing education and experiencing successful outcomes (Cummins, 1996, 2000; Fabian, 2013; Gay, 2000; Jenkins, 2004; Miller, 2003, 1999; Noddings, 2006). The stakeholders involved in transition seemed unaware of this critical knowledge, and failed to prioritize opportunities for the formation of caring relationships, such as when Moo Dar Eh was assigned friends who spoke a different language. Students were not provided sufficient time to build and sustain friendships prior to transition, and while caring relationships with teachers at the ELS already existed, these were not extended to relationships or even basic connections with teachers at the high school, resulting in limited support in academia and broader school processes. Such coercive practices (Cummins, 2000) reflected underlying power structures where the minority, RB learners had become subordinated by the dominant majority, the impact of which was to increase students' anxiety in transition and impair their readiness for high school.

Perhaps at the core of this limited focus on social connections was an overarching lack of prioritization for EAL and RB students in mainstream schools as reflected by the macro-interactions in wider society (Cummins, 2000). Often school communities were not welcoming to newly transitioning students. Although schools outwardly espoused rhetoric of inclusivity and diversity, in reality students and their needs were not mentioned in school policy, literacy frameworks or targeted provisions, with some school leaders even perceiving students to be a burden. Cummins notes that low prioritization of students is not surprising, as 'few school systems are willing to commit themselves beyond a rhetorical level to challenging coercive relations of power' (Cummins, 1997, p. 112). He argues that educating EAL students must become a whole-school issue and responsibility for the entire school staff rather than just EAL specialists, as this then relegates EAL students as a minority issue in a mainstream system (Cummins, 1996; also supported by Dare & Polias, 2001; Department of Education and Training, 2016; Hammond, 2014; Miller & Windle, 2010).

3. *RB students are optimistic, resilient, resourceful and capable agents of their own transition*

Students and families of this study had extensive funds of knowledge (González, Moll, & Amanti, 2005) to support their transition. Students were literate in multiple languages; technologically literate; had their own unique set of skills and abilities in a number of school subjects; and brought prior experiences of education and study skills to mainstream schooling. Students were proficient in cross-cultural interactions, holding a broad worldview from diverse cross- and inter-cultural backgrounds. They had distinctive personality traits and strengths, also exhibiting vast reserves of resilience shown in their ability to bounce forward through great adversity (Hutchinson & Dorsett, 2012). Students were optimistic and surrounded by highly supportive and proud families, who in turn were supported by the wider Karen community and various religious affiliations.

Each student and his/her family brought substantial skills and capacities of significant value to transition. However, often their needs and aspirations were presumed or overruled, and rarely were they provided opportunity to be actively involved in their own transition. In order for learners to become active agents in the process, all aspects of transition should be made transparent and fully involve all key stakeholders, placing the learners themselves at the centre of their own transition. Students and their families must have access to knowledge about the Australian education system, how it operates (explicitly and implicitly), the phases of transition, and where and how throughout these phases support can be accessed. Such knowledge would empower learners to make informed decisions about their education and advocate for their own needs. Cummins (2000) defines 'empowerment' to be the collaborative creation of power, however institutions such as schools may erroneously perceive empowerment to be at the expense of the dominant majority. In fact, when one minority group is uplifted and power is shared, it is to the advantage of all groups concerned (Cummins, 2000; Delpit, 2006). Empowering learners to be active agents along the process has the capacity not only to facilitate transition, but also to resolve current issues of equity and social justice.

Conclusion

This study reveals the experiences of Karen RB students in their move from ELS to mainstream schooling, and explores the educational policies and practices in place during the critical period of transition. Transition was deeply challenging for students: many well-intentioned practices were inadequate to support learners in their journey and resulted in coercive relations of power (Cummins, 2000). Findings of the study illustrate a need for school practices and wider education policy to recognize the significance of transition not only for learners and their families, but also for the whole school community. A more collaborative approach needs to be taken to identify and build on strengths, and to reconceptualise school readiness as a mutual experience of participation. Instead of placing the responsibility of 'readiness' on students, schools might also consider their readiness for transitioning students.

More efficient and effective operationalization of transition is needed to challenge common subtractive models about students' capacities, offering a strengths-based and additive lens to view students' wealthy funds of knowledge (González, Moll, & Amanti, 2005) and contributions in transition. Integrating this lens with these new and multi-faceted understandings about transition will ensure more equitable and socially just processes to support learners during a time that can lay down positive foundations for lifelong learning and integration into Australian society.

Recommendations born of this research are three-fold:

Recommendation 1: Include RB student transitions in educational policy
The role of government is vital in providing top-down support and direction in educational priorities for all learners. Policy demonstrates to schools, teachers, and communities what is of value in education. The current absence of top-down policy structures from federal and state education departments to direct schools in RB student transitions is of great concern. Initiating a transition-specific policy would support schools to include and prioritize RB learners in transition. Schools would be guided on how to make transition a smooth process for learners and in establishing necessary frameworks to formalize the operationalization of transition across schools. This would guarantee a system which is equitable, consistent, and sustainable, and lead RB students towards more fruitful outcomes in their education.

Recommendation 2: Designate transition-specific funding for RB EAL learners
Resources and provisions for RB learners in transition are currently insufficient. Transition-specific funding is required in the same way it is provided to all Victorian students transitioning from primary Grade 6 into high school Grade 7. The needs of RB learners in transition are complex and require sustained support over a long-term period. Funding provisions would recognize the considerable challenges involved for learners during this critical time by initiating such measures as:

- Extended time at the ELS to better prepare learners (ideally to two years over the six months currently offered in Victoria)
- Formalized bridging programs between ELS and mainstream schools
- Teacher exchange programs between the ELS and mainstream schools
- On-going professional development about RB EAL learners and their needs for mainstream teachers
- Integrated networks made up of stakeholders working together to support learners and families
- Intensive and consistent support for learners and families during all phases of transition

Schools would be accountable to the Department of Education and Training for the use of such funding, and the reporting of transition outcomes would ensure that evidence-based data informs on-going transition planning and improved supports for learners. These expanded provisions would have a significant, positive, and long-lasting impact on learners not only during transition but also for their long-term future in Australian society.

Recommendation 3: Establish Transition Support Networks where students lead their own transition

A student-centred approach to transitions where learners are recognized as being capable partners in transition would support the process significantly. Transition Support Networks would position learners at the centre to collaborate with all key stakeholders in an on-going dialogue about learners' individual and collective transition journeys and needs. Networks would involve students' families, representatives and leadership teams from the ELS and mainstream schools, Departmental representatives, external service providers, and community partners. These networks would work together to optimize all members' shared expertise and to implement policies and practices to support learners across all phases of transition.

This study was born from the desire to better understand students' experiences of transition, and to explore the structures in place which support learners' educational access in Australia. Although results of this study refer to this particular context and case of students, it is expected that findings and recommendations will resonate and have relevance for other similar cohorts of newcomer students. Transition for RB EAL learners is a field of research as yet not explored thoroughly. Much work is to be done to build knowledge about the phenomenon of transition in a variety of contexts and cohorts. Longitudinal tracking of students would also provide new understandings as to the long-term impact of transition and learners' inclusion into wider society. I call on my academic peers to advance this work, and to support students' hopes for their new futures.

References

Alerby, E. (2000). A way of visualizing children's and young people's thoughts about the environment: A study of drawings. *Environmental Education Research, 6*(3), 205–222.

Alerby, E. (2003). 'During the break we have fun': A study concerning pupils' experience of school. *Educational Research, 45*(1), 17–28.

Alikhan, S. (2016). Making schooling more humane for refugee and asylum seeker students. *New Community, 14*(3), 25–28.

Apple, M. (2014). *Official knowledge: Democratic education in a conservative age* (3rd ed.). New York, NY: Routledge.

Bell, J. (2005). Approaches to research. In J. Bell (Ed.), *A guide for first-time researchers in education, health, and social science* (pp. 7–27). New York, NY: Open University Press.

Birman, D., & Tran, N. (2017). When worlds collide: Academic adjustment of Somali Bantu students with limited formal education in a U.S. elementary school. *International Journal of Intercultural Relations, 60*, 132–144.

Bodde, R. (2011). *Karen refugee ministries: Needs and priorities study.* Melbourne: Anglican Diocese of Melbourne & Australian Karen Foundation.

Brown, J., Miller, J., & Mitchell, J. (2006). Interrupted schooling and the acquisition of literacy: Experiences of Sudanese refugees in Victorian secondary schools. *Australian Journal of Language and Literacy, 29*(20), 150–162.

Catholic Education Office. (2010). *Transition and engagement.* Melbourne: Catholic Education Office.

Centre for Multicultural Youth Issues. (2006). *Refugee young people and resettlement: Information sheet.* Melbourne: Centre for Multicultural Youth.

Cohen, L., Manion, L., & Morrison, K. (2011). *Research methods in education* (7th ed.). New York, NY: Routledge.

Collier, V. (1987). Age and rate of acquisition of second language for academic purposes. *TESOL Quarterly, 21*, 617–641.

Commonwealth of Australia. (2009). *Belonging, being and becoming: The early years learning framework for Australia.* Barton: Commonwealth of Australia.

Correa-Velez, I., Gifford, S., & Barnett, A. (2010). Longing to belong: Social inclusion and well-being among youth with refugee backgrounds in the first three years in Melbourne, Australia. *Social Science and Medicine, 71*, 1399–1408.

Craighead, E., & Ramanathan, H. (2007). Effective teacher interactions with English language learners in mainstream classes. *Research in the Schools, 14*(1), 60–71.

Cummins, J. (1996). *Negotiating identities: Education for empowerment in a diverse society* (2nd ed.). Ontario, CA: California Association for Bilingual Education.

Cummins, J. (1997). Cultural and linguistic diversity in education: A mainstream issue? *Educational Review, 49*(2), 105–114.

Cummins, J. (2000). *Language, power and pedagogy: Bilingual children in the crossfire.* Clevedon: Multilingual Matters.

Cummins, J. (2007). *What works? Research into practice.* Ontario, CA: The Literacy and Numeracy Secretariat.

Cummins, J. (2009). Pedagogies of choice: Challenging coercive relations of power in classrooms and communities. *International Journal of Bilingual Education and Bilingualism, 12*(3), 261–271.

Dare, B., & Polias, J. (2001). Learning about language: Scaffolding in ESL classrooms. In J. Hammond (Ed.), *Scaffolding teaching and learning in language and literacy education* (pp. 91–110). Newtown: Primary English Teaching Association.

Deiro, J. (2005). *Teachers do make a difference: The teacher's guide to connecting with students.* Thousand Oaks, CA: Corwin Press.

Delpit, L. (2006). *Other people's children.* New York, NY: The New Press.

Denzin, N. (1999). Interpretive ethnography for the next century. *Journal of Contemporary Ethnography, 28,* 510–519.

Department of Education and Early Childhood Development. (2009). *Transition: A positive start to school resource kit.* Melbourne: Department of Education and Early Childhood Development.

Department of Education and Training. (2003). *Blueprint for government schools: Future directions for education in the Victorian government school system.* Melbourne: Department of Education and Training.

Department of Education and Training (DET). (2016). *The EAL handbook.* Melbourne: Department of Education and Training.

Department of Education and Training. (2017a). *Tools for enhancing assessment literacy for teachers of English as an Additional Language (EAL).* Retrieved from http://www.teal.global2.vic.edu.au

Department of Education and Training. (2017b). *Student resource package.* Retrieved from http://www.education.vic.gov.au/school/principals/finance/Pages/srp.aspx

Department of Education and Training. (2017c). *EAL.* Retrieved from http://www.education.vic.gov.au/school/teachers/support/diversity/eal/Pages/default.aspx

Department of Immigration and Border Protection. (2017). *2015–16 humanitarian programme outcomes.* Retrieved from https://www.border.gov.au/ReportsandPublications/Documents/statistics/humanitarian-programme-outcomes-offshore-2015–16.pdf

Dockett, S., & Perry, B. (2013). Families and the transition to school. In K. Margetts & A. Kienig (Eds.), *International perspectives of transition to school* (pp. 111–120). London: Routledge.

Earnest, J., Housen, T., & Gillieatt, S. (2007). *A new cohort of refugee students in Perth: Challenges for students and educators.* Retrieved from http://clt.curtin.edu.au/events/conferences/tlf/tlf2007/refereed/earnest.html

Einarsdottir, J. (2007). Research with children: Methodological and ethical challenges. *European Early Childhood Education Research Journal, 15*(2), 197–211.

Fabian, H. (2013). Towards successful transitions. In K. Margetts & A. Kienig (Eds.), *International perspectives of transition to school* (pp. 45–55). London: Routledge.

Gay, G. (2000). *Culturally responsive teaching: Theory, research and practice.* New York, NY: Teachers College Press.

Gibbons, P. (2006). *Bridging discourses in the ESL classroom.* London: Continuum.

Gifford, S., Correa-Velez, I., & Sampson, R. (2009). *Good starts for recently arrived youth with refugee backgrounds.* Melbourne: La Trobe Refugee Research Centre.

González, N., Moll, L., & Amanti, C. (2005). *Funds of knowledge: Theorizing practices in households, communities, and classrooms.* New York, NY: Routledge.

Hamilton, R., & Moore, D. (2004). *Educational interventions for refugee children.* London: RoutledgeFalmer.

Hammersley, M. (2002). Ethnography and realism. In M. Huberman & M. Miles (Eds.), *The qualitative researcher's companion* (pp. 65–80). Thousand Oaks, CA: Sage Publications.

Hammond, J. (2014). *The transition of refugee students from intensive English centres to mainstream high schools: Practices and future possibilities.* Sydney: NSW Department of Education and Communities.

Henry, J. (2009). *Refugee transition into American public schools: An emergent study of major influences* (Doctor of education dissertation). The University of North Carolina, Chapel Hill.

Hiorth, A. (2017). *Drawings reveal the struggles and triumphs of child refugees in their first six months of high school.* Retrieved from https://theconversation.com/drawings-reveal-the-struggles-and-triumphs-of-child-refugees-in-their-first-six-months-of-high-school-74628

Hiorth, A., & Molyneux, P. (2018). Bridges and barriers: Karen refugee-background students' transition to high school in Australia. In S. Shapiro, R. Farrelly, & M. J. Curry (Eds.), *Educating refugee-background students: Critical issues and dynamic contexts* (pp. 125–143). Bristol: Multilingual Matters.

Hutchinson, M., & Dorsett, P. (2012). What does the literature say about resilience in refugee people? Implications for practice. *Journal of Social Inclusion, 3*(2), 55–78.

Hyman, I., Vu, N., & Beiser, M. (2000). Post-migration stresses among Southeast Asian refugee youth in Canada: A research note. *Journal of Comparative Family Studies, 31*(2), 281–293.

Isakson, K., & Jarvis, P. (1998). The adjustment of adolescents during the transition into high school: A short-term longitudinal study. *Journal of Youth and Adolescence, 28*(1), 1–26.

Jenkins, R. (2004). *Social identity* (2nd ed.). London: Routledge.

Kanu, Y. (2008). Educational needs and barriers for African refugee students in Manitoba. *Canadian Journal of Education, 31*(4), 915–940.

Kervin, L., Vialle, W., Herrington, J., & Okely, T. (2006). *Research for educators.* South Melbourne: Cengage Learning.

Kienig, A. (2013). Children's transition from kindergarten to primary school. In K. Margetts & A. Kienig (Eds.), *International perspectives of transition to school* (pp. 22–32). London: Routledge.

Liamputtong, P. (2007). *Researching the vulnerable.* London: Sage Publications.

Lincoln, Y., & Guba, E. (1990). Judging the quality of case study reports. *Journal of Qualitative Studies in Education, 3*(1), 53–59.

Margetts, K. (2002). How transition programs help students adjust. *EQ Australia, 3,* 15–16.

Matthews, J. (2008). Schooling and settlement: Refugee education in Australia. *International Studies in Sociology of Education, 18*(1), 31–45.

McBrien, J. (2005). Educational needs and barriers for refugee students in the US: A review of the literature. *Review of Educational Research, 75*(3), 329–364.

McBrien, J. (2014). *I ōrea te tuatara ka patu ki waho: Competing priorities in the New Zealand refugee resettlement strategy.* Wellington: Fullbright New Zealand.

McBrien, J., Dooley, K., & Birman, D. (2017). Cultural and academic adjustment of refugee youth: Introduction to the special issue. *International Journal of Intercultural Relations, 60,* 104–108.

McBrien, J. L. (2009). Beyond survival: School-related experiences of adolescent refugee girls and their relationship to motivation and academic success. In G. Wiggan & C. Hutchinson (Eds.), *Global issues in education: Pedagogy, policy, school practices and the minority experience* (pp. 294–330). Lanham, MD: Roman & Littlefield.

Miller, J. (1999). Becoming audible: Social identity and second language use. *Journal of Intercultural Studies, 20*(2), 149–165.

Miller, J. (2003). *Audible difference: ESL and social identity in schools.* Sydney: Multilingual Matters.

Miller, J. (2009). Teaching refugee learners with interrupted education in science: Vocabulary, literacy and pedagogy. *International Journal of Science Education, 31*(4), 571–592.

Miller, J., Mitchell, J., & Brown, J. (2005). African refugees with interrupted schooling in the high school mainstream: Dilemmas for teachers. *Prospect, 20*(2), 19–33.

Miller, J., & Windle, J. (2010). Second language literacy: Putting high needs ESL learners in the frame. *English in Australia, 45*(3), 31–40.

Moll, L., & Greenberg, J. (1990). Creating zones of possibilities: Combining social contexts for instructions. In L. C. Moll (Ed.), *Vygotsky and education: Instructional implications and applications of sociohistorical psychology* (pp. 319–348). Cambridge: Cambridge University Press.

Molyneux, P., & Hiorth, A. (forthcoming). Encountering and accommodating diversity: Contrasting approaches to refugee-background students from the early to middle years of schooling. *The European Journal of Applied Linguistics and TEFL. Global perspectives for teaching English to refugee-background students* (Special Issue).

Noddings, N. (2006). Educational leaders as caring teachers. *School Leadership and Management, 26*(4), 339–345.

Patel, S., Saudenmeyer, A., Wickham, R., Firmender, W., Fields, L., & Miller, A. (2017). War-exposed newcomer adolescent immigrants facing daily life stressors in the United States. *International Journal of Intercultural Relations, 60*, 120–131.

Pink, S. (2004). Visual methods. In C. Seale, G. Gobo, J. Gubrium, & D. Silverman (Eds.), *Qualitative research practice* (pp. 391–406). London: Sage Publications.

Poppitt, G., & Frey, R. (2007). Sudanese adolescent refugees: Acculturation and acculturative stress. *Australian Journal of Guidance and Counselling, 17*(2), 160–181.

Punch, K. (2011). *Introduction to research methods in education.* London: Sage Publications.

Punch, S. (2002). Research with children: The same or different from research with adults? *Childhood, 9*(3), 321–341.

Refugee Education Partnership Project (REPP). (2007). *The education needs of young refugees in Victoria.* Brunswick: Refugee Education Partnership Project.

Richardson, L. (2000). Writing: A method of inquiry. In N. Denzin & Y. Lincoln (Eds.), *Handbook of qualitative research* (3rd ed., pp. 923–948). Thousand Oaks, CA: Sage Publications.

Richardson, L., & St. Pierre, E. A. (2005). Writing: A method of inquiry. In L. Yates & N. Denzin (Eds.), *The Sage handbook of qualitative research* (3rd ed., pp. 959–978). Thousand Oaks, CA: Sage Publications.

Rutter, J., & Jones, C. (1998). *Refugee education: Mapping the field* (J. Rutter & C. Jones, Eds.). London: Trentham Books Limited.

Stake, R. (2000). Case studies. In N. Denzin & Y. Lincoln (Eds.), *Handbook of qualitative research* (2nd ed., pp. 435–454). Thousand Oaks, CA: Sage Publications.

Stake, R. (2005). Qualitative case studies. In N. Denzin & Y. Lincoln (Eds.), *The Sage handbook of qualitative research* (3rd ed., pp. 443–466). London & New York, NY: Sage Publications.

State Government of Victoria. (2008). *A fairer Victoria: Strong people, strong communities.* Melbourne: State Government of Victoria.

State Government of Victoria. (2015). *New guide to help refugee students and families succeed at school* [Media release]. Retrieved from https://284532a540b00726ab7e-ff7c063c60e1f1cafc9413f00ac5293c.ssl.cf4.rackcdn.com/wp-content/uploads/2015/06/150616-New-Guide-To-Help-Refugee-Students-And-Families-Succeed-At-School.pdf

Szente, J., Hoot, J., & Taylor, D. (2006). Responding to the special needs of refugee children: Practical ideas for teachers. *Early Childhood Education Journal, 34*(1), 15–20.

Taylor, S., & Sidhu, R. (2012). Supporting refugee students in schools: What constitutes inclusive education? *International Journal of Inclusive Education, 16*(1), 39–56.

United Nations High Commissioner for Refugees. (2017). *Figures at a glance.* Retrieved from http://www.unhcr.org/en-au/figures-at-a-glance.html

Victorian Curriculum Assessment Authority. (2016). *Supporting EAL at transition to school.* Retrieved from http://www.vcaa.vic.edu.au/Pages/resources/eyeal/welcome.aspx

Victorian Foundation for Survivors of Torture. (2004). *School's in for refugees: Whole-school guide to refugee readiness.* Melbourne: Victorian Foundation for Survivors of Torture.

Walsh, C., Este, D., Krieg, B., & Giurgiu, B. (2011). Needs of refugee children in Canada: What can Roma refugee families tell us? *Journal of Comparative Family Studies, 42*(4), 599–613.

Weekes, T., Phelan, L., Macfarlane, S., Pinson, J., & Francis, V. (2011). Supporting successful learning for refugee students: The Classroom Connect project. *Issues in Educational Research, 21*(3), 310–329.

Wilkin, A., & Liamputtong, P. (2010). The photovoice method: Researching the experiences of Aboriginal health workers through photographs. *Australian Journal of Primary Health, 16*, 213–239.

Yates, L. (2010). The story they want to tell, and the visual story as evidence: Young people, research authority and research purposes in the education and health domains. *Visual Studies, 25*(3), 280–291.

Yin, R. (2008). *Case study research: Design and methods* (4th ed.). Thousand Oaks, CA: Sage Publications.

CHAPTER 4

Systemic Policy Barriers to Meaningful Participation of Students from Refugee and Asylum Seeking Backgrounds in Australian Higher Education

Neoliberal Settlement and Language Policies and (Deliberate?) Challenges for Meaningful Participation

Caroline Lenette, Sally Baker and Asher Hirsch

Introduction

When 23-year-old Arash Bordbar received the 2016 *Young People's Human Rights Medal*,[1] he shared his experiences of living as an asylum seeker in Malaysia for six years before coming to Australia, to illustrate the central importance of education: *'It's the most basic form of human rights; with an education it can develop your skills and help you gain knowledge of your future and it helps you give back to the community'* (see https://www.humanrights.gov.au/news/stories/asylum-seeker-young-leader-arash-bordbar). He has since become an international advocate for higher education opportunities for refugee and asylum seeker students, particularly women and girls. Advocates like Arash are battling against two ideological drivers underpinning settlement, involving language and higher education policy in Australia: neoliberal efficiency and cost effectiveness on the one hand, and protectionist migration discourses on the other. In this chapter, we explore how Australian government policies on settlement and language learning impact students from refugee and asylum seeker backgrounds' possibilities for participating in higher education. We argue that current policy instruments can *restrict their educational imaginaries* by (i) maintaining uncertainty about visa status for extended periods of time (i.e. withholding opportunities to feel settled), and more importantly (ii) deliberately limiting their exposure to English language (i.e. denying opportunities to attain proficiency). Consequently, meaningful participation in higher education in Australia remains illusive for many students with lived experiences of forced migration.

As academics, we are committed to principles of social justice and privileging the perspectives of people from refugee and asylum seeker backgrounds in

© KONINKLIJKE BRILL NV, LEIDEN, 2019 | DOI: 10.1163/9789004401891_004

scholarly dialogues. We recognise from the outset that, as we have not experienced forced migration, this is a limitation in terms of speaking about this topic. We have included quotes from people with lived experiences throughout, drawing from the Refugee Council of Australia (RCOA) community consultations for which ethics approval was granted, to illustrate the complexity of the issues we discuss. We opened our discussion with words from an advocate with lived experience to be guided by his motivations and hopes. As scholars and advocates, we let our knowledge of the circumstances of Arash and others like him, who are working tirelessly to ensure that higher education opportunities are not elusive, permeate our discussions and ensure that our endeavours lead to meaningful outcomes for people with lived experiences.

Background

As at June 2017, there were an estimated 65.6 million people displaced worldwide, with over 22 million refugees and many in critical need of resettlement (United Nations High Commissioner for Refugees [UNHCR], 2017a). Due to continuing global concerns and political tensions over the increasing mass movement of refugees and migrants, the United Nations General Assembly (UNGA) issued the New York Declaration Addressing Large Movements of Refugees and Migrants in September 2016. As well as reaffirming commitments to the *1951 Refugee Convention* and the *1967 Protocol Relating to the Status of Refugees*, Member States committed to provide increased and coordinated protection for refugees and migrants. The New York Declaration tasked the UNHCR to present a Global Compact on Refugees (GCR) for adoption at the 2018 UNGA. The GCR will provide an international policy framework in response to the urgent need for a comprehensive and collaborative approach to addressing pressing issues of forced migration (UNHCR, 2017b). Higher education featured as an important topic in thematic discussions in Geneva (in October 2017) in the lead up to the drafting of a *Program for Action* to implement the GCR from 2018 onwards, which is a positive step towards ensuring better access. This process strengthens the UNHCR's existing efforts to make higher education an attainable goal for people with lived experiences.[2]

Refugee Settlement in Australia

Australia has a long history as a resettlement country, dating back to the early 1800s (Refugee Council of Australia [RCOA], 2017a). Australia became a state party of the *1951 Refugee Convention* when it was made legally binding in 1954, and is currently one of the top three resettlement countries after the United

States and Canada (Refugee Council of Australia [RCOA], 2016b). Over 870,000 refugees and humanitarian entrants have been resettled to Australia since the end of World War II. The country's current scheme offers 13,750 places to Onshore and Offshore applicants every year; in 2015, Australia committed to resettling an additional 12,000 people from Middle Eastern countries following a sharp increase and visibility in the movements of asylum seekers mainly from Syria (Department of Immigration and Border Protection [DIBP], 2017a). In 2015–2016, 15,552 visas were granted to offshore applicants from Iraq, Syria, Myanmar, Afghanistan, and Democratic Republic of Congo (DIPB, 2017b). The 2017–2018 Federal Budget announced that the humanitarian scheme would be expanded by 2,500 places in 2017–2018 (to 16,250 places) and will increase again in 2018–2019 to 18,750 places annually (Refugee Council of Australia [RCOA], 2017a). However, the total numbers will be lower in 2017–2018 than in the 2016–2017 total, which includes the additional intake of Syrian refugees announced in 2015.

The less controversial aspect is the offshore program (protection visas granted before arriving to Australia), while the contested element relates to the onshore program (asylum seekers processed once they reach Australian waters or land; see White, 2017), because many asylum seekers seeking protection arrive through irregular means, i.e., mostly by boat. This issue has garnered significant international criticism over the past 15 years[3] for clear breaches to Australia's obligations under international law, but successive governments have continued to introduce strict border security legislation with bipartisan support (Baker, Ramsay, Irwin, & Miles, 2018; Lenette, 2016). As such, despite this long history of successful humanitarian resettlement, it is difficult to extend a sentiment of a 'proud immigration nation' to policies relating to asylum seekers who seek protection in Australia. Over the past few years, an 'impenetrable system of visa allocation has been developed by successive governments, who have lost sight of the compassion shown by earlier generations' (White, 2017, pp. 2–3). Indeed, Australia's initial attitude towards asylum seekers who arrived by boat in the 1970s was aligned with an ethos of welcome and the need to contribute to shouldering the world's 'refugee problem.' However, the current situation is vastly different to those days of ensuring new arrivals were treated with care and respect. While this is not unique to the Australian context, government policy directed at asylum seekers has been scrutinized on the national and international scene because the measures are deemed 'inhumane and expensive' and are characterized by 'cruelty and abuse' (White, 2017, p. 2; see also Baker et al., 2018; Refugee Council of Australia [RCOA], 2015a). For instance, the UNHCR Commissioner and the Special Rapporteur on the

Human Rights of Migrants continues to express grave concerns about the treatment of asylum seekers in processing centres (International Detention Coalition, 2017).

Such policies materialise and become accepted as necessities because of on-going political discourses of fear and moral panic that have permeated public consciousness (Martin, 2015; White, 2017), even though most asylum seekers are eventually recognised as refugees and granted (depending on the policy of the day) permanent or temporary protection visas. Issues surrounding the country's unique policy of indefinite mandatory detention, its impact, and the trauma associated with such circumstances dominate the literature on asylum seekers (Lenette, 2016). Additionally, there are currently approximately 30,000 people living in Australia who arrived prior to 2014 and were thus subjected to different sets of rules that created a situation of protracted precariousness (Refugee Council of Australia [RCOA], 2015a; Refugee Council of Australia [RCOA], 2015b; White, 2017). The abundance of literature on the impact of this state of limbo for asylum seekers, paired with frequent policy changes, can easily be confusing. Amidst this Kafkaesque policy-scape, 'educational issues certainly get lost' (White, 2017, p. 3), and so the topic of access and meaningful participation in higher education has received limited attention, including in terms of media reporting on the barriers created intentionally through government policy.

For people who are offered permanent protection visas via the Offshore program, their permanent residency offers them access to a similar suite of provisions to higher education as is afforded to Australian citizens. As 'domestic' students from refugee backgrounds, they are eligible for government-subsidised higher education on a Commonwealth Supported Place and have access to the Higher Education Loan Program (HELP) to defer payment of fees. In contrast, the case of asylum seekers in Australia illustrates a deliberate approach to denying educational opportunities by maintaining uncertainty. They are currently classified as international students because they are 'temporary' entrants and so have to apply for entry to university as full-fee paying students (Baker et al., 2018). This comes in sharp contrast with most state governments' willingness to allow primary and secondary aged asylum seeker children to attend public schools (White, 2017). While there has been renewed commitment recently to offer generous scholarships for asylum seekers to attend university (Refugee Council of Australia [RCOA], 2017b), mainly in response to worldwide concerns about increasing intakes of Middle Eastern refugees, scholarships are described as 'stopgap measures' that simply offer a charitable substitute to the social justice imperative of making higher education more accessible for asylum seekers (White, 2017, p. 8; see also Lenette, 2016). Importantly, while the Australian Government funds (to varying degrees) initiatives that promote access and inclusion in higher education, asylum seekers who pay full fees or are on scholarships are generally not eligible to access such programs. As one person seeking asylum highlighted during the RCOA's consultations:

> I lost my dad, I lost my brother and I couldn't stay anymore. I came to be safe here. I came here in 2012, I'm not allowed to work, there are no funds for me to study. When I arrived I was 17. Imagine if you are 17 and you are not allowed to go to school, there are no funds for you to go to school. Now I'm almost 20. The best years of my life are gone. When can I go to school? When can I go to college? When can I have my education? (Refugee Council of Australia [RCOA], 2015b, p. 3)

The major ethical issue about this persistence with discouraging asylum seekers who arrived by boat from accessing higher education institutions is that it *achieves nothing* beyond extending border policies of deterrence. There is no valid explanation for the government's illogical stance, which results in years of missed opportunities particularly for younger generations, considering that most asylum seekers are eventually recognized as refugees under the *1951 Refugee Convention* (White, 2017).

Importance of Higher Education

As Arash's words conveyed, education is a basic human right enshrined in the *1948 Universal Declaration of Human Rights, the 1989 Convention on the Rights of the Child* and the *1951 Refugee Convention.* This is even more compelling for refugee children who can experience severe disruptions to their education in situations of conflict and exile (UNHCR, 2017c). For example, the UNHCR (2017c) highlights that only 1% of young people who are refugees have access to higher education (compared to 34% around the world). This means that only one refugee young person out of 100 will ever go to university or access vocational and technical education. This alarming trend suggests enormous untapped potential and clear educational disadvantage due to lack of viable pathways to access higher education, making this issue integral to the UNHCR's mandate. However, as Zeus (2011) contends, expanding access to higher education is hampered by a perception that it is a longer-term development effort, rather than an immediate need. The abysmal proportion of 1% of young people who have access to tertiary education provides a clear impetus to do much more in this area. A whole generation is at serious risk of being further disadvantaged and of contributing to a shortage of 40 million tertiary-educated workers worldwide by 2020 (UNHCR, 2017c). This is cause for grave concern, and comes in sharp contrast with the world-class facilities, research and educational programs that universities in resettlement nations like Australia have to offer.

Over the past decade, a number of praiseworthy refugee-camp based initiatives have been set up to give young people in particular an opportunity to study overseas-accredited tertiary courses (Crea, 2016; MacLaren, 2010; Wright & Plasterer, 2010); other programs such as the German DAFI scholarships scheme enable refugees to attend university classes in their countries of first asylum. Still, the UNHCR finds that 'too many ... refugees do not have the opportunity to go to university. For them, tertiary education is the exception, not the norm' (www.unhcr.org, 2017c). Given the extremely small numbers of refugees who are resettled in host countries each year – only 1% of the world's refugees (UNHCR, 2016), access to higher education in countries of exile, transit and resettlement continues to be hugely problematic.

The growing research on refugees in higher education in countries like Australia (Harris & Marlowe, 2011; Hirsch & Maylea, 2016; Lenette, 2016) highlights significant barriers and lack of support, preventing them from achieving their dreams of engaging with further education successfully. Overwhelmingly, the literature argues that supporting refugees to access higher education brings broad benefits across the lives of individuals, their immediate family and friends, and wider society (Bajwa et al., 2017; Naidoo et al., 2015; Olliff, 2010; Ramsay, Baker, Miles, & Irwin, 2016; Stevenson & Baker, 2018, 2010; UNHCR, 2016). Although the literature emphasises that refugees are not a homogenous group, there is a general consensus that students from such backgrounds have specific experiences that make access to and participation in higher education distinct. These factors can include:

- Interrupted education (Earnest, Joyce, deMori, & Silvagni, 2010; Harris, Spark, & Watts, 2015; Naidoo, 2009; Shapiro & MacDonald, 2017);
- Continuing psychological and emotional effects of trauma experiences (Earnest et al., 2010; Joyce, Earnest, DeMori, & Silvagni, 2010; McMichael, Nunn, Gifford, & Correa-Velez, 2014; Olliff, 2010);
- Lack of familiarity with language, writing and literacy demands (Cocks & Stokes, 2013; Hirsch, 2015; Ramsay et al., 2016);
- Lack of familiarity with social conventions around higher education (Cocks & Stokes, 2013);

- Difficulties making friendships or developing a sense of belonging (Joyce et al., 2010; Lawson, 2014; Olliff, 2010);
- Poverty (Gately, 2014, 2015; Olliff, 2010); and
- General difficulties in balancing family responsibilities and study (Glen, Onsando, & Kearney, 2015; Harris & Marlowe, 2011; Harris, Spark, & Watts, 2015; Hatoss & Huijser, 2010).

Many individuals end up with little or no access to primary, secondary, or tertiary education over the course of their lives. Even when they live in resettlement countries like Australia, women and men from refugee backgrounds experience difficulties with accessing higher education, despite immense knowledge, leadership capabilities, and intellectual capacity to work in research and policy roles, community development, and human services. Yet, there is a striking gap in the literature on the role that settlement and language learning policy play in adding to the complexities students may face, which we address here. To further illustrate the impact of government policy, we offer an overview of the policy-scape in terms of what language support people from refugee backgrounds can access. We draw predominantly on the case of New South Wales, the second largest state education system in the world. According to government figures, this state has a significant number of linguistically diverse students, with Watkins, Lean, and Noble (2016) reporting that 18% of the total school population in NSW required English as a Second Language (ESL[4]) support in 2012.

Australian Humanitarian Policy-Scape: Where Does Education Feature?

As with its visa policies, Australia's humanitarian settlement model discriminates between Offshore and Onshore refugees, creating a two-tier system of support based purely on mode of arrival. Those who are resettled at Australia's choosing benefit from one of the most successful settlement programs to assist new arrivals, including on-arrival support, orientation, intensive casework support for six to 12 months, and on-going community development and casework services up to five years. However, those who arrived in Australia without prior authorisation are not eligible for these services. People awaiting an outcome of their refugee applications receive minimal casework support through the Status Resolution Support Service (SRSS), while those who are found to be refugees after arriving by boat have no settlement support (Refugee Council of Australia [RCOA], 2015a). This two-tier system has significant implications for new arrivals, in terms of the supports and services they are able to access, and this in turn impacts on their opportunities to engage in higher education.

For resettled refugees, recent policy changes have introduced the Humanitarian Support Program (HSP), which combines a number of services into one and reduces the number of providers across the country (Department of Social Services, 2017). In line with neoliberal policies, the Australian Government has outsourced settlement services to agencies that competitively tender to receive contracts, leading to a race to reduce costs and services. Another neoliberal landmark is the HSP prioritising the 'three E's' – Employment, English and Education – and agencies must report against these key performance indicators. However, the HSP is primarily a casework program and so does not provide comprehensive English, education or employment services. Instead, refugees receive English tuition through the Adult Migrant English Program (AMEP) (discussed below), employment support through the mainstream Jobactive program, and education through Australia's vocational and tertiary education system (notably, not higher education). This policy confusion sees HSP settlement providers measured on outcomes for which they are not primarily responsible.

While the 'three E's' can support quicker employment outcomes, there are concerns that it undermines other important settlement outcomes including social integration, trauma recovery, and understanding the sociocultural context. One settlement worker highlighted the impact of the intense focus on employment at a consultation with the RCOA:

> In the past, while they were doing the [Adult Migrant English Program (AMEP)], which was 15 hours a week, they were exempt from looking for jobs ... But students now have pressure to look for a job, go on a computer and apply. In the last couple of weeks I have enrolled 20 mothers into a computer class and for every single one of them I have to use an interpreter. If it is their first time seeing a computer, you can only imagine how hard it is for them to apply for twenty-odd jobs that they have to in two weeks' time ... It does seem to be a policy conflict. (Refugee Council of Australia [RCOA], 2016, p. 72)

Several refugee community members have reiterated this requirement as in this example from NSW:

> [The] Jobactive consultant said I cannot continue to do the English course at Navitas to improve my English. I had an appointment for an English test to enrol into [an English] program. She cancelled my appointment

and said to stop the beauty TAFE[5] course I was doing on Fridays for the past 10 weeks. She said she found a job for me as a kitchen hand and that I need to start the job in a few days' time; if I don't Centrelink[6] will stop my money. (Refugee Council of Australia [RCOA], 2017b, p. 9)

Likewise, numerous settlement services have reported increased pressure to get newly arrived refugees into employment, before they have adequately settled in, improved their English language proficiency, and updated their skills and qualifications. This undermines longer-term settlement goals, and traps refugees into a cycle of low-skilled work, where they are unable to improve their language and professional skills to secure more meaningful employment or become reluctant 'circumstantial law breakers' by taking cash-in-hand work (see Morrice, 2011). This can significantly impact on a person's likelihood and opportunities to engage in higher education: getting trapped in low-skilled jobs precludes people from developing the kinds of formal literacies and higher-level qualifications that offer currency for access to higher education.

Education and Language Support

Developing effective Basic Interpersonal Communicative Skills (BICS) is key to 'successful' settlement, and to participating in civic and social life in a settlement country; however, mastering what Cummins (1981) calls Cognitive/Academic Language Proficiency (CALP) requires sustained engagement in language learning, especially for people who have experienced interrupted education and may have underdeveloped first language literacy. In this section, we outline how Australian policy fails to provide the appropriate engagement with language learning required to develop the kinds of formal literacies and academic register for meaningful participation in higher education studies.

When someone arrives in Australia through the resettlement program, they are offered access to English language support, depending on age and location, and these vary for school-aged children and adults. We focus on NSW but note that there are state/territory variations in the provisions described below. For example, the public-school system assumes responsibility for supporting children and young people with language and literacy development needs. However, as is the case for all schooling in Australia, the division of education provision and oversight between individual states and territories makes it difficult to offer a simple description of how federal policy is enacted in local practice.

Young People, Schooling and English Language Tuition

In NSW, caseworkers help newly arrived young people to enter the local school system where they have access to a state/territory-variation of the New Arrivals Program (NAP), which provides on-arrival intensive English language tuition via the schooling system. English as an Additional Language/ Dialect (EAL/D) teachers and supports (like bilingual teaching assistants) are funded through school equity funding, as well as through the targeted individual student funding component of the Resource Allocation Model (RAM). EAL/D teachers are university graduates, trained in either primary or secondary teaching with a TESOL (Teaching English to Speakers of Other Languages) component. The national Australian Curriculum and Assessment Reporting Authority (ACARA) offers a standardised typology of EAL/D learning progressions that teachers can use to assess students' English language proficiency: Beginning English (with a sub-category included of Limited Literacy Background), Emerging English, Developing English, and Consolidating English.

For those in established urban settlement areas that have a high concentration of people who speak languages other than English, a young person is likely to be placed initially in a government-run Intensive English Centre (IEC) or an Intensive English High School (IEHS). IECs are generally attached to 'host' public schools and offer up to one year of English language tuition (generally up to three terms) before a student is transitioned into 'mainstream' schooling. For students outside urban hubs of major cities, there is no IEC provision; instead, these students are immediately placed into 'mainstream' schools and the majority are supported by EAL/D teacher(s), or by class teachers. However, as Watkins et al. (2016, p. 53) reported, in NSW in 2012, only 86,661 of 137,487 students who were eligible for ESL support actually received it. The authors suggested that recent neoliberal policies aiming at decentralizing funding and increasing cost-efficiency in the public schooling budget has further complicated this provision of support, by pushing responsibility to individual schools to use existing funding (rather than historic allocation of ESL teaching positions) to support students' language needs (see also Pugh, Every, & Hattam, 2012). The reallocation of liability away from the state thus impacts individual students and their families. As Due and Riggs (2009) contend, seemingly benign discourses of 'inclusion' and 'integration' conceal the underpinning intention for students to conform and assimilate, 'rather than creating an environment in which NAP students are able to shape the space to the same extent as non-NAP students' (p. 56).

If the number of new arrivals warrants it, a regional school can apply temporarily for an EAL New Arrivals Program teacher allocation, or can access support to pay for a School Learning Support Officer (Ethnic), as well as bilingual support. These supports are dependent on the number of eligible students. Unfortunately, this means that in regional areas where students are dispersed in smaller numbers among several local schools, the provision of targeted supports that can facilitate children's acclimatisation to new spaces, practices, and languages may not be warranted (Due, Riggs, & Mandara, 2015). As Pugh et al. (2012) argue, this policy hinders inclusive education for many students from refugee backgrounds, particularly those who are immediately moved into mainstream schooling. They argue that '[p]olicy reform which appoints teachers to NAP schools based on their skills, and which allows for a more stable teaching body, is necessary to support localised school reforms' (p. 135).

The regional diversity of intensive English provision – both in terms of state and territory-based education, and the divide between metropolitan and rural Australia – has significant impacts on opportunities to develop English language proficiency, and to transition into 'mainstream' (or 'whitestream', according to Andersen, 2009[7]) schooling. In their analysis of children's learning experiences in IECs, Due and Riggs (2009, 2011) make a strong case that this model offers children a 'soft landing' to facilitate their transitions into the Australian educational system, by offering small classes and 'safe' spaces where they learn social norms and practices of western schooling systems and develop English language proficiency. In addition to opening important spaces for developing common experiences, friendships and a sense of belonging (for example, Due et al., 2015; Due, Riggs, & Augoustinos, 2016; de Heer, Due, Riggs, & Augoustinos, 2016), the expertise of English language teachers allows for identification and differentiation between language and learning difficulties. As Due et al. (2016) suggest, teacher-participants in their study identified that 'learning difficulties would be misconceived in mainstream classes as undeveloped EALD skills, resulting in a late diagnosis, or ... an incorrect assumption that a student may have learning difficulties when in fact they do not' (p. 1292).

For students who are not able to access an IEC, and whose intensive English support occurs outside of their usual classroom, the possibilities to learn are significantly constrained. As Ferfolja and Vickers (2010) lament:

> While much emphasis is placed on the need for improved academic skills, it appears that for refugee students, acculturation to the social expectations and institutional practices of the mainstream must come first. Without an understanding of these institutional practices, students cannot 'work the classroom' and, therefore, are less able to engage with learning. (p. 156)

Other challenges in the language provision space for children are related to resource allocation. Many researchers and educators have argued that a general maximum of four terms of intensive English tuition is insufficient, and the impacts of fragmented prior education and low levels of literacy cannot be ameliorated in such a short time (Due et al., 2016; Ferfolja & Vickers, 2010; Pugh et al., 2012).

A further concern relates to collapsing issues relating to language proficiency and literacy acquisition, particularly for students who are pre-literate in their first language (Sidhu & Taylor, 2007; Woods, 2009). For Woods (2009), socially just schooling for students from refugee backgrounds is hampered by the conflation of English language and literacy; she argues for a 'qualitatively, and not just quantitatively different' form of support from what she calls 'traditional ESL instruction' (p. 88). At the centre of this approach is the separating of teaching away from print-based textual engagement with school subjects that disadvantage students with limited literacies. Due et al. (2015) and de Heer et al. (2016) make a similar point about the affective, social and linguistic possibilities offered by engaging newly arrived students in commonly valued, low-print text subjects like art, music and sport (see also Riggs & Due, 2011).

A fundamental issue relating to language development in particular is the question of whose responsibility it is to provide language support. Even in areas that have IECS or an IEHS, students will ultimately transition into mainstream schooling before they have necessarily reached the Developing English stage (ACARA, n.d.). A recent survey of over 5000 NSW public school teachers revealed that only 27.4% of teachers have expertise in ESL, with a significantly higher percentage noted in primary teachers (Watkins et al., 2016). This means that in the cases of students whose schools do not have the numbers to warrant NAP support or sufficient EAL/D provision – which affected over 50,000 children in NSW in 2012 (Watkins et al., 2016) – mainstream teachers with limited or no ESL experience have to work harder to support their students, as the complex needs that second language and literacy acquisition involve both require specialist training. As Woods (2009) contends, for students with limited literacy backgrounds being compared with students who 'have been involved in continuous, print-based textual engagement with school subjects across the compulsory years of schooling' opens conditions for 'othering' and sustains deficit framing of students from refugee backgrounds (p. 89).

Adults and English Language Tuition

For newly arrived adults (including people aged 15–17 years old in areas that do not have capacity to support them in mainstream schooling), accessing English language tuition is significantly less complex. Unlike the Australian schooling system, the Adult Migrant English Program (AMEP) is a program administered by the Australian Department of Education and Training (DET), and its policy, provisions, and reporting are implemented uniformly across the country. It serves two sets of legislation: the *Immigration (Education) Act* of 1971, and the *Immigration (Education) Regulations* 1992 (DET, 2017). The AMEP offers new arrivals 510 hours of English language tuition and childcare in the first five years of settlement in Australia, with an optional 490 additional hours for those who require it. Accessing the AMEP is voluntary, and must be within six months of arrival. However, people seeking asylum are not eligible for English language tuition, as one person recalled at the RCOA community consultations:

> My English is not good, it's just a little bit and only reasonable as it is not my first language. Actually I have no opportunities to improve my English here, just friends and neighbours help me to learn a little bit more. I cannot pay for any education. (Refugee Council of Australia [RCOA], 2017b)

The overall aim of the AMEP is to help adults reach a 'functional' level of English, which equates to the 'Basic Social Proficiency' level according to the ISLPR (International Second Language Proficiency Rating)[8]. The Department of Social Services (2017) information sheet, *Settlement Services for Humanitarian Entrants,* describes the AMEP as offering the chance to learn 'foundation English skills' to help with 'successful settlement' in Australia. Furthermore, some humanitarian entrants may also be eligible for an additional 400 hours of tuition in Special Preparatory Programs (SPP) as recognition of 'their greater learning and support needs arising from difficult pre-migration experiences, such as torture or trauma, and/or limited prior schooling', through the Settlement Language Pathways to Employment and Training (SLPET), and the Skills for Education and Employment (SEE) programs. These are offered as English classes by Registered Training Organisations (RTOs) with AMEP service provider contracts across Australia. However, if students are unable to attend a class, they are able to use their AMEP hours through the Home Tutor Scheme or access e-learning options.

Similar to the laments about encroaching neoliberal logics in the provision of school English language tuition, the AMEP, which includes a suite of sub-programs, has also been subject to the same market forces and cost-efficiency strategies. AMEP service provision is allocated on a tender basis, meaning that while it is still available in each region, the provision may be moved to new RTOs and new locations, with new teachers and resources. The regularity of these potential changes results in the erosion (or depletion) of existing networks, relationships, and expertise. In 2017, the AMEP underwent significant changes, with reduced funding and the development of two streams: the Social Stream and the Pre-Employment Stream, and impactful amendments to minimum class sizes – which, in effect, meant increasing class sizes from 12 to 25 and reducing TESOL qualifications for teachers in the Social Stream (although teachers need to be actively enrolled in a postgraduate TESOL qualification). During the consultation phase, the proposed changes drew strong criticism from community 'stakeholders'; for instance, the Australian Council of TESOL Associations (ACTA) described the changes as 'a mean, backdoor attempt to undermine vulnerable refugees and new migrants' legal entitlements to English classes', with the 'best these classes can produce will be *stigmatised speakers of "broken" English on a road to discrimination, unemployment and social isolation*' (ACTA, 2016; bold in original). The RCOA (2016c) expressed similar concerns, particularly with regard to the increased employment focus in the program, larger class sizes, reduction of funding, and diminished professional requirements.

Refugee communities continue to raise the inadequacy of the hours in the AMEP program as a key issue. As one former refugee from South Sudan highlighted in community consultations with the RCOA:

> 510 hours of English is not enough. Some people at the end of five years don't know how to communicate. We need to do something about the intensive English course … People from refugee/migrant backgrounds should be included in the delivery of English language programs. (Refugee Council of Australia [RCOA], 2017b)

Nevertheless, the English language tuition offered in Australia (precluding the situation of many people claiming asylum) is generous compared to the UK, for instance, which in its equivalent adult English language programme offers eight hours a week for the first year of settlement, then four hours a week in subsequent years if one is claiming Jobseeker's Allowance. However, despite the relatively substantial provision of English language hours in Australia, the ideology underpinning the decision to limit the target level to 'functional' is inherently hegemonic and disadvantageous, serving to limit potential and imaginaries and creating a significant underclass. 'Functional' English will not meet the language proficiency requirements of universities, nor will it be sufficient for meaningful participation in higher education. We readily acknowledge that learning language and literacy can be a convoluted and deeply complex experience, particularly for people whose circumstances include interrupted education, poverty, low levels of literacy, and incongruent cultural practices which impede 'successful' (e.g., quick, smooth) settlement; we are also mindful that this learning requires significant investment in terms of time and resources. However, we argue that capping the expected level of proficiency at 'functional' results in constraints on economic, sociocultural, and aspirational opportunities.

Discussion and Conclusion

Recent Australian government policy pertaining to students from refugee and asylum seeker backgrounds work to maintain uncertainty in terms of visa processes and restrict their educational imaginaries by explicitly focusing on moving new arrivals into quick employment, while simultaneously denying opportunities to develop their English language skills. The example of recent changes to the AMEP and the 'three Es' can be seen as serving a hegemonic project to contain people from refugee and asylum seeker backgrounds in low-skilled, service work, creating hurdles for ideas and aspirations for professional careers and further study. Arriving in a settlement country with professional qualifications and work experience does not provide a buffer against such situations; as Morrice (2011) argues:

> Refugees are firmly placed into symbolic structures of inequality, determining what economic and educational opportunities are available to them and limiting their access to different forms of capital ... The store of social and cultural capital which had enabled them to achieve educational and professional status in their own country was generally not recognised and valued in the UK and could not be converted into symbolic capital. (pp. 131–132)

We share concerns raised by McPherson (2010) who argued that the AMEP is a tool that promotes a form of integration that is based on a tacit set of Australian 'national values', ideas about employment and migrants' willingness to assimilate, and positions refugees as problematic in relation to normalised subject positions and subjectivities. Writing in the US context, Koyama (2013) argues that the urgent imperative for refugees to become economically self-sufficient often results in people delaying language education, thus 'limit[ing] initial employment opportunities and narrow[ing] families' livelihood strategies upon resettlement' (p. 962). We agree with Koyama's (2015) recommendations for a longer period of financial support and increased access to ESL teaching and workforce training to give people from refugee backgrounds (especially those with minimal language and literacy on arrival) a better chance than being pigeon-holed into low-level work, which could have myriad economic and social benefits to individuals and the nation.

A major issue is that higher education issues are subsumed into broader education policies with social justice orientations based on an 'undifferentiated ethnoscape' (Sidhu & Taylor, 2007, p. 283), which ignores and collapses the distinct needs of students from refugee backgrounds under a broad umbrella term. The resulting absence of a nuanced understanding of the complex suite of linguistic needs that refugees have as a result of their often lengthy forced displacement, compared with other kinds of economic or familial migrants (Creagh, 2016; Sidhu & Taylor, 2007), remains alarming. Amidst this chaotic policy-scape, the circumstances of asylum seekers – for whom educational opportunities are particularly limited – remain unresolved. Gender participation and politics are continually silenced in these debates, and women are still largely disadvantaged by the current context (Harris, Spark, & Watts, 2015; Hatoss & Huijser, 2010).

We have focussed on one state here as example, and we acknowledge the diversity in experiences in more rural areas of Australia and interstate, where challenges are context-specific. However, the contributions from people with lived experiences and practitioners that are included in this chapter clearly suggest a collective experience, whereby issues of language support and the race for *any* job are positioned as deterrents from engaging with meaningful higher education opportunities. While the literature on the topic largely focuses on practical aspects that prevent people from refugee and asylum seeker backgrounds from accessing and benefitting from a tertiary education, we have identified here some clear links between policy rhetoric and directions and the resulting lack of opportunities. Further research in close collaboration with people with lived experiences to explore such links in more detail is warranted to shed more light on how neoliberal and reductionist policies continue to exacerbate the lack of educational opportunities for people from refugee and asylum seeker backgrounds.

We have endeavoured to outline the policy-scape affecting higher education opportunities in Australia in all its complexity, to demonstrate key challenges to participation. Paired with divisive political rhetoric, such as the Minister for Immigration and Border Protection dubbing refugees as 'illiterate' and largely unemployed[9], it can be tempting to feel discouraged about the current situation. But based on our collaborative work with advocates with lived experiences like Arash, we can say with confidence that momentum is gathering – on the national and international scenes – to 'push back' against neoliberal policy that denies educational opportunities to a group of people with high motivations. The creation of an Education Special Interest Group (SIG) in 2015 (people from the community, higher education, vocational education and school sectors who have an interest in supporting educational opportunities for students from refugee and asylum seeker backgrounds) represents one example of how increased collaborative efforts can challenge slow policy reforms in the sector. While our discussion suggests that major issues remain unaddressed at this point, we are hopeful about the potential for higher education opportunities to be expanded through participatory advocacy efforts and further research on the topic.

Notes

1 The highest human rights award of Australia, bestowed by the Australian Human Rights Commission at the Human Rights Day Ceremony on 10 December in each year. See https://www.humanrights.gov.au/news/stories/asylum-seeker-young-leader-arash-bordbar
2 See http://www.unhcr.org/education
3 See article entitled *All The Times The UN Has Slammed Australia's Asylum Seeker Policy* at http://www.huffingtonpost.com.au/2017/07/25/all-the-times-the-un-has-slammed-australias-asylum-seeker-polic_a_23046469
4 English as a Second Language does not adequately capture the pluri-lingual backgrounds of many students who may be learning English as a third, fourth or sixth language, but we use the term here to connect with its dominance in the international scholarly and practitioner literature.
5 Technical and Further Education (TAFE) is the government-funded vocational education and training provision in Australia.
6 Centrelink is the Australian welfare system.
7 Anderson (2009) discussed Indigenous issues; however, we contend there is much to be learnt in the Australian context from such discussions.
8 See http://islpr.org/why-use-islpr/summary-of-islpr
9 See https://www.theguardian.com/australia-news/2016/may/18/fact-check-was-peter-dutton-right-about-illiterate-refugees-taking-jobs

References

Anderson, C. (2009). Critical indigenous studies: From difference to density. *Critical Studies Review, 15*(2), 80–100.

Australian Council of TESOL Associations [ACTA]. (2016). *Downgrading migrant English teaching hits the most vulnerable* [Media release]. Retrieved from http://www.tesol.org.au/files/files/569_ACTA_Media_Release_-_Downgrading_Migrant_English_Teaching_16_Sept_2016.pdf

Australian Curriculum, Assessment and Reporting Authority [ACARA]. (2016). *Reporting*. Retrieved from https://www.acara.edu.au/reporting

Bajwa, J., Couto, S., Kidd, S., Markoulakis, R., Abai, M., & McKenzie, K. (2017). Refugees, higher education, and informational barriers. *Refuge: Canada's Journal on Refugees, 33*(2), 56–65.

Baker, S., Ramsay, G., Irwin, E., & Miles, L. (2018). 'Hot', 'cold' and 'warm' supports: Towards theorising where refugee students go for assistance at university. *Teaching in Higher Education, 23*(1), 1–16.

Cocks, T., & Stokes, J. (2013). Policy into practice: A case study of widening participation in Australian higher education. *Widening Participation and Lifelong Learning, 15*(1), 22–38.

Crea, T. (2016). Refugee higher education: Contextual challenges and implications for program design, delivery, and accompaniment. *International Journal of Educational Development, 46*, 12–22.

Creagh, S. (2016). A critical analysis of the Language Background Other Than English (LBOTE) category in the Australian national testing system: A Foucauldian system. *Journal of Education Policy, 31*(3), 275–289.

Cummins, J. (1981). Empirical and theoretical underpinnings of bilingual education. *Journal of Education, 163*(1), 16–29.

de Heer, N., Due, C., Riggs, D., & Augoustinos, M. (2016). "It will be hard because I will have to learn lots of English": Experiences of education for children newly arrived in Australia. *International Journal of Qualitative Studies in Education, 29*(3), 297–319.

Department of Education and Training (DET). (2017). *English classes for eligible migrants and humanitarian entrants in Australia*. Retrieved from https://docs.education.gov.au/system/files/doc/other/amep_factsheet_program_info_june_2017.pdf

Department of Home Affairs [DHA]. (2017). *Australia's offshore humanitarian program: 2017–18*. Retrieved from https://www.homeaffairs.gov.au/research-and-stats/files/australia-offshore-humanitarian-program-2017-18.pdf

Department of Social Services. (2017). *Humanitarian settlement program*. Retrieved from https://www.dss.gov.au/settlement-and-multicultural-affairs/programs-policy/settlement-services/humanitarian-settlement-program

Due, C., Riggs, D., & Mandara, M. (2015). Educators' experiences of working in intensive English language programs: The strengths and challenges of specialised English language classrooms for students with migrant and refugee backgrounds. *Australian Journal of Education, 59*(2), 169–181.

Due, C., Riggs, D. W., & Augoustinos, A. (2016). Diversity in intensive English language centres in South Australia: Sociocultural approaches to education for students with migrant or refugees backgrounds. *International Journal of Inclusive Education, 20*(12), 1286–1296. doi:10.1080/13603116.2016.1168874

Earnest, J., Joyce, A., deMori, G., & Silvagni, G. (2010). Are universities responding to the needs of students from refugee backgrounds? *Australian Journal of Education, 54*(2), 155–174.

Ferfolja, T., & Vickers, M. (2010). Supporting refugee students in school education in Greater Western Sydney. *Critical Studies in Education, 51*(2), 149–162.

Gately, D. E. (2014). Becoming actors of their lives: A relational autonomy approach to employment and education choices of refugee young people in London, UK. *Social Work and Society, 12*(2), 1–14.

Gately, D. E. (2015). A policy of vulnerability or agency? Refugee young people's opportunities in accessing further and higher education in the UK. *Compare: A Journal of Comparative and International Education, 45*(1), 26–46.

Glen, M., Onsando, G., & Kearney, J. (2015). *Education pathways for humanitarian background refugees in southeast QLD: Focus on Logan community.* Brisbane: Griffith University.

Harris, A., Spark, C., & Watts, M. (2015). Gains and losses: African Australian women and higher education. *Journal of Sociology, 51*(2), 370–384.

Harris, V., & Marlowe, J. (2011). Hard yards and high hopes: The educational challenges of African refugee university students in Australia. *International Journal of Teaching and Learning in Higher Education, 239*(3), 186–196.

Hatoss, A., & Huijser, H. (2010). Gendered barriers to educational opportunities: Resettlement of Sudanese refugees in Australia. *Gender and Education, 22*(2), 147–160.

Hirsch, A. (2015). *Barriers to education for people seeking asylum and refugees on temporary visas.* Refugee Council of Australia. Retrieved from http://www.refugeecouncil.org.au/wp-content/uploads/2014/08/1512-Education.pdf

Hirsch. A., & Maylea, C. (2016). Education denied: People seeking asylum and refugees trapped in limbo. *New Community, 14*(3), 19–24.

International Detention Coalition. (2017). *Two damning UN expert reports of Australia's detention regime.* Retrieved from https://idcoalition.org/news/two-damning-un-expert-reports-of-australias-detention-regime/

Joyce, A., Earnest, J., DeMori, G., & Silvagni, G. (2010). The experiences of students from refugee backgrounds at universities in Australia: Reflections on the social, emotional, and practical challenges. *Journal of Refugee Studies, 23*(1), 82–97.

Koyama, J. (2013). Resettling notions of social mobility: Locating refugees as 'educable' and 'employable.' *British Journal of Sociology of Education, 34*(5–6), 947–965.

Koyama, J. (2015). Learning English, working hard, and challenging risk discourse. *Policy Futures in Education, 13*(5), 608–620.

Lawson, L. (2014). "I have to be my own mother and father": The African student experience at university, a case study using narrative analysis. *The Australasian Review of African Studies, 35*(1), 59–74.

Lenette, C. (2016). University students from refugee backgrounds: Why should we care? *Higher Education Research and Development, 35*(6), 1–5.

MacLaren, D. (2010). Tertiary education for refugees: A case study from the Thai-Burma border. *Refuge: Canada's Journal on Refugees, 27*(2), 103–110.

Martin, G. (2015). Stop the boats! Moral panic in Australia over asylum seekers. *Continuum, 29*(3), 304–322.

McMichael, C., Nunn, C., Gifford, S., & Correa-Velez, I. (2014). Studying refugee settlement through longitudinal research: Methodological and ethical insights from the Good States study. *Journal of Refugee Studies, 28*(2), 238–257.

McPherson, M. (2010). 'I integrate, therefore I am': Contesting the normalizing discourse of integrationism through conversations with refugee women. *Journal of Refugee Studies, 23*(4), 546–570.

Morrice, L. (2011). *Being a refugee: Learning and identity. A longitudinal study of refugees in the UK*. Stoke on Trent: Trentham Books.

Naidoo, L. (2009). Developing social inclusion through after-school homework tutoring: A study of African refugee students in greater western Sydney. *British Journal of Sociology of Education, 30*(3), 261–273.

Naidoo, L., Wilkinson, J., Langat, K., Adoniou, M., Cuneen, R., & Bolger, D. (2015). *Case study report: Supporting school-university pathways for refugee students' access and participation in tertiary education*. Penrith: University of Western Sydney.

Olliff, L. (2010). *Finding the right time and place: Exploring post-compulsory education and training pathways for young people from refugee backgrounds in NSW*. Sydney: Refugee Council of Australia.

Onsando, G., & Billett, S. (2009). African Students from refugee backgrounds in Australian TAFE institutions: A case for transformative learning goals and processes. *International Journal of Training Research, 7*, 80–94.

Pugh, K., Every, D., & Hattam, R. (2012). Inclusive education for students with refugee experience: Whole school reform in a South Australian primary school. *The Australian Educational Researcher, 39*(2), 125–141.

Ramsay, G., Baker, S., Miles, L., & Irwin, E. (2016). Reimagining support models for students from refugee backgrounds: Understandings, spaces and empowerment. In M. Davis & A. Goody (Eds.), *Research and development in higher education: The shape of higher education* (Vol. 39, pp. 279–288). Fremantle.

Refugee Council of Australia [RCOA]. (2012). *History of Australia's refugee program.* Retrieved from https://www.refugeecouncil.org.au/getfacts/seekingsafety/refugee-humanitarian-program/history-australias-refugee-program/

Refugee Council of Australia [RCOA]. (2015a). *Eroding our identity as a generous nation: Community views on Australia's treatment of people seeking asylum.* Retrieved from http://www.refugeecouncil.org.au/wp-content/uploads/2015/12/1512-Asylum.pdf

Refugee Council of Australia [RCOA]. (2015b). *Barriers to education for people seeking asylum and refugees on temporary visas.* Retrieved from https://www.refugeecouncil.org.au/wp-content/uploads/2014/08/1512-Education.pdf

Refugee Council of Australia [RCOA]. (2016a). *Australia's response to a world in crisis: Community views on planning for the 2016–17 Refugee and Humanitarian program.* Retrieved from http://www.refugeecouncil.org.au/wp-content/uploads/2016/04/2016-17-Intake-submission-FINAL.pdf

Refugee Council of Australia [RCOA]. (2016b). *UNHCR global trends 2015 – How Australia compares with the world.* Retrieved from https://www.refugeecouncil.org.au/getfacts/statistics/unchr2015/

Refugee Council of Australia [RCOA]. (2016c). *Letter to minister for education and training regarding the adult migrant English program.* Retrieved from https://www.refugeecouncil.org.au/wp-content/uploads/2017/02/FECCA-RCOA-Letter-re-AMEP.pdf

Refugee Council of Australia [RCOA]. (2017a). *Not working: Experiences of refugees and migrants with Jobactive.* Retrieved from https://www.refugeecouncil.org.au/wp-content/uploads/2017/08/Jobactive.pdf

Refugee Council of Australia [RCOA]. (2017b). *Unpublished consultation responses.* RCOA.

Shapiro, S., & MacDonald, M. (2017). From deficit to asset: Locating discursive resistance in a refugee-background student's written and oral narrative. *Journal of Language, Identity & Education, 16*(2), 80–96. doi:10.1080/15348458.2016.1277725

Sidhu, R., & Taylor, S. (2007). Educational provision for refugee youth in Australia: Left to chance? *Journal of Sociology, 43*(3), 283–300.

Stevenson, J., & Baker, S. (2018). *Refugees in higher education: Debate, discourse and practice.* Sheffield: Emerald Publishing Group Ltd.

Summers, H. (2016, November 16). Language barrier leaves refugees facing struggle to rebuild their lives. *The Guardian.* Retrieved from https://www.theguardian.com/society/2016/nov/16/language-barrier-refugees-english-classes-integration-esol

United Nations High Commissioner for Refugees [UNHCR]. (2016). *Missing out: Refugee education in crisis.* Retrieved from http://www.unhcr.org/missing-out-state-of-education-for-the-worlds-refugees.html

United Nations High Commissioner for Refugees [UNHCR]. (2017). *Comprehensive refugee response framework.* Retrieved from http://www.unhcr.org/comprehensive-refugee-response-framework-crrf.html

Vickers, M., McCarthy, F., & Zammit, K. (2017). Peer mentoring and intercultural understanding: Support for refugee-background and immigrant students beginning university study. *International Journal of Intercultural Relations, 60*, 198–209. Retrieved from http://dx.doi.org/10.1016/j.ijintrel.2017.04.015

Wache, D., & Zufferey, C. (2013). Connecting with students from new and emerging communities in social work education. *Advances in Social Work and Welfare Education, 15*(1), 80–91.

Watkins, M., Lean, G., & Noble, G. (2016). Multicultural education: The state of play from an Australian perspective. *Race, Ethnicity and Education, 19*(1), 46–66.

White, J. (2017). The banality of exclusion in Australian universities. *International Journal of Inclusive Education, 21*(11), 1142–1155. doi:10.1080/13603116.2017.1350321

Windle, J., & Miller, W. (2012). Approaches to teaching low literacy refugee-background students. *Australian Journal of Language and Literacy, 35*(3), 317–333.

Woods, A. (2009). Learning to be literate: Issues of pedagogy for recently arrived refugee youth in Australia. *Critical Inquiry in Language Studies, 6*(1), 81–101.

Wright, L., & Plasterer, R. (2010). Beyond basic education: Exploring opportunities for higher learning in Kenyan refugee camps. *Refuge: Canada's Journal on Refugees, 27*(2), 42–54.

Zeus, B. (2011). Exploring barriers to higher education in protracted refugee situations: The case of Burmese refugees in Thailand. *Journal of Refugee Studies, 24*(2), 256–276.

PART 2

North America

CHAPTER 5

Community Initiatives to Support Refugee Youth
A Canadian Perspective

Jan Stewart

Introduction

The Human Development Report indicates that more than 1.5 billion people live in countries affected by conflict (United Nations Development Programme, 2016). This represents about a fifth of the world's population, creating significant cost to human development and repercussions for national progress (Malik, 2014). The United Nations High Commissioner for Refugees reports that over 68.5 million people (an estimated 31 people per minute) were forcibly displaced from their homes by the end of 2017 representing the highest number of displaced people since the post-World War II period (UNHCR, 2018). Fuelling this massive migration of people are situations of protracted conflict and civil war affecting the world's most vulnerable populations who are already living in extreme poverty and deprivation (Malik, 2014). Refugee agencies are calling out for a renewed global commitment to the protection of people fleeing persecution and conflict (UNHCR, 2015). The involuntary movement of people due to crisis and conflict has become a defining issue of the 21st century and a critical issue for today's world leaders. Unlike other immigrants, refugees are often fleeing war, violence, oppression, persecution, or torture; circumstances that often complicate the settlement process (UNHCR, 2015). This makes it imperative that schools, social service agencies, and health professionals better understand the challenges faced by refugee youth (Young & Chan, 2014) and how best to provide support as they settle in Canada.

Literature related to refugees has frequently concentrated on political, medical, social, and linguistic issues pertaining primarily to adult populations. Less research has been conducted on issues directly concerning refugee children, and there is a paucity of literature related to the unique issues of refugee children who have been affected by armed conflict (McBrien, 2005; Stewart, 2011). Given that over 50% of the world's refugees are children (Young & Chan, 2014), there is a pressing need for research and policy to better understand and support the post-migration needs and challenges of refugee youth (Shakya et al., 2010). It is imperative to investigate the effects of conflict and displacement on children more closely and to explore the best practices and interventions

© KONINKLIJKE BRILL NV, LEIDEN, 2019 | DOI: 10.1163/9789004401891_005

necessary to assist children in post-conflict situations. Shifting demographics in the Canadian population require increased intercultural knowledge and more preparation for professionals who work with refugee children (Stewart, 2011). The aim of this chapter is to examine the programs and services that support refugee children in Manitoba and also to consider some of the challenges that arise both within and between community-based organizations and schools.

Background and Context

Canada accepted 260,351 new permanent residents in 2014. Of this number, approximately 9% (23,281) were refugees. In the same year, Manitoba recorded the highest number of refugees per capita brought to Canada (Manitoba Labour and Immigration, 2015). Since 2000, Manitoba has received more than 125,000 immigrants, of which approximately 9% were refugees (Manitoba Immigration, and Multiculturalism, 2013). Just over half of the government-assisted refugees originated from Somalia, Iraq, Democratic Republic of Congo, and Eritrea with the majority (over 85%) settling in Winnipeg (Manitoba Labour and Immigration, 2015). With increasing numbers of children coming from war-affected regions and civil unrest, more research is needed to understand how war affects children and their long-term development and what programs and services will ultimately assist with their adjustment to life after conflict.

Children are among the most vulnerable in all societies and in all conflicts, which can have a devastating impact on their lives (Office of the Special Representative of the Secretary-General for Children and Armed Conflict, 2014). Modern wars are killing, exploiting, and maiming children more callously and more systematically than ever before (Machel, 2000). Machel (2001) states, 'War undermines the very foundation of children's lives, destroying their homes, splintering their communities and shattering their trust in adults' (p. 80). It is estimated that one in every 230 people in the world is a youth who has been forced to urgently leave his or her home (UNHCR, 2015). Countless children have suffered from malnutrition, disease, sexual violence, and forced recruitment into fighting (Machel, 2000). Children living in conflict are often denied their basic right to an education. Out of the 61 million children worldwide who are not enrolled in school, approximately 42% are from conflict-affected states (Inter-Agency Network for Education in Emergencies [INEE], 2013).

The challenges and obstacles that refugees encounter are often clustered among pre-migration (experiences before migration); transmigration (the journey and process of relocation); and post-migration (adjustment in the host-culture) experiences (Fazel & Stein, 2002; Hamilton & Moore, 2004). Barriers to learning are often complicated by pre-migration and trans-migration stressors including trauma, family separation, injury, violence, and harsh living conditions (Fazel & Stein, 2002). Additional long-term difficulties related to settlement include discrimination in the host country, limited employment opportunities and career experience, living in poverty, lack of adequate housing, and low educational achievement (Shakya et al., 2010; Stewart, 2011; Yau, 1995). Children who have not been directly affected by trauma may also experience the effects of secondary and trans generational traumatization (Kirmayer, Lemelson, & Barad, 2007). Research suggests that there is a need to understand how 'the interaction of the individual and collective processes contribute to resilience and reconstruction in the aftermath of political violence' (Kirmayer et al., 2007, p. 10). Together, these collective experiences can affect the well-being of children and their long-term adjustment to life in Canada. Similarly, a research program must also be comprehensive and holistic in nature and include the contexts of community, family, and the school system to understand how best to support the academic and psychosocial well-being of refugee students (Stewart, 2011).

School and Community Connections

The context of the school environment is crucial to the pro-social development and the acculturation of the refugee student (McBrien, 2005; Rutter, 2006) as the school is often the first contact a child has with the host community. Having said this, schools frequently report that they are ill-equipped to meet the diverse needs of refugee children (Stewart, 2011); and teachers indicate that they need more training and preparation in order to provide adequate psychosocial support to meet the adjustment needs of children. Suarez-Orozco, Onaga, and de Lardemelle (2010) note that middle and high schools that serve refugee students in the United States are unprepared resulting in them being 'overlooked and underserved' (Ruiz-de-Velasco, Fix, & Clewell, 2000, p. 1). While many refugee children adjust quite successfully to life in Canada (Fazel, Reed, Panter-Brick, & Stein, 2012), there are others who do not, and their post-migration trajectories are underscored with persistent and pervasive challenges and complications relating to poverty, lack of housing, psychosocial issues, language difficulties, and academic barriers (Stewart, 2011).

Because it is not typically a part of teacher preparation programs and professional development agendas, training in the area of refugee education for teachers and school leaders is often limited (Stewart, 2011). School personnel are now frequently looking to community organizations and settlement services to establish partnerships that will assist them in providing the necessary services and supports to refugee youth (Noam & Tillinger, 2004). Due to the interconnectedness of issues concerning refugees, researchers argue that establishing partnerships among agencies and organizations is a requirement if the purpose of a program or service is to serve refugee children, youth, and/or families (Chavkin, 1998; Noam & Tillinger, 2004). Moreover, educational researchers are examining the connections between schools and the community to take a closer look at the diversity of programs offered in the community including recreation, homework clubs, project-based learning, sports, arts, and leadership opportunities (Noam & Tillinger, 2004). The overarching purpose of this research program was to better prepare teachers to meet the needs of refugee youth. To do this most effectively, we investigated influences from the various systems that most directly affect the child and we explored programs and services that were considered to be 'best practices' in terms of supporting refugee youth. In addition, we worked in collaboration with teachers and community organizations to build on best practices and to delineate recommendations for policy makers.

As Young and Chan (2014) note, school-based programs that are designed to address the mental health needs of refugees are limited in the Canadian context. While there are meritorious programs offered in pockets across the country, there appear to be more services offered in community settlings, rather than at the school level (White et al., 2009). In addition, White et al. (2009) note that professionals trained within Western settings have certain expectations and methods of serving their populations that may not be culturally appropriate for populations when considered in the context of diversity. It is possible that some interventions will need to be reconsidered to determine if they are culturally appropriate and inclusive to the needs of children and youth from diverse backgrounds (Stewart, 2011). As migration and resettlement continue to increase in North America, it is critical for scholars and practitioners to conduct research that seeks to address the challenges of living in varied contexts. Concomitantly, it is essential to also know what programs, services, and models best support adjustment and what can be done to strengthen the connections among service providers, community agencies, and schools.

Theoretical Framework Informing the Study

Stewart's (2011) adaptation of Bronfenbrenner's Bioecological Model (2001) provided the theoretical framework for a three-year investigation into the programs and services that support refugee youth in Manitoba (see Figure 5.1). According to Bronfenbrenner (2001), there are five ecological systems that shape the psychosocial development of the individual, ranging from the family to the broader host culture. Represented in a series of concentric circles, the ecological systems are grouped from the closest most inner circle of influence to the larger context in which all systems exist. As a brief summary, Bronfenbrenner (2005) describes the microsystem is the closest circle of influence to the child representing the relationships and contexts that are most prominent in the child's life. The adapted model includes the addition of a nanosystem as adapted by Stewart (2011). The nanosystem represents the smallest most immediate support that is provided to the student. It is the prevalence of a nanosystem that was observed to be the catalyst for refugee students staying connected to the microsystem (Stewart, 2011). The nanosystem is a network, a connection, and a close relationship that forms in the microsystem. It may exist for only a short period of time in the person's development, or it may be a life-long connection. Individuals could be a part of a microsystem, but only those who had a deeply rooted and more intimate meaningful relationship with an individual or group within this microsystem, felt a sense of belonging and acceptance. It was this sense of belonging that was instrumental in keeping the individual connected to the system or systems.

As Bronfenbrenner (2001) explains, the mesosystem represents the connections and intersections between the systems. The mesosystem can also be referred to as a system of microsystems. Relating to the more distant systems that can indirectly affect the development of the child, such as school division policies or community organizations, is the exosystem. The macrosystem is the outer system in which all other systems exist and might include the overarching ideologies of the culture, social structure and subculture embedded in society. The chronosystem represents the changes over time to the individual. The impact of prior life events and experiences are also reflected in the chronosystem.

Bronfenbrenner's theory purports that the individual is both a producer and a product of development (Bronfenbrenner, 2001). The individual and the environment are in a reciprocal relationship and the individual is both influenced by, and influences, the environment. Moreover, the environment is not a single entity; rather, it is the compilation of several multi-level systems and the interconnections between them. This fundamental principle influenced this study and the investigation as we focused on both the direct and the indirect interactions that refugee children encounter in their immediate and more distant ecological systems. The reciprocal relationship between the child and the environment and the nature of these influences was also explored. Due to the

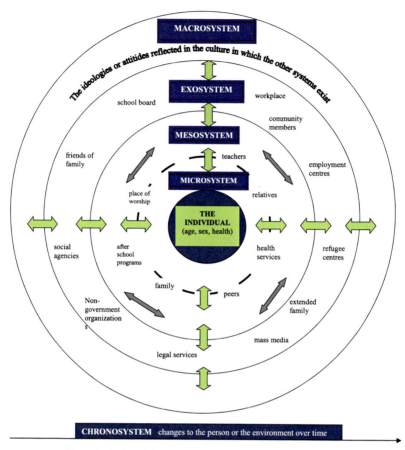

FIGURE 5.1 Bioecological model

inherent connections between the systems and the aforementioned importance of forging partnerships between them, we believed it was essential to extend the investigation to include perspectives from a variety of participants representing the various ecological systems.

According to Bronfenbrenner (2001), youth develop with influences and interactions within a variety of systems. We examine the adjustment and settlement of refugee students through the various perspectives or systems interacting with the child. We explore how these ecological systems interact with community-based organizations to either support or subvert the integration of refugee youth into Canadian society. Our examination of the various ecological systems that affect the development of the child takes into account the reciprocal influence of settlement workers and refugee youth as they interact and connect in schools and community agencies. The first phase of this research specifically examined the influence of the exosystem – the more distant organizations and the people who indirectly affect the child's life. Working from this outer circle of influence, we endeavoured to learn about the community support systems and the organizations working with the families to inform our understanding of best practices for supporting adjustment. With the overarching assumption that there will be several factors that hinder and facilitate the development and implementation of programs and services, this discussion will focus on the perspective of the settlement workers in Manitoba and what they perceive to be the best practices for supporting refugee children. Approaching the investigation from the perspective of those in the exosystem allowed individuals to define and identify what programs and services they observed and perceived to be helping refugee students. As we moved into the systems that had more direct influence on the students, we were able to ask more focused questions on how these programs supported students and what posed challenges or difficulties for adjustment.

Overview of Research Program

This chapter is derived from data collected in Manitoba from phase one of a multi-year research program that included research sites in Manitoba, Alberta, and Newfoundland. The research program is part of a partnership development grant whereby investigators from three institutions – University of Winnipeg, University of Calgary, and Memorial University of Newfoundland – have interacted closely with government and non-government partners to examine best practices for supporting refugee youth in Canada. Phase one, as reported in this chapter, examines the exosystem and includes data from 40 semi-structured qualitative interviews with executive directors, outreach workers, mentors, community liaison officers, and staff members at 24 service providing organizations in Manitoba. A qualitative design has provided the opportunity to gather in-depth responses and narratives from individuals with first-hand knowledge of issues affecting refugees. Data collection and analysis occurred as a continual and dynamic process (Bogdan & Biklen, 2003; Creswell, 2003) as the researchers identified themes and developed concepts and propositions to be investigated further in subsequent research phases. Phase two consisted of observations and interviews with the microsystems in each province to gather data indicative of how schools support the integrative capacity of refugee students.

In total, the study included a total of 320 interviews with community members, teachers, immigrant and refugee students, Canadian-born students, school administrators, and school division consultants in all four cities; representing different communities where there are large numbers of refugee children. Subsequent phases of this research involved the development and implementation of youth advisory councils, regional focus group consultations, and formal professional development and training for in-service teachers. The research team also developed policy recommendations and professional development activities and resources to better prepare teachers who work with refugees.

The methodology of this research program was designed for knowledge transfer and mobilization activities. Preparation and engagement with the regional focus groups and the final national consultation was intended to inherently involve dialogue and share consensus among participants from schools, school divisions, communities, and policy and agency partners. Data collected from these groups, as well as the collective interviews, were used to inform and develop a comprehensive support guide, *Bridging Two Worlds: Supporting Newcomer and Refugee Youth* (Stewart & Martin, 2018). A final culminating activity was held at the University of Winnipeg in the form of a conference and connected course training for in-service teachers. This event disseminated findings and training over a period of ten days with participants from various levels of service participating. Focus was on supporting a sense of belonging that includes respect for differences and an understanding of the complexities of settlement and integration including, but not limited to, forced migration, refugee characteristics, trauma, resilience, and relationship building.

There were two broad questions guiding the research: (1) How do community-based organizations support the integration of refugee youth? and (2) What issues arise as refugees are integrated within, and navigate across, different ecological systems? By investigating best practices for supporting refugee youth we endeavoured to understand what was working and how we could build on that to strengthen the capacity of schools to provide healthy and productive environments. We also wanted to learn how to effectively foster more meaningful and supportive relationships between individuals and organizations throughout the various ecological systems. Although the focus of the research was to maintain a strength-based perspective by investigating what was 'working' in the exosystem, we invariably learned about the challenges and obstacles that stood as barriers to success.

Best practices

The collective findings of this research have demonstrated the importance of schools embracing a holistic approach designed to engage with the students, their families, and their communities. It is important for educators to familiarize themselves with support services available within and around their school environment. Whenever necessary and possible, it is encouraged that teachers take time to work with parents in an effort to help them understand the expectations and procedures of the Canadian education system. If it is not possible for the classroom teacher to do this, support workers can be utilized to assist students and families, acting as a liaison or cultural broker. As a settlement worker shared, '... it's about supporting whole families. Youth-specific interventions are great. Adult-specific interventions are great. But also looking at the family more holistically is very important, too.'

Educators and students expressed the importance of the physical classroom in terms of providing a welcoming environment. Consideration of factors such as class size and expectations are important when program planning for refugee students so that students are not overwhelmed or lost in terms of following daily routines and procedures. Further consideration should be given to the design and spatial layout and represent the demography of the students.

Further findings reveal the need for transitional centres to support student learning and settlement. This is of particular importance when learning has been interrupted as part of the migration experience. Staff education and training should also be a priority so they are familiar with the needs and experiences of students and can provide appropriate support. This lends itself to the commonly addressed need for professional development, education, and training for teachers and school staff that focuses on how best to meet the needs of their refugee students.

After School Programs, Clubs and Community Engagement Activities

As previously indicated, school is often the first integrated contact for refugee students (Stewart, 2011). As such, our research found that schools have the unique opportunity, and responsibility, to offer programming supportive of student needs and social development. Students participating in extracurricular programming offered by both school and community programs were found to have a more successful settlement and adjustment experience. Students who were involved in groups and clubs were more connected to school and were more apt to ask for help when encountering a problem. Attending school regularly and engaging in classroom activities was considered to be a sign of more positive adjustment. Co-curricular and extracurricular programs offered by schools were bike shop, computer clubs, cooking, gardening, music/jazz clubs, and open gym. Community programs, often making use of available school space, included Mini-University, Boys and Girls Club opportunities, summer camps, and Peaceful Village, a program offering intensive homework assistance and bursary opportunities for students wishing to continue with post-secondary studies after graduation. One NGO Program worker stated,

> I know programs like the Peaceful Village that do some kinds of in-school support for refugee youth. These are very helpful in terms of creating social support, as well as supporting academics. They also play a role in linking youth with each other and the broader community.

After school programs were dependent on funding from external sources, and participants noted that there was considerable uncertainty about the sustainability of programs and clubs. One community organizer noted that even stellar programs could be gone overnight due to the government pulling funding. Facilitators for the programs felt overburdened with the numbers of students attending programs and noted that some programs had funding for 20 students and over 100 would show up any given night. Programs that provided transportation to and from the activity were attended more frequently and most programs included food.

Mentorships and Internships

Participants noted the importance of mentorships and internships in helping refugees connect with Canadian-born people and learn about different career options available to them. These opportunities also provided experiences for integrated learning about Canadian career culture. The mentoring process usually involved an informational interview where the student expresses what kind of job he/she would like to learn about to the coordinator. The coordinator then attempts to match the client with a mentor in that career. Typically this begins with an interview being arranged where the client is able to learn more about the career as well as the path that was followed by the interviewee to get to where they are. One government organization worker discussed a method of speed mentoring where there might be a room full of various mentors and the clients who move from one to the next in a timed session gathering information. The coordinator might also set up workplace tours where clients can go and learn more about a particular sector. While traditional mentoring and internship programs do exist, participants noted that they were able to form more valuable and lasting relationships when they had the opportunity to get to know employers. One NGO settlement worker stated,

> What is working is the openness of certain individuals or community groups or agencies, who have found ways to go beyond the minimum of what their job requires. We've had some great mentors, for example, in

COMMUNITY INITIATIVES TO SUPPORT REFUGEE YOUTH

our agency that treated families just like family. Without those mentors, I would imagine that some of those families would be in much more difficult situations.

Although the mentoring existed, participants noted that to really help people, mentors needed to forge a family-like connection to make a difference. Another unique form of mentoring described by an NGO director is 'Up-mentoring.' In this case, the youth or child serves as the mentor and the mentee is an adult.

> Well, it is interesting because we call it 'up-mentoring.' So here, even I did a thing with our junior staff mentorship program, the grade 10 students. I said, You are going to be leaders. You probably think of leaders as you helping young children to look up to you and do what you do and all that, and I said, That might be part of it. Here is the other thing. It is your ability to listen. Are you ready to learn from a 10 year old? Because when a 10 year old sees that you are paying attention to them, and listening to them – you are going to fill them with confidence. They will feel important and valued.

In this case, the refugee student is in a position of power and the older student is the 'listener' or the 'learner.' In doing this, the intent is to show the younger student that he/she is in a position of power and is important. This could be a particularly helpful strategy in the case of refugee children and their families given that they have lost power and control over their own situations through forced migration and often numerous pre-migration stressors.

Participants also mentioned that paid internships would help to both provide youth and their families with income and also keep youth who are at risk of becoming involved in marginalized activities connected to employment. The importance of being proactive by engaging in preventative programs to keep students connected to the world of work is illustrated in the following quote from an NGO program worker:

> I would say government-sponsored mass-scales internship paid programs for youth [is needed], you know because if you look at the research it shows that if you look at countries with high youth unemployment, [they] have more presence of crime, upheaval, violence like we've seen all over the world, right? And we're moving in that direction in terms of being a country where we have higher youth unemployment and it creates problems for our society and we need to act before it becomes a bigger problem.

Participants also identified the importance of having former refugees serve as mentors to share their stories of success to encourage others. One NGO settlement worker stated, 'We really identified that there are many successful refugees and that we aren't capitalizing on them and sharing the story'. In addition, participants suggested that having Canadian-born mentors assist refugees with learning the nuances of the Canadian work culture and learning social skills would be beneficial. An NGO settlement worker noted,

> [the intent is] for our refugee youth to spend the day, or the time, with that person to teach them the values of Canada, the culture – and then to integrate that into their culture as well as their background. So there are social skills related to that, and then maybe to go out and shop.

Although the importance of acquiring skills and meaningful work knowledge was discussed, underscoring this was also the need to just go out and shop, in other words, just to be with a Canadian doing things that Canadians might like to do where they can begin to forge meaningful relationships.

Employment Programs and Career Development

> Career development must include creativity and the building of creative imagination. It must be transformational and not reduced to finding a job. It is about dreaming about possibilities with hope and awareness of personal strengths and abilities. (NGO Program Director)

Research participants were nearly unanimous in indicating the importance of a focus on career development and employment programs. Helping both teachers and students understand that career development starts in the early years of education and continues throughout life and learning is a dissemination outcome of this project. A variety of meaningful programs were shared noting that career development begins with an awareness of self, engagement with the community, and developing relationships with others. This means facilitating programs focused on building intra- as well as interpersonal skills. As a director of an after school program stated,

> We have a fine arts component to the program as well. They play games, they do a lot of improving just some really different things to build their confidence. It gets them to take risks and it's great, it's been really, really, really good for them. They talk a lot in there about emotions and that's really where we focus on the emotions and the self-awareness. One of the

COMMUNITY INITIATIVES TO SUPPORT REFUGEE YOUTH

things they did the last group was made masks and it was about when I'm in public, this is my face, and behind my mask these are my emotions.

Interviewees also noted the importance of employment to refugees who are trying to help family members back home. An employment counselor noted,

> I think employment is a really, really important piece, because most of them are supporting people back home and so in their minds, employment is one of the, if not the most important thing. It doesn't matter is they are government-sponsored or privately-sponsored. They're supporting people back home and they want a job.

The availability of, and participation in, extracurricular school and community programs, as indicated earlier, offers youth the opportunity to engage in enjoyable activities while also building social and community capacity. Summer camps (art, science, music, sport, etc.) and youth employment agencies offer further options to engage in career development activities. One individual shared,

> … whether its employment or access to music or sports programs … those kind of things are important to help integrate refugees into the community and for others to also get to know who these – who are the neighbours across the street?

Support offered by community service providers who focus on employment and integration is helpful in allowing refugees the opportunity to participate in skill building programs and training. One settlement service program indicated that their in-house training program offers an allowance for two, four or six weeks of training that focuses on language, settlement, and employment. This allows participants to focus on these things without the added stress of where supplementary income is going to come from. A participant indicated, 'Beyond the basic pieces … employment support, career readiness, credential recognition, helping folks getting into appropriate training, and employment readiness'.

In addition to professional development and training recommendations for teachers, the research team developed suggested learning activities to support career development from kindergarten through Grade 12. These activities have been assigned to various learning outcomes using the 'Blueprint for Life/Work Designs' found in *Bridging Two Worlds* and are meant to be infused in core curriculum areas such as language arts, guidance programs, health education, and social studies (Stewart & Martin, 2018).

Social Connections, Relationships, and Nanosystems

The need for social connections and positive community connections was a strong theme emerging from interviewed service providers. Finding a sense of belonging within the community contributes to required connections within the nanosystem. One participant indicated,

> Finding ways for our refugee communities to interact in a positive way with the mainstream community, [and] with indigenous communities. And for mainstream and indigenous communities to be open to having a dialogue with refugees and see integration as a two-way process and find ways to build those bridges to make connections.

Several parties interviewed expressed the importance of establishing a network to assist with successful settlement. Integrative experiences with established or settled refugee families as well as Canadian-born neighbours contribute to building a support network and facilitate learning of the Canadian structures and systems. These networks can help refugees access necessary and desired resources in terms of education, healthcare, and employment. Further, social interactions contribute to an overall wellbeing and may reduce a sense of isolation. It was suggested that there is need for space where further dialogue and storytelling opportunities can take place and contribute to building relationships based on establishing an understanding of one another and our experiences. An interviewee observed,

> I think ... if you're listening to someone's stories, you're then humanizing them. It helps to build that relationship, it builds peace ... I think that's important and sort of creating a sense of community. I love Winnipeg because it's so ethnically diverse and there's people from all over the place, but I think we need to come out of our silos and engage with our community and find out who people are. I think it goes a long way because if you know who your neighbour is and who other people are it builds trust and solid relationships.

Further insights suggested that genuine efforts toward inclusion and opportunities for meaningful integration created a stronger sense of community. As a parent stated, 'My advice to how we help refugees integrate, just be decent people, help each other, be friends and neighbours.' Suggestions for forging these relationships include inviting refugee families to participate in activities considered normal in terms of Canadian culture such as ice skating or spending a day at the lake.

Integrating learning with recreational opportunities is another way to promote relationship building and social inclusion while also maintaining a focus on gaining an education. One program described the interrelated design of their activities in that students attended a homework program as part of a social contract that then allows them to participate in recreational activities such as soccer. In exchange for the academic efforts of students, the program pays for the soccer registrations fees and provides uniforms and transportation. This encourages students to stay in school while still participating in a fun social activity. The program facilitator noted, 'the things that they are passionate about and that they thrive in and do … their place of success … is guaranteed for them in exchange for this continued learning'.

Conclusion

Refugee youth represent a unique subset of the immigrant population whose needs are best served when connections between service providers and community agencies are strong (MacKay & Tavares, 2005). While there have been publications by community organizations on 'best practices' for supporting refugee youth, the organizational challenges which undermine integration efforts among refugees in Manitoba are poorly understood. Research that explores how the community can work in partnership with other ecological systems to support the needs of refugee students is also limited. The research conducted in Manitoba underscored the need for the family, school, and community systems to work collaboratively to support refugee children. More importantly, the findings revealed that the lack of connections between the systems was a key factor in complicating the settlement process and contributing to the overall stress for refugee students and their families. In some cases, participants were not accessing services because they did not know about the programs and others suggested that there was duplication of services. It was suggested that case managers or cultural brokers would be beneficial to help connect the students and their families to all available services. When a more holistic or 'wrap around' approach is achieved, the student's settlement and integration trajectory was perceived to more successful partly because it provided students with more comprehensive access to services and more long-term support.

While the benefits of the programs and services were frequently noted, one overarching concern was that most of the programming occurs in conjunction with the school, but outside of school hours. Respondents suggested more interaction with the school was necessary and more connection with the teachers was needed for these programs to more successful. Providing teachers with specific training on how best to support refugee students was noted as being necessary as well as providing curriculum within the school day that fostered peace and included understanding of diversity and cultural competence.

Increased interdisciplinary and cross-sector discussions are required to determine additional best practices and new approaches to supporting refugee children in Canada.

References

Bogdan, R., & Biklen, S. (2003). *Qualitiative research for education.* Boston, MA: Pearson.

Bronfenbrenner, U. (2001). The bioecological theory of human development. In N. J. Smelser & P. B. Baltes (Eds.), *International encyclopedia of the social and behavioural sciences* (Vol. 10, pp. 6963–6970). New York, NY: Elsevier.

Bronfenbrenner, U. (2005). Lewinian space and ecological substance (1977). In U. Bronfenbrenner (Ed.), *Making human beings human: Bioecological perspectives on human development* (pp. 41–49). Thousand Oaks, CA: Sage Publications.

Chavkin, N. (1998). Making the case for school, family and community partnerships: Recommendations for research. *The School Community Journal, 8*(1), 9–21.

Creswell, J. (2003). *Research design: Qualitative, quantitative and mixed methods approaches* (2nd ed.). Thousand Oaks, CA: Sage Publications.

Fazel, M., Reed, R. V., Panter-Brick, C., & Stein, A. (2012). Mental health of displaced and refugee children resettled in high-income countries: Risk and protective factors. *Lancet, 379*(9812), 266–282. doi:10.1016/S0140-6736(11)60051-2

Fazel, M., & Stein, A. (2002). The mental health of refugee children. *Archives of Disease in Childhood, 87*(5), 366–370. doi:10.1136/adc.87.5.366

Hamilton, R., & Moore, D. (Eds.). (2004). *Educational interventions for refugee children.* New York, NY: RoutledgeFalmer.

Inter-Agency Network for Education in Emergencies (INEE). (2013). *Conflict sensitive education.* New York, NY: International Rescue Committee.

Kirmayer, L. J., Lemelson, R., & Barad, M. (2007). Introduction: Inscribing trauma in culture, brain, and body. In L. J. Kirmayer, R. Lemelson, & M. Barad (Eds.), *Understanding trauma: Integrating biological, clinica, and cultural perspectives* (pp. 1–20). New York, NY: Cambridge University Press.

Machel, G. (2000, September). *The impact of armed conflict on children.* Report presented at the International Conference on War-Affected Children, Winnipeg, MB.

Machel, G. (2001). *The impact of war on children.* London: Hurst & Company.

MacKay, T., & Tavares, T. (2005, October 20). Building hope: Appropriate programming for adolescent and young adult newcomers of war-affected backgrounds and Manitoba schools. Winnipeg: Manitoba Education, Citizenship and Youth.

Malik, K. (2014). *Human development report 2014 sustaining human progress: Reducing vulnerabilities and building resilience.* New York, NY: United Nations Development Programme.

Manitoba Labour and Immigration. (2015). *Manitoba immigration facts: 2014 statistical report.* Retrieved from https://www.immigratemanitoba.com/wp-content/uploads/2015/09/MIF-2014_E_Web_Programmed.pdf

McBrien, J. L. (2005). Educational needs and barriers for refugee students in the United States: A review of literature. *Review of Educational Research, 75,* 329–364.

Noam, G. G., & Tillinger, J. R. (2004, Spring). After-school as intermediary space: Theory and typology of partnerships. *New Directions for Youth Development, 101,* 75–113.

Office of the Special Representative of the Secretary-General for Children and Armed Conflict. (2014). *The six grave violations against children during armed conflict: The legal foundation.* New York, NY. Retrieved from http://childrenandarmedconflict.un.org

Ruiz-de-Velasco, J., Fix, M., & Clewell, B. C. (2000). *Overlooked and underserved: Immigrant students in the U.S. secondary schools.* Washington, DC: The Urban Institute. Retrieved from http://www.urban.org/uploadedpdf/overlooked.pdf

Rutter, J. (2006). *Refugee children in the UK.* Berkshire: Open University Press.

Shakya, Y. B., Guruge, S., Hynie, M., Akbari, A., Malik, M., Htoo, S., ... Alley, S. (2010). Aspirations for higher education among newcomer refugee youth in Toronto: Expectations, challenges, and strategies. *Refugee, 27*(2), 65–78.

Stewart, J. (2011). *Supporting refugee children: Strategies for educators.* Toronto: University of Toronto Press.

Stewart, J., & Martin, L. (2018). *Bridging two worlds: Supporting newcomer and refugee youth: A guide to curriculum implementation and integration.* Ottawa: CERIC.

Suárez-Orozco, C., Onaga, M., & de Lardemelle, C. (2010). Promoting academic engagement among immigrant adolescents through school-family-community collaboration. *Professional School Counseling, 14*(1), 15–26. Retrieved from http://dx.doi.org/10.5330/prsc.14.1.xl6227108g624057

United Nations Development Programme. (2016). *Human development report 2016: Human development for everyone.* Retrieved from http://hdr.undp.org/sites/default/files/2016_human_development_report.pdf

UNHCR. (2015). *Worldwide displacement hits all-time high as war and persecution increase.* Retrieved from www.unhcr.org/558193896.html

UNHCR. (2018). *Figures at a glance: Statistical yearbooks.* Retrieved from http://www.unhcr.org/figures-at-a-glance.html

White, J., Franklin, D., Gruber, K., Hanke, C., Holzer, B., Javed, N., ... Weighill, C. (2009). The moving forward project: Working with refugee children, youth, and their families. In S. McKay, D. Fuchs, & I. Brown (Eds.), *Passion for action in child and family services: Voices from the prairies* (pp. 143–164). Regina: Canadian Plains Research Center. Retrieved from http://cwrp.ca/sites/default/files/publications/prairiebook2009/Chapter7.pdf

Yau, M. (1995). *Refugee students in Toronto schools: An exploratory study* (Research Services No. 211). Toronto: Toronto Board of Education.

Young, M., & Chan, J. (2014). School-based interventions for refugee children and youth. In C. A. Brewer & M. McCabe (Eds.), *Immigrant and refugee students in Canada* (pp. 31–53). Edmonton: Brush Education.

CHAPTER 6

In the Era of Bans and Walls

The Integration of Education and Immigration Policy and the Success of Refugee Students

Asih Asikin-Garmager, Duhita Mahatmya, Leslie Ann Locke and Ain A. Grooms

Introduction

The year 2017 marked two key policy events affecting refugees and immigrants in the United States. Shortly after the inauguration of the 45th president of the United States, the White House administration issued Executive Order (EO) 13769 (2017): *Protecting the Nation from Foreign Terrorist Entry into the United States*. Signed on January 27, 2017, the executive order banned all entries of individuals from Iran, Iraq, Libya, Somalia, Sudan, Syria, and Yemen, which are majority Muslim countries. EO 13769 also reduced the admission ceiling for refugees from 110,000 to 50,000, and suspended the U.S. refugee programme for 120 days to put in place additional procedures to screen individuals seeking refuge in the United States 'to ensure that those approved for refugee admission do not pose a threat to the security and welfare of the United States' (Executive Order 13769 sec. 5.). Amidst the largest global refugee crisis (United Nations High Commissioner for Refugees [UNHCR], 2015), the U.S.' proposed refugee admissions limit for 2017 was the lowest since 1980 (Patrick, 2004). The current political climate has also increased fear among refugee and immigrant communities (Goodman, 2017), and the threat of raids in schools with student populations from refugee and immigrant communities (American Federation of Teachers, 2016).

Coincidentally, 2017 also marked the 35th anniversary of the 1982 *Plyler v Doe* case, in which the U.S. Supreme Court ruled it unconstitutional to deny a public education to children based on their immigration status. The Court, in refusing to allow public school districts to charge undocumented immigrants an annual tuition, argued that 'without an education, these undocumented children, [a]lready disadvantaged as a result of poverty, lack of English-speaking ability, and undeniable racial prejudices, … will become permanently locked into the lowest socioeconomic class' (Plyler v Doe, 1982, para. 20). The importance of access to education for non-native born children persists as a common theme in conversations about comprehensive immigration reform;

© KONINKLIJKE BRILL NV, LEIDEN, 2019 | DOI: 10.1163/9789004401891_006

for example, with the Development, Relief, and Education for Alien minors (DREAM) Act, a bi-partisan supported bill, undocumented children of good moral character (often defined as being academically strong students) would receive access to institutions of higher education and a pathway to legal status (Mahatmya & Gring-Pemble, 2014).

Broadly speaking, access to education for students from traditionally under-served groups has been a focal point in educational policy in recent years. The passage of the *No Child Left Behind Act* (NCLB) in 2001 – a reauthorization of the 1965 Elementary and Secondary Education Act (ESEA) – brought increased attention to student proficiency, academic standards, and accountability for students, educators, and schools. Under NCLB, all students, regardless of background, were to reach academic proficiency by 2014. To facilitate this, NCLB placed emphasis on equity and educational access and provided additional funding to schools for subgroups of students, including students of colour, low-income students, English Language Learners (which includes immigrant and refugee populations), and students with disabilities (US Department of Education [US DOE], 2018a). NCLB proficiency goals required schools an annual assessment of student performance using the state assessments to ensure Adequate Yearly Progress (AYP) was made. Schools or districts failing to make AYP for at least two consecutive years are identified for improvement (US Department of Education [US DOE], 2018b).

Unfortunately, the lofty proficiency goals of NCLB were not met. Darling-Hammond (2007) suggests that under the structure and implementation of the bill, the schools serving students that need the most resources were the schools that were penalized the most. These schools lost funding and received sanctions because they did not consistently meet AYP requirements. Abedi (2004) critiqued the impact of NCLB on ELL students. He argued that an important factor in assessing ELL students is the lack of consistency in classifying students as ELLs. NCLB did not require a uniform definition across states, meaning that individual districts could determine their own ELL standards. Another factor was the lack of stability within the subgroup, calling it a 'moving target' (p. 4). As individual students reach proficiency, they are moved out of the subgroup, coinciding with new students moving in. Given the fluctuation within the subgroup, Abedi (2004) contends that reaching AYP would be highly unlikely. In 2015, ESEA was again reauthorized, and is now known as the *Every Student Succeeds Act* (ESSA). Under ESSA, states still hold schools accountable for student achievement, but have more flexibility in determining what constitutes proficiency. ESSA also required that states develop a uniform definition for ELL classification to which all districts must adhere (US Department of Education [US DOE], 2018c).

IN THE ERA OF BANS AND WALLS

There is a growing need to understand the complex experiences of children from displaced communities and the structures and policies that support or undermine these children's educational success. For refugee and immigrant students living at the intersection of education and immigration policies in the United States, there exists an additional layer of complexity and underscores their experiences as students from kindergarten through college (Skattebol, 2016).

The Current Study

This chapter uses 'Smalltown,' a small, rural town in Iowa, as a bounded case (Yin, 2014) with which to offer an initial exploration for this intersectionality and how schools, through their educators, help and/or hinder resettled students' progress. In particular, this chapter explores academic and demographic characteristics of the Smalltown Community School District (SCSD) and how educators in SCSD describe and offer support to refugee and immigrant students within the context of state and federal education and immigration policies.[1] The U.S. Department of Education describes foreign-born or immigrant populations to include 'immigrant children and the children of immigrants, Deferred Action for Childhood Arrivals (DACA) children and youth, immigrant families, adult immigrants (e.g. refugees, asylees), foreign-born professionals, migrant students, teachers of English learners and foreign languages, and receiving communities' (https://www2.ed.gov/about/overview/focus/immigration-resources.html). Accordingly, for the purpose of our chapter, we use the term 'refugee and immigrant students' to broadly refer to those whose parents were born outside of the U.S., and so were not U.S citizens at birth. Additionally, our definition encompasses children whose parents arrived in the U.S. legally or illegally.

For this exploratory study, our unit of analysis consisted of one school district. We used quantitative and qualitative data sources to support our research. Quantitative data consisted of state administrative data from 2006–2017 and was used to examine correlations between student enrolment and achievement trends in SCSD over the past decade. Our qualitative data draws from interviews with members of the SCSD to present insights about the realities and perceptions of educators in the era of bans and walls. Interviews were conducted with two educators (Educator 1 and Educator 2) at SCSD. The interview participants were identified through a snowball sampling method. Prior to conducting the interview, we sent an email to potential participants to invite them to be interviewed. Both agreed. We explained that participation was voluntary and that the study was intended to serve as an exploratory pilot study. The interviews lasted approximately 60 minutes and were recorded with the participants' consent. The recordings were transcribed and the transcriptions were coded following Strauss and Corbin's (1998) strategies of open coding, axial coding, and selective coding. The summary of the interviews was sent to the participants for member checking.

Context for the Study: Iowa

Iowa is a state in the Midwest region of the United States. It has long been considered to be a rural, as well as a racially and ethnically homogenous state. Although the ancestral homeland of the Ioway, Otoe, Ponca, and other Native American tribes and bands, only the Meskwaki remain, in addition to small land trusts managed by the Omaha and Winnebego (Foster, 2009). Current data from the U.S. Census Bureau (2016) reflect that only 0.5% of the approximately 3.1 million state residents identify as American Indian/Alaska Native. The remainder of the population is 91.4% White, 3.7% African American/Black, 2.5% Asian/Pacific Islander, and 5.8% Hispanic/Latino. Only 1.8% of the population identified with two or more races, or multiracial.

There have been, however, significant population shifts in recent decades (Locke & Schares, 2016). From 2000 to 2010, Iowa's population grew by 6.2%, which is about 3% lower than the national rate (Statewide Population Trends, n.d.). In spite of the overall slow population growth in the state, Iowa is becoming more diverse, and children are leading this trend. Specifically, 'all parts of the state are becoming more diverse, and population growth among children of colour and/or Hispanic descent is the sole driver of population growth in that age group in Iowa' (Statewide Population Trend, n.d., p. 8). According to the Statewide Population Trend (n.d.), the population growth rate for children under the age of 6 years in Iowa between 2000 and 2010 was 6.7%, compared to the national rate of 4.8%. Within this growing child population, 10.2% of these children were identified as being of Latinx[2] heritage. In general, there was a 110.5% change in the Latinx population in Iowa from 2000 to 2014. The Asian population grew by 88.5% and the Black population grew by 71.5%; this is compared to the 4.1% change in the White population in that same time period (Krob, 2016).

These population changes shape the state's public schools. The percentage of White students in the state's public schools has been on a downtrend for decades. Table 6.1 shows the demographic breakdown of students enrolled in Iowa during the 2016–2017 academic year. The students of colour, or from minoritised[3]

IN THE ERA OF BANS AND WALLS 135

groups collectively, represent slightly more than 23% of the total student population in Iowa. This is up from slightly over 21% in the 2013–2014 academic year (Locke & Schares, 2016). There are parallel shifts in the languages represented in Iowa's public schools. According to the Iowa Data Center (2017), 7.7% of Iowans speak a language other than English at home. Those languages include Spanish (4%), an Asian/Pacific Islander language (1.6%), and Other (2.1%). The number of English Language Learners (ELLs) in schools has also continued to increase in recent years. Currently, there are well over 100 different languages spoken in the state's schools (Ryan, 2017). The majority of ELLs in Iowa claim Spanish, Arabic, or Karen languages as their home language (Winn & Winn, 2016). These languages reflect the increases in the Latinx population as well as refugees from Burma and Iraq (Table 6.2). According to Ryan (2017), 'over the past 25 years, the percentage of students learning English has grown far faster than their native English-speaking peers, increasing 500 per cent to 27,241 students during the 2015–16 school year' (n.d.). All districts in Iowa serve some population of ELL students. A few serve student populations with over 30% ELLs.

TABLE 6.1   Demographic characteristics of Iowa and SCSD (2016–2017)

	Iowa public schools	SCSD
Total PreK-12 Enrolment	510,932	714
Total K-12 Enrolment	481,588	695
Race[a]		
American Indian/Native American	1,905 (0.4%)	4 (0.6%)
Asian	12,678 (2.5%)	8 (1.1%)
Black	30,298 (5.9%)	75 (10.5%)
Hispanic	54,171 (10.6%)	362 (50.7%)
Pacific Islander	1,237 (0.2%)	0 (0%)
White	391,449 (76.6%)	254 (35.6%)
Multiracial	19,186 (3.8%)	11 (1.5%)
Immigrant[b]	8,486 (1.8%)	59 (9%)
English Language Learners	28,604 (5.9%)	237 (34.1%)
Free or Reduced Lunch	198,885 (41.3%)	576 (82.88%)

SOURCE: IOWA DEPARTMENT OF EDUCATION (2017)

a Race numbers and percentages are based on PreK-12 enrolment numbers, all else are drawn from the K-12 enrolment.

b Immigrant enrolment information is pulled from the 2015–2016 (the most recent year of data available).

TABLE 6.2   Top 5 largest groups resettled in Iowa, 2006–2017

Country of origin	Number of individuals
Burma	2,813
Bhutan	1,061
Iraq	688
Democratic Republic of Congo	581
Somalia	500

SOURCE: WORLDWIDE REFUGEE ADMISSIONS PROCESSING SYSTEM (WRAPS), 2017. RETRIEVED FROM HTTP://IREPORTS.WRAPSNET.ORG/INTERACTIVE-REPORTING/ENUMTYPE/REPORT?ITEMPATH=/RPT_WEBARRIVALSREPORTS/MX%20-%20ARRIVALS%20BY%20DESTINATION%20AND%20NATIONALITY

A Brief History of Iowa's Refugee Policies

Iowa's shifting demographics includes its decades-long history of welcoming refugees into the state. In 1975, Iowa Governor Robert Ray established the Governor's Task Force for Indochinese Resettlement in response to President Gerald Ford's request to offer resettlement to Tai Dam refugees displaced by the Vietnam War. He was the only governor to respond. However, by 1976, the Task Force expanded the scope of its services to include all refugees in Iowa. In the 1970s, many of Iowa's refugees came from Southeast Asia, which increased the number of school districts enrolling ELLs tenfold (Peterson, 1983). By the 1980s, refugees from Eastern Europe were resettling in Iowa. The 1990s and 2000s brought to Iowa refugees from Sudan and Bosnia. Since 2006, Iowa has welcomed close to 7,000 individuals seeking refuge in the United States (Refugee Processing Center, 2017). Figure 6.1 shows the number of refugee arrivals in Iowa from 2006–2017 and Table 6.2 shows the top 5 largest groups resettled in Iowa within the same time period.

Currently, the state of Iowa is home to one of only nine official field offices affiliated with the United States Committee for Refugees and Immigrants. However, in recent years, federal and state appropriations to support Iowa's refugee resettlement efforts have decreased, leaving non-profit organizations to carry more of the weight. For example, in February 2017, a cadre of refugee service providers in Iowa participated in Refugee Day on the Hill (Tendall, 2017) in Des Moines. They advocated for continued funding of English language programmes in the education budget and for the Refugee Revitalize Iowa's Sound Economy (RISE) Bill (SF 2298) as part of the Department of Human Services budget. Both bills would provide support for refugee workforce development

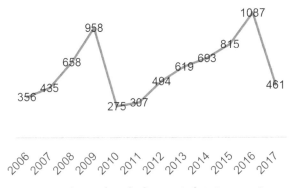

FIGURE 6.1 The number of refugee arrivals in Iowa, 2006–2017

(Gruber-Miller, 2014; Tendall, 2017). At the end of the 2017 legislative session, $210,000 of the education budget (0.01%) was allocated toward workforce training programmes, but only $105,000 was budgeted for the 2018–2019 fiscal year (HF 642). Financial support of the Refugee RISE programme was cut by two-thirds, from $300,000 to $100,000. The dwindling of state government support can be traced to 2010 when the U.S. Department of State notified Iowa's Bureau of Refugee Services that it would no longer receive financial support as a national resettlement agency. In this way, the funding to support refugee and immigrant well-being in the state of Iowa has been split across different agencies, thus placing refugee and immigrant families and students in the intersection of state and federal education and immigration policies.

A Closer Look at Smalltown

Smalltown is a town of approximately 2,000 people, located in northeast corner of a Midwestern state in the United States. As of the 2010 U.S. Census, the racial/ethnic demographics were 77% White, 4% African American, 0.6% Native American, 1.7% Asian/Pacific Islander, 2% Multiracial, and 14% Other. Approximately 32% of Smalltown's population identified as being of Latinx origin (of any race). (Hispanic or Latino origin was asked as a separate question from race, which is why percentages add up to over 100%). With immigrants comprising approximately 25% of its population (Flakus, 2017), Smalltown prides itself on its diverse immigration history (Hsu, 2008); the town has received immigrants from Eastern European, African, and Latin American communities through the decades (Jones, 2012). The unique immigration history of Smalltown began in the 1980s when an Orthodox Jewish family from New York City started a kosher meatpacking plant, which later became the largest producer of kosher meats in the United States (Flakus, 2017). The opening of the kosher meatpacking plant drew newcomers, which included other Hasidic Jewish families, and people from Mexico, Guatemala, and Ukraine to the area (Minikwu, 2017; Reynolds, 2013).

As is common in small, rural communities, the meatpacking industry draws workers who are willing to work in low-wage and low-status jobs; this often means migrants, refugees, and documented and undocumented immigrants as the main source of labour (Grey, 1997). In May 2008, Smalltown experienced one of the largest immigration raids by the U.S. Immigration and Customs Enforcement (ICE). The raid resulted in the arrest of nearly 400 workers assumed to lack significant documentation for legal employment in the U.S. (Preston, 2008), which led to the deportation of many workers with children in Smalltown schools. Eighteen of those arrested and facing deportation were juveniles, and in some instances, the youth faced refugee resettlement proceedings (Hsu, 2008). The raid reduced Smalltown's population by 20% (Grey, Devlin, & Goldsmith, 2009). Replacing the lost workers were people from the island nation of Palau, who were later replaced by Muslim refugees from Somalia (Drash, 2008; Jones, 2012), creating a cultural shift in the community. Members of the Latinx community are also returning slowly to the town (Minikwu, 2017).

The raid, and changing cultural landscape after the raid, shaped the Smalltown schools (Mehaffey, 2013). The dependence on foreign labour bears consequences for local schools, such as the ones in Smalltown. On one hand, the influx of students helped to keep the local Smalltown schools from closing (Jones, 2012; Juby & Kaplan, 2011). However, on the other, there are on-going issues related to student attendance as refugee and immigrant students move to areas with more family or community members, or where migrant students drop out of school to work in the local factories (Reynolds, 2013; Zehr, 2008). Following the raid, many students, in addition to parents, disappeared, fuelling trauma and fear in the students in the community even months later (Juby & Kaplan, 2011). The day following the raid, almost 90% of the school's Latinx population were absent because their parents were arrested or they were hiding because they were afraid of further raids (Hsu, 2008; Zehr, 2008). School personnel also reported more behaviour and mental health issues among students following the raid (Juby & Kaplan, 2011). Now, almost a decade after the raid, new communities of refugees and immigrants have arrived in Smalltown (see Table 6.1 for SCSD demographic statistics) bringing with them new challenges and opportunities for the community and schools. In the current political climate, old fears have resurfaced and anti-immigration sentiment has escalated.

Educating Refugee Students in SCSD

Despite being among the smallest school districts in Iowa (see Table 6.1 for a comparison between SCSD demographics and the state of Iowa School Districts), SCSD has a relatively large minoritised student population (50%) and the highest immigrant student population in the state at 9% (Iowa Department of Education [IDOE], 2018). Additionally, there are 17 different primary languages represented in the student body (Grey et al., 2009). The district also has the highest number of students eligible for free or reduced lunch and is fourth in the state for the number of ELL students enrolled in the schools. Currently, SCSD is one of the 13 districts (out of 332 districts) in Iowa receiving state funding as part of the U.S. Department of Education Title III (English Instruction for Limited English Proficient and Immigrant Student) appropriations. In Iowa, Title III funds are used to provide evidence-based programmes that increase English proficiency and professional development to educators around how to improve instruction for ELLs (Iowa Department of Education [IDOE], 2017a). The following sections outline how the district addresses the academic and non-academic needs of its students and fosters community engagement.

Addressing Academic and Language Needs

Drawing upon the years of data available from the state that span the last decade (2006–2017), there was a statistically significant, $t(10) = 3.86, p < .01$, decline in the average number of students identified as immigrants in the academic years preceding (2006–2008 mean = 101.50, SD = 19.09l) and following (2009–2017 mean = 49.90, SD = 17.04) the Smalltown raid; the population essentially decreased by half. As seen in Figure 6.2, there was a decrease in the total number of ELL, and immigrant students in SCSD during the 2006–2007 through 2008–2009 academic years. There was a continued decrease in the total enrolment of immigrant students through the 2009–2010 academic year, before the numbers level off. This drop parallels the 70% decrease in the number of refugee arrivals in the state of Iowa between 2009 and 2010 (Figure 6.1). There were also general decreasing trends for the total number of White students over the past decade in SCSD. Interestingly, the total enrolment of non-White and ELL students (the numbers include refugee and immigrant students) saw an increasing trend in SCSD after the raid. Number of non-White student enrolment surpassed White students starting in the 2011–2012 academic year.

Even though SCSD has been culturally diverse for decades, it was not until recently that the district implemented programmes aimed at meeting the academic needs of their refugee and immigrant student populations. Addressing

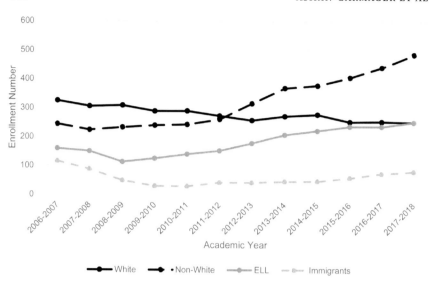

FIGURE 6.2   SCSD student enrolment trends, 2006–2017

the educational needs of newcomers can pose a challenge for schools because the students may vary in their exposure to formal education, first language skills, and age of arrival (Francis, Rivera, Lesaux, Kieffer, & Rivera, 2006). Furthermore, newcomers often come with limited or no English language proficiency, which is a prevailing issue that negatively affects refugee students' resettlement process in general (McBrien, 2005). According to the educators we interviewed, the district saw a high number of drop outs among their newcomer ELL population when those students were placed in mainstream classes without having received support in acquiring English. As a result, in 2010, SCSD started offering a Newcomer Programme for students. According to SCSD's ELL plan,[4] this programme is intended for 'students who have been in the U.S. for less than 2 years and/or have had very limited educational background' (p. 7).

The Newcomer Programme is a self-contained programme, and has been described by a SCSD educator as 'a school in a school pathway' (Educator 1, July 14, 2017). A challenge for small rural districts, such as SCSD, in educating their newcomers is balancing the need to integrate those students with their mainstream peers and, at the same time, addressing the academic needs of the students with limited resources (Rah, 2007). At SCSD, the Newcomer Programme aims to provide students with basic English language instruction (e.g., vocabulary, phonics, letter identification) and instruction on cultural and educational norms. A transitional programme, such as the Newcomer Programme, allows teachers to develop lessons and provide instructions that specifically address the language and cultural needs of their newly arrived refugee and immigrant students so that those students are able to follow instructions and understand the content of mainstream academic classes (Rah, 2007).

At SCSD, students enrolled in the Newcomer Programme are expected to exit the programme within two years, after which they are integrated into mainstream classes with their peers and get additional support from ELL teachers. The district recognises that two years is not sufficient for ELL students to acquire language proficiency beyond basic communication skills. An educator we interviewed revealed that the two-year time frame was determined based on 'other successful programme nation-wide' and to ensure that students are able to get into grade-level content classes before they 'age out or graduate' (Educator 2, January 4, 2018).

In the grade-level or mainstream classes, students who have exited the Newcomers Programme are given additional support to address remaining needs in their cognitive/academic language proficiency. At the elementary level, Newcomer Programme graduates are placed in mainstream classes co-taught by classroom and ELL teachers. Secondary students are put in Foundation classes that are co-taught by content and ELL teachers. In the Foundation classes, students receive academic content aligned with the state's academic standards. The purpose of the foundation classes are to support refugee and immigrant students in acquiring the basic knowledge in academic classes, which they may not already have due to their limited formal educational background, and vocabulary for concept development. Classes such as these have the advantage to better prepare students linguistically and academically before they join the mainstream classes, which, in turn, helps reduce frustration for both the students and teachers (Rah, 2007). A challenge for SCSD in offering Foundation classes is the limited resources that not only meet students' needs, but also comply with federal and state requirements. For example, as explained by Educator 2, Foundation for Science teachers had to create their materials that are aligned with the recently published national science standards – the Next Generation Science Standards because currently none specifically designed for ELL students exist.

Despite the practices put in place by the district to meet the academic and language needs of its refugee and immigrant populations, student achievement data indicate a large gap in the academic performance of the minoritised population in the district. Even though the school district as a whole is over 60% non-White, White students outperformed all other racial groups and students who qualify for free and reduced lunch, commonly used to indicate socioeconomic status (Iowa Department of Education [IDOE], 2017b). We took a closer look at correlations among changes in the immigrant student enrolment and changes in the districts' math and reading achievement over the last decade. Math and reading achievement was available for grades 3, 4, 5, 6, 7, 8, and 11. There were no significant correlations between changes in the immigrant enrolment and SCSD math and reading achievement. There were significant, negative correlations between the non-White enrolment numbers and grade 5 ($r = -0.89, p < .01$) and grade 11 ($r = -0.92 p < .01$) reading achievement. There were also negative correlations between the ELL enrolment numbers and grade 4 ($r = -0.63, p < .05$), grade 5 ($r = -0.87, p < .01$), and grade 11 ($r = -0.82, p < .01$) reading achievement, and grade 11 math achievement ($r = 0.66, p < .05$).

An educator at SCSD attributed the low academic performance of the non-White students in the district, which is predominantly made up by refugee and immigrant students, to the state's policy requiring all students who have attended schools for a full academic year to take the Iowa assessments. School assessment results, as outlined by first by NCLB and now by ESSA, are disseminated to the public by way of the State Report Card. In 2016, Smalltown's elementary/middle school was classified as 'Needs Improvement' by the State Report Card, while its high school was rated 'Priority.'[5] Educator 1 explained,

> If you look at our District Report Card ... ours is awful because after one year of these kids being in our district, they're required to take the Iowa Assessment, and it's counted against us. And the kids get a 6th grade education, they're 10th grader, and they've been in the country for one year barely learning English, and you make them take the Iowa Assessment in English and they obviously do terrible on it and then you calculate it as part of my group ... It is what it is. We just go with it because there's not much we can do at our end at the local level. (Educator 1, July 14, 2017)

Limited resources constrain the district's efforts to adequately support the varied educational backgrounds and needs of the students.

Adding to the challenge in closing the achievement gaps between White and non-White students is the Iowa State policy limiting state residents' right to receive free public education after they are 21 years old (Iowa Department of Education [IDOE], 2017c). This policy presents a challenge to SCSD, as stated by an SCSD educator we interviewed, 'We're trying to get [newcomer students] caught up as fast as we possibly can because everybody wants kids to graduate. I get it. But I get kids at 19 years old with no English, and, the last time they were in 5th grade, that are supposed to graduate by 21, it's not going to happen' (Educator 1, July 14, 2017). Age of arrival has documented effects on the educational experiences and outcomes of immigrant students, whereby students who come to the US in their teenage years have lower attainment than those students who arrived as pre-teens (Chiswick & DebBurman, 2004; Cortes, 2006). Variation in age of arrival poses a challenge for the district in ensuring that all students get the support they need to be successful. Students who arrive at older ages, such as 19, may need more assistance, but are limited by the state's age policy as well as potentially longer gaps in their educational exposure (Thomas & Collier, 1997). When students arrive at younger ages, they have more time to get support and adjust to the school's culture. State assessments also assume a continuity in the students who take the tests each year, which fails to account for the variable migration histories of refugee and immigrant students (Grey, 1997).

The need to comply with state education policies around annual student assessment and aging-out complicates SCSD's local efforts to support the academic and language success of SCSD refugee and immigrant students. Students with interrupted educational histories, such as refugees, not only have language as a barrier in catching up with their peers, but they are also confronted with other barriers including limited prior knowledge and understanding of the school culture and norms around 'proper' student behaviour (Miller, Mitchell, & Brown, 2005). According to Cummins (1992), it may take a minimum of five years for ELLs to acquire cognitive/academic language proficiency. And yet, as the quotes from district administrators illustrate, the district does not have five years to help refugee and immigrant students catch up with their native peers or acclimate to school culture in the US. In SCSD, students and educators have, at most, the two years of the Newcomers Programme to offer intensive academic and language support for refugee students.

Addressing Students' Non-Academic Needs

The district has also implemented efforts to attend to students' psychosocial needs. As demonstrated by studies investigating the intragroup differences of academic experiences among minoritised students (e.g., Chen & Stevenson, 1995; Gibson, 1997), there exists a more complex interplay among the students' multiple identities, stemming from immigration status, ethnicity, language, and generational status; all of which affect their educational experiences. For current refugee and immigrant students, the larger U.S. political climate informs students' educational experiences as well (Goodman, 2017). According to an educator we interviewed, the immigration policies issued by the Trump Administration have indirectly affected the minoritised students in the district. He recounted:

> We had a situation this spring. Facebook blew up: ICE is in town. I had 30 kids that were scared to walk home. So I got a Suburban out instead of

running a bus service. Because the minute they walk off the school property, they're 18 years of age ... In the school property, they're safe, unless [ICE agents] have a warrant or something. But we drove them home and made sure they got in their house. (Educator 1, July 14, 2017)

Members of the Smalltown community offered similar assistance to children after the raid in 2008, and school personnel worked with community members to ensure students' safety (Juby & Kaplan, 2011; Zehr, 2008).

Refugee and immigrant students' mental health is another important factor to consider in an effort to support their resettlement and acculturation process (Cole, 1998). Students' past experiences with violence and living in refugee camps likely affect their resettlement process in their host countries (Rah, 2007). Researchers have found that refugee students' past traumatic experiences are what set them apart from the experiences of immigrant/migrant students (McBrien & Day, 2012). An educator in the district recognized that many of the refugee students experienced trauma, which manifests in their behaviour and difficulty to retain information. Currently, SCSD does not have staff trained to work with students with trauma, but it has scheduled to bring in a trainer with the expertise to work with the district staff. She acknowledged the need for teachers and district staff to be properly trained to provide ongoing support to their students affected by trauma.

Fostering School and Community Engagement

The district educators we interviewed recognized important areas of improvement and that the district was purposeful in its efforts to include the refugee and immigrant communities in making decisions on how to best support their students. The educators, at least those to whom we spoke, considered the families as partners, and ensured that students' needs were met, despite the limited resources provided by the state. For example, they hired people with ties to the community to serve as translators. The Spanish translator was one of the first Latinx who graduated from Smalltown High School, and the Somali translators are also members of the community. Not only did the translators help the district to communicate with the families, they also helped district staff to understand different cultural norms so that district staff can interact more effectively with students and families.

Additionally, the district engaged the community to acquire a better understanding of the students' home cultures. Educator 1 recounted a time when he met with Somali community members. They engaged in conversations about academic, cultural, and religious values and expectations. According to him, understanding the cultural and religious expectations of their students and

IN THE ERA OF BANS AND WALLS

families helped school staff to be more flexible in accommodating the needs of their students and families. He stated,

> It was just kind of a necessity for us to start understanding the different [cultural] things, why they did what they did, what the expectations were for them, so that we knew enough not to ... start jumping on their case. Well, they're gone because it's an excuse for religious events, which is 100% excused in the district. We don't want teachers jumping down their throats and get themselves in a bid with the parents because we just didn't quite understand what was taking place. So it's just that. We continue to understand that and make adjustments ... So we're just trying to be very cognizant of things [that are] going on, and flexible ... We really just had to tap on to those resources of people in the community. (Educator 1, July 14, 2017)

The district also recognized the need to support its teachers in their work with refugee and immigrant students and families. The educators in the district with whom we communicated discussed initial frustrations among teachers toward the refugee students as a result of cultural misunderstandings:

> Something we learned right away was when our new refugees would come, they would not look you in the eye. And a lot of teachers felt that was a disrespect. Because if they were in trouble or something, they would not make eye contact. So, that was an issue where teachers were getting students in trouble for not having that eye contact. In reality, it was a cultural barrier. So we had to teach the teachers that that was a barrier, and we have to teach [the students] that here, that's something they need to do. [Students] can't be in trouble for that until they understand. (Educator 2, December 19, 2017)

Teachers in the district have various formal and informal opportunities to learn about the cultural and religious values of their students, including learning basic vocabulary words in the native languages of their refugee and immigrant students, so that they can interact more effectively with their students and families. Additionally, the district incorporates discussions on the different cultures represented in the community and the district into their orientation programme for new teachers.

An educator we spoke with explained that the community had not always reacted well to the diversity, and schools played an important role in bringing the community together:

I think it started when we first started getting diversity. We had a lot of community members who are not open to that. You know, we're in … [a] very small rural farm town. So change is hard, I feel, for communities around here. And new things are a little bit scary, maybe. So I know there used to be quite a bit of negativity towards diversity in general … And then with this new population [the Somalis] … in the community I would hear people talking about how they need to learn our culture and just that theirs is a hard culture to get along with. I think it started here in school. I think school has a huge impact on a community because we had to do a lot of education with our teachers as well. (Educator 2, December 19, 2017)

In connecting with community members to help them better understand the refugee population, Educator 2 focused on individual stories:

[When I hear people] made comments about the Somalis … I feel that's my opportunity to jump in and say, 'hey, let me tell you a little bit about them and explain the culture' … I felt that the best way that we've been able to make a difference in the community is to tell good stories about what's happening with [the people from] that culture. I have so many students' stories of what they've been through and how far they've gotten and how they're succeeding. I try to share those stories … It really helps to make that personal connection. If you know someone, then it makes it totally different than just talking about a group of people. (Educator 2, December 19, 2017)

Discussion

Our findings inform the literature on refugee students' educational success by revealing how one rural school district works to support their refugee and immigrant students within the boundaries of changing state and federal policies and lingering trauma following one of the largest immigration raids in U.S. history. Extensive scholarship examines immigrant students' language acquisition (Faltis & Arias, 2007) and acculturation (Fuligni, 2001). There is a dearth of research, however, on the influence of education policy and leadership in addressing the unique needs of refugee students specifically.

As demonstrated in our analysis, schools can partner with refugee students and families to create a culture of inclusion and mutual respect in the classroom and larger community. Typical of school districts in small rural towns, community life in Smalltown is centred around its schools (Chalker, 2002). As the town became more diverse, teachers and administrators found themselves to be essential players not only in the educational, but also acculturation, process of their refugee and immigrant students. Despite the limited human and fiscal resources, the district was and continued to be committed to providing on-going support for both its educators and students to ensure student success, while also complying with federal and state education and immigration policy.

Policy Considerations

Iowa, and other states, should consider affording schools the capability to further disaggregate student data. In Iowa, refugee, migrant, and immigrant students are included in the same subgroup for data collection purposes, yet as we have outlined, there exist significant differences in the needs and experiences of various student groups. Disaggregated data would encourage schools, districts, and the state to more closely examine the needs of their students as well as the methods by which access to high quality education is provided.

School administrators and leaders in Smalltown may also benefit from implementing professional development that trains educators on adopting socially just practices to ensure all students have equal opportunities to succeed (Theoharis, 2007). These practices include providing inclusive education for ELL and newcomer students, increasing staff capacity to develop cultural humility, providing staff with resources focusing on equity, and incorporating culturally relevant curriculum for students. In addition, college of education should incorporate specialized curriculum and training into their teacher and leadership preparation programmes to proactively address the changing demographics of public schools.

Finally, Iowa's ESSA plan – approved by the US Department of Education in May 2018 – has changed the ways in which ELL students are assessed. Rather than assessing ELL students via their scores on the state's academic assessments in the English language, the state will now use growth over time as the measure of academic progress (Iowa Department of Education [IDOE], 2018b). Educators in Smalltown continue to do their best with the limited resources available and believe that previous federal and state policies created additional and unnecessary obstacles. These concerns echo the critiques made by Abedi (2004) and Darling-Hammond (2007). The Iowa ESSA plan will go into effect during the 2018–2019 school year, making us hopeful about the future academic success of the state's ELL students.

Theoretical Considerations

Ogbu's (1992) cultural-ecology theory of minoritsed school performance is often cited to understand how institutional and community factors shape the schooling experiences and outcomes of traditionally minoritised students. In Ogbu's theory, non-White minorities are placed into two broad categories: voluntary and involuntary (Ogbu, 1992). Voluntary minorities are communities who came, more or less, willingly to the U.S. in pursuit of better opportunities. This group includes immigrants to the U.S., and this group's willingness to assimilate into the culture of the majority (i.e., the White American ways) is key to their academic success. Conversely, involuntary minorities are those who are in the U.S. not as a result of their volition. This group often includes Blacks and Native Americans who were forced to come or leave by the majority group, and, thus, are less likely to view the majority culture favourably (Ogbu & Simons, 1998). In this interpretation, refugee, immigrant, and migrant students are viewed similarly as voluntary minorities. The U.S. Department of Education generally holds this same view and categorizes refugees, asylees, migrant students, as immigrants (https://www2.ed.gov/about/overview/focus/immigration-resources.html).

A major critique of Ogbu's theory is that it tends to hold a deficit perspective of minoritised students' academic engagement, hints at fixed notions of race/ethnicity, and lacks consideration of intragroup differences of educational experiences (Foley, 2004; Gibson, 1997; McBrien, 2005). We agree with these critiques and that the theory perpetuates the misconception that students who belong to one group (i.e., voluntary minorities) will have more positive attitudes toward schooling and educational experiences compared to those belonging to other group (i.e., involuntary minorities). Nevertheless, Ogbu's theory is useful in recognizing historical, socio-political, and community factors that influence the schooling experience of students from traditionally minoritised groups. For the refugee students at SCSD, their educational experiences cannot be divorced from their migration histories, traumas, and the strength of their cultures and communities (Dryden-Peterson, 2016; Strekalova-Hughes, Nash, & Erdemir, 2017). Their histories also intersect with the long immigration history of their local community, Smalltown.

McBrien and Day's (2012) research highlighted how refugee students' acculturation process is marked by 'considerable pain: the loss and inability to be in touch with family members and friends from their native countries; the trauma of death, war, separation, and on-going uncertainty in their homelands; and discrimination and person/economic uncertainty in their current lives' (pp. 562–563). These experiences distinguish refugee experiences from other immigrant populations. In Smalltown, students of the refugee and immigrant communities have also experienced traumas related to separation and discrimination, which may make the distinction between refugee and immigrant, at least in SCSD, small.

Still, our conversations with SCSD educators revealed a purposeful effort to build a school environment and climate based on mutual respect. According to them, learning about cultures was perceived as a two-way process, and was, in part, intended to foster a culture of belonging for the students. Both the educators with whom we spoke considered families and community members to be an integral part in the education of the refugee and immigrant student populations. They reached out to and partnered with families and community members to support their work with students; an important step in creating a socially just school (Theoharis, 2009). However, our findings also indicate that educators still tended to define the immigrant and refugee students by the past trauma they experienced. Learning difficulties and behavioural issues among these population are attributed to their past experiences in their country of origin or refugee camps. Consequently, school efforts to educate the refugee student population are geared toward helping them overcome trauma. In doing so, educators in Smalltown narrowly define who and what a refugee student looks like and inadvertently contribute to the popular narrative of the refugee population as needy and lacking agency to overcome their challenges (Strekalova-Hughes et al., 2017).

RefugeeCrit theory, currently being developed by Strekalova-Hughes et al. (2017), can serve as a stepping stone to gain insights into how educators can continue working with their refugee students and families to design an educational approach that takes into account their complex identity and the complexity of their experiences. RefugeeCrit situates people who are refugees within the context of globalism, colonialism, and other societal level mechanisms that have functioned to oppress groups of people. Through this theoretical perspective, refugee students are students who, by way of certain circumstances, are given (but do not choose, per se) refugee status and identity. Defining, understanding, and interpreting students' experiences beyond their status is crucial to address the needs of immigrant/refugee students. Foremost, refugee students are not all the same. As the theory purports, it is time for 'agential voices and counter-narratives' (Strekalova-Hughes et al., 2017) to emerge from refugee communities that start to unchain their stories from their status.

Limitations and Recommendations for Future Study

A limitation of our study is that, officially, refugee students in Iowa are categorized with other immigrant and non-White students. Our discussion of refugee students' experiences in SCSD is confounded with the experiences of immigrant students and students of colour, generally. The administrative data on student demographics and test scores combines refugee and immigrant into the non-White and ELL student groups. In practice, for educators, especially those in rural schools such as SCSD, the structure of federal and state funding also necessitates the mixing of these students (Rah, 2007). Nevertheless, the SCSD educators with whom we spoke, gave a more nuanced description of the students, recognizing that within their Newcomers Programme, ELL students came from varied immigration, migration, and educational backgrounds. Likewise, the educators could identify the different communities served by their school and reached out to alumni and community members to serve as translators, or engaged in conversations with community members about their cultural values and expectations. SCSD attempted to address the unique needs of the students in their population by providing a space for different cultures to contribute and integrate (Berry, 2001), while simultaneously complying with state education testing and funding policies and recognizing the lingering fears and traumas in the community after the 2008 raid (Love, 2017). For future analyses, we would like to explore how school leaders and educators are changing their practices to meet the needs of immigrant/refugee students and families in this unique geographical and socio-political context. The district employees we interviewed discussed connecting with community members to create a space for mutual understanding. We would be interested in conducting an in-depth case study on how the district engages with community members and community-based organizations to address the needs of the immigrant and refugee students in the district.

Furthermore, our interviews with district educators pointed to the need of attending to students' psychosocial needs, which influence students' educational experience and acculturation process (Cole, 1998; McBrien & Day, 2012; Rah, 2007). As this issue transcends the field of education, an interdisciplinary research approach is called for to effectively support schools in meeting the psychosocial needs of their immigrant and refugee students. Findings from an interdisciplinary research in the fields of education and public health, for example, may inform educators on how to address students' academic needs while simultaneously addressing mental health or behavioural issues in the classroom. An integrated and holistic approach to education may best serve the overall well-being of immigrant and refugee students.

Notes

1 Official school data in Iowa classifies immigrant, migrant, and refugee students into one category: immigrants. While we acknowledge the differences between refugees, immigrants, and migrants, our discussion of refugee students' experiences will also

encompass the experiences of immigrant and migrant students. As such, henceforth, we will use refugee and immigrant in our chapter.

2   The term 'Latinx' is gender-neutral and refers to individuals and groups who can link their heritage and/or identity (culture, ethnicity) to Latin America.

3   We use the term 'minoritised' rather than 'minority.' The term 'minoritised' best reflects the systemic nature of how groups and individuals are reduced in terms of their social, political, and economic power in the U.S. Further, the term 'minority' is not only a misnomer, as some racial/ethnic groups now outnumber Whites, but the term carries with it inherit inferiority.

4   Iowa Codes § 280–280.4 and § 280.1-60.1-6 require all school districts in Iowa to develop a plan to serve the academic needs of English language learners (Iowa Department of Education [IDOE], 2017a).

5   The performance of schools in Iowa is evaluated annually using state-wide student assessment data, student academic growth, narrowing achievement gaps among students, college and career readiness, student attendance, graduation rates, and staff retention. Based on their performance, schools are placed into 6 categories: exceptional, high-performing, commendable, acceptable, needs improvement, and priority (Iowa Department of Education [IDOE], 2017c).

References

Abedi, J. (2004). The no child left behind act and English language learners: Assessment and accountability issues. *Educational Researcher, 33*(1), 4–14.

American Federation of Teachers. (2016). *Immigrant and refugee children: A guide for educators and school support staff.* Retrieved from https://www.aft.org/sites/default/files/im_uac-educators-guide_2016.pdf

Berry, J. W. (2001). A psychology of immigration. *Journal of Social Issues, 57*(3), 615–631.

CBS News. (2008, July 27). Immigration raid hurts small Iowa town. *CBS News.* Retrieved from https://www.cbsnews.com/news/immigration-raid-hurts-small-iowa-town/

Chalker, D. M. (Ed.). (2002). *Leadership for rural schools: Fewerons for all educators.* Lanham, MD: R&L Education.

Chen, C., & Stevenson, H. W. (1995). Motivation and mathematics achievement: A comparative study of Asian-American, Caucasaion-American, and East Asian high school students. *Child Development, 66*(4), 1215–1234.

Chiswick, B., & DebBurman, N. (2004). Educational attainment: Analysis by immigrant generation. *Economics of Education Review, 23,* 361–379.

Cole, E. (1998). Immigrant and refugee children: Challenges and opportunities for education and mental health services. *Canadian Journal of School Psychology, 14*(1), 36–50.

Cortes, K. E. (2006). The effects of age at arrival and enclave schools on the academic performance of immigrant children. *Economics of Education Review, 25*, 121–132.

Darling-Hammond, L. (2007). Race, inequality and educational accountability: The irony of 'No Child Left Behind.' *Race Ethnicity and Education, 10*(3), 245–260.

Drash, W. (2008, October 14). Mayor: Feds turned my town 'topsy turvy.' *CNN*. Retrieved from http://www.cnn.com/2008/US/10/14/postville.raid/#

Dryden-Peterson, S. (2016). Refugee education: The crossroads of globalization. *Educational Researcher, 45*(9), 473–482.

Exec. Order No. 13769. 82 FR 8977. 8977–8982 (2017).

Faltis, C., & Arias, B. (2007). Coming out of the ESL ghetto: Promising practices for Latino immigrant students and English learners in hypersegregated secondary schools. *Journal of Border Educational Research, 6*(2), 19–35.

Flakus, G. (2017, June 2). Small Iowa town celebrates its diversity. *VOA*. Retrieved from https://www.voanews.com/a/small-iowa-town-celebrates-diversity/3884931.html

Foley, D. (2004). Ogbu's theory of academic disengagement: Its evolution and its critics. *Intercultural Education, 15*(4), 385–397.

Foster, L. M. (2009). *The Indians of Iowa*. Iowa City, IA: University of Iowa Press.

Francis, D. J., Rivera M., Lesaux, N., Kieffer, M., & Rivera, H. (2006). Practical guidelines for the education of English language learners: Research-based recommendations for serving adolescent newcomers. *Center on Instruction*. Retrieved from https://www2.ed.gov/about/inits/ed/lep-partnership/newcomers.pdf

Fuligni, A. J. (2001). A comparative longitudinal approach to acculturation among children from immigrant families. *Harvard Educational Review, 71*(3), 566–578.

Gibson, M. A. (1997). Exploring and explaining the variability: Cross-national perspectives on the school performance of minority students. *Anthropology & Education Quarterly, 28*(3), 318–329.

Goodman, A. (2017). The long history of self-deportation: Trump's anti-immigrant policies build on more than a century of attempts to create fear and terror within US immigrant communities. *NACLA Report on the Americas, 49*(2), 152–158.

Grey, M. A. (1997). Secondary labor in the meatpacking industry: Demographic change and student mobility in rural Iowa school. *Journal of Research in Rural Education, 13*(3), 153–164.

Grey, M. A., Devlin, M., Goldsmith, A. (2009). *Postville U.S.A.: Surviving diversity in small-town America*. Boston, MA: GemmaMedia.

Gruber-Miller, S. (2014, December 14). Progress in Iowa City's refugee services, but needs persist. *Iowa City Press Citizens*. Retrieved from http://www.press-citizen.com/story/news/2016/12/14/progress-iowa-citys-refugee-services-but-needs-persist/95426604/

Hsu, S. S. (2008, May 18). Immigration raid jars a small town. *Washington Post*. Retrieved from http://www.washingtonpost.com/wp-dyn/content/article/2008/05/17/AR2008051702474.html?noredirect=on

IN THE ERA OF BANS AND WALLS

Iowa Data Center. (2017).

Iowa Department of Education. (2017a). *English language learners*. Retrieved from https://www.educateiowa.gov/pk-12/learner-supports/english-language-learners

Iowa Department of Education. (2017b). *Iowa school report card*. Retrieved from http://reports.educateiowa.gov/schoolreportcard

Iowa Department of Education. (2017c). *About the Iowa education system*. Retrieved from https://www.educateiowa.gov/about-iowas-education-system

Iowa Department of Education. (2018). *Student demographic data*. Retrieved from https://educateiowa.gov/education-statistics#Student_Demographic_Information

Iowa Department of Education. (2018). *Every student succeeds act*. Retrieved from https://www.educateiowa.gov/pk-12/every-student-succeeds-act

Iowa Department of Education. (2018). *Student demographic data*. Retrieved from https://educateiowa.gov/education-statistics#Student_Demographic_Information

Jones, M. (2012, July 11). Postville, Iowa, is up for grabs. *The New York Times Magazine*. Retrieved from https://www.nytimes.com/2012/07/15/magazine/postville-iowa-is-up-for-grabs.html

Juby, C., & Kaplan, L. E. (2011). Postville: The effects of an immigration raid. *The Journal of Contemporary Social Services, 92*(2), 147–153.

Krob, G. (2016). *Iowa's changing demographic* [PowerPoint Slides]. Retrieved from https://www.legis.iowa.gov/docs/publications/ID/794317.pdf

Krogstad, J. M. (2013, May 9). Iowa raid helps shape immigration debate. *USA Today*. Retrieved from https://www.usatoday.com/story/news/nation/2013/05/09/iowa-raid-helps-shape-immigration-debate/2149039/

Locke, L. A., & Schares, D. (2016). Diversity within Iowa's K-12 public schools and the role of school leaders. In L. Hollingworth & C. Manges (Eds.), *Organization & administration of Iowa public and private schools* (2nd ed., pp. 101–118). Dubuque, IA: Kendall Hunt.

Love, B. (2017, May 11). Life after the raid: Postville 9 years later. *KCRG*. Retrieved from http://www.kcrg.com/content/news/Life-After-the-Raid-Postville-9-years-later-422051183.html

McBrien, J. L. (2005). Educational needs and barriers for refugee students in the United States: A review of the literature. *Review of Educational Research, 75*(3), 329–364.

McBrien, J. L., & Day, R. (2012). From there to here: Using photography to explore perspectives of resettled refugee youth. *International Journal of Child, Youth and Family Studies, 4*(1), 546–568.

Mahatmya, D., & Gring-Pemble, L. M. (2014). DREAMers and their families: A family impact analysis of the DREAM Act and implications for family well-being. *Journal of Family Studies, 20*(1), 79–87.

Mehaffey, T. (2013, May 5). Five years later: Ever-changing diversity maintains Postville. *The Gazette*. Retrieved from http://www.thegazette.com/2013/05/05/five-years-later-ever-changing-diversity-maintains-postville

Miller, J., Mitchell, J., & Brown, J. (2005). African refugees with interrupted schooling in the high school mainstream: Dilemmas for teachers. *Prospect, 20*(2), 19–33.

Minikwu, J. (2017). *Lessons from Postville: How an immigration raid changed a small town and its schools*. Retrieved from http://www.colorincolorado.org/article/lessons-postville-how-immigration-raid-changed-small-town-and-its-schools

Ogbu, J. U. (1992). Adaptation to minority status and impact on school success. *Theory into Practice, 31*(4), 287–295.

Ogbu, J. U., & Simons, H. D. (1998). Voluntary and involuntary minorities: A cultural-ecological theory of school performance with some implications for education. *Anthropology & Education Quarterly, 29*(2), 155–188.

Patrick, E. (2014, June 1). The U.S. Refugee resettlement program. *Migration Policy Institute*. Retrieved from https:www.migrationpolicy.org/article/us-refugee-resettlement-programme#3

Peterson, M. L. (1983). The Indo-Chinese refugee child in Iowa: Talking with the teachers. *Contemporary Education, 54*(2), 126–129.

Preston, J. (2008, November 5). Large Iowa meatpacker in illegal immigrant raid files for bankruptcy. *The New York Times*. Retrieved from http://www.nytimes.com/2008/11/06/us/06immig.html

Rah, Y. (2007). *How school leaders address the needs of refugee students* (Doctoral dissertation). Retrieved from ProQuest Dissertations and Theses Global database. (UMI No. 3261531)

Refugee Processing Center. (2017). *Admissions & arrivals*. Retrieved from http://www.wrapsnet.org/admissions-and-arrivals/

Reynolds, J. F. (2013). (Be)laboring childhoods in Postville, Iowa. *Anthropological Quarterly, 83*(3), 851–889.

Ryan, M. (2017, May 12). Iowa schools struggle to keep non-English speakers on path to graduation. *Des Moines Register*. Retrieved from https://www.desmoinesregister.com/story/news/education/2017/05/12/iowas-evolving-approach-educating-english-learners/100482154/

Skattebol, J. (2016). 'It's hard to blend it': Everyday experiences of schooling achievement, migration and neoliberal education policy. In C. Hunner-Kreisel & S. Bohne (Eds.), *Childhood, youth and migration* (pp. 83–99). Cham: Springer.

Statewide Population Trend. (n.d.). *Statewide population trends*. Retrieved from https://www.legis.iowa.gov/docs/publications/SD/16442.pdf

Strauss, A., & Corbin, J. (1998). *Basics of qualitative research: Techniques and procedures for developing grounded theory*. Thousand Oaks, CA: Sage Publications.

Strekalova-Hughes, E., Nash, K. T., & Erdemir, E. (2017). *Towards a refugee critical race theory in education (RefugeeCrit)* [PowerPoint Slides].

Tendall, M. (2017, February 21). Iowa refugee program advocates ask lawmakers to maintain funding. *The Gazette*. Retrieved from http://www.thegazette.com/subject/news/government/iowa-refugee-programme-advocates-ask-lawmakers-to-maintain-funding-20170221

Theoharis, G. (2007). Social justice educational leaders and resistance: Toward a theory of social justice leadership. *Educational Administration Quarterly, 43*(2), 221–258.

Theoharis, G. (2009). *The school leaders our children deserve: Seven keys to equity, social justice, and school reform.* New York, NY: Teachers College.

Thomas, W. P., & Collier, V. (1997). School effectiveness for language minority students. In *NCBE resources collection series* (pp. 48–64).

United Nations High Commissioner for Refugees (UNHCR). (2015, June 18). Worldwide displacement hits all-time high as war and persecution increase. *News.* Retrieved from http://www.unhcr.org

U.S. Census Bureau. (2016).

US Department of Education. (2018a). *No child left behind: Elementary and secondary education act.* Retrieved from https://www2.ed.gov/nclb/

US Department of Education. (2018b). *Guidance on standards, assessments, and accountability: Adequate yearly progress.* Retrieved from https://www2.ed.gov/policy/

US Department of Education. (2018c). *Every student succeeds act.* Retrieved from https://www.ed.gov/esea

Winn, K. M., & Winn, P. J. (2016). Social justice leadership for Iowa's K-12 refugee students. In L. Hollingworth & C. Manges (Eds.), *Organization & administration of Iowa public and private schools* (2nd ed., pp. 173–189). Dubuque, IA: Kendall Hunt.

Yin, R. K. (2014). *Case study research: Design and methods* (5th ed.). Thousand Oaks, CA: Sage Publications.

Yofee, E. (2005, June). In Postville, Iowa, kosher is kosher. *National Geographic Magazine.*

Zehr, M. A. (2008, May 14). An immigration raid and a subpoena in Postville, Iowa. *Education Week.* Retrieved from http://blogs.edweek.org/edweek/learning-the-language/2008/05/an_immigration_raid_and_a_subp.html

CHAPTER 7

Utilising Digital Storytelling as a Way to Understand the Complexities of the Haitian Refugee Transmigration Experience

Elizabeth Paulsen Tonogbanua

Introduction

If schools are to support the education of refugee students, they must take seriously their capacity to socialize, acculturate, accommodate, integrate, involve and care:

> It is no exaggeration to say that refugee children's wellbeing depends to a major degree on their school experiences, successes and failures. Because they are unfamiliar with the education system and particularly when they do not speak English, parents cannot help their children as they would wish to, and children may be left to deal with difficulties alone. School policies are a powerful tool for helping a refugee child feel safe and normal again, and begin to learn. They can promote the child's confidence and integration, and prevent isolation and frustration. Failure in school can have a disastrous impact on children who are trying to reconstruct their lives and their self-esteem, and develop hope for the future. Educational progress and emotional well-being are mutually dependent. (Richman, 1998 as cited in Hek, 2005, p. 29)

These words were written by Richman twenty years ago, and are as timely and relevant today as they were then. How refugee students adapt may impact both students' emotional and academic investment in their schooling. As Matthews (2008) maintains, 'literacy is critically important, but schools are not simply literacy delivering machines' (p. 42). Urban public schools are comprised of culturally, linguistically, racially, and socioeconomically diverse learners. Teachers need to know how to construct learning environments that provide all learners a haven to participate, communicate, and form relationships.

This interpretive study explored how Haitian refugee English Language Learners (ELLs) in Boston Public Schools (BPS) made sense of their transmigration experiences through a digital storytelling project. By focusing on

© KONINKLIJKE BRILL NV, LEIDEN, 2019 | DOI: 10.1163/9789004401891_007

Haitian youth, I extend the notion of 'refugee' to include those forcibly displaced by natural disaster (Fagen, 2013; 'Should International,' 2014). Article 1A, paragraph 2, of the 1951 Convention relating to the Status of Refugees and the updated 1967 Protocol define a refugee as any person that: 'owing to well-founded fear of being persecuted for reasons of race, religion, nationality, membership of a particular social group or political opinion, is outside the country of his nationality and is unable or ... unwilling to return to it' (United Nations High Commissioner for Refugees, 2010). However, this definition is not inclusive of a refugee from a natural disaster. In 2010, the year of the 'mega-disaster' in Haiti, there were approximately 42 million people displaced around the world as a result of massive weather-related hazards. Extreme weather events are increasing in their intensity and frequency, and it seems that this trend is not going away. 'With all probability, the number of those affected and displaced will rise as human-induced climate change comes into full force,' said Elisabeth Rasmusson, the secretary general of the Norwegian Refugee Council (as cited in 'Natural Disaster,' 2011).

Compounding matters, in international law, there are no safeguards that currently exist to permit those who have been displaced due to environmental disasters to enter a State against the will of the State, unless they have a refugee designation. As international law stands, there is no solution for how to handle or consider people who are displaced as a result of climate change-induced facts, particularly slow onset environmental issues. No legal framework has been developed as yet ('Should International,' 2014).

The relationship between refugee students' transmigration experiences and their future educational attainment has been established in the literature on immigration and education (Gozdziak & Martin, 2005). However, students who have not been exposed to grade-level academic content in their country of origin, due to a natural disaster, may require a more specific type of instruction that is tailored to ensure that they are strategically positioned and equipped to make academic gains in a timely manner. Supporting students as they hone their voice is a vital component of success for students from diverse backgrounds (Northedge, 2003 as cited in Earnest, Joyce, de Mori, & Silvagni, 2010).

In this study, the participants are refugees who have moved to the United States within the last one to three years and represent a range of educational, linguistic, cultural, and socioeconomic backgrounds. As a participant-observer and facilitator of the project, I worked with refugees who were former newcomers because I wanted to learn about students' reflections on the numerous transitions they have made after spending some time living in the United States.

Drawing on qualitative and ethnographic methods, I designed a project with a small group of Haitian refugees who entered BPS as newcomer students. The refugees engaged in a digital storytelling project that captured their perceptions of how they adapted and adjusted to their new academic environments within the BPS. This study brings 'English-only' governmental policies into the conversation with the daily realities of students, as recounted by them. In doing so, the study suggests ways that school practices could help with resettled refugee students' progress. ELLs in Massachusetts are the state's fastest growing group of students and experience the largest proficiency gap, with Haitians comprising the second largest share of immigrants in Boston.

Refugee ELLs bring with them additional needs that go beyond those of U.S.-born, monolingual students. Along with the pressures of taking large-scale assessments in a relatively short amount of time, refugees must also adjust to a new school environment and learn a second language and culture at an intense pace. Furthermore, refugees also have to process what it means to be displaced, as families weigh the temporary or permanent nature of the displacement. In Massachusetts, the state's fastest growing group of students are ELLs and, as a group, 'experience the largest proficiency gap when compared to their native English speaking peers' (Massachusetts Department of Elementary and Secondary Education [MA DESE], 2014). The findings suggest that strategies honing participants' English language development, technological skill development, opportunity to tell their stories, and meeting as a Haitian student community with shared and unique experiences were outcomes that had implications for research and teaching refugee ELLs.

Background

Unz Initiative

In the late 1990s, the Unz Initiative dominated the press, and reporters listened intently to Ron Unz's every word, demonstrating how bilingual education can be presented as a controversial issue in the mainstream news. In 1998, Ron Unz, a successful businessman from California who had aspirations for political office, seized the opportunity to make bilingual education his niche campaign issue, garnering much state-wide fame, despite his lack of experience in education or knowledge of English language learners. The goal of the Unz initiative was to strip students of their right to access their native language as they acquire English in an academic setting. Outrageous assertions by Unz – such as, 'most bilingual programs [do] not teach English' – went un-scrutinized by the press, which printed his allegations as though they were facts (Gandara &

Contreras, 2010, pp. 143–144). During one debate, Unz admitted he had never been in a bilingual classroom but instead based his ideas about the failure of bilingual education on things he had read 'in junior high school.'

Somehow, little or no attention was paid to the fact that the majority of ELLs, who were thought to be failing because of bilingual education, were not enrolled in bilingual education programs. The same currently holds true for the overwhelming majority of ELLs in BPS; they are enrolled in monolingual schools and receive sheltered instruction in an English-only learning environment. Gandara and Contreras (2010) maintain that the absurdity of blaming a bilingual model of education on the educational failure of children who have never been instructed by that model was never raised during the campaign. Moreover, comparisons that should have been drawn were not. English-speaking Latinos and poor Black students were not held up by the press as counterexamples to Unz's claims, though they also fared very poorly in school but were monolingual English-speaking students.

There was in fact an estimated shortage of 27,000 bilingual teachers, and fully certified instructors taught only 20% of ELLs – a shortage that has also not been remedied in Massachusetts. The overwhelming majority of ELLs have been taught in settings that did not meet their academic or social needs, as determined by educational researchers. Therefore, if programs were 'failing' at the time Unz was making his claims, it was more reasonable to blame English-only methodologies, an observation that eluded most reporters (Crawford, 2000). The challenges faced by ELLs in under-resourced, under-staffed settings and taught by teachers unqualified to effectively teach second language acquisition should have motivated politicians to invest in sound educational practices, not the opposite.

Indeed, ELLs are not a monolith, and their instructional needs should not be decided by the uniformed or misled. Unz won in California and succeeded in Arizona in 2000. Massachusetts, with a total ELL population of 5%, also voted 61% in favour of the Massachusetts English Language Education in Public Schools initiative, also known as Question 2 (Ballotpedia, 2012). Supporters claimed that bilingual education had been a failed experiment in Massachusetts, leaving ELLs unable to speak English after years of instruction. Opponents, on the other hand, among whom were members of the state legislature's Joint Committee on Education, Arts and Humanities, believed the law to be 'overly simplistic and inflexible,' making the case that the initiative disregarded research indicating that there is more than one effective method of teaching English. They held that the initiative mandated all students to be taught by a single method and greatly restricted how local school districts chose to instruct ELLs (Ballotpedia, 2012). Framing the issue as an 'either/or' decision benefitted Unz's campaign and placed opponents in new territory – as defenders of the status quo (Crawford, 2000). The initiative was defeated in Colorado, however, by a carefully crafted counteroffensive, paid for largely by a wealthy White parent of a child in a dual-language program (Gandara & Contreras, 2010). It is worth noting that for ELLs in Massachusetts, their education remains restricted, leaving districts to apply for waivers when the curriculum is modified to meet the cultural and linguistic needs of its students.

Given the current state of affairs of ELLs in BPS, it seems ironic to look back at Massachusetts' accomplishment as the first state to approve transitional bilingual programs in public schools (Gort, de Jong, & Cobb, 2008). More than a decade later, Boston Public Schools' ELL student population is floundering, given these restrictions. Doucet (2014) argues 'in the same way that language is a stand-in for contests over social status in Haiti and among Haitians in the Diaspora, the English-only war is a thin disguise for xenophobia' (p. 17).

Boston Public Schools

Boston Public Schools, the oldest school district in the United States, has 125 schools with an enrolment of 55,843 students. Student demographics indicate that learners within the district are 42% Hispanic, 35% Black, 14% White, 9% Asian, and <1% other/multiracial. ELL students in BPS speak 71 different languages, the most widely spoken being Spanish, Haitian Creole, Cape Verdean Creole, Chinese, Vietnamese, Portuguese, Somali, French, and Arabic. BPS has a sizable and diverse ELL population of 16,694 (30% of the total BPS student body), designated as limited English proficient (LEP) (BPS Communications Office, 2017).

In BPS, how best to educate ELLs remains complex since the overwhelming majority of ELLs have been taught in an English-only setting since 2002, and there are limited spaces in Sheltered English Immersion (SEI) programs. Understanding how refugee newcomer ELLs make meaning of their experiences in an English-only context will help to inform educators about how their professional practice can be enhanced to meet ELLs' needs. This, in turn, will contribute to the development of more welcoming and supportive policies and practices by teachers and administrators as they receive newcomers in the future.

Based on current data, I found that no solid, district-wide policy existed in BPS that informed schools about how newcomers should be welcomed into their new environment. Thus, this study sought to help fill the gap between policy and practice by exploring students' transmigration experiences as they related to educational practices in BPS. BPS' learners' rich cultural and linguistic backgrounds necessitate educational services that go beyond the needs of general education. BPS staff and schools must be prepared to educate all learners while meeting the stringent requirements established by a settlement agreement the district entered into in 2010.

BPS and the U.S. Departments of Justice and Education have been working together to address the violation of ELLs' civil rights in the district. Federal agencies faulted BPS for inappropriately categorizing students as having 'opted out' of ESL classes, when, in fact, that was found not to be the case at all (Zehr, 2010). The U.S. Justice Department cited that since 2003, BPS 'failed to properly identify and adequately serve thousands of ELLs as required by the Equal Educational Opportunities Act of 1974 and Title VI of the Civil Rights Act of 1964' (as cited in Zehr, 2010). In order for ELLs to be successful in the U.S., as maintained by the Justice Department and the Office for Civil Rights, they need ESL classes at the beginner and intermediate levels, and embedded ESL strategies used in instruction for advanced-level ELLs. Both federal agencies are working with the BPS to ensure that all ELLs have access to ESL classes. To meet this need, ESL-licensed teachers have been hired, and general educators within BPS have been offered trainings to ensure that their instructional strategies adhere to current best practices.

The settlement agreement, described above, sought to remedy the social and emotional, and academic damage done from the implementation of Question 2. In Boston in 2003, there was a decline in the identification of students with limited English proficiency, and programs for ELLs saw a decline in their enrolments as well. These numbers rebounded somewhat in the school years that followed, but did not return fully to the values noted during the school year of 2003. During the years following Question 2, ELLs were tested and designated as needing special education services in much higher numbers than in the years prior. There was also an increase in suspensions and grade retention, as well as a rise in the drop-out rate. The participants of this study began their education in BPS after it entered into the settlement agreement. With professional development for teachers who instruct ELLs, such as SIOP training, Category 1, 2, 3, and 4 training, and how with the mandated RETELL courses (which replaced the recommended Category trainings), the climate in which the participants of this study began BPS was entirely different from the practices in place during the years that immediately followed the implementation of Question 2, the Massachusetts English in Public Schools Initiative that required English be the only language of instruction.

Haitian Migration

Massachusetts has the third largest Haitian community in the United States, behind southern Florida and the New York metropolitan area (Kitchen, 2010).

According to recent data, there are an estimated 47,000 Haitian-born immigrants living in the Boston area, with Haitians comprising the second largest share of immigrants in the city (8.5%), behind China (8.6%) and ahead of the Dominican Republic (7.9%) (Boston Redevelopment Authority, 2009; Schulz & Batalova, 2017). This number has increased dramatically in the aftermath of the devastating 2010 earthquake but has not been accurately counted.

When Haiti was struck by the largest earthquake it had experienced in over 200 years in January 2010, the country was sent into crisis mode. More than one million people were displaced. And 750,000 children were directly affected as a result. They had to live in crowded camps without a way to make a living, all the while shelter and services made it so children were barely able to stay healthy and maintain access to education (United Nations Children's Fund, 2011). Families did what they could to reunite with relatives in Boston. According to Eric Johnson, the Director of Newcomers Academy (in BPS) at that time, families in Boston sought to have their extended and distant relatives join them (Nicas, 2010). Although the exact total number for the years following is difficult to determine, as Haitians are classified as Black, Haitians entered schools throughout the school year and most often with little notice to their teachers that they were coming. Upon arrival, students found established Haitian Creole (SEI) and Students with Limited or Interrupted Formal Education (SLIFE) programs staffed with Haitian Creole speaking teachers at many of the schools to which they were assigned (Merrigan, 2010). Transitional bilingual education programs, where students could use their native language as a bridge to English, were not available due to the Massachusetts governmental policy restrictions; however, many of the newcomers found themselves in Haitian Creole speaking communities within their schools. The specific educational programming they needed was already established in the neighbourhoods where Haitians settled, and the groundwork was in place to receive them.

One issue was that the specific linguistic programs that these newcomers needed could reach a limit due to over enrolment at a particular school. Although Governor Patrick declared that 'step[ping] up and step[ping] forward and look[ing] out for each other in times of trial and trauma' was acting as 'full human beings,' Boston did not see any increase in budget to assist with this humanitarian crisis (Corcoran, 2010; Nicas, 2010). Boston's Mayor Menino avowed, 'as a city, we will come together to support the Haitian community both here in Boston and abroad in any way possible' (Kitchen, 2010). However, additional Haitian Creole-speaking staff had to be hired at some schools, new classes were opened, and crisis counsellors had to be available at several schools with large populations of Haitian immigrants and Haitian-American

UTILISING DIGITAL STORYTELLING 163

students and faculty (Corcoran, 2010). These types of strains affected entire school communities, not only the Haitians within them.

Critiquing the English-Only Movement

James Crawford, the foremost critic of the official English movement, posits a firm argument for why making English the official language of the U.S. would be a grave mistake. He has testified to Congress, maintaining that the English-only movement 'ignites ethnic conflicts' and is harmful to national priorities (Crawford, 2006). He holds that official English is unnecessary as English is already the dominant language and remains unthreatened. The danger of proliferating non-English languages is a recurrent theme in the anti-immigrant ethos of the U.S., but there has not been any evidence of a serious threat. In addition, an English-only measure is punitive because it restricts the government's ability to communicate in other languages, which would threaten the rights and welfare of millions of people, including many American citizens. Crawford also views official English as pointless because English-only legislation does not give practical assistance to anyone who wants to learn English. Official English laws have been declared unconstitutional in state and federal courts because they violate guarantees of freedom of speech and equal protection of the laws. Lastly, Crawford maintains that English-only policies are self-defeating. They make no sense in an era of globalization, where multilingual skills are essential to economic prosperity and national security (Crawford, 2000). Social and economic opportunities abound for university-educated, multilingual individuals who are interculturally competent.

Furthermore, the U.S. government has recognized the need to channel resources to fund the learning of languages other than English that are deemed critical to national security, as evidenced by the 2006 National Security Language Initiative. However, such efforts are aimed at students who do not speak those languages. At the same time, the language resources of those bilingual Americans who already speak those languages are not recognized or developed in schools (García, Zakharia, & Otcu, 2013); rather, these students and their languages are viewed as 'foreign' in the context of English-only policies.

At the heart of English-only mandates is a mechanism of exclusion rather than assimilation (Citrin, Reingold, & Walters, 1990). Schools are fitting sites for examining this exclusion:

> Schools that enforce an 'English-only' policy are, willingly or not, sending students a message about the status and importance of languages other than English. In some of these schools, students are forbidden to speak their native language not only in the classroom, but even in the halls, the

cafeteria, and the playground. To students who speak a language other than English, the message is clear: Your language is not welcome here; it is less important than English. (Nieto, 2010, pp. 43–44)

Despite how well-intended English-only policy may be, or how it may have been designed with a genuine desire to foster proficient English-speaking students, the effect on students is a feeling of disapproval of their very identities.

Literature

English-speaking countries are among the top countries for permanent refugee resettlement. In this section, research on identity, student voice, and social integration is discussed as they pertain to the experiences that refugees have had as they enter the Boston Public Schools. The relationship between language use and identity has never been more relevant than it is today, as immigrant student populations in urban areas continue to increase, with many of them being refugees. Along these lines, as teachers create spaces in their classrooms for all students to share their ideas, refugee students can exercise their voices regarding how they integrate to their new schools and engage in their education. Lastly, successfully integrating newcomer refugee students into the classroom is a bi-directional process. In the section on Social Integration, I consider how teachers and students can develop mutual respect and understanding of the other's cultures, values, and beliefs (Trueba & Bartolome, 2000).

Identity

As refugee ELL students consider and further develop their identities, Dryden-Peterson (2015) has noted some commonalities faced by these students. The curricula are usually not inclusive of the history and culture of refugee students' countries of origin, but rather emphasize the receiving country's history and culture. Refugee students may also be confronted with tension and hostility from students in the dominant culture of the host country, particularly if refugee students are of a nationality that is associated with terrorism.

While refugee students are grappling with the ideas above, identity theory is significant because of how the participants – that is, refugee ELLs-view themselves – underpin how they make sense of their transmigration experiences. At its core, identity theory is defined as 'the categorization of the self as an occupant of a role, and the incorporation, into the self, of the meanings and expectations associated with that role and its performance' (Stets &

Burke, 2000, p. 225). Understanding how one's identity impacts his or her educational experience and role in society is at the centre of one's perception of how a learner integrates socially. Identity is also a major factor in acquiring a second language; this is directly relevant to my study, as participants made sense of who they were as students before they left their home countries and how they have changed during transmigration (Suarez-Orozco, Darbes, Dias, & Sutin, 2011). Despite having interrupted access to schooling as a result of the earthquake, all of the participants had been enrolled in school in Haiti.

Children's day-to-day lives span very different worlds – home and school life – and through an immersion process in each, children form identities vis-à-vis their experiences in those communities. Language is intimately bound with identity, and whose language is used in the public sphere not only relates to political power, but also to how much one belongs. The language one uses influences how a group constructs its identity, while at the same time the identity of the group shapes the patterns of attitudes and language uses (Liebkind, 1999 as cited in García & Zakharia, 2010).

Migrants immerse themselves simultaneously in multiple sites and aspects of the transnational social fields in which they live (Levitt & Jaworsky, 2007). Navigation between two worlds-the homeland and the host country – is at the heart of transnationalism, as both countries shape one's identity. Thus, a transnational identity emerges when individuals hold themselves to be a reflection of two or more cultures (Pedraza, 2006 as cited in Orbe & Drummond, 2011, p. 1692). Transnational identity is pertinent to this study because it offers a means for understanding how identity is viewed from the perspectives of immigrants within the receiving communities.

Bryce-Laporte (1972) notes, 'Haitians are seen as Blacks by Whites and as foreigners by native-born Blacks' (as cited in Cone, Buxton, Lee, & Mahotiere, 2014, p. 54). This is problematic because Haitian newcomers are more likely to enrol in urban schools that have a large percentage of African American students and are located in high-poverty neighbourhoods. Facing prejudice from U.S. society at large and from staff and classmates at school, Haitians are frequently subject to negative peer critiques of their school identities, both by African American students and by other Haitians who have been in the United States longer and have become more 'Americanized.'

Student Voice

Understanding the significance of student voice and determining how to draw on it were essential elements to this study. Student voice can 'become an organizing force to negotiate and construct multiple interpretations of school life within the reality of institutionalized ways of being in school' (Roberts & Locke, 2001, p. 376). By building upon what has been established in literature about student voice, students shared their thinking about their unique transmigration experiences, empowering themselves and their peers in the process. Student voice represents more than physical vocalizations. Researchers and teachers alike consider student voice to be demonstrated in any activity in which students exercise a degree of control as they communicate their feelings (Johnson, 1991). Over time, student voice has come to be associated with empowerment, meaning that students have the opportunity to provide input into decisions affecting their education. Participants had complete creative control over what aspects of their transmigration experiences they chose to share.

Social Integration

Social integration and how students experience it comprise the heart of this study. Social integration is the degree to which immigrant and refugee students interact positively with U.S.-born peers and the school community as a whole. Schools that implement social integration policies and procedures support immigrants as they adjust to their new environment. The reality, however, is that it is more common for schools not to recognize the unique needs of immigrant students; schools have been shown to disregard their unique emotional experiences, treating them instead in the same way they would a monolingual, U.S.-born student who is new to the school. Newcomer students are often left to themselves to negotiate the educational environment, which only further contributes to their academic difficulties. When schools neglect to establish a practice to integrate newcomers, they are at least partly responsible for the problems that arise (Lasso & Soto, 2005).

Crawford (2016) posits with even more specificity. She holds that districts need to take into account how much schooling the student has had in his country of origin and have programming that matches the student's linguistic and cultural needs. She also cautions school districts to monitor late-entry students closely, particularly those who arrive as unaccompanied minors. High school-age students will need educational and English-language supports to make the content accessible, as well as opportunities to hone their social integration skills. Mental and physical health should be assessed shortly after arrival. Poor health will impact all aspects of a refugee student's transmigration experience. Regular access to healthcare is essential. Finally, Crawford maintains that integration can be a lengthy process for some, and affects students who have not had access to formal schooling disproportionately.

Research Design

This interpretive, qualitative study drew on ethnographic methods and digital storytelling to investigate the following research question: How do former newcomer ELLs who are refugees make sense of their transmigration experiences through a digital storytelling project? The participants took pictures or used existing imagery to add to a digital story, which expressed their views of how they adapted and adjusted to their new environment. This chapter is based on a larger study that examined circumstances around participants' move to Boston and the types of initial interactions they recalled having in their schools, as well as their perception of social integration at their schools in the context of an English-only education. This work informs what an inclusive school setting-that is, one which values new students' languages, cultures, and identities-'looks like' in the context of an English-only education.

In July 2014, I conducted my study at a community centre in the Boston area. The community centre offers youth development programs and social responsibility programs. My rationale for choosing this locale was because it yielded a wider sample of diverse experiences than working with students from one high school. I recruited six high school students who were able to commit to the 12-session timeframe. In my convenience sample, participants who lived in the United States for one to three years were selected based on their ability to attend all the sessions (Bryman, 2001).

The six participants each had use of their own MacBook for the duration of the project. I kept the laptops secured when not in use to ensure the integrity of the students' work. Participants used an interview guide that contained questions asking participants to consider the circumstances around their move, their initial experiences upon arrival in Boston, questions that target social integration, and finally, the effectiveness of digital storytelling when exploring students' transmigration experiences. We used Word to draft the scripts, and Google image to select images that reflected their memories or experiences. Once the words and images were finalized, participants shared them with each other for feedback. Next, we used iMovie to create the digital story. Participants were able to select how long to let an image play. They were also encouraged to select quotes from their scripts to type out and play as they read their script during recording. The result was a digital story roughly three minutes in length, describing participants' most compelling memories of their transmigration created entirely from their own perspective. Though my research set out to explore participants' transmigration experiences, participants autonomously selected what went in, or was left out of, their digital story.

All of the participants hailed from Haiti, and the majority had lived in the capital, Port-au-Prince. Following the earthquake that levelled their city in January 2010, the participants were unable to remain in that area of Haiti, as there was a shortage of food, shelter, and work, due to the city nearly becoming completely destroyed. People who had lost their homes were able to stay in one of the temporary tent shelters, though this was the least desirable option for families. Instead, families tried to find solace and refuge elsewhere in Haiti. However, this choice was largely unappealing as well because other urban centres outside of Port-au-Prince were too poor to take on additional people, and little aid was received to buffer this sudden addition to their population. This meant that families found the support inadequate and became displaced again. The most desirable choice was for Haitians who had family in the US to be evacuated and join them. Authorities had not anticipated the extent and volume of migration, nor were they able to address it in other ways (Fagen, 2013). Through these familial connections, all of the participants came to Boston. Cousins, aunts, uncles, and siblings all opened their doors to the participants and one of their parents, as each participant experienced parental separation.

Data Collection Methods

I used a combination of methods to examine the refugees' transmigration experiences: interviews, participant observations, photography, digital storytelling, and analysis of student work. Throughout the study, my intent was for student participants to have a voice in the research as I conveyed the details about the data collection.

Instrument Interviews

I asked the questions from an interview guide to the whole group, and the participants shared their experiences aloud and wrote their own responses in the guide. As a qualitative researcher, I am interested 'not just in *what* people say but also in the *way* that they say it' (Bryman, 2001, p. 321). I developed questions that honed refugees' ideas about how their prior educational experiences had affected their identities as students.

Participant Observation

I facilitated the sessions and used digital recorders and a teaching assistant to help me spend the entire time engaged with the participants. As the researcher, I needed to rely on my memory and write down my observations as soon as each session ended. Writing down everything that was (or could have been) significant to my study while at the same time engaging with and observing participants was no small feat. Students worked on group-based activities, and I observed students engaging with their peers. This was another important source of information in my research; as Hays (2004) held, case studies that involve the interaction of individuals cannot be understood without observation.

Photography

I wanted students to capture moments that were important and representative of social integration, adaptation, and adjustment in their new surroundings according to them. Photo voice and its application stem from Paulo Freire's (1970) work that grew out of critical education, feminist theory, and a participatory approach to documentary photography. Freire's problem-posing education starts with issues that people see as central to their lives and then enables them to identify common themes through dialogue (as cited in Paiewonsky, 2005). In this sense, I guided participants as I explained that what they chose to photograph would be a reflection of what they perceived a visual representation of social integration to be, and that their ability to select images that expressed their perceptions of particular issues was critical to their digital story.

Digital Storytelling

Digital storytelling has come to be a vehicle for cultural analysis. Digital storytelling creates space for former newcomer ELLs to affirm their identity and become agents of social change, as it is a creative work and both represents and invites the construction of meaning (Lambert, 2010). Images-either still or moving-drive the story and explain the relationship between the narrator and the audience. The storyteller carefully selects images as he or she refines the message to be conveyed. Participants had the time and space to reflect on their experiences and describe them in as much detail as possible. In my study, participants were each guided to develop their own digital story. They wrote their own scripts, highlighting aspects of their transmigration experiences; and they selected images to convey their ideas. Each digital story was approximately three minutes long.

Data Analysis

I analysed, took participant-observation notes, categorized, and coded all of the data I collected. By conducting a thematic content analysis, I was able to determine what participants focused on and was able to connect their texts back to the thematic areas (Berg, 2001).

Findings/Discussion

Despite recommendations from researchers and education scholars, many school systems in poorer neighbourhoods have not adapted educational curricula or teaching styles that support immigrants and refugees in their educational pursuits (Contreras, 2002). Haitian children who are new to the U.S. want to do well in school, but unfortunately their socioeconomic status will largely predict their educational attainment more so than their academic aspirations. Immigrant children are vulnerable, often settling in low-income neighbourhoods and becoming students in an educational system that is unable to meet their unique academic, social, and linguistic needs. Therefore, as Nicolas, DeSilva, and Rabenstein (2009) urged, the time has come for society to stop blaming the social construct of race for the achievement gap that exists amongst racial groups. Instead, the researchers maintain that the context in which immigrant students are educated, as well as the current policies that influence the way these schools instruct, may be inhibiting the educational attainment of immigrant children in the United States. These are some of the reasons that exploring refugees' transmigration experiences in Boston Public Schools is both timely and valuable.

As students engaged in the digital storytelling process, it became clear that they made sense of their move from Haiti to Boston Public Schools in different ways. Furthermore, throughout the study, digital storytelling emerged as a pedagogical process that served as an effective tool for working with refugee ELLS, both as a means to facilitate meaning making and give significance to their transmigration experiences. As such, digital storytelling may also offer a process by which teachers may better understand the circumstances of students' transmigration and thus how better to support them. In this section, I describe some of the insights provided by students regarding their displacement and subsequent transmigration experiences, as well as the utility of the digital storytelling process.

Participants in this project demonstrated an understanding of the circumstances regarding their move in different ways. Participants also made sense of their move in various ways. Some chose to reveal personal details, while others were vague about what they knew about their moves and when they knew it. As participants made sense of their move, some crosscutting themes emerged. There was a change in roles within families from all of the participants, and there was separation and loss for all of them as well.

Participants changed roles within their families as they pertained to gender and moved from living with extended families to partial nuclear families. Some of the participants became the head female in their house, which meant taking on domestic responsibilities for younger siblings and fathers. Other participants transitioned from a two-parent household to a single parent home, as nearly every participant experienced separation and loss from one parent, which Duman and Snoubar (2017) deem as one of the most serious problems faced by refugee children, as they then become more vulnerable to exploitation. They spoke fondly of having the freedom to visit extended family nearby during our discussions, as they lost the ability to feel the support and connection to their extended families. They tried to utilize technology, to the extent that it was possible, but Skype could not take the place of stopping by one's grandmother's house for a home-cooked meal.

Participants had had little control over being uprooted and relocated; yet, through the storytelling project, they were given an opportunity to make meaning of their experiences, and in some sense, regain some control over their transmigration story. Some challenged themselves to use more English, while others felt the highlight was getting to collaborate with other refugee students who were also Haitian. Their parallel journeys were difficult to put into words for them at points, for numerous reasons, but the bond that was created through trying was invaluable to creating a cohesive group. The implication is that teachers who capture students' interest by using digital stories would be able to link content matter to aspects of students' lives. Students' sense of belonging and motivation to be part of their school community would increase, as their affective filter was lowered.

Overall, participants recognized how much had changed for them since they arrived. They expressed varying degrees of pride regarding the extent to which they have integrated socially in their schools. They all acknowledged that it took time to adjust during these major transitions, and many could cite teachers as having a direct hand in helping to ease some of the isolation that was described. For example, there was the guidance counsellor at one high school who spoke Haitian Creole. She played a pivotal role in three of the participants' academic lives. She helped them to get situated and because of her linguistic expertise, they were able to adapt in their new educational expectations and surroundings. One successful strategy for English-language learning, according to the refugee students themselves, was having teachers and school staff who were representative of students' home languages and cultures. Over time, the participants categorized themselves as students who fit in with the culture of their high schools, and reflexively now refer to themselves as students, per Stets and Burke's (2000) identity theory. Even though everyone could name ways in which they have integrated, exploring this topic left me wondering how they each will grow and adapt further.

Conclusion

Governmental policies may hinder the education that refugee students receive. Current governmental policies in Massachusetts prohibit and/or greatly diminish the opportunity for refugee students to obtain an education in any language other than English, which may negatively impact refugee students' educational experiences, as they then receive the message that their dominant language has little or no value in an educational setting. In the case of this study, participants cited that being instructed in an English-only setting might have hindered their educational achievement. Most of the participants had hardly any opportunity to clarify their ideas during lessons in their first language. Regardless, all of their standardized testing and proficiency indicators in multiple content areas were conducted and measured solely in English.

In terms of school practices, schools that employ staff that are proficient in refugee students' first languages may be more efficient in resettling students. Refugee students may be able to seek out those bilingual teachers, guidance counsellors, and staff in other capacities while going through an adjustment period as they get used to learning in their new educational settings. However, this study found no formal guidelines for welcoming refugee students, which made happenstance encounters with classmates or teachers who were fellow Haitian Creole speakers all the more meaningful.

As a pedagogical process, digital storytelling was shown to be an effective tool for working with refugee newcomer ELLs, both as a means to facilitate meaning making and give significance to their transmigration experiences, as well as to support language development. Student voice was exercised, as participants had the ability to determine all aspects of their products. The findings of this study suggest that teachers may also utilize digital storytelling as a way to better understand the circumstances of students' transmigration and thus how better to support them.

Language development, technological skill development, opportunity to tell their stories, and meeting as a Haitian student community with shared and unique experiences were other outcomes that had implications for research and teaching ELLs. The data showed that some participants challenged themselves to use more English, while others held that a highlight for them was getting to collaborate with Haitians. They demonstrated a great deal of empathy towards each other. The findings suggest that teachers may benefit from taking the time to get to know each of their students and become knowledgeable about their strengths as individuals and learners in order to make authentic connections with them. By utilizing digital stories in the classroom, students

UTILISING DIGITAL STORYTELLING 173

may be able to learn content matter as they engage in a creative approach to mastering standards.

Furthermore, the findings suggest that community centres in urban areas, such as the one where I did my study, may be able to organize and implement digital story projects with great success. Being completely removed from the high-stakes testing environment, community centres have the autonomy and resources to recruit students during after school hours, intersessions, and summer breaks. Students may be able to strengthen their voices in their own work by immersing themselves in a topic of their choosing and then interpreting the visual images that they believe best tell their stories.

References

Ballotpedia. (2012). *Massachusetts English in public schools initiative, question 2 (2002)*. Retrieved on January 5, 2013 from http://ballotpedia.org/wiki/index.php/ Massachusetts_English_in_Public_Schools_Initiative,_Question_2_(2002)

Berg, B. (2001). An introduction to content analysis. In B. Berg (Ed.), *Qualitative research methods for the social sciences* (pp. 238–267). Boston, MA: Allyn and Bacon.

Boston Public Schools Communications Office. (2017). *Boston public schools at a glance 2016–2017*. Retrieved from https://www.bostonpublicschools.org/cms/ lib/MA01906464/Centricity/Domain/238/BPS%20at%20a%20Glance%202016- 17_online.pdf

Boston Redevelopment Authority, Research Division. (2009). *Imagine all the people: Haitian immigrants in Boston*. Boston, MA: Mayor's Office of New Bostonians.

Bryman, A. (2001). Interviewing in qualitative research. In A. Bryman (Ed.), *Social research methods* (pp. 311–333). New York, NY: Oxford University Press.

Citrin, J., Reingold, B., & Walters, E. (1990). The "official English" movement and the symbolic politics of language in the United States. *The Western Political Quarterly, 43*(3), 535–559.

Cone, N., Buxton, C., Lee, O., & Mahotiere, M. (2014). Negotiating a sense of identity in a foreign land: Navigating public school structures and practices that often conflict with Haitian culture and values. *Urban Education, 49*(3), 263–296.

Contreras, A. R. (2002). The impact of immigration policy on education reform: Implications for the new millennium. *Education and Urban Society, 34*(2), 134–155.

Corcoran, A. (2010). Boston area schools (and students!) suffer with influx of Haitian students. *Refugee Resettlement Watch*. Retrieved from https://refugeeresettlementwatch.wordpress.com/2010/03/19/boston-area- schools-and-students-suffer-with-influx-of-haitian-students/

Crawford, J. (2000). *At war with diversity: US language policy in an age of anxiety.* Tonawanda, NY: Multilingual Matters.

Crawford, J. (2006). *Official English legislation: Bad for civil rights, bad for America's interests, and even bad for English (Testimony before the House Subcommittee on Education Reform).* Institute for Language and Education Policy.

Crawford, V. (2016). 10 ways countries can help refugees integrate. *Word Economic Forum.* Retrieved from https://www.weforum.org/agenda/2016/05/10-ways-countries-can-help-refugees-integrate/

Cresswell, J., & Miller, D. (2000). Determining validity in qualitative inquiry. *Theory into Practice, 39*(3), 124–130.

Doucet, F. (2014). Panoply: Haitian and Haitian-American youth crafting identities in U.S. schools. *Trotter Review, 22*(1), 7–32.

Dryden-Peterson, S. (2015). *The educational experiences of refugee children in countries of first asylum.* Washington, DC: Migration Policy Institute.

Duman, N., & Snoubar, Y. (2017). Role of social work in integrating refugee and immigrant children to Turkish schools. *European Journal of Social Sciences Education and Research, 10*(2), 334–344.

Earnest, J., Joyce, A., de Mori, G., & Silvagni, G. (2010). Are universities responding to the needs of students from refugee backgrounds? *Australian Journal of Education, 54*(2), 155–174.

Fagen, P. W. (2013). *Receiving Haitian immigrants in the context of the 2010 earthquake. The Nansen initiative: Disaster-induced cross-border displacement.* Geneva: International Environment House. Retrieved from https://www2.nanseninitiative.org/wp-content/uploads/2015/03/DP_Receiving_Haitian_Migrants_in_the_Context_of_the_2010_earthquake.pdf

Gandara, P., & Contreras, F. (2010). Is language the problem? In P. Gandara & F. Contreras (Eds.), *The Latino education crisis: The consequences of failed social policies* (pp. 121–150). Cambridge, MA: Harvard University Press.

García, O., & Zakharia, Z. (2010). Positioning language and ethnic identity. In J. Fishman & O. García (Eds.), *Handbook of language and ethnic identity* (2nd ed., pp. 521–525). Oxford: Oxford University Press.

García, O., Zakharia, Z., & Otcu, B. (Eds.). (2013). *Bilingual community education and multilingualism: Beyond heritage languages in a global city.* Bristol: Multilingual Matters.

Gort, M., deJong, E. J., & Cobb, C. D. (2008). Seeing through a bilingual lens: Structural and ideological contexts of structured English immersion in three Massachusetts districts. *Journal of Educational Research & Policy Studies, 8*(2), 41–67.

Gozdziak, E. M., & Martin, S. F. (Eds.). (2005). *Beyond the gateway: Immigrants in a changing America.* Lanham, MD: Rowman & Littlefield Publishing Group, Inc.

Hays, P. (2004). Case study research. In K. deMarrais & S. Lapan (Eds.), *Foundations for research: Methods of inquiry in education and the social sciences* (pp. 217–234). Mahwah, NJ: Lawrence Erlbaum Associates, Inc.

Hek, R. (2005). *The experiences and needs of refugee and asylum seeking children in the UK: A literature review*. Birmingham: University of Birmingham. Retrieved from http://dera.ioe.ac.uk/5398/1/RR635.pdf

Johnson, J. (1991). Student voice: Motivating students through empowerment. *OSSC Bulletin, 35*(2), 1–25.

Kitchen, M. (2010). Boston Public schools reach out to Haitian population. *Examiner. com*. Retrieved from http://www.examiner.com/article/boston-public-schools-reach-out-to-haitian-population

Lambert, J. (2010). *The digital storytelling cookbook*. Berkeley, CA: Digital Diner Press.

Lasso, C., & Soto, N. (2005). *The social integration of Latino newcomer students in Midwestern elementary schools: Teacher and administrator perceptions*. Retrieved from http://www.usca.edu/essays/vol142005/lasso.pdf

Levitt, P., & Jaworsky, B. N. (2007). Transnational migration studies: Past developments and future trends. *The Annual Review of Sociology, 33*, 129–156.

Massachusetts Department of Elementary and Secondary Education. (MA DESE) (2014). *Rethinking Equity and Teaching for English Language Learners (RETELL)*. Retrieved from http://www.doe.mass.edu/retell/

Matthews, J. (2008). Schooling and settlement: Refugee education in Australia. *International Studies in Sociology of Education, 18*(1), 31–45. Retrieved from http://www.tandfonline.com/doi/pdf/10.1080/09620210802195947?needAccess=true

Merrigan, T. (2010). Children of the quake: Young survivors learn in a new land. *Dorchester Reporter*. Retrieved from http://www.dotnews.com/2010/children-quake-young-survivors-learn-new-land

Natural Disaster. (2011, June 6). Natural disaster refugees more than doubled to 42 million: Monitoring group worries climate change is playing big role in 2010 jump. *MSNBC News*. Retrieved from http://www.nbcnews.com/id/43295013/ns/world_news-world_environment/t/natural-disaster-refugees-more-doubled-million/#.Wly6iq2ZOCQ

Nicas, J. (2010, March 1). Group in Mattapan welcomes Haiti quake's school-age victims. *Boston Globe*. Retrieved from http://www.boston.com/yourtown/boston/mattapan/articles/2010/03/01/group_in_mattapan_welcomes_haiti_quakes_school_age_victims/

Nicolas, G., DeSilva, A., & Rabenstein, K. (2009). Educational attainment of Haitian immigrants. *Urban Education, 44*, 664–686.

Nieto, S. (2010). *Language, culture, and teaching: Critical perspectives* (2nd ed.). New York, NY: Routledge.

Orbe, M., & Drummond, D. (2011). Competing cultural worldviews in the United States: A phenomenological examination of the essential core elements of transnationalism and transculturalism. *The Qualitative Report, 16*(6), 1688–1714.

Paiewonsky, M. (2005). *See what I mean: Using photovoice to plan for the future. Bilingual community education and multilingualism: Beyond heritage languages in a global city* (Doctoral dissertation). University of Massachusetts, Boston. Retrieved from ProQuest Dissertations and Theses database. (UMI No. 3172767)

Roberts, A., & Locke, S. (2001). Tending school: A forum on the experiences of refugee and immigrant students in the United States system. *Interchange, 32*(4), 375–393.

Schulz, J., & Batalova, J. (2017). Haitian immigrants in the United States. *Migration Policy Institute*. Retrieved from https://www.migrationpolicy.org/article/haitian-immigrants-united-states

Should International. (2014, July 3). Should International refugee law accommodate climate change? *UN News Centre*. Retrieved from http://www.un.org/apps/news/story.asp?NewsID=48201#.WlzFlK2ZOCR

Stets, J. E., & Burke, P. J. (2000). Identity theory and social identity theory. *Social Psychology Quarterly, 63*(3), 224–237.

Suarez-Orozco, M. A., Darbes, T., Dias, S. I., & Sutin, M. (2011). Migrations and schooling. *Annual Review of Anthropology, 40*, 311–328.

Trueba, E. T., & Bartolome, L. I. (2000). *Immigrant voices: In search of educational equity*. Lanham, MD: Rowman & Littlefield.

United Nations Children's Fund. (2011). *Children in Haiti one year after – The long road from relief to recovery*. UNICEF. Retrieved from https://www.unicefusa.org/sites/default/files/assets/pdf/Children-in-Haiti-One-Year-After.pdf

United Nations High Commissioner for Refugees. (2010). *Convention and protocol related to the status of refugees*. Communications and Public Information Service. Retrieved from http://www.unhcr.org/3b66c2aa10.pdf

Zehr, M. A. (2010). Boston settles with federal officials in ELL probe. *Education Week, 30*(7), 10.

CHAPTER 8

Expanding Educational Access to Create Self-Sufficiency

The Post-Secondary Educational Experiences of Resettled Refugees in Florida

Tara Ross, Jody L. McBrien and Briana Byers

Introduction

The global refugee crisis necessitates an understanding of policymaking governing the resettlement of refugees in the United States. The United States emphasises rapid employment over post-secondary education for adult resettled refugees in order to compel their self-sufficiency. However, self-sufficiency does not fully address the manifold aspects that account for a refugee's adaptation and adjustment to living in the United States. The resources that they need to become self-sufficient, such as post-secondary education, are difficult to obtain due to immediate employment needs, language barriers, poor guidance on educational options, lack of childcare, and/or lack of cultural capital. Using the lens of acculturation theory, this phenomenological study explores the value and influence of post-secondary educational experiences in the lives of seven first generation adult refugees living in Florida.

The work of Strang and Ager (2010) provides the support for examining refugee integration in terms of identifying specific markers or achievements that indicate greater self-sufficiency within society. McPherson (2010) provides support for operationalizing acculturation by examining how refugees identify themselves within their new culture, and the importance of post-secondary education within their self-actualisation. Zeus (2011) provides the impetus for examining higher education as a human right for refugees throughout their migration process, and the international policies and dominant discourses that hinder educational attainment. In-depth, semi-structured, one-on-one interviews with seven resettled refugee participants were conducted to explore the educational experiences of resettled refugees and participant attitudes and beliefs about the importance of education in their process of acculturation. Implications for resettlement and educational policy follow.

© KONINKLIJKE BRILL NV, LEIDEN, 2019 | DOI: 10.1163/9789004401891_008

Backgrounds

In the aftermath of World War II, as European refugees fled genocide and war, the newly formed United Nations (UN) created a refugee office to deal with the crisis. Governed by a limited mandate, the UN refugee office helped refugees affected by the violence on the European continent to repatriate to their home countries, integrate in the local communities where they fled, or resettle into a new country, such as the United States, Canada, or countries in South America (United Nations High Commissioner for Refugees [UNHCR], 2010). As the Cold War and decolonisation of the developing world replaced World War II as the leading causes of involuntary migration, a 3-year mandate for the newly formed UN refugee agency – the UNHCR – grew into a permanent mandate to protect refugees who involuntarily fled their home countries. With the end of the Cold War in the 1990s; the ethnic warfare in Bosnia, Rwanda, and Darfur; and the global war on terror in the first decade of the new century; the refugee crisis has continued to grow (UNHCR, 2005).

The UNHCR has identified three durable solutions for the protracted refugee crisis, which include voluntary return to the refugee's home country, integration into the local community to which the refugee fled, and permanent resettlement to one of just over 30 countries in the world that UNCHR identifies as resettlement countries (UNHCR, 2012b). Of these countries, which include the United States, Australia, Canada, the United Kingdom, and countries from Europe and Latin America, the United States has historically resettled more than twice the number of refugees as all other countries combined (Singer & Wilson, 2006; UNHCR, 2012a).

Existing refugee resettlement policy derives its legal foundation from the Refugee Act of 1980, providing entrance into the United States for refugees who cannot return home (US Department of State, 2001). The policy is implemented through anti-poverty programmes in the United States, such as Temporary Assistance to Needy Families (TANF) and Medicaid, and through service providers who seek to help refugees gain rapid self-sufficiency. In practice, however, policies shift as global crises change, exacerbating the need for relevant research demonstrating the benefits of self-sufficiency for refugees when they have access to post-secondary education (Dawood, 2011; Georgetown University, 2009).

On-going global emergencies contribute to the refugee crisis. Since the civil war began in Syria in 2011, nearly 13 million Syrians have fled their homes (60% of the pre-war population). Of those, approximately 6 million are internally displaced (Migration Policy Center, 2014). As of early 2018, over 6 million Syrians fled the country to become asylum seekers and refugees (Connor, 2018; The Guardian, 2014),

The body of research on international and national policies governing refugee resettlement indicates that barriers to acculturation exist for newcomers. Education is important to acculturation because it provides the means by which students can learn the language of their new country, and develop an on-going understanding of the customs and culture (Dawood, 2011; Farrell, Barden, & Mueller, 2008; Georgetown University, 2009; Koehler, 2009; McBrien, 2005; Schiller, Boggis, Messenger, & Douglas, 2009; Shakya et al., 2010; Stevenson & Willot, 2007; Valenta & Bunar, 2010). Education aids newcomers in building skills that will expand their opportunities within their new country as well as assist in their acculturation (Brooker & Lawrence, 2012).

Education at all levels – primary, secondary, and post-secondary – is one marker of societal integration for resettled refugees. Education aids the process of a refugee building intra-ethnic (within an ethnic community) and inter-ethnic (between ethnic communities) alliances; and in acquiring the skills, licenses, and degrees needed for meaningful employment (Ager & Strang, 2004). Barriers to education exist, however, due to policies that prioritise rapid self-sufficiency through employment over acculturation.

Students who emerge from the initial trauma of the refugee experience – experiencing war or natural disaster, loss of loved ones, flight from their home and home country, arrival in a new location, and ultimately resettlement in a third country – have varied experiences in education related to their cultural inclusion. Those who are more committed to integrating into the new society appear to have a more positive experience in education (Brooker & Lawrence, 2012).

The purpose of this study was to examine post-secondary educational experiences of first-generation refugees who have resettled in Florida and how these experiences influenced their acculturation process. Important to this study was the focus on acculturation theory, which is the process by which a person changes because of experiences in a new society, and how the society changes to accommodate the new resident.

The central research question of this study was the following: How do resettled refugees in Florida perceive that their post-secondary education received during resettlement influenced their acculturation?

Opportunities and Barriers to Education

Disruption of education begins in the refugee's home country due to violence or socio-political upheaval (Shakya et al., 2010). Little post-secondary education is available in refugee camps (MacLaren, 2010; Zeus, 2011). Part of the challenge of refugee education is that education is often one of the first programmes to be cut when a nation is in conflict (Burde, Kapit, Wahl, Guven, & Skarpeteig, 2017). Once a nation is classified as a conflict zone, humanitarian aid organisations typically provide the only opportunities for youth to continue their education (Burde et al., 2017). Unfortunately, these humanitarian aid efforts tend to focus their efforts on primary education as it is critical and complicated, leaving tertiary education students with limited access to obtain a degree, through no fault of their own (Milton & Barakat, 2016). However, inroads by groups such as Jesuit Commons: Higher Education at the Margins are being made to bring college courses into the camps. Additionally, some US-based institutions partner with community-based organisations located near refugee camps. For instance, Southern New Hampshire University works to connect refugee communities to advance higher education by partnering with an East African INGO (CLCC, 2017).

Upon arrival to the United States, issues tangential to the educational environment affect refugees' access to education. Lack of English language comprehension, isolation from the broader society, and money concerns are barriers not just to education, but to acculturation as well (Brooker & Lawrence, 2012). Transportation, health-related problems, and childcare needs often frustrate refugees' educational options.

Newcomers are welcome to participate in language classes, attend college, or enrol in recertification courses. However, the quality of English language classes varies widely (Georgetown University, 2009), with location of classes or lack of childcare often preventing attendance (Schiller et al., 2009). The cost may also be prohibitive to their enrolment. Because they must prioritise work in order to subsist, a job becomes a more immediate need. Such an approach emphasises employment over education, yet sustainable, living wage employment is unlikely given the many obstacles refugees face, most of which are also obstacles to higher education (Georgetown University, 2009).

The requirement of refugees to take the first job available in order to become self-sufficient also prevents a focus on education that exacerbates their ability to acculturate within society (Dawood, 2011; Georgetown University, 2009). Recertification for professionals is costly, not widely available, and requires high levels of English ability (Dawood, 2011; Georgetown University, 2009; Schiller et al., 2009). Such obstacles to obtain a primary goal such as education create frustration and hinder resettled refugees' processes of acculturation (Schiller et al., 2009).

As part of the admissions process, students are expected to submit proof of an official high school diploma or equivalent. Institutions committed to advancing the education of refugee students must implement policies that allow for flexibility in this requirement, given that it is unlikely or impossible for refugee applicants to obtain these official records (Connected Learning in

Crisis Consortium, 2017). In addition, many international students, including refugees, are required to submit both standardised tests scores (such as the SAT/ACT) and language proficiency test scores (e.g., TOEFL). Such tests have fees that create additional burdens for refugee applicants. The US-based Institute of International Education (IIE) has provided limited support with some US universities to admit and fund a few refugees annually (Loo, Streitwieser, & Jeong, 2018). The IIE also encourages partner institutions to waive or make exceptions to admission criteria by offering interviews when free for English language proficiency exams are not affordable and accepting scanned copies of academic transcripts if the original was lost (Binkley, 2016).

When accepted into a higher education programme, most refugee students struggle to finance their education. In the United States, there is no comprehensive programme for assistance or even for information leading to assistance, such as a national database. The US Department of State (n.d.) advocates for private sector companies to aid refugees by ensuring access to quality education, aiding refugees as they enter the workforce, providing technical assistance, assisting with financial services and affordable housing, and expanding services to aid refugee education. However, especially in the last two years and a presidential policy of anti-immigration, there is little to support such advocacy. Rather than a national plan to support these students, there are local success stories, such as a University of California Irvine student who fundraised for a refugee scholarship and a partnership between two Michigan community organisations that partnered to establish refugee scholarships (Loo et al., 2018). While admirable, such efforts cannot begin to create a national strategy to support the students in their efforts for higher education.

In addition to educational expenses, refugees in higher education must find means to support their living expenses. Here again, although the US Refugee Resettlement Programme, a division of the US State Department, offers refugees an opportunity to rebuild their lives in the United States, there is limited financial federal support (Hess, Isakson, Githinji, Roche, Vadnais, Parker, & Goodkind, 2014). Again, there are small, unconnected programmes, such as an initiative started by a professor at Guilford College in North Carolina (Loo et al., 2018), and the Weslyan Refugee Project in Connecticut founded by student volunteers to assist refugee students with housing and energy subsidies (Rubenstein, 2015).

Acculturation Theory

Acculturation theory provides the framework to undergird the study on post-secondary education for resettled refugees. Acculturation theory helps researchers explore how immigrants or refugees adapt to a new society (Berry, 2001). The theory proposes that when an individual arrives to live in a new country, there is an exchange of ideas, values, cultural identities, and perspectives (Hickey, 2007). Acculturation involves a two-way relationship, with the merging of traditions and practices within society when groups have prolonged exposure to one another (Atfield, Brahmbhatt, & O'Toole, 2007; Morris, Popper, Rodwell, Brodine, & Bower, 2009; Smyth & Kum, 2010). What follows are specific markers that occur during this process.

Cultural Identity and Self-Reflection

The process of integration, time, and self-reflection provides refugees with the opportunity to recreate their cultural identities and their sense of belonging. Refugees can then merge their cultural identities. Self-reflection allows refugees to evaluate who they are within the context of their new society. They may discard elements of their identities that are no longer applicable in their new lives (Djuraskovic & Arthur, 2009).

Creating Knowledge of Self

Creating social connections within society cannot come without first allowing the refugee to create self knowledge. Refugees have noted that education can provide an opportunity for self-empowerment through learning about one's abilities and determining one's goals. From that knowledge of self comes the ability for newcomers to engage with others who may hold different points of view (McPherson, 2010).

Social Capital

Social capital involves the mechanisms by which refugees can engage within society and increase their acculturation (Strang & Ager, 2010). Connections within an ethnic group, how members of ethnic groups support newcomers, and family relationships to relatives already in the new country are examples of social bonds. Social networks in which refugees can connect with others outside of their family and ethnic group, (such as school, work, and refugee service providers) create social bridges.

Cultural Capital

Cultural capital is the knowledge one has of the surrounding culture and reciprocal skills they bring to it (Camblin, 2003). Education helps newcomers navigate societal rules and cultural norms. Lack of understanding cultural cues creates barriers to acculturation and feelings of inferiority (Berry, 2001; Hickey, 2007; Koehler, 2009; McPherson, 2010; Stevenson & Willot, 2008).

Key Findings

The process of interviewing seven resettled refugee adults in Florida uncovered several key themes related to the above framework of acculturation as well as barriers identified in the literature. Below we provide examples related to each theme.

Self Knowledge and Identity
All participants expressed a need to retain their identity, while at the same time accepting new elements to their lives in the United States that would necessitate changes to their identity. The topic of identity was discussed throughout the interviews, but the idea of creating a new identity is effectively elucidated by Cira:

> I started going out more, and I started meeting people and interacting. Because everybody at the jewellery store was Spanish, *I had to start there. The only way to move to ... get adapted was to use my own culture and do that.* (emphasis added)

Each noted the need of the newcomer to adopt the language in order to access the benefits of living in the country and to be respectful in learning the language of the country that accepted them. Some of them noted that acculturation was a two-way street for the newcomer and the society. They looked for native residents to show signs of welcoming. However, it is not an easy status to achieve. There were many comments indicating that native residents expected the newcomers to make changes to fit into their new country, but few indicating that the established communities should, likewise, be open to change in order to be welcoming.

Social Capital
Education provided the participants in this study with the opportunity to create social bonds within society that extended beyond their own group. English classes often provided the initial contact with other immigrants and refugees with whom they could share experiences. Education provided the participants with the opportunity to create support networks. Brena, who arrived from Bosnia as a 16 year old with severe medical trauma from the war, remembers what she asked for first:

> When I actually I got to Cumberland, Maryland hospital they asked me what I wanted to do, and I was like, 'Just take me to the high school. Just take me to school.' And at this point you have to understand, all I'm

seeing is adults: doctors, medical, physical therapists. Nobody my age. So, I was like, give me somebody that's under 18, in a high school setting, in a school setting, because I needed to have that. Any kind of school setting. I needed to have that ... it was just really great to go and visit the school and go to the gym. Just like see kids. That whole school smell ... Backpacks and books.

One consistent theme among the participants was the belief that education would help them create a sense of belonging in the United States. Shakya et al. (2010) mentioned the importance of education in helping newcomers create that connection. Sonja, who had been a published writer when she lived in Belgrade and was a literature student at the university there, explained her realisation of needing to figure out how she was going to make education possible, despite the barriers:

Then there is this moment when I thought, okay I'm not going to be able to go to college here. There is dignity in that, too. I'll read books and be like low paid factory worker who reads Hegel and loves obscure things, and art, and again I met a lot of people there – I was amazed at the stuff they knew and things they'd been through. *But, I also started to feel that in order to feel like I belonged in this country I had to go through the education system. I have to learn it ... So, it felt like I needed to do this. I needed to have this acknowledgement like I belonged more.* (emphasis added)

Cultural Capital

Informal lessons, such as academic skills, communication, learning 'the rules of the game,' and understanding diversity learned in their college experiences helped participants build their cultural capital. Education also helps resettled refugees learn to navigate societal rules and cultural norms (Berry, 2001; Hickey, 2007; Koehler, 2009; McPherson, 2010). Sometimes, for the participants, that meant learning cultural rules, even when those were rules that lacked fairness. As Mirella explained, it took an acceptance of the rules to move on:

You have to understand it's not your country. You have to follow their rules. It's not your rules. You have to adapt to their environment. That is difficult; that is the truth. You want to live here? You have to adapt here in all the affairs of your life. For everything. An acceptance, you know?

Participating in post-secondary education opened participant experiences to working with others in a diverse culture. Inevitably, this exposure created openness to other types of people that led the participants to seek the opportunity to work with diverse groups. Brena described a positive experience:

> Another thing I really liked about college was the exposure to different things and different people and different walks of life. I mean that was really ... even for a small, Catholic school I had exposure to a lot of different diversity. And ... um, that's something I wouldn't be able to get at home ... In Bosnia we're all the same, we're all Bosnians, you know, it's how it is. Forget the whole religious thing in the war, but in general we're all the same, we're all like somebody stamped us, and very similar. Here it's very ... it's really like a melting pot. There's very much a diversity. That's something I really kind of appreciated and kind of looking back now, I probably would have wanted to go to state school to even have a bigger diversity in the state school, but at the time I didn't know.

Barriers to Acculturation and Education

This section elucidates the obstacles that participants felt as they pursued higher education. Again, their comments closely follow barriers identified in the literature.

Learning the English Language

Learning a new language was the most important thing participants mentioned they needed to do before they could integrate into society. All participants speak English comfortably now. Academic English was much more difficult to learn. Luay, who came from Iraq having completed his Bachelor's degree in Communications in Baghdad, described the challenges of improving his academic English when starting graduate school:

> The difference when you are reading words from a book as academic level will be really different from reading it in newspapers ... So when I was reading, it was really hard, it's not you're building from English one by one ... I'm taking English immediately as a master's level, but this year, in English, your first year in education in this country, master's level, in English. And you studied all your life reading in Arabic. Is this one way that universities can expand educational access?

Luay's comment clearly describes the challenge Cummins (1979) describes in extra years needed to learn academic English. Conversational English takes a relatively short amount of time, at 1-3 years, but academic skills can take 5–7 years.

Recertification of Existing Credentials

Those with professional backgrounds from their native countries had varying levels of success in re-entering their fields. Participants had a variety of credentials, including medical school and teacher training at the university level. These credentials could not be renewed, but did help when they returned to school to start over. One participant was able to have a family member get his transcript from his university in Baghdad, verifying his bachelor's degree. This enabled him to start on his graduate degree in the United States. See Appendix for list of participants and their educational backgrounds.

Cost and Time

The cost and time involved with education proved to be challenging, but participants in this study were able to combine grants, scholarships, and loans to achieve their educational goals. Participants used creative scheduling to be able to work and attend college at the same time. Several participants emphasised the importance of taking a systematic approach. Mirella explained how she thought of the step-by-step process as one that would lead the newcomer to a greater place in five years, but that it takes planning and cooperation within the family:

> When we come to this country, everybody has to work to earn some money. Nobody thinking they have to learn ... Believe me, if I know each person [I tell them]: Go ahead and go slowly, go step-by-step. Go to school in the morning, and go part time in the night. If everybody in the family does it in this way and puts in their money they can get any problem solved. After five year, you be very great. In five year, you can't throw away this very great opportunity you have in your life. You can become a technician and receive very good pay salary. It would be great. Most of the people [don't] understand this.

Using this method among family members, Mirella exhibited a positive use of social capital to make it possible for not only herself, but also other family members, to attain higher education.

Transcripts

Obtaining transcripts to demonstrate proof of educational background ranged from complicated to life threatening (if they had to do so during migration).

EXPANDING EDUCATIONAL ACCESS TO CREATE SELF-SUFFICIENCY   187

Boro's university was destroyed in the Bosnian war. Luay's university remained, but he had to flee due to political persecution.

Support Networks

Support networks were important for participants in their school success. Luay described connecting with classmates in school to study and work on projects:

> You do your assignment or you know people will help each other to do, you know, like I will help my friend to understand more, this is the only thing as a group, we helping each other to understand more.

Luay's comment suggests the use of cultural capital to advance. Support networks were often difficult to create, however, due to constraints on time as well as being an adult student with limited English language capabilities. Participants did not get to have the traditional university experience.

Inaccurate Information

Participants often received inaccurate information at the community colleges, state colleges, and universities they attended in the United States. Refugees often lack reliable information about what rights they have and where they can access benefits (Atfield et al., 2007; Goodson & Phillimore, 2005). Participants in this study noted that they received inaccurate information about their educational options. The participants explained an overall lack of familiarity among professors and administrators regarding refugees and their educational rights.

Participants often relied on informal connections among classmates, which were not always accurate, either. As Sonja noted,

> I got really depressed because then I was just going to work and I felt like I'm stuck here in this life that I didn't actively choose, so I started asking around. 'How can I start any kind of school? 'So now this guy from Bosnia told me, 'Oh you cannot go to college here, because they don't recognise your high school diploma, so you have to have your high school diploma to do something about that. And plus, you can't go to college in Florida until you've been living here a year.' He was talking about out-of-state tuition, which is not even true. But that made me depressed even more ... And I had no way ... I had internet ... but I had no way ... I didn't know how to look for information. I didn't know who to ask.

Sonja's comment indicates a lack of cultural capital that would have facilitated her educational journey.

Policy

Participants were asked to share their recommendations for US policy governing refugee resettlement and university approaches to expanding educational access. As noted by McPherson (2010), refugees have limited opportunities to share their experiences and influence policy. Empowering the participants to give voice to their ideas for improvement based on their personal experiences helps to mitigate the loss of control participants had throughout their pre-migration and post-migration experience.

Specific recommendations included lengthening the cultural orientation process prior to migration, and reducing the disconnect participants felt existed between federal, state, and local resettlement policies.

Educational Recommendations
Scaffold learning The participants each emphasised the importance of educational policy that would scaffold a newcomer's learning, while helping them to become independent. Such scaffolding included greater resources for English language education and allowing refugees one year to go to school and have integration classes. Boro, who arrived from Bosnia having attended a year of university in Sarajevo, stated:

> Just give them [resettled refugees in the United States] one year in school and classes for one year, pay rent, just make them feel comfortable in this society. To have sense of belonging. That's very important. To have sense of belonging here. And to get that belonging to succeed and to move on. If you don't feel that you belong here, if you feel that you're just ignored, you don't speak English, it's just hard. Because I have a sense of belonging here.

Improving the Recertification Process

The three participants who had professional degrees before migrating all noted the importance of improving the recertification process, as ultimately bringing professionals to the United States can benefit the society. The time spent away from their profession during migration and resettlement resulted in weakening skills. Mirella, a doctor in Cuba who had nine years of medical school training, highlighted this problem:

> As a time passes, if you don't practice you lose your ability. You lose ability to hear ... our ear is very important. Our fingers is important. We can

listen, we can see, we can feel ... I mean you lose all of the ability that you got during your practice in Cuba or whatever country, you know? You lose all of those things.

Create Liaisons

A few of the participants believed that social connections were extremely important to the integration of newcomers. They advocated for programmes (such as foster families for newcomers or connections for the first year between an American family and a refugee family) that would promote such connections. University liaisons consisting of upperclassmen as mentors could help newcomers to the country as well as to the institution develop connections that supported their learning efforts.

Key Points of Analysis

Social connections have a multiplier effect. Threadgold and Court (2005) mentioned the benefit of 'mobility multipliers' (p. 22), which were those public benefits, including education, that helped resettled refugees work toward self-sufficiency. In this study, the multiplier effect meant that when new connections were made in the resettled refugees' lives, they created opportunities that not only increased their employment options in society, but also created opportunities for enjoyment and happiness.

Making social connections with classmates, colleagues, and other refugees helped in the participants in our study adjust to the culture. Some of the participants used these social connections to help with study in school, while others benefited from social connections by gaining advice on educational and career options or just enjoying social gatherings.

Building Personal Capacity

The skills developed in their educational programmes, and the cultural awareness created by learning about their society, helped participants to build personal capacity and cultural capital. While capacity is a term that implies organisational readiness in meeting the needs of constituents or clients, the participants expanded their personal capacity by developing the skills through post-secondary education and training that they needed to provide for their self-sufficiency and support their families. They also helped to expand the capacity of the organisations they worked with by developing the skills that made them valuable working members of society.

Taking the Long View

The three participants who arrived with college degrees each used that understanding and perspective to motivate themselves to continue with further education in the United States. For these participants, education helped them to take the long view of the acculturation process. They developed a perspective that helped them to balance their priorities between their lives and their goal attainment.

While all of the participants experienced manifold frustrations and barriers to enrolling in college and successfully completing classes, those who had already completed their college degrees prior to migration each explained that their prior education helped them to understand the importance of continuing their education in the United States for their own self-actualisation.

While not definitive based on the participant group size and varied experiences, the experiences and comments of the three participants who completed their education prior to arrival appear to suggest an easier process of initial acceptance of their circumstances, and understanding that acculturation takes time and patience.

Rapid Self-Sufficiency Versus Lasting Self-Sufficiency

Empowerment has that multiplier effect, as mentioned previously. It is created out of the personal identity and awareness mentioned by McPherson (2010), and the means and markers created when resettled refugees engage in education, as mentioned by Ager and Strang (2004). Current US policy forces resettled refugee adults to find employment as soon as possible, rather than to hava time to reach their golas and potentials, some of which were realised in their native countries where they became teachers, lawyers, doctors, and managers. Ulitmately, their ability to find similar positions in the United States would add to the US economy more than their current need to find any job, often low-paying jobs. Because education is strongly implicated in its ability to teach newcomers about themselves, their abilities, and their desire to help others, refugee policy needs to provide educational options to newcomers. Postsecondary education benefits society, and creates lasting sufficiency, rather than just rapid sufficiency.

Implications for Practice

While policy surrounding refugee resettlement emerges from a variety of government offices and the resettlement agencies contracted to handle resettlement, it is useful to consider options for carrying out practices mentioned in the study. The fundamental implication for practice derived from this study is that the federal government provide greater support for resettled refugees to prioritise education. This would mean loosening the requirements on rapid employment and self-sufficiency, and in its place, allowing for a longer period of support while refugees learn English and work towards a diploma or degree. English language education ideally would begin in the pre-migration period, while in the refugee camps or through an extended orientation in the country of departure.

To facilitate refugee opportunities in higher education, colleges and universities could provide professional development to staff regarding the rights of resettled refugees to enrol in classes as well as their rights to receive financial aid and grants. Some frustration and barriers could be lessened if staff and faculty were enlightened about the refugee students and their specific needs as well as their potential contributions to society.

Social connections have the multiplier effect that help refugees to maximize the aid and opportunities they have in meaningful ways. While resettlement agencies help to establish newcomers with their initial benefits, an outreach family could show them where to shop for groceries, how the bus system works, and where they can take classes. Colleges and universities could use peer mentoring programmes to reach out to refugee students who might benefit from help in registering for classes, receiving tutoring, or developing peer networks. Family programmes or student mentoring programmes would have the benefit of enhancing the two-way acculturation process mentioned in the literature.

The US Department of Education, in conjunction with regional accrediting agencies, should establish acceptable practices for universities to use when evaluating the credentials and practices of refugees who were doctors, nurses, other medical workers, engineers, lawyers, or other professionals in their home countries. Existing practices of determining credit for life experience are cumbersome, costly to the student, and slow. Recertification programmes are often too costly for a former professional to be able to pay or are not readily available.

Bridge programmes that link prior experiences to the needed skill training for certification for doctors, nurses, teachers, and other professionals could be more readily available throughout the country, especially in areas where a high number of refugees resettle. Combined with academic English training specific to these fields of study, such programmes could quickly train professionals with diverse talents, enabling them to use their skills and experience, fill critical shortages in the United States, earn a good income, and contribute more to the tax base.

The option to create bridge programmes could benefit from funding provided through the Affordable Care Act for institutions and students. Passed in

2009, the Act provides an initial investment of $250 million for the training for medical professionals, especially primary care physicians, physician assistants, practitioners working in preventative medicine, and nurses.

Encouraging the Department of Health and Human Services, which oversees the Affordable Care Act as well as the Office of Refugee Resettlement, to promote bridge programmes for highly-qualified refugees makes sense given the critical shortage of medical personnel – a shortage that will only become more acute as 30 million more people are added to the health care system in 2014 (Healthcare.gov, 2012).

Research to explore the refugee experience from personal perspectives informs policymakers, international organisations, and educational leaders with relevant perspectives and fresh approaches to understanding their reality. Researchers have the unique opportunity to provide refugees with a voice to share their stories and suggest novel approaches to address complex problems; such was a goal of this study. Policymakers, administrators, and educators have an obligation to hear these perspectives and consider them when engaging in policy planning and institutional planning that will affect the lives of so many within a vulnerable, but resilient, population.

References

Ager, A., & Strang, A. (2004). *Indicators of integration: Final report.* London: Home Office Development and Practice Report. Retrieved from www.homeoffice.gov.uk/rds/pdfs04/dpr28.pdf

Atfield, G., Brahmbhatt, K., & O'Toole, T. (2007). *Refugees' experiences of integration.* London: Refugee Council and University of Birmingham. Retrieved from http://www.refugeecouncil.org.uk/Resources/Refugee%20Council/downloads/researchreports/Integrationresearchreport.pdf

Berry, J. W. (2001). A psychology of immigration. *Journal of Social Issues, 57*(3), 615–631.

Binkley, C. (2016, May 24). US colleges offer Syrian refugees scholarships. *The Spokesman-Review.* Retrieved from http://www.spokesman.com/stories/2016/may/24/us-colleges-offer-syrian-refugees-scholarships/

Brooker, A., & Lawrence, J. (2012). Educational and cultural challenges of bicultural adult immigrant and refugee students in Australia. *Australian Journal of Adult Learning, 52*(1), 66–88.

Burde, D., Kapit, A., Wahl, R. L., Guven, O., & Skapeteig, M. I. (2017). Education in emergencies: A review of theory and research. *Review of Educational Research, 87*(3), 619–658. doi:10.3102/0034654316671594

Camblin, S. J. (2003). *The middle grades: Putting all students on track for college.* Honolulu, HI: Pacific Resources for Education and Learning.

EXPANDING EDUCATIONAL ACCESS TO CREATE SELF-SUFFICIENCY 193

Connected Learning in Crisis Consortium (CLCC). (2017). *Quality guidelines playbook: Lessons learned through contextualized practice.* Retrieved from http://www.connected learning4refugees.org/wp-content/uploads/CLC_playbook_screen.pdf

Connor, P. (2018, January 29). *Most displaced Syrians are in the Middle East, and about a million are in Europe.* Pew Research Center. Retrieved from http://www.pewresearch.org/fact-tank/2018/01/29/where-displaced-syrians-have-resettled/

Cummins, J. (1979). Linguistic interdependence and the educational development of bilingual children. *Review of Educational Research, 49*(2), 222–251.

Dawood, N. (2011). From persecution to poverty: The costs of the US refugee resettlement program's narrow emphasis on early employment. *Policymatters.* University of California Berkeley. Retrieved from http://policymatters.net/?p=912

Djuraskovic, I., & Arthur, N. (2009). The acculturation of former Yugoslavian refugees. *Canadian Journal of Counselling, 43*(1), 18–34.

Farrell, M., Barden, B., & Mueller, M. (2008). *Synthesis of findings from three states. The evaluation of the Refugee Social Service (RSS) and Targeted Assistance Formula Grant (TAG) programs: Synthesis of findings from three sites.* U.S. Department of Health and Human Services, Office of Refugee Resettlement. Retrieved from http://www.acf.hhs.gov/programs/orr/resources/synthesis_of_finding_contents.htm#top

Georgetown University. (2009). *Refugee crisis in America: Iraqis and their resettlement experience.* Retrieved from http://www.law.georgetown.edu/news/releases/documents/RefugeeCrisisinAmerica_000.pdf

Goodson, L., & Phillimore, J. (2005). *New migrant communities: Education, training, employment and integration matters.* University of Birmingham, Centre for Urban and Regional Studies. Retrieved from http://www.download.bham.ac.uk/curs/pdf/new_migrant_communities.pdf

Healthcare.gov. (2012). *Creating jobs and increasing the number of primary care providers.* Retrieved from http://www.healthcare.gov/news/factsheets/2010/06/creating-jobs-and-increasing-primary-care-providers.html

Hess, J. M., Isakson, B., Githinji, A., Roche, N., Vadnais, K., Parker, D. P., & Goodkind, J. R. (2014). Reducing mental health disparities through transformational learning: A social change model with refugees and students. *Psychological Services, 3*, 347–356. doi:10.1037/a0035334

Hickey, M. G. (2007). Burmese refugees' narratives of cultural change. In C. Park, R. Endo, S. Lee, & X. L. Rong (Eds.), *Asian American education: Acculturation, literacy development, and learning* (pp. 25–53). Charlotte, NC: Information Age.

Koehler, M. (2009). The role of education in teaching norms and values to adult newcomers: An analysis of integration policy in the Netherlands, with emphasis on the city of Rotterdam. *Intercultural Education, 20*(2), 161–172.

Loo, B., Streitwieser, B., & Joeng, J. (2018, February 6). Higher education's role in national refugee integration: Four cases. *World Education News + Reviews.* Retrieved from https://senr.wes..org/2018/02/higher-educations-role-national-refugee-integration-four-cases

MacLaren, D. (2010, May 23). ACU refugee program on the Thai-Burma border. *Jesuit Commons*. Retrieved from http://www.jesuitcommons.org/index.asp?bid=13&pid=41

McBrien, J. L. (2005). Educational needs and barriers for refugee students in the United States: A review of the literature. *Review of Educational Research, 75*(3), 329–364.

McPherson, M. (2010). 'I integrate, therefore I am': Contesting the normalizing discourse of integrationism through conversations with refugee women. *Journal of Refugee Studies, 23*(4), 546–570. doi:10.1093/jrs/feq040

Migration Policy Center. (2014). *Syrian refugees: A snapshot of the crisis – Din the Middle East and Europe*. European University Institute. Retrieved from http://syrianrefugees.eu/

Morris, M., Popper, S., Rodwell, T., Brodine, S., & Brouwer, K. (2009). Healthcare barriers of refugees post-resettlement. *Journal of Community Health, 34*(6), 529–538. doi:10.1007/s10900-009-9175-3

Milton, S., & Barakat, S. (2016). Higher education as the catalyst of recovery in conflict-related societies. *Globalisation, Societies and Education, 14*(3), 403–421.

Rubenstein, R. (2015, November 24). *Wesleyan Refugee project aids refugees from around the world*. Retrieved from http://newsletter.blogs.wesleyan.edu/2015/11/24/wesleyanrefugeeproject/

Schiller, N. G., Boggis, J. A., Messenger, M., & Douglas, E. M. (2009). *Refugee resettlement in New Hampshire: Pathways and barriers to building community*. University of New Hampshire. Retrieved from ttp://www.rcusa.org/uploads/pdfs/Refugee%20Resettlement%20in%20NH,%202009.pdf

Singer, A., & Wilson, J. H. (2006). From 'there' to 'here': Refugee resettlement in metropolitan America. *Living Cities Census Series*. The Brookings Institute. Retrieved from http://www.brookings.edu/~/media/Files/rc/reports/2006/09demographics_singer/20060925_singer.pdf

Shakya, Y., Guruge, S., Hynie, M., Akbari, A., Malik, M., Htoo, S., ... Alley, S. (2010). Aspirations for higher education among newcomer refugee youth in Toronto: Expectations, challenges, and strategies. *Refuge, 27*(2), 65–78.

Smyth, G., & Kum, H. (2010). 'When they don't use it they will lose it': Professionals, deprofessionalization and reprofessionalization: The case of refugee teachers in Scotland. *Journal of Refugee Studies, 23*(4), 503–522.

Stevenson, J., & Willott, J. (2007). The aspiration and access to higher education of teenage refugees in the UK. *Compare, 37*(5), 671–687.

Stevenson, J., & Willott, J. (2008, July). *The role of cultural capital theory in explaining the absence from UK higher education of refugees and other non-traditional students*. Paper presented at the 38th annual meeting of the Standing Conference of University Teaching and Research in the Education of Adults (SCUTREA), University of Edinburgh, Edinburgh.

Strang, A., & Ager, A. (2010). Refugee integration: Emerging trends and remaining agendas. *Journal of Refugee Studies, 23*(4), 589–607.

The Guardian. (2014, August 29). *Three million refugees have fled Syria, says UN.* Retrieved from http://www.theguardian.com/world/2014/aug/29/three-million-refugees-fled-syria

Threadgold, T., & Court, G. (2005). *Refugee inclusion: A literature review. Cardiff School of Journalism.* Cardiff: Cardiff University. Retrieved from http://www.werconline.org.uk/pdf/Terry2005.pdf

United Nations High Commissioner for Refugees (UNHCR). (2005). An introduction to international protection: Protecting persons of concern to UNHCR. Self-study module 1. *Refworld.* Retrieved from http://www.unhcr.org/refworld/docid/4214cb4f2.html

United Nations High Commissioner for Refugees (UNHCR). (2010). *Annex.* Retrieved from http://www.unhcr.org/4ef9c7269.html

United Nations High Commissioner for Refugees (UNHCR). (2012a). *A new beginning in a third country.* Retrieved from http://www.unhcr.org/pages/4a16b1676.html

United Nations High Commissioner for Refugees (UNHCR). (2012b). *Durable solutions.* Retrieved from http://www.unhcr.org/pages/49c3646cf8.html

US Department of State. (n.d.). *Diplomacy in action: Private sector cooperation on refugees.* Retrieved from https://www.state.gov/j/prm/partnershipforrefugees/

US Department of State. (2001). *Appendix E: Overview of U.S. refugee policy.* Retrieved from http://www.state.gov/j/drl/rls/irf/2001/5562.htm

Valenta, M., & Bunar, N. (2010). State assisted integration: Refugee integration policies in Scandinavian welfare states: The Swedish and Norwegian experience. *Journal of Refugee Studies, 23*(4), 463–483. doi:10.1093/jrs/feq028

Zeus, B. (2011). Exploring barriers to higher education in protracted refugee situations: The case of Burmese refugees in Thailand. *Journal of Refugee Studies, 24*(2), 256–276. doi:10.1093/jrs/fer011

PART 3

Europe

∵

CHAPTER 9

Refugee Children and Young People in Ireland
Policies and Practices

Merike Darmody and Samantha Arnold

Introduction

The social change experienced by Ireland is remarkable in comparison with other Western countries in that it transformed from a country of emigration and declining population in the 1980s due to weak economy and high rates of unemployment to a prosperous country experiencing economic revival during the period that came to be known as the Celtic Tiger. Unprecedented large-scale immigration to Ireland since the 1990s has given rise to a large body of research exploring the impact of immigration on Irish society and the situation of new arrivals in Ireland, mainly focussing on labour market integration of adult migrants (O'Connell & McGinnity, 2008; Barrett & Duffy, 2008). In addition to the new arrivals, immigration was also driven by returning Irish nationals from the mid-1990s to early 2000s. There was additionally a dramatic rise in the number of asylum applicants from 1997, peaking in 2002 (Arnold et al., 2018). The numbers stabilised from 2004 onwards.

Rapid social change in Ireland can be evidenced by the fact that by 2016, the number of non-Irish nationals living in the country had reached 11% of the total population (CSO, 2017). This group is very heterogeneous, representing 196 nationalities and 182 languages, with the largest communities originating from the UK, Brazil and Poland (CSO, 2012, 2017). The status and rights of new arrivals varies between migrant workers, asylum seekers and refugees who all are likely to have diverging challenges, needs and strengths. The response to large-scale rapid immigration has been reactionary in policy terms, partially due to expectations of temporary immigration in the earlier years. As many people moved to Ireland to fill gaps in the labour market, the policies tended to focus on migrant workers.

Reflecting the immigration trends, immigrant-origin children have become an important part of the Irish society. Growth in immigrant numbers, including children of immigrant origin, has resulted in increased policy focus on the integration of the new arrivals, especially after the European Union expansion in 2004. Over time the empirical research on immigrant-origin children, particularly in school contexts, has grown (Smyth et al., 2009; Darmody et al.,

© KONINKLIJKE BRILL NV, LEIDEN, 2019 | DOI: 10.1163/9789004401891_009

2011a, 2011b; Darmody & Smyth, 2016), although the knowledge of some groups and individuals, such as refugees and asylum seekers and their experiences in the new country has remained relatively scant. The reasons for this may be on the one hand relatively small numbers of such children and youth within the wider 'immigrant' category, and on the other hand difficulty in accessing these children and young people for research purposes. Yet, their experiences and needs are likely to differ from those of other immigrant groups. This chapter addresses the gap in knowledge by giving an overview of the situation of unaccompanied minors and refugee children in Ireland, drawing on a variety of second hand data sources. After defining the groups under discussion the chapter then moves on to discussing school-level supports available to all immigrant-origin children in Irish primary and post-primary schools and identifies specific support to unaccompanied minors and refugee children.

Unaccompanied Minors and Child Refugees in Ireland – Definition and Figures

There are three main categories in Ireland as regards refugee children and young people. All three categories present unique challenges to the educational infrastructure in Ireland and to the refugee families themselves. The first category of child refugee in Ireland is comprised of those who arrive through Irish Refugee Resettlement Programme, or Programme Refugees. Programme Refugees are persons with an international protection need who are re-settled to Ireland upon request from the United Nations High Commissioner for Refugees (UNHCR). Programme Refugee children often travel in the company of their parents; indeed family units are prioritised for resettlement by the Irish government. Programme Refugee children have access to free primary and post-primary education. In addition, refugee children may access free third level education if they have lived in Ireland for three years or more.

The second category is comprised of children who arrive, or who are re-unified in the host country, with their families to seek asylum. Upon recognition as a refugee, persons falling within this category are referred to as 'Convention Refugees.' Like Programme Refugees, Convention Refugee children may access free primary and post-primary education and may be eligible for free third level education if they have been living in Ireland for three years or more. While the applicants await a decision on their claim, they are commonly referred to as 'asylum seekers.' While asylum-seeking children await a decision on their claim, they may access free primary and post-primary education as well. However, these young people are not eligible for free third level education. Those who wish to attend third level education would have to cover the costs of the degree themselves and they will often be charged international fees, which are significantly higher than EU fees.[1] The paradox of studying in Irish secondary school alongside indigenous students, all the while preparing for college entrance exams, and being effectively precluded from third level education is discussed in greater detail below in the context of separated children.

Many (if not the majority of) asylum-seeking children will ultimately receive permission to remain on protection grounds (i.e. refugee or subsidiary protection), for example as 'Convention Refugees', or on humanitarian grounds. When this happens, they have the same rights to access the third level[2] education system as Irish citizens. They must however prove residency of 3 or more years in Ireland to be eligible for free third level education. Years spent in Direct Provision do not ordinarily count towards the residency requirement.

The third category is comprised of unaccompanied minors and separated children. Unaccompanied minors are children who travel on their own to seek protection in a country other than their own. Separated children are children who travel alone or in the company of someone other than their primary care giver to seek protection in a country other than their own. Separated children are not a feature of the Irish Resettlement Programme (Arnold & Quinn, 2016, p. 31). Therefore, all separated children arrive in Ireland without a legal status and must seek protection or immigration permission, with the exception of those arriving from Calais as part of the Calais Special Project (discussed below).

In Ireland, the term unaccompanied minor is typically used in the context of immigration policy and refugee law whereas the term separated children is typically used in the literature, good practice guidance (such as the Statement of Good Practice of the Separated Children in Europe Programme, 2009) and by the Child and Family Agency (Tusla), the agency responsible for improving wellbeing and outcomes for children in Ireland. Both terms, unaccompanied minor and separated children, are used throughout this chapter.

The number of unaccompanied minors increased in 2017 due to the Government's commitment to take up to 200 children from the refugee camp in Calais, France. Some 41 unaccompanied minors were brought to Ireland as of April 2018. Additionally, unaccompanied minors form part of the Irish Relocation Programme. The Irish government committed to relocating a total of 2,622 persons as part of the EU Resettlement and Relocation Programmes agreed in 2015 to support Greece and Italy (Arnold & Quinn, 2016, p. 10). Tusla confirmed they could take up to 20 relocated unaccompanied minors into their care.

Unaccompanied minors arriving through the relocation programme enjoy prioritisation in the asylum application process. As a result, their applications are processed faster than ordinary spontaneous refugees. Unaccompanied minors arriving through the Calais Special Project arrive with Programme Refugee Status. In other words, the unaccompanied minors accessing targeted support services therefore have varying statuses and related rights.

Vulnerabilities

Child refugees are likely to present specific challenges to the schools of host countries as they are often characterised in the literature as vulnerable; their vulnerability is most often attributed to experiences of war, violence, separation from family, exposure to domestic harm, etc. (Machel, 2001; Bhabha & Young, 1999, pp. 85–86). Hence, it is likely that children and young people in Ireland falling under the three categories described above are likely to have high levels of vulnerability arising from their personal circumstances. In addition, moving into a new jurisdiction, they need to navigate their way through its education system (Darmody et al., 2011). UNHCR note that refugees in Ireland generally require information, advice and support to access opportunities for integration, including educational services (UNHCR, 2013, pp. 8, 27–28). Teachers and other education professionals need to be aware of the possible issues (discussed below) arising from the backgrounds of these children and how to address any potential difficulties. While acknowledging the specific needs these children have, it is equally important to acknowledge their agency. There is a growing trend in the research to recognise the resilience of child refugees, in particular in the context of separated children. Research suggests that while refugee children may indeed be vulnerable, these children have made use of optimism, hope and strategies for developing a sense of cultural identity as sources of resilience (Maegusuku-Hewett et al., 2007). Kholi (2006, p. 7) has referred to separated children as 'elastic in their capacity to survive and do well', while Ní Raghallaigh (2011, p. 9) has argued that it is 'through the use of multiple strategies' that '[t]hey display remarkable resilience.'

Although this chapter focuses on the vulnerabilities associated with refugee children, it is important to remember, as Kholi (2006, p. 7) notes in the context of separated children, that they are 'ordinary' despite coping with extraordinary circumstances. Vulnerability and resilience should thus be seen side-by-side (Ní Raghallagih, 2011, p. 9) in developing policy and practice including in the context of education.

Importantly, existing studies, both international (Machel, 2001; Digidiki & Bhabha, 2017; Bhabha & Young, 1999) and domestic (Coulter 2013; Martin et al., 2016; Arnold 2012; O'Riordan et al., 2014; Ogbu, Brady, & Kinlen, 2014) indicate that there are also different vulnerabilities which are more commonly associated with one category or another thus impacting upon their potential to engage/thrive in the Irish educational setting.

Potential Challenges

This section outlines the different challenges the three broad categories of child refugees face in Ireland to emphasise the complexities of their needs, both educational and pedagogical. The discussions in this section suggest that Convention Refugees, Programme Refugees, asylum seekers and unaccompanied minors have particular needs that may be overlooked in the largely 'mainstream' approach to education in Ireland.

Among the circumstances contributing to the vulnerability of child Programme Refugees is their experience of protracted stays in refugee camp settings (see Ogg, 2016). Children living in refugee camps often experience periods of time outside of the mainstream school setting (see Zeus, 2011; Machel, 2001). In addition to their experience of interrupted education, refugee camps are often criticised for being unsafe, lacking electricity and basic hygiene facilities as well as not having a sufficient food supply to cater to the population, in particular in times of crisis (Digidiki & Bhabha, 2017; Harrell-Bond, 2000). In addition, while Programme Refugees often arrive to Ireland as a family unit, some family, close friends or close relatives may for one reason or another remain behind. This is an experience that contributes to the vulnerability of all three categories of refugee children, but perhaps less so for accompanied Programme Refugee and asylum seeking children.

Many of the child asylum seekers in Ireland may have been very young when they fled their home country (see Figure 9.2). However, their parents, who may have suffered trauma and/or experienced persecution, accompany them. Research also suggests that Direct Provision centres, government funded full board accommodation for persons seeking asylum, may cause or exacerbate mental health difficulties, including those brought on by experiences of trauma (Coulter, 2013). While accompanied children await a decision on their claim, they reside in Direct Provision. Residents receive a modest payment of €21.60 per resident each week. Residents of Direct Provision are not eligible for child benefit, an otherwise universal payment of €140 per month per child. Ireland has been widely criticised for the approach to those in Direct Provision.

Research highlights the impact the generally stressful environment in Direct Provision has on children in school. Research has found that the conditions associated with Direct Provision and the immigration restrictions placed on asylum seeking families impact negatively on children's education and educational opportunities (Martin et al., 2016, p. 3). Several studies note that there is limited or no access to quiet study space (Arnold, 2012; O'Riordan et al., 2013; Ogbu, Brady, & Kinlen, 2014) and that participation in afterschool homework clubs or other study supports are not available to asylum seeking children either due to the small fees associative with attendance or because no transportation is provided to enable the children to attend (Arnold, 2012).

Indirect factors have also been identified in the research, such as the impact institutionalisation may have on children in terms of their growth and development. Residents living in Direct Provision made written submissions to a government Working Group on the Protection Process citing concerns that children felt stigmatised and were bullied in school because they live in DP. In addition, parents noted that they were unable to meet costs associated with school (McMahon Report, 2015, p. 205).

Separated children in Ireland are typically aged between 15 and 17. Therefore given their age the majority of separated children are attending post-primary schools. The State is bound by law, specifically the International Protection Act 2015 and the Child Care Act 1991, as amended, and international treaties, specifically Article 22 of the Convention on the Rights of the Child, to provide care to separated children. Tusla operates an equity-of-care principle meaning unaccompanied children receive the same care and priority as any other child in State care. All separated children except those under 12 are placed initially in residential care. The majority are then placed either in foster homes or supported lodgings. Others are placed in six bed residential units with other separated children (Ní Raghallaigh, 2013).

A number of unique circumstances which apply specifically to separated children also contribute to their vulnerably and their ability to access education. Firstly, research shows that separated children may be sent by their families whose role is to obtain residency permission and to then apply for family reunification so that they can be joined by the family left behind (Engebrigtsen, 2003, pp. 193–194). Separated children thus not only have to cope with the pressure of the family left behind, but also the pressure of obtaining status (prior to turning 18 so that they are eligible to be joined by family) so that the family can all reach Ireland.

The issue of transitioning from being a minor to an adult is also a challenge specific to separated children. Separated children are in some form of care until they turn 18. If they have status (i.e. they are a recognised refugee) they will likely receive aftercare support and typically have the option to remain in their foster family if they are pursuing third level education or other full time education (such as training or apprenticeships). They will also have access to free third level education if they fulfil habitual residence criteria (3 years continual residence in Ireland).

If they do not have status, they will transition to a form of aftercare where they will be able to access an aftercare worker, but they will be placed in Direct Provision to share a room with adult asylum seekers, sometimes far from their residential or foster home (Ní Raghallaigh, 2013; Arnold, 2013). It has been argued that this transition does not take into account the needs and often vulnerabilities of separated children (Ní Raghallaigh & Thornton, 2017) and thus preparing for this transition has proved to be a challenge for (foster or residential) carers, social workers, aftercare workers and other support services (Ní Raghallaigh, 2013; Arnold, 2013). The uncertainty of status and whether or not they will be able to access third level education, vocational education and training or apprenticeships may impact separated children's abilities to focus on their studies or indeed affect their motivation to succeed in post-primary school.

Only a small number of separated children submit applications for refugee protection each year. In 2016, just 34 separated children applied for protection in 2016. Critics argue that separated children are not facilitated to make an application until they are approaching 18 years of age, noting that this adds to the challenges associated with aging out of State care (Arnold et al., 2015; Arnold & Ní Raghallaigh, 2017). Persons without refugee or subsidiary protection or permission to remain may not access free fees at third level. The delay in submitting applications thus affects their ability to progress to third level education. Where the outcome of an application for international protection is yet outstanding, separated young people seeking asylum may not access the third level free fees scheme available to other resident young people, including Convention and Programme Refugees. Nevertheless, research indicates that separated young people with and without 'status' often thrive in education, including third level. Migration research has also pointed to obtaining better quality education as a reason for migration in the case of separated children (EMN, 2009). In addition, separated children themselves have identified education as something that is important to them (Charles, 2009, p. 44; Quinn et al., 2014, p. 57). Indeed, recent research on separated children in Ireland has identified their 'passion to succeed' (One Foundation, 2014, p. 51). In recognition of this gap in policy and the capabilities of separated children, an annual scholarship programme was established (One Foundation, 2014).

The Proportion of Unaccompanied Minors and Refugee Children in Ireland

In Ireland, most immigrant children are children of migrant workers. A relatively small number is made up of refugees, separated children/unaccompanied minors and asylum seekers. While Irish Census collects information on individuals' country of birth, ethnicity, religion and other areas, it is difficult to identify individuals' legal background in terms of immigration. In order to provide background information, Figure 9.1 shows the residence permissions of non-European Economic Area (EEA) nationals in Ireland aged 16 and over. Some 113,914 non-EEA nationals held live residence permissions in Ireland in 2015, 1% (1,430) of whom were registered for protection reasons (either with refugee status or as beneficiaries of subsidiary protection). Data on registrations by children under the age of 16 are not available.[3] While the number of persons registered in Ireland for protection reasons is small in contrast to the number of non-EEA nationals and indeed non-Irish nationals in Ireland, it would still be useful from a policy-making perspective to have access to data on children with residence permits for protection reasons in Ireland. This is one of the many data gaps that exist in the area of international protection.

Figure 9.1 also shows the number of asylum applications per year. Asylum applications increased from 2013 to 2015, decreasing in 2016. However, there is no disaggregation of children within the figures provided by the International

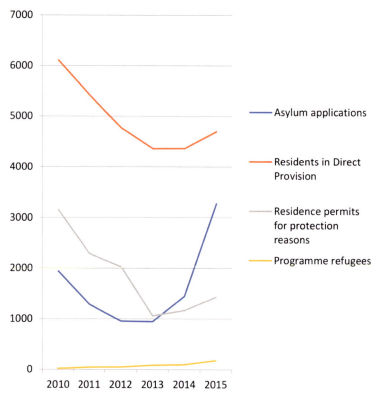

FIGURE 9.1   Overview of trends of asylum seekers and refugees in Ireland, 2010–2015 (Office of the Refugee Applications Commissioner [now International Protection Office]; Reception and Integration Agency; Eurostat; Office of the Promotion of Migrant Integration; Tusla. Note: 2012 and 2015 based on December monthly report – no annual report available on website)

Protection Office (IPO, formerly the Office of the Refugee Applications Commissioner), aside from the small number of applications submitted on behalf of unaccompanied minors. We know from national and international research in this area that children are most often subsumed within head-of-household claims and as such are less visible within asylum procedures and data. Figure 9.1 also provides figures for programme refugees who have arrived to Ireland between 2010 and 2015. The Irish Government has increased their resettlement pledge arising from their participation in the EU Resettlement and Relocation Programmes (Arnold & Quinn, 2016). The number of programme refugees has increased annually from 2013. Some 356 programme refugees arrived to Ireland in 2016, an increase of 103% from 2015 (176 persons were resettled in 2015). However, like the figures available for asylum applications, the publicly available data are not disaggregated by age. Lastly, Figure 9.1 refers to persons resident in Direct Provision. It shows that the number of residents in Direct Provision has remained largely constant since 2012/2013. On average, 1/3 of all residents in Direct Provision are children (McMahon Report, 2015).

Figure 9.2 shows that in 2016, the majority of children living in Direct Provision were under the age of 13. Only 14% of the children in Direct Provision were between 13 and 17 years old (162 out of 1,131 total minor residents). In 2016, there were 1,131 children under the age of 18 living in Direct Provision, 969 of whom were under the age of 13. As at 26 May 2017 there were a total 5,140 residents living in Direct Provision accommodation. Some 1,230 (24%) of the

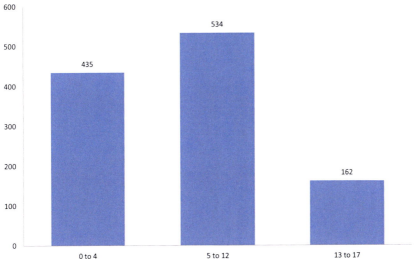

FIGURE 9.2   Age of minor residents in Direct Provision, 2016 (Reception and Integration Agency, 2016)

5,140 residents are under the age of 18. While the data on residents living in Direct Provision gives us an idea of the scale of the asylum seeking population in Ireland, it does not provide a full-picture as not all asylum seekers reside in Direct Provision.

Across the EU, separated children tend to be 16 to 17 years of age (EMN, 2009, p. 10). This is indeed the case in Ireland as well. The number of separated children referred to the Social Work Team for Separated Children (SWTSC) of Tusla between 2010 and 2015 is small (see Figure 9.2) relative to other EU Member States (EMN, 2016, p. 6) and also relative to the number of accompanied children seeking asylum and living in Direct Provision.

Much like the figures available for residents in Direct Provision, the figures available for separated children do not provide a complete picture. The data available only comprise referrals made to the SWTSC based in Dublin. No national data on separated children is collected (Quinn et al., 2014). While it is a national service for separated children, separated children may enter into and indeed remain in State care in other local health areas.

The numbers of refugees and asylum seekers in Ireland are very small compared to the wider non-Irish population/demographic. Integration supports, including educational supports, are not typically tailored to any one group of migrants and while the number of refugee and asylum seeking children is small, they do have needs that are different to other groups of migrant children and they have experiences such as torture or exposure to conflict and violence (UNHCR, 2009) that may set them apart from other migrant students. Both the educational supports available to migrant children and the particular needs and experiences of refugee and asylum seeking children were discussed above and are revisited in subsequent sections of this chapter.

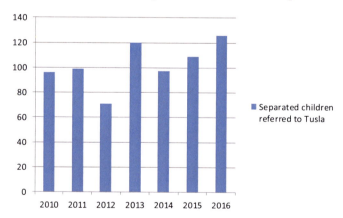

FIGURE 9.3   Separated children referred into State care, 2010–2016 (Social Work Team for Separated Children, 2017)

The section demonstrated that while data are available on refugees and asylum seekers, there are gaps concerning child refugees and asylum seekers. Due to the differences in needs and vulnerabilities between the various new communities groups and indeed amongst the refugee and asylum seeking populations, availability of better quality/more detailed data is essential for informing policy making and initial teacher education and continuous professional development.

An Overview of Irish Educational System and School-Level Supports for Immigrant-Origin Children and Youth

Types of Primary and Post-Primary Schools in Ireland

In Ireland there is now a growing body of research highlighting the impact of structural and institutional factors on social and academic outcomes of immigrant-origin students (Darmody et al., 2012a, 2012b; Devine, 2011a, 2011b). Ireland pursues a policy of mainstream integration. However, some targeted supports are available to refugees and refugee and asylum seeking children. This section outlines the educational supports available to these children.

Policy on immigrant children is part of the general education policy. The main organisation responsible is the Department of Education and Skills. National Council for Curriculum and Assessment (NCCA) is responsible for curricular content. The DES collaborates with the Department of Justice and Equality regarding the protection of immigrant children.

Education is compulsory for all children from the ages of six to sixteen or until students have completed three years of post-primary education. In practice, most 4 and 5 year olds join junior infants' classes. All children (including asylum seekers, refugees or children of migrant workers), are entitled to free primary and post-primary education. School attendance is monitored and steps are taken to combat absenteeism. The process is overseen by Tusla. There are various types of primary schools in Ireland including denominational (e.g. Catholic and Church of Ireland), multi-denominational (e.g. community national schools) and non-denominational (e.g. Educate Together). Although most schools teach the curriculum through English, there are also some Irish-medium schools. Single sex schools teach boys and girls separately. Mixed schools teach boys and girls together. In principle, the variety of school types allows greater choice for parents. In practice, however, choices are often limited by school admission policies and other structural factors (Darmody et al., 2012b). Primary schools act as 'feeder' schools for specific post-primary schools in the area. The post-primary sector comprises voluntary secondary schools (largely denominational), community schools and comprehensive schools, which are generally denominational (for example, Roman Catholic or Protestant). Vocational schools and community colleges are non-denominational.

Each school in primary and post-primary sector exercises admission policies. Schools that are over-subscribed may select their pupil intake based on these policies. In the past, certain admission criteria disadvantaged newly arrived children (Smyth et al., 2009). The recently enacted Education (Admission to Schools) Act 2016 is expected to give all children a more equal footing.

Asylum seeking children in Direct Provision accommodation centres most often attend their local school, unless such school is over-subscribed. Evaluation of primary and post-primary schools and centres of education is the responsibility of the Inspectorate, the division of the Department of Education and Skills. Inspectors also provide advice on a range of educational issues to school communities, policy makers in the Department and to the wider educational system. The Intercultural Education Strategy 2010–2015, put forward by DES aims to ensure that: 1. all students experience an education that 'respects the diversity of values, beliefs, languages and traditions in Irish society and is conducted in a spirit of partnership' (Education Act, 1998) and 2. all education providers are assisted with ensuring that inclusion and integration within an intercultural learning environment become the norm. Unfortunately, the monitoring of the implementation of the IES was impacted by the austerity measures due to the economic downturn. Integration Unit within departments were disbanded and staff re-assigned.

School-Based Support Available to Migrant Children

Academic and social integration of migrants is often influenced by issues around proficiency in the language of the receiving country. Supporting migrant children in the development of language proficiency has become an important topic in public debates and policy-making. At school level, in Ireland, main efforts focus on the provision of newly-arrived immigrant-origin children with English language skills – language of instruction in the majority of Irish schools. Additional tuition in English is generally provided by withdrawing migrant students from some subject classes (mainly Irish or Religious Education). The schools have designated language support (LS) teachers across primary and post-primary schools. The allocation of resources to employ such teachers depends on the number of students with English as a second language, with additional teaching hours made available for students with very poor proficiency or no English. According to Smyth et al. (2009), immigrant students are generally identified for language support on an informal basis. This would mainly occur when meeting the student and their parents regarding entry to the school.

The majority of primary schools with immigrant intake used withdrawal for certain class periods while almost a quarter provided intensive courses in separate base classes for immigrant children (see Figure 9.4). A similar approach could be found in post-primary schools where most schools withdrew students from class for extra support. In schools where there were full-time learning support teachers available immigrant children received intensive approach provided in separate base classes. In both sectors teachers and peers played an important role in providing language support to the new arrivals.

Over time an increasing number of higher education institutions that provide initial teacher education have focussed on increasing diversity in Irish classrooms. However, there is no specific policy for supporting teachers who teach immigrant-origin students. Existing policies concern all students, whatever their background. In addition, there is no explicit policy at the government level for (immigrant) parental involvement. It is generally up to individual schools to engage all parents, including those of immigrant background, in school activities. A study by Smyth et al. (2009) found that the majority of teachers interviewed observed that low language proficiency acted as a significant barrier to parents' involvement in school. It was also evident that schools had put some thought into how these parents could be included. Low proficiency in English became a barrier when accessing educational or general resources and supports for their children.

While additional tuition in English is the main targeted measure for immigrant-origin children, these children and young people can avail of already existing supports for all disadvantaged children. Delivering Equality of Opportunity in Schools (DEIS), the Action Plan for Educational Inclusion, is the Department of Education and Skills policy instrument to address educational

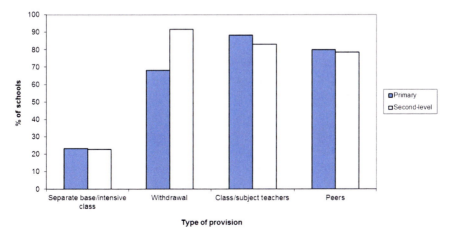

FIGURE 9.4   Type of language support provision

disadvantage. It prioritises the educational needs of children and young people from disadvantaged communities, from pre-school through second-level education (3 to 18 years). DEIS schools receive additional resources from the government. In addition, (pastoral) care teams operate in schools to offer support to students who need it. In general, the term refers to a small group of staff members with a specialist role, typically a guidance counsellor, deputy principal and/or one other member of staff, who meet weekly to address the urgent needs of a small number of students. This system is central in the whole school approach to the development and progress of each student. Smyth et al. (2009) noted that their study schools varied in the extent to which they provided specific support for immigrant-origin students: while in post-primary schools, such could avail of the support of the pastoral care team and other designated staff members, in primary schools formal support was mainly provided by student mentors, home-school links and language support teachers

Despite some progress in providing targeted support for migrant children in Irish schools in the form of additional English language provision, the recent economic downturn has resulted in significant cuts in the education sector that have also reduced initiatives supporting linguistic and socio-cultural inclusion of migrant students. The Department of Educational Skills (2012a, 2012b) has identified examples of good practice across the schools in Ireland in supporting EAL students. However, both evaluations have found scope for more effective differentiation of class programmes and lessons for EAL pupils and closer collaboration between mainstream class teachers and EAL support teachers. At post-primary level there is a need for a broader acceptance that every subject teacher is also a language teacher. Across both levels, the reports identify a need to provide further professional-development opportunities for teachers.

Martin et al. (2016, p. 2) argue that while the Irish government commits to encouraging active partnership between education providers, students and parents from new communities, the goals are focussed on English-language learning and data collection, failing to recognise the different challenges faced by other migrants, such as asylum seekers.

Some children (immigrant or not) require specialist support. If a child has a health problem e.g. hearing or speech or psychological/trauma difficulties, then experts from the local Health Board will be asked to help the child. There can be delays in obtaining such specialist help. The National Educational Psychological Service (NEPS) provides psychological services in public and private primary and post-primary schools and in related educational centres. NEPS is a service of the Department of Education and Skills (DES). The psychologists employed by NEPS are located in 8 regions throughout the country. They work directly with a number of schools and their work includes engaging in individual casework with children and young people; providing a consultation service for teachers and parents; participating in school-based projects relevant to educational psychology; promoting mental health in schools.

Career and Guidance Councillors as well as Home School Community Liaison teachers provide important support. Existing research indicates that immigrant-origin youth rely on the advice of Guidance Councillors when planning for post-school pathways as they may not be as familiar with options available compared to their native peers (McCoy et al., 2014). HSLTs provide an important link between families and schools, whereby the teacher is often seen as a 'person of trust', especially by more disadvantaged and vulnerable groups.

Specific Supports for Unaccompanied Minors and Programme Refugee Children in Ireland

In general, support for refugee and asylum-seeking students is part of a mainstream approach targeting all migrants with special or additional educational needs in the case of all other supports. There are two programmes in Ireland that target refugee/asylum-seeking children specifically. The first relates to the orientation programme provided to programme refugees and the second relates to the education service available to separated children. The separated children who avail themselves of the education services described below may be refugees or they may be asylum seekers; most often they are asylum seekers. Therefore, of the three typologies discussed above, it is only the accompanied asylum-seeking children that do not have access to a targeted education programme. In 2017, however, the Youth and Education Service (YES) for Refugees and Migrants received funding from the Dormant Account Fund to provide targeted education support to other migrant children, including those who are accompanied, irrespective of status and/or nationality. The service targets English as an Additional Language students in Dublin. While Programme Refugees and Convention Refugees ultimately obtain the same residence permission in Ireland, the support they receive upon arrival is different (Programme Refugees arrive with refugee status and Convention Refugees must first apply for asylum and await a decision on their applications) (Kinlen, 2011). It is possible to suggest that the difference in access to educational opportunities will impact upon the outcomes of Convention Refugee young people.

As discussed earlier in the chapter, separated children, like all children in Ireland, have access to mainstream education. In addition, once in the care of Tusla, they are referred to the YES for Refugees and Migrants of the City of Dublin Education and Training Board (CDETB). This service has been in operation since 2001 and operates a Migrant Access Programme. It serves as a 'reception and transition programme' to prepare separated children whose first language is not English for mainstream post-primary school. The Programme focuses not only on English language skills, but also social and cultural aspects of life in Ireland. The core modules are English, Mathematics, IT and Life-Skills. The programme runs from September to July each year. Students can enrol any time. They may transition to mainstream education at any time as well. This is based on an assessment of their individual needs, abilities and circumstances.

In addition, the Service offers after and in school supports to students who require additional support with English and other subjects. Separated children may access a School Support Programme, including a study buddy programme which operates twice a week in Dublin City centre. The students are matched with a volunteer tutor who will help them with their school work. After school and holiday camps are also provided whereby students may sign up to more intensive language support interventions. Separated children may join the Access Programme for six weeks in June and July to improve their English language skills. These additional programmes are only available to separated children who are within travelling distance to Dublin City centre. Lastly, the Service offers an outreach and drop-in service for young asylum seekers, refugees and migrants provided by youth workers. Accompanied children based may also access the drop-in service. They can support young people with school placement and course work, among other day-to-day issues.

According to Ward (2004), Reception or 'Access Programmes' are important for students with little or no English, but specialist centres need to be based within mainstream schools. The study found that 'effective schools tried to understand and work with the 'whole child' (pp. 28–31). The Convention on the Rights of the Child provides for the right to survival and development (Article 6). The UN Committee on the Rights of the Child expects States to interpret 'development' in its broadest sense as a holistic concept, embracing the child's physical, mental, spiritual, moral, psychological and social development. Implementation measures should be aimed at achieving the optimal development for all children. Ward does not define the 'whole child', but refers to the other needs separated children may have, separate to their language needs. Ward notes that separated children may benefit from reception or access programmes that also focus on school and youth culture, for example, and not just English. While separated children are provided with equitable care and access to mainstream education and have access to a targeted education support service, they face new challenges once they reach the age of 18 as discussed above.

Programme Refugees are also provided with an orientation programme on arrival. Part of the orientation programme focuses on education. Parents are provided with information about the school system. At the same time

Programme Refugee children access English language tuition and an induction programme to prepare them for entry into mainstream education via the Education and Training Boards (ETBS). A resettlement support worker is provided following resettlement in the community in order to provide on-going support to refugee families (Arnold & Quinn, 2016, p. 42).

Conclusion

Over the last decades migration across Europe has continued to increase. Consequently, the issue of offering an appropriate educational support for migrant students has been extensively debated across Europe and further afield, especially in countries with a history of immigration. However, less is known about how education systems in the 'new' immigration countries have responded to the needs of recently arrived migrants. Immigration to Ireland has increased significantly over the decades. While there was some decrease in the rate of flow of migrants during the recession but non-Irish nationals still make up 11.6% of the population in 2016, down somewhat from 12.2% in 2011 (CSO, 2017). The migrant population in Ireland is very heterogeneous, representing 196 nationalities and 182 languages (CSO, 2012). In addition, the category 'migrant children' is highly diverse including children of migrant workers as well as refugees and asylum seekers. While the majority of immigrant-origin children and young people are children of migrant workers, small but important proportion have arrived to Ireland as refugees, presenting specific needs in terms of their support in the Irish education system.

This chapter has explored the situation of refugee children and young people in the Republic of Ireland regarding policies adopted and support services available. While education at primary and secondary school level is free to all children, including those of refugee background, their needs tend to differ from those young people who have arrived with their parents from EU countries. However, the main targeted support for all immigrant-origin children is the provision of additional English language tuition. The 'one size approach' may not be the best as some migrant-origin children may have had interrupted schooling and may have experienced significant trauma. Pastoral care teams operating in Irish primary and secondary schools play an important role in identifying and addressing the needs of children that are not purely educational. These teams, in collaboration with relevant state agencies play a key role in providing multi-faceted support to refugee children. However, care and support of refugee and other vulnerable children and young people should not be the responsibility of these teams or individual teachers. Schools need to adopt a whole school approach in supporting all vulnerable children, whereby all teachers are aware of the differences between various migrant groups and how best to address their needs. Furthermore, having an intercultural policy in place that includes examples of best practice goes a long way in ensuring that the needs of different migrant groups are met at institutional level. Culturally responsive leadership and pedagogies adopted further support the school engagement of children and young people of immigrant background. While the providers of initial teacher education have introduced modules of intercultural education in their programmes, the content of such modules tends to vary, possibly resulting in uneven preparedness of young teachers entering into multicultural and pluralingual classrooms.

Notes

1 Since 2015, students who have been enrolled in school in Ireland for a minimum of five years can avail of the free frees scheme. Only two students were able to avail of this scheme in 2015.
2 Third level refers to education or training following secondary/high school.
3 New legislation has removed the exemption for those under 16 to register for residency with the Garda National Immigration Bureau (GNIB), however, the provision has not yet been rolled out (Barrett et al., 2017 p. 11).

References

Arnold, S. (2012). *State sanctioned child poverty and social exclusion.* Dublin: Irish Refugee Council.
Arnold, S. (2013). *Implementing the core standards for guardians of separated children in Europe Country Assessment: Ireland.* Dublin: Irish Refugee Council.
Arnold, S., & Ní Raghallaigh, M. (2017). Unaccompanied minors in Ireland: Current law, policy and practice. *Social Work & Society, 15*(1).
Arnold, S., Ní Raghallaigh, M., Conaty, M., O'Keeffe, E., & Roe, N. (2015). *Durable solutions for separated children in Europe: National Report Ireland.* Dublin: Irish Refugee Council.
Arnold, S., & Quinn, E. (2016). *Resettlement of refugees and private sponsorship in Ireland* (EMN Ireland. Research Series No. 55). Dublin: Economic and Social Research Institute.
Arnold, S., Ryan, C., & Quinn, E. (2018). *Ireland's response to recent trends in international protection applications* (EMN Ireland. Research Series No. 72). Dublin: Economic and Social Research Institute.

Barrett, A., & Duffy, D. (2008). Are Ireland's immigrants integrating into its labour market? *International Migration Review, 42*(3), 597–619.

Barrett, A., McGinnity, F., & Quinn, E. (2017). *Monitoring report on integration 2016.* Dublin: Economic and Social Research Institute.

Bhabha, J., & Young, W. (1999). Not adults in miniature: Unaccompanied child asylum seekers and the new U.S. guidelines. *IJRL, 11*(1), 84–125.

Charles, K. (2009). *Separated children living in Ireland: A report by the Ombudsman for Children's Office.* Dublin: Office of the Ombudsman for Children.

Central Statistics Office (CSO). (2012). *Profile 6: Migration and diversity.* Retrieved from http://www.cso.ie

Central Statistics Office (CSO). (2017). *Profile 7: Migration and diversity.* Retrieved from http://www.cso.ie

Coulter, C. (2013). *Child care law reporting project interim report.* Child Care Law Reporting Project.

Darmody, M., & Smyth, E. (2016). *Entry to programmes of initial teacher education.* Dublin: The Teaching Council & Economic and Social Research Institute.

Darmody, M., Smyth, E., Byrne, D., & McGinnity, F. (2011). New school, new system: The experiences of immigrant students in Irish schools. In Z. Bekerman & T. Geisen, (Eds.), *International handbook of migration, minorities and education – Understanding cultural and social differences in processes of learning.* London: Springer.

Darmody, M., Byrne, D., & McGinnity, F. (2012a). Cumulative disadvantage? Educational careers of migrant students in Irish secondary schools. *Race, Ethnicity and Education.* doi:10.1080/13613324.2012.674021

Darmody, M., Smyth, E., & McCoy, S. (2012b). *School sector variation among primary schools in Ireland.* Dublin: Economic and Social Research Institute.

Devine. D. (2011a). Securing migrant children's educational well-being: perspective of policy and practice in Irish schools. In M. Darmody, N. Tyrrell, & S. Song (Eds.), *The changing faces of Ireland: Exploring the lives of immigrant and ethnic minority children.* Rotterdam, The Netherlands: Sense Publishers.

Devine, D. (2011b). *Immigration and schooling in the Republic of Ireland.* Manchester: Manchester University Press.

Digidiki, V., & Bhabha, J. (2017). *Emergency within an emergency: The growing epidemic of sexual exploitation and abuse of migrant children in Greece.* Cambridge, MA: FXB Centre for Health and Human Rights, Harvard University.

Education Act. (1998). Retrieved from http://www.irishstatutebook.ie/eli/1998/act/51/enacted/en/print.html

Engebrigsten, A. (2003). The child's – or the state's – best interests? An examination of the ways immigration officials work with unaccompanied minors in Norway. *Child and Family Social Work, 8*(3), 191–200.

European Migration Network (EMN). (2009). *Unaccompanied Minors – an EU comparative study.* Brussels: EMN.

European Migration Network (EMN). (2016). *EMN annual report on immigration and asylum 2015.* Brussels: EMN.

Harrell-Bond. (2000). *Are refugee camps good for children? New Issues in Refugee Research Working Paper No. 29.* Cairo: UNHCR.

Kholi, R. (2006). The sound of silence: Listening to what unaccompanied asylum-seeking children say and do not say. *British Journal of Social Work, 36*(5), 707.

Kinlen, L. (2011). Welcome to Ireland: Seeking protection as an asylum seeker or through resettlement – Different avenues, different reception, *Refuge, 28*(2), 31.

Machel, G. (2001). *The impact of war on children: A review of progress since the 1996 United Nations Report on the Impact of Armed Conflict on Children.* London: C. Hurst & Co.

Martin, S., Horgan, D., O'Riordan, J., & Christie, A. (2016). Advocacy and surveillance: Primary schools teachers' relationships with asylum-seeking mothers in Ireland. *Race Ethnicity and Education, 2*(13). doi:10.1080/13613324.2016.1248827

Maegusuku-Hewett, T., Dunkerlet, D., Scourfield, J., & Smalley, N. (2007). Refugee children in Wales: Coping and adaptation in the face of adversity. *Children & Society, 21,* 309–321.

McCoy, S., Smyth, E., Watson, D., & Darmody, M. (2014). *Leaving school in Ireland. Longitudinal study of post-school transitions.* Dublin: Economic and Social Research Institute.

McMahon Report. (2015). *Working group to report to government on improvements to the protection process, including direct provision and supports to asylum seekers.* Dublin: Department of Justice and Equality.

Ní Raghallaigh, M. (2011). Social work with separated children seeking asylum. *Irish Social Worker.* Autumn. Retrieved from https://researchrepository.ucd.ie/handle/10197/5471

Ní Raghallaigh, M. (2013). *Foster care and supported lodgings for separated asylum seeking young people in Ireland: The views of young people, carers and stakeholders.* Dublin: HSE/Barnardos.

Ní Raghallaigh, M., & Thornton, L. (2017). Vulnerable childhood, vulnerable adulthood: Direct provision as aftercare for aged-out separated children seeking asylum in Ireland, *Critical Social Policy, 1*(19). doi:10.1177/0261018317691897

O'Connell, P., & McGinnity, F. (2008). *Immigrants at work – Ethnicity and nationality in the Irish Labour Market.* Dublin: Economic and Social Research Institute.

Ogbu, H., Brady, B., & Kinlen, L. (2014). Parenting in direct provision: Parents' perspectives regarding stresses and supports. *Child Care in Practice, 20*(3), 256.

Ogg, K. (2016). Protection from 'refuge': On what legal grounds will a refugee be saved from camp life? *IJRL, 28*(3), 384–415.

One Foundation. (2014). *2004–2013 impact report.* Dublin: One Foundation.

O'Riordan, D. (2014). Early childhood care and education policy: Ireland country note. *New Zealand Research in Early Childhood Education, 17*(21), 21.

Quinn, E., Joyce, C., & Gusciute, E. (2014). *Policies and practices of unaccompanied minors in Ireland*. European Migration Network. Dublin: Economic and Social Research Institute.

Separated Children in European Programme. (2009). *Statement of good practice* (4th ed.). Copenhagen: Save the Children.

Smyth, E., Darmody, M., McGinnity, F., & Byrne, D. (2009). *Adapting to diversity: Irish schools and newcomer students*. Dublin: Economic and Social Research Institute.

UNHCR. (2009). *Guidelines on international protection: Child asylum claims under article 1(A)2 and 1(F) of the 1951 convention and/or 1967 protocol relating to the status of refugees*. Geneva & New York, NY: UNHCR.

UNHCR. (2013). *Towards a new beginning: Refugee integration in Ireland*. Dublin: UNHCR.

Ward, T. (2004). *Education and the language needs of separated children*. Dublin: City of Dublin Vocational Educational Committee (CDETB).

Zeus, B. (2011). Exploring barriers to higher education in protracted refugee situations: The case of Burmese refugees in Thailand. *Journal of Refugee Studies, 24*(2), 256–276.

CHAPTER 10

Smoothing the Bumpy Road? An Examination of Some Targeted Initiatives for the Education of Refugee and Minority Ethnic Children and Young People in Ireland

Rory Mc Daid

Introduction

While often overlooked in academic and broader popular discourse, Ireland has a long history of inward migration, with associated ethnic, linguistic, cultural and religious diversity (Lentin, 2012; Fanning, 2018). These observations notwithstanding, it is the case that Ireland has historically been a site of outward migration, resulting in a concomitant relatively low level of ethnic diversity. The main traditional minority religious and/or minority ethnic groups, Jews, Protestants and Irish Travellers, have, historically, registered very low numbers in comparison with the dominant white settled Catholic population. For example, only 3,907 Jews were resident in Ireland in 1945 (Keogh, 1998); the Protestant population numbered 126,156, or 3.7% of the total population, in 1981 (Tovey & Share, 2003); and 30,987 Irish Travellers were enumerated in the 2016 Census (Central Statistics Office [CSO], 2017). Indeed, such was the absence of focus on this issue that the generation of ethnic based data in national instruments was not properly considered prior to 1996, and these data were gathered for the first time in the 2006 Census (King-O'Riain, 2007).

Recently, Ireland has experienced a significant surge in inward migration. Free movement of people through an expanded European Union (EU) coupled with an economic boom, often referred to as the 'Celtic Tiger,' has radically altered the ethnic diversity of the state (Coolahan, Hussey, & Kilfeather, 2012). In 2004, CSO data indicated an Irish population, which identified themselves as white at 2,983,000; black 20,000; Asian 28,000; and other 29,000 (King-O'Riain, 2007). Between 2002 and 2011, the number of minority ethnic people living in Ireland increased by 143% (CSO, 2012). Census data from 2016 indicate that 11% of the total population may be classified as 'non-Irish nationals' and 18% identify as something other than white Irish (CSO, 2017). This is as a percentage of a total population of 4.76 million inhabitants.

© KONINKLIJKE BRILL NV, LEIDEN, 2019 | DOI: 10.1163/9789004401891_010

It is important to situate this issue contextually, both with regard to levels of Irish outward migration and broader movements of globalisation. With regard to emigration, it is estimated that there are tens of millions of people worldwide who claim some Irish descent (Department of Foreign Affairs and Trade [DFAT], 2015). There is a significant historical trajectory to this number with, for example, a quarter of a million emigrants leaving Ireland in the year 1851 as a result of the famine (Beckett, 1981). Throughout the 20th century, emigration was seen as a recurrent solution to high rates of unemployment; most recently, for example, in post-2008 recessionary Ireland. While there was a general decline in population, with many previous immigrants moving to other jurisdictions, it is noteworthy that, for example, in the twelve months preceding April 2013, 50,900 Irish people emigrated (Glynn, Kelly, & MacÉinrí, 2013). From a globalisation perspective, Ireland is routinely positioned as one of the most globalised countries in the world; in 2017, Ireland ranked 2nd on the KOF Swiss Economic Institute (Konjunkturforschungsstelle) Index of Globalization (KOF, 2017), down from first place in 2015 (KOF, 2015). This index employs data across three dimensions of Globalisation: economic, social and political, and provides evidence of Ireland's deep globalisation across a broad assortment of indicators, ranging from trades in goods, international income payments, foreign direct investment, migration, international tourism, international NGOs and UN peace keeping missions (Gygli, Haelg, & Sturm, 2018). Thus, Ireland is a highly globalised nation; migration is one component of such globalisation and reactions to migration should always be contextualised within this frame of reference.

Immigration has considerably altered the ethnic profile of the population of children and young people in the country (Devine, 2011). Migrant children constituted 8% of the total child population in Ireland in 2011 (Department of Children and Youth Affairs [DCYA], 2016). Multi-ethnicity is now a fixed characteristic of the Irish school-going population. Data from 2007 indicate that 6% of post-primary and 10% of the primary pupil cohort come from immigrant backgrounds (Smyth, Darmody, McGinnity, & Byrne, 2009). Given that 24% of total births in Ireland in 2012 were to mothers who were, themselves, born outside of Ireland (Röder et al., 2014), it is projected that this percentage will continue to rise. The overwhelming majority of these children come from non-refugee backgrounds and have either come to Ireland with their parents, or have been born in Ireland, as part of broader movements of economic migration.

Refugees and Asylum Seekers in Ireland
Thus, while Ireland has become a resettlement nation, the numbers of people seeking asylum and the numbers who have been successful in this process are

particularly low, both from an absolute numeric perspective, and as a percentage of the overall population of immigrants and the population of the country. The corresponding Irish chapter in this volume highlights a dearth of robust data pertaining to the whole area of refugee and asylum seeking children and young people in Ireland. In part, this may be explained as a result of the relative recentness of refugee and asylum seeking component to migration into Ireland.

While it is accurate that Ireland accepted Hungarian refugees following the Hungarian uprising in November 1956, Chilean refugees in 1973–1974, Vietnamese refugees in 1979, members of the Baha'i community fleeing persecution in Iran in 1985 and refugees from Bosnia in 1992 (Fanning, 2012), these were always in relatively small numbers, making no real dent into the overall ethnic profile of the country. With regard to more recent arrivals, between the years 1993 and 2015, a total of 92,884 applications for asylum were made in Ireland. Of these, 21,034 were made by, or on behalf of children, establishing an adult to child ratio of 3.4:1. Official records indicate the first arrival of an unaccompanied minor into Ireland in 1996 (Horgan & Ní Raghallaigh, 2017). These numbers increased year to year, culminating in a peak of 1085 children in 2001 (Abunimah & Blower, 2010). Numbers in this category declined rapidly since 2001, with only 35 applications for asylum registered by unaccompanied minors in 2015, out of a total of 88,300 across all members of the European Union (Eurostat, 2016). This remained relatively stable in 2016, with only 34 applications received, representing 1.6% of the total number of applications received in Ireland in 2016. It is important to note that almost 90% of asylum applications made in Ireland since 2008 have been turned down (Fagan, 2018). Department of Justice and Equality (DJE) spokespersons signal that this has much to do with geographical location, and the attendant countries of origin for those seeking asylum in Ireland. It is argued that the granting of asylum to people from countries which are recognised as conflict zones tends to be much higher than for those from countries not experiencing conflict, and Ireland has had a much higher number of applications from people from the latter category.

As noted above, there is an absence of comprehensive and robust data that have been generated with and on refugee and asylum seeking children and young people. While certain academics have made a significant contribution to the field (see, for example, the work of Ní Raghallaigh (2013), Arnold (2012) and Fanning (2018, 2012), there exist considerable lacunae in our knowledge of the *educational* experiences of these youth in Ireland. This observation is consistent with international findings that refugees and education remains relatively under-researched (Pinson & Arnot, 2007). Any attempt at a composite picture must be assembled through interrogation of studies into the experiences, more generally, of immigrant students in education, which sometimes include a focus, if often tangential, to refugee and asylum seeking youth, coupled with interrogations of the wider facets of the lives of these youth, for example, in relation to housing (McMahon, 2015), the right to work (Jesuit Refugee Service [JRS], 2015) and mental health (O'Connell et al., 2016).

Meeting Basic Material Needs?

Provision for meeting the material needs of people seeking asylum is an important first component in painting this composite picture. For most asylum seekers, these needs are delivered by the state on the basis of a system known as Direct Provision. Through this, the state provides accommodation on a full board basis of three meals per day. The Direct Provision centres themselves are often hotels and holiday camps deemed economically unviable by their owners, now contracted to the Reception and Integration Agency (RIA) for the singular purpose of provision of accommodation and meals. Families, including single parents with children, are accommodated together. Single people normally share rooms, often with two or more other people of the same gender but whom they may not have known before arriving at their designated centre. Some centres cater exclusively for single males and single females respectively, others for families, with a number of centres housing a mixture of families and single people (Ombudsman, 2018). Adults and children are given a payment of €21.60 each per week, from which they must meet all other material needs. Occasional exceptional needs payments may be made available, though these are quite infrequent. Applicants are also entitled to a medical card to assist with some medical bills. Children have access to pre-school, primary and secondary education (Martin et al., 2016) and ancillary supports such as school transport on the same basis as Irish citizens (McMahon, 2015). Residents spend an average of more than four years in Direct Provision (RIA, 2013), with 27% having stayed for over six years (Lentin, 2016). This is despite the original idea that this would be limited to no more than six months (Irish Refugee Council [IRC], 2013).

This system has been roundly criticised. Fanning, for example, has described it as a 'deliberatively punitive separate welfare system' (Fanning, 2009, p. 63). It is helpful to try to understand the system within what Moreo (2012) describes as the Irish state's problematic history of refugee reception, arguing, as she does, that the state continues to disregard refugees' specific resettlement needs thus keeping them on the margins of social citizenship. Kitching (2014, p. 72) locates a more overt political goal in the system and has described the geographic isolation of Direct Provision settings from the nearby community as 'largely as a means of facilitating deportation with minimal protest' and proceeds to characterise the entire system as premised on the terror of deportation. This percipient contribution to the field helps frame the totalising experience for both adults and children of living in Direct Provision, while trying to (re)gain some degree of autonomy over their lives. In this context, Ní Raghallaigh (2013) reflects that many separated children understand that the Irish public do not want asylum seekers in their country.

Citing numerous reports into the system, Moreo (2012, p. 163) argues that the policy violates fundamental human rights to 'housing, food, work, family life, education [and] health.' A government established independent working group charged with reporting on the 'existing protection process and to recommend improvements to Direct Provision and to other supports for asylum seekers' (McMahon, 2015, p. 10) found that the settings themselves, coupled with the excessive length of time spent in the settings, exacerbated the following concerns among the residents:

– the lack of personal autonomy over the most basic aspects of their lives and daily living – cooking, going to the shops, cleaning,
– the lack of privacy and the challenges of sharing with strangers,
– the boredom and isolation,
– the inability to support themselves or their family and contribute to society in a meaningful way,
– the impact on children of being born and/or living their formative years in an institutional setting,
– the impact on parents' capacity to parent to their full potential and on normal family life,
– the loss of skills and the creation of dependency, and
– the negative impacts on physical, emotional and mental health (McMahon, 2015, p. 19).

One of the main criticisms of the system is that it was illegal for asylum seekers to work in Ireland prior to February 2018. This law was only overturned on the basis of a constitutional challenge by a Burmese asylum seeker who had spent eight years living in Direct Provision (Doras Luimní, 2018). In June 2018, the DJE announced new measures for access to the Irish labour market for international protection applicants, as part of the transposition of the EU (recast) Reception Conditions Directive. This directive lays down standards for the reception of applicants for international protection. The availability of access to paid employment is important as, in its absence, asylum seekers have been found to become de-skilled and depressed, with often negative impact on mental health (AkiDwA, 2010). The detrimental impact of this exclusion is of real importance when considering the educational experiences of the children; one of the many results is that it has undermined a parent's ability to act as a role model and/or make decisions to improve the welfare of their children (JSR, 2015). Furthermore, the ability of parents to earn will also enable them to help with costs of schooling, including co-curricular activities, such as attending after-school activity clubs or homework supports (Arnold, 2012) and has the potential to contribute to general social inclusion.

Asylum Seeking and Refugee Children and Youth in Irish Education

Certain contributions to the literature are quite positive about the experiences of asylum seeking children in Irish schools. Work with unaccompanied minors is particularly strong in this regard, demonstrating the very positive impact school and individual teachers can have on their lived experience. It has been claimed, for example, that school can very often be used to supress and distract them from past experiences or their current situation (Ni Raghallaigh & Gilligan, 2010). Vekic (2003) reports that all of the 18 participants in his study demonstrated 'extremely positive reactions' to their teachers across three inner city second level schools in Dublin. These minors were particularly observant of the caring and understanding nature of their teachers and highlighted their teachers' commitment and dedication to their work, including their work with these individual students. These observations have to be balanced, however, with other work in the field demonstrating racist and linguistic practices, and highlighting the institutionalised racism prevalent within Irish schools and assessment systems (Bryan, 2009, 2012; Devine, 2011; Fitzsimmons, 2017; Kitching, 2010, 2011a, 2011b; Mc Daid, 2011).

A number of studies have illuminated the negative consequences for the education of children living in Direct Provision. In addition to the social exclusion directly related to the economic precarity of these children, there exist structural barriers, which further contribute to isolation and exclusion. For example, owing to the regulations within the settings, children are not able to invite their friends to their place of residence for play dates or to celebrate their birthdays (Fanning et al., 2001; White, 2012). The impact of this is made depressingly clear through the contribution of one participant in a study into the system of Direct Provision when she recounts, 'I have two friends ... but I can't invite them here, it is a hotel, ... I'm not sure you would be allowed, but you can't sit in one room ... everybody else has their own house, they invite you for birthday party but here ... I feel sad' (Fanning et al., 2001, p. 43). This work proceeds to identify the following challenges to education experienced by child residents of Direct Provision:
– difficult or impossible to get pre-school facilities for children,
– lack of parental involvement with school due to the distance of the hotel from the school and parents' inability to meet transport costs,

- lack of participation in afterschool clubs or activities because of cost and transport difficulties,
- difficulty making friends,
- no space to do homework in the bedroom,
- language difficulties (Fanning et al., 2001, p. 43).

While these observations are dated, more research investigations find very little real change in the educational lives of these children (Arnold, 2012; Uchechukwu Ogbu, Brady, & Kinlen, 2014; McMahon, 2015). The disruption caused by the very act of children and families being moved from setting to setting has been criticised by Devine (2011) as being damaging to children's positioning within school. While school itself was seen as very important by parents in Direct Provision in a study by Uchechukwu Ogbu, Brady, and Kinlen (2014), these parents also reported that their children were not able to participate in school activities and tours, had worn out uniforms, lacked correct school materials and had no choice of food for school lunches. Some parents even reported that the provision of basic items such as body care essentials and underwear were also unaffordable. Such material deprivation poses a myriad of potential difficulties for children trying to negotiate their way through the education system. Arnold (2012, pp. 26–27) highlights three further areas of concern regarding education: access to education, participation and transportation. In relation to access to education, evidence is provided of some asylum-seeking parents failing to find a place for their child in local schools because of oversubscription to those schools. This occurrence must also be understood through the on-going dilemma of the management of schools in Ireland along religious lines (Faas, Darmody, & Sokolowska, 2016; O'Toole, 2015).

The fact that 96% of primary schools in Ireland are under denominational patronage is unique among developed countries (Coolahan, Hussey, & Kilfeather, 2012). While moves are being made to remove the right of schools to prioritise places for children from particular religious backgrounds in the case of a school which is oversubscribed, children of minority faiths or none may still face *de facto* religious discrimination during the school day (Fischer, 2016). Arnold highlights other elements of barriers to participation in education, many of which are rooted in material poverty, including a lack of books and other educational materials, and children arriving to school hungry and without uniforms. Under the theme of transport, Arnold refers to travel arrangements that can pose threats to the safety of children as they navigate public transport or wait for busses at inappropriate sites. She concludes that 'life in Direct Provision is not conducive to active participation in education and limits children from taking full advantage of their school experiences to reach their full potential' (Arnold, 2012, p. 26). This observation is echoed in a report for the Ombudsman for Children (2008, p. 5) with a description of asylum seeker children in Ireland as among the 'most vulnerable in our society' and an argument that they face multiple and stringent barriers to the realisation of their rights. The following section of this chapter provides a synopsis of two initiatives that seek to reduce these barriers to the realisation of the rights to education for asylum seeking children and young people. It commences with an analysis of the highly centralised structure of the Irish education system, which is particularly important when considering how educational institutions can best address what Stewart refers to as asylum seeking students' 'insatiable appetite for education' (Stewart, 2011, p. 67).

Centralisation of Education Provision in Ireland: Missing the Glocal

In order to make sense of the processes of immigration, resettlement and integration, and associated educational issues, it is necessary that the reader is made aware of relevant components of structure and organisation of the landscape of Irish education. This is important as it is, *inter alia,* this educational infrastructure that frames policy and practical responses to the education of and care for refugee children and young people in Ireland.

The education system in Ireland is highly centralised. Lynch (1990, p. 4) argues that the administrative structure of Irish education has 'much in common with other highly centralised systems.' The Department of Education and Skills (DES) sets the general regulations for the recognition of schools, prescribes curricula, establishes regulations for the management, resourcing and staffing of schools and centrally negotiates teachers' salary scales (Houtsonen et al., 2010, p. 601). While it is argued that recent restructuring has led to the creation of external agencies with responsibilities, for example, for state examinations or special educational needs (Houtsonen et al., 2010), power and decision making remains centralised within these national bodies. Thus, there are no real Local Education Authorities (LEA) or similar structures with whole scale responsibility for the management and delivery of education and schooling at a local level. The closest structure available in Ireland to that of LEAs is the 16 Education and Training Boards (ETB). However, these ETBs only have responsibility for eleven primary schools out of a total of over 3,200. The majority of the rest, as noted above, are under the management of religious authorities, while in receipt of public funding for infrastructure and salaries. Provision of schooling at second level is more disparate, though more than 50% of the almost 750 schools remain managed by religious authorities. While these will have local representation on their boards of management, they are not managed on a localised basis, and neither is there localised coordination of schools across an area. Thus it is accurate that 'our current system ensures that not only is there no institution responsible for the public of collective good, conceived of at local community level in ensuring equality of access and treatment of each children ... but high degree of competition between local schools almost ensures inequality of access and treatment' (Hannan, 1993 cited in O'Sullivan, 2005, p. 160).

Navigating this system is particularly fraught for refugee and asylum seeking populations, who very often lack the economic, social and cultural capital to enable to manage these systems and structures. This becomes apparent, for example, when considering how and when to apply for entrance to schools or how to access developmental supports such as speech and language therapy (SLT). Competent local government educational authorities *can* help in this regard, offering coordinated, holistic support and expertise which does not always reside within individual schools, while also decentralising decision making, away from national authorities who may not appreciate the complexities of local situations. The Council of Europe (COE, 2018), for example, highlight the importance of local authorities within its 47 member states in helping to protect refugee children's rights by developing services and enforcing quality standards. With regard to education, the Council argues that access to quality education and training 'are recognised as a key factor in successful integration of refugee families' (COE, 2018, p. 14). In support of this, it offers evidence of a number of effective local authority initiatives, such as the establishment of 'welcome classes,' modelled on the 'Willkommensklassen,' financed in Berlin by the local authorities, the development of the 'Open Schools' program in Athens, and the decision by the municipality of Florence to acknowledged the right of all children, regardless of legal status, to attend nursery school (COE, 2018, p. 15).

LEAS have previously played an important role in the provision of high quality education for refugee and asylum seeking children in England. The move towards the privatisation of school provision (West, 2014; Mortimore, 2013) has led to the ongoing erasure of this provision. Within the privatisation movement, schools are increasingly envisaged as self-managing businesses in competitive market places (Gunter & McGinity, 2014, p. 301), and the ideology prioritises parental choice in the selection of schools for their children (Hicks, 2015). It is well established, however, that this 'ideology of school choice obscures the negative impact of the market system on less well-resourced students' (Baker et al., 2009, p. 147); refugee and asylum seeking children may be particularly vulnerable in this regard. The former provision for education for refugee and asylum seeking children through LEAs in England offers a helpful structural model when considering best practice in this regard. A report for the Research Consortium on the Education of Asylum-Seeker and Refugee Children (Arnot & Pinson, 2005) identified good practice in LEAs when they had 'taken account of the complex needs of these pupils (learning, social and emotional needs), they foster home-school links and community links, they employ a multi-agency approach, and they all take a child-centred approach towards the education of these pupils' (Arnot & Pinson, 2005, p. 41). This was supported within a holistic model of support. These holistic models vary from LEA to LEA but are characterised by a number of important considerations, which are underpinned by the development of multi-agency structures committed to providing a comprehensive and targeted approach to the education of refugee and asylum seeking children and young people. The coordination of these activities, often through an Ethnic Minority Achievement Support worker, located within the LEA, was seen to be particularly important. Arnot and Pinson analysed these models through the lenses of policy development, organisation of the service, data collection and support services. This approach provides a helpful framework for assessing provision in other jurisdictions. The two Irish initiatives synopsised below try to pull some of these strands together. They are hampered, however, by, among other issues, the lack of a LEA structure in Ireland. It is noticeable, that in some respects, these initiatives strive to provide some of the resources and supports, which would better be served by such a structure.

Integration of Migrant Students Project

One important initiative, striving to help asylum seeking young people achieve their education potential, is the Integration of Migrant Students Project, run by the Education Service for Refugees and Migrants within the City of Dublin Education and Training Board (CDETB). This project is comprised of a Migrant Access Programme, a School Support Programme and a training/Continuing Professional Development (CPD) element. The project commenced in January 2017 and initial funding has been secured to run the project until December 2019. The author of this chapter is evaluating the project. The Education Service for Refugees and Migrants has worked with unaccompanied minors and other young people from refugee and migrant backgrounds since 2001, providing a range of education and youth support programmes, interventions and activities. While cognisant of the myriad of important approaches often necessary for supporting the actualisation of refugee and migrant youth potential (see, for example, Mc Brien, 2005; Candappa, 2000; Rutter, 2001; Stewart, 2011; Pinson, Arnot, & Candappa, 2010), this project specifically targets the teaching of English language to ensure the successful inclusion of these children and young people into post-primary education and to their integration into Irish society.

The Migrant Access Programme is a pre-immersion programme for newly arrived young people from refugee and migrant families, and unaccompanied minors, aged 13 to 18, located in Dublin city centre. It centres around three core modules: English language; Maths and Life Skills, and basic information technology (IT) skills. It also provides a range of after school activities for participating young people. The programme runs for 42 weeks a year and has on on-going intake and progression policy. The School Support Programme aims to support English as an Additional Language (EAL) learners who are in mainstream education. It supports their continued language development in order for them to engage with the school curriculum and develop, in particular, their written skills, required in Irish second level schools.

The programme is underpinned by a competency framework, which provides an overview and guide for teachers. The framework is divided into strands; four core strands of Reading, Writing, Listening and Speaking; and three additional strands of Language awareness and Literacy, Grammar and Vocabulary. Each aspect of the core strands is further comprised of four sub-strands, classified under the genres of communication as outlined in the DES Senior Cycle English curriculum: Language of Information, Persuasion, Argument and Narration. Concrete examples of 'text' are provided (for example: Diary, Instructions, Poster, Letter, Story). The examples represent Input and Output in the target language, that is, text that the learner has produced and text which the learner has received. Each text type is cross-referenced with a range of competencies to aid with planning, recording, monitoring, tracking, evaluating and reporting. The content of this element of the programme is very well thought through and rooted in a clear understanding of teaching English as an Additional Language. Another key strength of this programme is the deliberate linkage between the content and competencies delivered during the Migrant Access Programme with those embedded within the new English curriculum for the lower end of second level school in Ireland.

Koehler et al. (2018) describe three stages of education for young refugees and asylum seekers from first arrival to mainstream education in Europe. The majority of EU countries have some provision to smooth refugee children's' entry into mainstream education. These range from separate immersion classes, in a mainstream school, for up to two years, to immediate enrolment in mainstream classes with targeted language and other support. Sometimes the immersion classes are centralised into one school, with children moving to other schools following completion of their time in the immersion class, and at times these classes are held in asylum centres (Koehler, 2017). Stand-alone language or reception programmes, especially those that lie outside of a mainstream educational setting, have been subject to criticism. The main approaches to English language learning for migrants and refugee youth in Ireland continue to take place within schools. The DES provides an allocation of teaching hours or full teaching posts depending on the number of children in need of specific English language teaching. Integrate Ireland Language and Training (IILT) provided training and support materials for these teachers until 2008 when it was closed due to the aforementioned financial crisis. In its absence, there is no formalised training for teachers in Irish schools; neither have the resources been appropriately updated. As a result, there is a shortage of appropriately qualified teachers working in the field.

Schools which 'lack the specialised resources necessary to help refugee children integrate into school activities' (UNHCR Central Europe, 2016) weaken the possibilities of successful education for refugee children. While research into the benefits of models of delivery are quite rare in Ireland, one study (Vekic, 2014) found significantly better academic results for students who were placed in mainstream classes, supported by targeted withdrawal and in-class support for English language learning. This is important contextual information when attempting to evaluate the benefits of a programme such as the Migrant Access Programme. However, it should also be borne in mind that the target group for the project are children over the age of 13, and many of the participants are aged 15 and over. Students of these ages can face particular difficulties in additional language learning. Furthermore, many of these children have also experienced significant periods of disrupted education, or indeed, complete absence from formal schooling for a number of years.

The sheltered approach provided by the programme can work well to cocoon these children and prepare them to enter mainstream schooling on a more stabilised basis. An evaluation of a previous similar initiative, the Refugee Access Programme (RAP), run by the CDETB (Gannon, 2014) points to this as a particular strength of that programme. One student quoted in the evaluation claimed, '[b]efore I join the main school I spent much in the RAP Program this help me to have confident not fear on going to the different school in Ireland' (Gannon, 2014, p. 5). It is important, however, that formalised communication structures are encouraged between the MAP and schools into which the young children will go. Further developments, including team-teaching by staff across both settings, would further improve the potential of the programme.

Schools' Cultural Mediation Project

The second project, the Schools' Cultural Mediation Project (SCMP), was organised on a collaborative basis between two community initiatives in a multi-ethnic area in Dublin, and is a good example of a grass roots project utilising alternative structures in the absence of an LEA. The Education Coordinator within one of the initiatives had a key role in the development of the project concept, securing project funding and remained centrally involved in the project delivery. Two core staff were appointed to the project. The full-time Project Coordinator managed the project on a day-to-day basis. The part-time Administrator had responsibility for the implementation of the project actions. An Advisory Group was formed of key members of the local education, academic and social-activist community. They played a key role in advising on the implementation of the project and the further development of the project. This sharing of expertise and experience was central to guiding and supporting the delivery of the project (Murray, 2008).

The aim of the project was to ensure that parents of minority ethnic and minority language students in a selection of schools in Dublin's north inner city could participate in the life of the school on the same basis as any other parents and therefore become integrated in the school community. The underlying concept behind this aim was that improved parental involvement would improve the educational experiences of their children (see Wilder, 2014). The geographical area covered by the project remains one of the most ethnically diverse areas in the country.

The main objectives of the project were to:

- Translate and distribute relevant information about the education system and schools, for example national education policies, school policies, and school notices.
- Provide interpreters for oral interpretation during important school meetings such as parent-teacher meetings and one to one meetings.
- Develop a team of cultural mediators to work with schools in regard to the orientation of new families, to facilitate dialogue between families and schools on education related issues and to mediate in situations of crisis and conflict.
- Document international best practice in an attempt to devise and pilot an acceptable form of interpretive, culturally appropriate psychological assessment for minority language and minority ethnic students.

Key achievements of the project included the development of a panel of 35 translators addressing 20 languages with very quick return of documents to schools. Furthermore, a panel of 25 interpreters provided interpretation services in 20 target languages. In addition to their own professional qualifications, these professional interpreters undertook training in 'Community Interpreting in the Irish Education System.' Interpreters were available for structured Parent/Teacher (P/T) parent and staff meetings, individual meetings and pupil/teacher meetings. This service removed the need for children to take on this job in meetings between their parents and school employees, reducing the identity confusion and conflict that often arises as a result of children taking on what might be understood as parental roles within families (McBrien, 2005).

These two services enabled schools to build more positive relationships with the students and their parents. One school principal offered the following commendable evaluation of the provision: 'the translation service is invaluable. Apart from getting messages clearly to all parents, it shows them and their children that we value them and make every effort to help them integrate into the community of the school' (Murray, 2008, p. 26). The experience of parents crying at parent teacher meetings assisted by an interpreter, with a sense of relief that for the first time they could ask questions and discuss their children's progress with the teacher is a clear indicator of this sense of involvement (Murray, 2008, p. 28).

With regard to cultural mediation, the project commenced designing an applicable model for working with its target groups. A key component of this was the compilation of examples of best practice through a review of the international literature and the generation of contextual data through needs analyses with various national interest groups. The project coordinated an international conference, drawing together evidence from three different yet complementary approaches to cultural mediation from a municipality-based service in Sarcelles in Paris, an intercultural and social-based service in Charleroi in Belgium, and a school-based approach from Battlefield Primary School, Glasgow, Scotland. Cultural mediation and cultural brokering have been proven to play a significant role in directly enhancing the educational experiences of refugee populations. Additionally, through mediator-engaged work with refugee families, they offer the types of holistic supports, such as linkages with housing agencies, medical practitioners, and even the world of employment, which have direct positive impacts on children's schooling (Yohani, 2010; Pinson, Arnot, & Candappa, 2010). Thus, the SCMP made a radical difference to the lives of immigrant children and young people, including refugee children, in these schools. The framework of the project was adapted and a similar initiative founded in a separate multi-ethnic region of Dublin.

Conclusion

Education has been described as 'one of the most important paths to the structural integration of young asylum seekers and refugees' (Koehler et al., 2018,

p. 4). Education systems, schools, and teachers across the English-speaking world are encountering significant numbers of asylum seekers and refugees, and this phenomenon is only set to increase. Developing an evidence-based approach, which proactively meets the educational needs of these children and young people is one of the defining educational challenges of our time. Like all good comparative education, it is vital that the contexts (historical, geographical, financial, social etc.) of a site are well known in advance of drawing out lessons for importation. This chapter has undertaken this task, by providing key information about the manner in which migration and refugee reception has grown and developed in Ireland. The chapter has provided important education-related contextual information regarding the centralised nature of the system and has critiqued the absence of a localised education structure, which may provide a framework for supports for these children and young people in other jurisdictions. In the absence of these structures, the chapter highlights two specific projects that enrich the educational experiences of asylum seeking and refugee youth in Ireland, with the hope that this information might provide a useful basis for similar conversations and initiatives in other jurisdictions.

References

Abunimah, A., & Blower, S. (2010). The circumstances and needs of separated children seeking asylum in Ireland. *Child Care in Practice, 16*(2), 129–146.

AkiDwA. (2010). *Am only saying it now: Experiences of women seeking asylum in Ireland.* Dublin: AkiDwA.

Arnold, S. (2012). *State sanctioned child poverty and exclusion: The case of children in state accommodation for asylum seekers.* Dublin: Irish Refugee Council.

Arnot, M., & Pinson, H. (2005). *The education of asylum-seeker and refugee children.* Cambridge: Research Consortium on the Education of Asylum-Seeker and Refugee Children.

Baker, J., Lynch, K., Cantillon, S., & Walsh, J. (2009). *Equality: From theory to action* (2nd ed.). Basingstoke: Palgrave Macmillan.

Beckett, J. C. (1981). *The making of modern Ireland 1603–1923.* London: Faber and Faber.

Bryan, A. (2009). Migration nation: Anti-racism and intercultural education as symbolic violence in Celtic Tiger Ireland. In: F. Vavrus & L. Bartlett (Eds.), *New approaches to comparative education: Vertical case studies from Africa, Europe, the Middle East, and the Americas* (pp. 129–148). New York: Palgrave MacMillan.

Bryan, A. (2012). "You've got to teach people that racism is wrong and then they won't be racist": Curricular representations and young people's understandings of 'race' and racism. *Journal of Curriculum Studies, 44*(5), 599–629.

Candappa, M. (2000). The right to education and an adequate standard of living: Refugee children in the UK. *The International Journal of Children's Rights 8*, 261–270.

Central Statistics Office. (2012). *Profile 6 – Migration and diversity*. Dublin: Stationary Office.

Central Statistics Office. (2017). *Census 2016: Summary results part 1*. Dublin: Stationary Office.

Coolahan, J., Hussey, C., & Kilfeather, F. (2012). *The forum on patronage and pluralism in the primary sector: Report of the forum's advisory group*. Dublin: Department of Education and Skills.

Council of Europe. (2018). *Unaccompanied refugee children: The role and responsibilities of local and regional authorities*. Strasbourg: Council of Europe.

Department of Children and Youth Affairs. (2016). *State of the nation's children: Ireland 2016*. Dublin: Government Publications.

Department of Foreign Affairs and Trade. (2015). *Global Irish: Ireland's diaspora policy*. Dublin: Department of Foreign Affairs and Trade.

Devine, D. (2011). *Immigration and schooling in the Republic of Ireland – Making a difference?* Manchester: Manchester University Press.

Doras Luimní. (2018, July 3). *Doras welcomes significant developments on right to work and reception conditions for asylum seekers*. Retrieved from http://dorasluimni.org/right-to-work/

Eurostat. (2016, May 2). *Almost 90,000 unaccompanied minors among asylum seekers registered in the EU in 2015* [Press release]. Retrieved from http://ec.europa.eu/eurostat/documents/2995521/7244677/3-02052016-AP-EN.pdf/

Faas, D., Darmody, D., & Sokolowska, B. (2016). Religious diversity in primary schools: Reflections from the Republic of Ireland. *British Journal of Religious Education, 38*(1), 83–98.

Fagan, M. (2018, February 12). *Republic of Ireland's record of granting asylum below EU average*. Retrieved from https://www.thedetail.tv/articles/republic-of-ireland-s-record-of-granting-asylum-below-eu-average

Fanning, B. (2018). *Migration and the making of Ireland*. Dublin: UCD Press.

Fanning, B. (2012). *Racism and social change in the Republic of Ireland* (2nd ed.). Manchester: Manchester University Press.

Fanning, B. (2009). *New guests of the Irish nation*. Dublin: Irish Academic Press.

Fanning, B., Veale, A., & O'Connor, D. (2001). *Beyond the Pale: Asylum seeking children and social exclusion in Ireland*. Dublin: Irish Refugee Council.

Fischer, K. (2016). *Schools and the politics of religion and diversity in the Republic of Ireland: Separate but equal?* Manchester: Manchester University Press.

Fitzsimmons, P. (2017). *A critical analysis of standardised testing of minority language children* (Unpublished masters dissertation). Marino Institute of Education, Dublin.

Gannon, M. (2014). *The city of Dublin education and training board refugee access programme: Its impact on students accessing mainstream school and integrating into Irish society*. Dublin: CDETB.

Glynn, I., Kelly, T., & MacÉinrí, P. (2013). *Irish emigration in an age of austerity*. Dublin: Irish Research Council.

Gunter, H. M., & McGinity, R. (2014). The politics of the academies programme: Nationality and pluralism in education policy-making. *Research Papers in Education, 29*(3), 300–314.

Gygli, S., Haelg, F., & Sturm, J. E. (2018, February). *The KOF globalisation index revisited* (KOF Working Papers, No. 439). Retrieved from https://www.ethz.ch/content/dam/ethz/special-interest/dual/kof-dam/documents/Globalization/2018/KOF_Globalisation%20Index_Revisited.pdf

Hicks, T. (2015). Inequality, marketisation and the left: Schools policy in England and Sweden. *European Journal of Political Research, 54*(2), 326–342.

Horgan, D., & Ní Raghallaigh, M. (2017). The social care needs of unaccompanied minors: The Irish experience. *European Journal of Social Work*. doi:10.1080/13691457.2017.1357018

Houtsonen, J., Czaplicka, M., Lindblad, S., Sohlberg, P., & Sugrue, C. (2010). Welfare state restructuring in education and its national refractions: Finnish, Irish and Swedish teachers' perceptions of current changes. *Current Sociology, 58*(4), 597–622.

Irish Refugee Council. (2013). *Direct provision: Framing an alternative reception system for people seeking international protection*. Dublin: Irish Refugee Council.

Jesuit Refugee Service. (2015, February). *Right to work evaluating the case for extending the right to persons seeking protection in Ireland* (Working Paper). Retrieved from http://www.justice.ie/en/JELR/Evaluating%20the%20Right%20to%20Work%20-%20JRS%20Ireland%20Working%20Paper%20(submitted%2024.02.2015).pdf/Files/Evaluating%20the%20Right%20to%20Work%20-%20JRS%20Ireland%20Working%20Paper%20(submitted%2024.02.2015).pdf

Keogh, D. (1998). *Jews in twentieth-century Ireland: Refugees, anti-semitism and the holocaust*. Cork: Cork University Press.

King-O'Riain, R. C. (2007). Counting on the 'Celtic Tiger' – Adding ethnic census categories in the Republic of Ireland. *Ethnicities, 7*, 516–542.

Kitching, K. (2014). *The politics of compulsory education: Research and learner-citizenship*. London: Routledge.

Kitching, K. (2010). An excavation of the racialised politics of viability underpinning education policy in Ireland. *Irish Educational Studies, 29*(3), 213–229.

Kitching, K. (2011a). Interrogating the changing inequalities constituting 'popular' 'deviant' and 'ordinary' subjects of school/subculture in Ireland: New migrant student recognition, resistance and recuperation. *Race Ethnicity and Education, 14*(3), 93–311.

Kitching, K. (2011b). Taking responsibility for race inequality and the limitless acts required: Beyond 'good/bad whites' to the immeasurably whitened self. *Power and Education, 3*(2), 164–178.

Koehler, C. (2017). *Continuity of learning for newly arrived refugee children in Europe* (NESET II ad hoc Question No. 1). Retrieved from http://nesetweb.eu/wp-content/uploads/2016/02/Refugee-children.pdf

Koehler, C., Kakos, M., Sharma-Brymer, V., Schneider, J., Tudjman, T., Van den Heerik, A., Ravn, S., Lippens, M., Nouwen, W., Belloni, M., Clycq, N., Timmerman, C., Denkelaar, M., Palaiologou, N., & Toumpoulidis, G. (2018). *Multi-country partnership to enhance the education of refugee and asylum-seeking youth in Europe.* Bamberg: European Forum for Migration Studies.

KOF. (2015). *KOF Index of Globlization, 2015.* Retrieved from http://www.globalization.kof.ethz.ch

KOF. (2017). *KOF Index of Globalization, 2017.* Retrieved from http://www.globalization.kof.ethz.ch

Lentin. R. (2012). Introduction: Immigration in Ireland and migrant-led activism. In R. Lentin & E. Moreo (Eds.), *Migrant activism and integration from below in Ireland* (pp. 1–20). Hampshire: Palgrave Macmillan.

Lentin, R. (2016). Asylum seekers, Ireland, and the return of the repressed, *Irish Studies Review, 24*(1), 21–34.

Lynch, K. (1990). Reproduction: The role of cultural factors and educational mediators. *British Journal of Sociology of Education, 11*, 3–20.

Martin, S., Horgan, D., O'Riordan, J., & Christie, A. (2016). Advocacy and surveillance: primary schools teachers' relationships with asylum-seeking mothers in Ireland. *Race Ethnicity and Education*, 2–13. doi:10.1080/13613324.2016.1248827

Mc Daid, R. (2011). GŁOS, VOCE, VOICE: Minority language children reflect on the recognition of their first languages in Irish primary schools. In M. Darmody, N. Tyrrell, & S. Song (Eds.), *The changing faces of Ireland: Exploring immigrant and ethnic minority children's experiences* (pp. 17–33). Rotterdam, The Netherlands: Sense Publishers.

McBrien, J. L. (2005). Educational needs and barriers for refugee students in the United States: A review of the literature. *Review of Educational Research, 75*(3), 329–364.

McMahon Report. (2015). *Working group to report to government on improvements to the protection process, including direct provision and supports to asylum seekers.* Dublin: Department of Justice and Equality.

Moreo, E. (2012). The Horn of Africa people's aid: Refugee empowerment and new forms of neo-liberal rationality. In R. Lentin & E. Moreo (Eds.), *Migrant activism and integration from below in Ireland* (pp. 159–181). Hampshire: Palgrave Macmillan.

Mortimore, P. (2013). *Education under seige.* Bristol: Policy Press.

Murray, E. (2008). *School cultural mediation project Dublin 7: Evaluation report.* Dublin: School Cultural Mediation Project.

Ní Raghallaigh, M. (2013). The causes of mistrust amongst asylum seekers and refugees: Insights from research with unaccompanied asylum-seeking minors living in the Republic of Ireland. *Journal of Refugee Studies, 27*(1), 82–100.

Ni Raghallaigh, M., & Gilligan, R. (2010). Active survival in the lives of unaccompanied minors: Coping strategies, resilience, and the relevance of religion. *Child and Family Social Work, 15*(2), 226–237.

O'Connell, M., Duffy, R., & Crumlish, N. (2016). Refugees, the asylum system and mental healthcare in Ireland. *British Journal of Psychology, 13*(2), 35–37.

O'Sullivan, D. (2005). *Cultural politics and Irish education since the 1950s: Policy paradigms and power.* Dublin: Institute of Public Administration.

O'Toole, B. (2015). 1831 to 2014: An opportunity to get it right this time? Some thoughts on the current debate on patronage and religious education in Irish primary schools. *Irish Educational Studies, 34*(1), 89–102.

Ombudsman. (2018). *The Ombudsman and direct provision: The story so far.* Dublin: Office of the Ombudsman.

Ombudsman for Children. (2008). *Separated children living in Ireland: A report by the Ombudsman for Children's Office*: Dublin: Ombudsman for Children.

Pinson, H., Arnot, M., & Candappa, M. (2010). *Education, asylum and the non-citizen child: The politics of compassion and belonging.* Basingstoke: Palgrave Macmillan.

Pinson, H., & Arnot, M. (2007). Sociology and education and the wasteland of refugee education research. *British Journal of Sociology of education, 28*(3), 399–407.

Reception and Integration Agency. (2013). *Annual Report 2013.* Dublin: reception and Integration Agency.

Röder, A., Ward, M., Frese, C., & Sánchez, E. (2014). *New Irish families: A profile of second generation children and their families.* Dublin: Trinity College Dublin.

Rutter, J. (2001). *Supporting refugee children in 21st century Britain: A compendium of essential* information. Stoke-on-Trent: Trentham Books.

Smyth, E., Darmody, M., McGinnity, F., & Byrne, D. (2009). *Adapting to diversity: Irish schools and newcomer students*: ESRI Research Series 8. Dublin: ESRI.

Stewart, J. (2011). *Supporting refugee children: Strategies for educators.* Toronto: University of Toronto Press.

Tovey, H., & Share, P. (2003). *A sociology of Ireland* (2nd ed.). Dublin: Gill and Macmillan.

Uchechukwu Ogbu, H., Brady, B., & Kinlen, L. (2014). Parenting in direct provision: Parents' perspectives regarding stresses and supports, *Child Care in Practice, 20*(3), 256–269.

UNHCR Central Europe. (2016, December 14). *Educating refugee children: Building a better future.* Retrieved from http://www.unhcr.org/ceu/92-enwhat-we-docaring-for-the-vulnerableeducating-refugee-children-html.html

Vekić, K. (2003). *Unsettled hope: Unaccompanied minors in Ireland, from understanding to response.* Dublin: Centre for Educational Services.

Vekić, K. (2014). *Mono-ethnic to Multi-ethnic: Exploring change in four schools which went from mono-ethnic to multi-ethnic student populations* (Unpublished doctoral dissertation). Dublin: Mater Dei Institute of Education.

West, A. (2014). Academies in England and Independent Schools (fristående skolor) in Sweden: Policy, Privatisation, Access and Segregation. *Research Papers in Education, 29*(3), 330–350,

White, A. (2012). 'Every Wednesday I am happy': Childhoods in an Irish asylum centre. *Population, Space and Place, 18*, 314–326.

Wilder, S. (2014). Effects of parental involvement on academic achievement: A meta-synthesis. *Educational Review, 66*(3), 377–396.

Yohani, S. C. (2010). *Challenges and opportunities for educational cultural brokers in facilitating the school adaptation of refugee children* (Working Paper Series, WP10-05). Thousand Oaks, CA: Prairie Metropolis Centre.

CHAPTER 11

An Underclass of 'the Underclass'? Critically Assessing the Position of Children and Young Refugees in the UK Educational System during a Time of Austerity

Helen Murphy

Introduction

The political and social transformations of nation states in the twentieth century, coupled with the impact of globalisation, have resulted in a process of forced migration as economic and political crises impact citizens. Populations flee from the tyranny of internal wars, processes of ethnic cleansing, and purges against religious and cultural sub-groups. Freedman (2007) comments that economic dislocation, political oppression, and infractions against human rights are intimately connected. Minority groups that were previously exploited and indentured to sustain colonisation in the last century are now aligned with current refugee populations, internally displaced from their home countries and then dependent on other state's refugee policies and international dictates on human rights (Castles & Miller, 1998).

Such movements of people seeking peace and prosperity have produced a 'refugee problem' in the UK with threats and demands on national resources, aided and re-enforced by negative and inflammatory political and media commentaries (for example, see the BBC News, 2015; Daily Mail Comment, 2016). This is despite the fact that immigration in the UK has little impact on wage deflation or decreasing employment opportunities for home nationals (Trades Union Congress, 2007). Compared to Germany, France, Spain and Italy, the UK has some of the harshest immigration policies in Western Europe (The Guardian, 2017). The UK does not allow asylum seekers to work, offers less financial aid, and usually provides sub-standard housing. The UK has the lowest rate of asylum approvals, forcing asylum seekers into homelessness and destitution because of bureaucratic delays in their applications (ibid.).

In the UK, there is no set of *unique educational* government policies for children and young people[1] who are seeking asylum or who have refugee status. It the responsibility of the local authority and local schools to ensure that

---

© KONINKLIJKE BRILL NV, LEIDEN, 2019 | DOI: 10.1163/9789004401891_011

schooling is delivered to children of compulsory school age. This includes the assignment and delivery of education to refugee children.[2] Such mandatory statutes may be in contrast to the concerns and advice of the UN Committee on the Rights of the Child (2008). They note that, generally, refugee and asylum-seeking children have not been fully able to access and enjoy their rights to education. Setting gold standards, pushing for further civil liberties for refugee children and/or increasing their quality of life and life chances through education is not a national political agenda item in the UK. The UK government has played a limited role in ensuring that refugee children get a better deal in the educational context.

The purpose of this chapter is to contextualise the position that refugee families, children, and young people find themselves in when they arrive in the UK with specific reference to the position education holds in refugee narratives. UK resettlement policies will be outlined alongside the initiatives advocacy groups and leading charities programs adopted in relation to looking after this vulnerable group of children and young refugees across the UK. The chapter will then pay particular attention to the psychological needs of refugee children during this transitional process and close with a commentary on the socio-political position refugee children and young people find themselves/ are located in during this period of austerity in the UK's history. A set of recommendations for educational practices for child refugees and young people in the UK is included.

Referencing the Narrative: Recent UK Responses to Displaced Peoples

Successive UK governments have accepted the plight of (individual) refugees who have fled from countries as a result of political persecution. To do so was to be seen by other nation states as politically liberating, and the UK was seen as pursuing a neo-liberal agenda. This involved *not* colluding with enemy nation states and was bolstered by British conceptions of liberty, democracy, and free speech. Marfleet (2012), however, argues that this led to selective inclusion of certain types of immigrants and produced a narrative of who is a 'genuine' refugee (e.g. one single political asylum seeker) and who is not. The 'genuine refugee' may be differentiated from large groups of individuals who escape from their home countries *en masse* avoiding death and seeking sanctuary in more economically well off and more peaceable societies. Interestingly, Korac-Sanderson (2018) asserted that in current political discourses, borders are described as 'vulnerable' but fleeing populations are not. Korac-Sanderson noted that the agency of the victimized is symbolically represented in the long road trails of asylum seeking people depicted in visual images from the media in the UK. Despite the moral panic that accompanies such images in the UK, most asylum cases are denied. Only 1 in every 5 immigration applications is approved with only 1 in every 3 appeals being successful (BBC News, 2018).

Nonetheless, an expansion of the Vulnerable Persons Relocation (VPR) scheme was announced by the UK government in 2015 (Department for Communities, 2017). This was specifically created to help re-settle up to 20,000 Syrian refugees as a result of conflict in Syria and the flight of its peoples across refugee camps in Turkey, Jordan and Lebanon (Department for Communities and Local Government, 2015). It was seen as a government policy on significantly improving the life chances and widening opportunities for some refugee populations. The fundamental difference between the VPR scheme and the previous Humanitarian Protection scheme is welfare based, with the VPR scheme giving full refugee status for 5 years with full access to employment rights and access to public welfare funds. The opportunity to be able to work and improve family circumstances was seen as motivational, self-reliant and self-determining when adapting to new cultures and lifestyles, and refugee people could also use the skills that they brought from their home country. Notably, Gupta (2012) comments that there are two different types of immigrants: those that are visible in that they are 'state documented'; and those who decide to remain 'invisible' and go underground, seeking to not engage in un-assured asylum processes and decisions. This renders them safe from deportation but vulnerable to violence, disease, and slavery.

Referencing the Narrative: Experiencing Education in the UK as a Child Refugee

Specific issues refugee children and young people face in accessing education include the lack of availability of school places for refugee children and young people, transition issues in Year 11, and the reluctance of schools to take in pupils in the middle of term time (Brownlees & Finch, 2010). Even though refugees of school age experience such issues in accessing education in the UK (Dennis, 2002; Doyle & McCorriston, 2008), refugee children tell us that education is a priority for them (Brownlees & Finch, 2010; Stanley, 2001). Developing friendships, meeting peers, and becoming familiar with local cultures through school attendance reduced feelings of social isolation and helped with psychological health for refugee children (Chase, Knight, & Statham, 2008).

Furthermore, children and young people who are refugees are often viewed predominantly through this status label rather than being seen as children who need an education (Pinson & Arnot, 2010). However, the success with which child refugees are able to successfully adapt to their new education is heavily dependent on the ways in which their whole family grouping adapts to the new schooling experience (Hart, 2009). In the UK, charitable organisations are more capable of identifying gaps in provision and push forward progress on educational policies and standards to ensure that such a vulnerable learner group experiences a quality of life. For example, the Supporting and Mentoring in Learning and Education (SMILE) project was set up by the UK Refugee Council and funded by the UK Department for Education in 2008 (Walker, 2011).

The SMILE project focused on the educational and social needs of refugee children and young people and carried out an assessment of befriending and mentoring activities provided by volunteers to the young refugee population. It also assessed the impact of educational talks in schools that raised awareness of refugee issues in ten schools across England (Greater London, Yorkshire and Humberside, and in the Midlands). The research produced information about volunteer motivations, expectations between refugees and volunteers, and how volunteers and refugee children and young people formed goals together (see also Hall, 2003). However, the overarching findings delineate the series of benefits that child refugees and young people experienced as a result of the befriending and mentoring project. This included help in accessing education, assistance with language, boosting young people's confidence and supporting a range of pastoral care issues (see Table 11.1 for a full account). Initiatives and research projects such as this tell us the intensity of support that is needed for child refugees and young people in the education system to allow them to thrive and flourish.

While the SMILE project was successful for the refugee children and young people involved, other refugee groups not participating in such projects may encounter more difficulties. Confusion and/or lack of knowledge about schools and schooling can determine early impressions of education in the UK and inductions into the UK education process can be negligible (Geraghty, McStravick, & Mitchell, 2010). There may also be segments of the curriculum that may not necessarily be sympathetic to the position of refugee children and young people. Sempowicz, Howard, Tambyah, and Carrington (2017) highlighted activities in a common curriculum that would prove difficult for children who had been adopted from overseas. The authors argue that teaching units that focus on family and family origin in a settled home population may be less likely to trigger emotional responses and may minimize social harm compared

TABLE 11.1   Synopsis of benefits of the UK Refugee Council SMILE programme for child refugees and young people

Help in accessing education:	Volunteers were largely successful in helping child refugees and young people begin school within 3 months of the start of the mentoring relationship. Mentors would contact schools, help with application forms, attend school interviews with the mentees, be an advocate for the mentee and help with local area orientations. This made finding a way through an unfamiliar a English education system much easier and more transparent for mentees coming from different countries.
Help achieving in education:	Settling into school settings, interacting with peers and understanding how education in a UK school is delivered were all-important forms of support that the mentors were able to provide for child refugees and young people.
Assistance with language skills:	Mentees reported that developing their skills in English was more achievable with the help and support of mentors in the SMILE programme. Initially, interpreters were used in the early stages of the mentor-mentee relationship but this diminished as the relationship grew. Mentees appreciated the opportunity to speak to the mentor on a one-to-one basis, so gathering skills and confidence in a supported manner.
Confidence building:	Building up social and educational capital positively impacted on how mentees felt about themselves. Young people felt less isolated and began to build up resilience through developing friendship networks and social support as their language abilities and opportunities for social interaction improved.
Social integration:	Mentors introduced and explained aspects of UK culture that mentees were unfamiliar with. This allowed mentees to feel more socially secure and become more socially integrated with home populations.
Alleviating loneliness:	Mentees who engaged in longer-term mentor-mentee relationships had strong attachments as they had a consistent caring adult in their lives. This was especially salient for refugee children who had become separated from their parents and/or family in the process of fleeing and seeking safety. Moreover, mentees did not feel 'judged' by their mentors. This was in contrast to the adults/Home Office officials they came across as a result of the UK asylum seeking process.

(cont.)

TABLE 11.1   Synopsis of benefits of the UK Refugee Council SMILE programme for child
refugees and young people (*cont.*)

Pastoral care:	The mentors became almost like parents according to the mentees and helped mentees feel more comfortable living in an unfamiliar country. Mentors would help child refugees and young people with everyday activities that went beyond the educational sphere e.g. going on trips out.
Support to families:	The mentor became part of the extended family for mentees as mentors often visited the family home and would get to know the rest of the mentee's family.
Interaction with Social Workers:	Through regular weekly contact, the mentors fulfilled a role that statutory services could not because of the nature of that role. The child refugee and young people's social worker recognized and appreciated that. Additionally, when frictions arose between young people and statutory services, mentors were able to advocate for the mentees.
Recreational activities:	Mentors helped support refugee children and young people by providing structured (and fun) UK based cultural activities when not in educational settings e.g. visiting Shakespeare's house in Stratford-upon-Avon, going along to the local cricket club, going to the cinema and to firework displays.

to a more vulnerable population of adoptees. Similarly, refugee children and young people may have issues in openly discussing autobiographies, family trees and personal timelines. Discrimination and racism at school are common against children who are from different racial and ethnic backgrounds, and refugee children who disclose their stories and their family backgrounds may feel especially vulnerable (Correa-Velez, Gifford, & Barnett, 2010). Sempowicz et al. (2017) recommended that teachers be sensitive and flexible in their approach in responding to the educational needs of such vulnerable groups of children and work with families and caregivers to help support students.

Referencing the Narrative: Delivering Education to Children and Young Refugees – Three Case Studies across the UK

Here, we consider a variety of case studies that deal with some of the issues arising in the dispersal of refugees for local authorities (the London case);

document issues that face regional governments, communities and schools in the UK (the Northern Ireland case); and finally, appreciate and begin to comprehend the demands that young refugees face when they choose to take part in higher education in a UK setting (the university case).

The London Case

Feldman (2012) comments that over a 20 year period from 1986–2006, London's foreign born population doubled from 1 million to 2 million. Over the same period, the population base also became more diverse, with 50% of immigrants coming from six principle countries. By the close of 2006, some 50% of immigrants came from 15 different countries. Ryan, D'Angelo, Sales, and Roddriguez (2010) carried out a review of issues newly arrived migrant and immigrant children and families face in London schools and colleges. Following a range of case study interviews with a set of 10 parents from diverse ethnic backgrounds (Afgani, Albanian, El Salvadorian, Indian, Iraqui, Nigerian and Black-British) as well as key informants across eight London boroughs, the researchers produced a set of key findings. This included the acknowledgement that London schools had more diverse school population samples due to the more random spatial dispersion of the current refugee and immigrant population.

Previously, migrant groups had tended to settle in specific geographical areas across the capital allowing school expertise to develop in community settings. As a result of more random dispersal of newly arrived migrant families, delivery of services is more complex and resource intensive. The financial, social, and educational support for this increased and more varied population group comes from local London Boroughs and the Greater London Authority (GLA). The context of the global financial crisis in 2008 and the ensuing periods of austerity, cuts, and under-funding in UK public services and public bodies were initiated (Financial Times, 2017); and, hence, conflicts and tensions about the 'cost of immigration' rose. As a counter, Ryan et al. (2010) recommended that community organisations play a more significant role in providing help, signposting, advice, and translation services in relation to overviews of the unfamiliar education system that newcomer families and children encounter in the UK.

The Northern Ireland Case

Northern Ireland, the smallest populated region of the UK, accepted a total of 632 Syrian refugees between December 2015 and August, 2017, as part of the VPR scheme mentioned previously (Department for Communities and Local Government, 2015). The Northern Ireland Assembly created a strategic planning group (led by the Northern Ireland Executive Office) and an operational planning group (led by the Northern Ireland Department for Communities) to accommodate the needs of the Syrian refugees. English classes were arranged through the Northern Ireland Department for the Economy and held in regional colleges across the Province (ibid.). The Northern Ireland Office acknowledged the vulnerability and complex needs of this population upfront and included a good practice charter covering adult and child safeguarding needs in the briefing paper.

However, as clean as the Department for Communities briefing report reads, this is in contrast to the lived experience of the refugees and asylum seekers who have been resettled in Northern Ireland. Murphy and Vieten (2017) collected information about asylum seekers and refugees' experiences of resettlement there. The authors recommended improvements in sub-standard housing and accommodation for a Northern Ireland refugee population as well as improved access to mental health services and substantive legal advice to pursue claims of asylum. According to Murphy and Vieten's[3] research findings, the ESOL (English for Speakers of Other Languages) strategy was found to be wanting and did not lead to the much desired level of English language skill that was needed for employment.

However, at the school level, one particular initiative has been noted in the Northern Ireland context. While the majority of schooling in Northern Ireland is segregated along religious lines, a small sector of education (circa 7% in 2014/15) is delivered through integrated schooling where Protestant and Catholic children attend the same school (Department of Education, 2015). In one particular integrated post-primary setting in Belfast, the Northern Ireland Council for Integrated Education (NICIE) and the Integrated Education Fund (IEF) worked together to develop an initiative that was designed to understand the issues that young people from newcomer and ethic minority communities faced (IEF & NICIE, 2010). This involved considering firstly, how educational outcomes could be improved for newcomer and ethnic minority students; secondly, identifying the range of stakeholders involved and how these stakeholders could be engaged; and thirdly, how to garner interest in this group from the community at large (ibid.).

The Belfast integrated school held a 'Citizens' Panel' where students from ethnic minority groups gave powerful accounts of their the prejudices they faced at school. This was delivered to a variety of invited stakeholders – other students from the school, students from other integrated colleges, parents, community groups and youth workers and local government and police. There were a series of recommendations at school and community level including engaging in projects to counter racist attitudes and behaviour, inviting specific cultural groups into schools to promote inter-cultural understanding and developing community programmes which would help integrate individuals and families into the home culture (see Table 11.2 for a detailed list of recommendations). The outcome of the Citizens' Panel supported the UK National Children's Bureau (NCB) position that schools should have safe spaces to speak about different ethnic groups; that teachers need support in understanding the needs of such groups, including understanding racism; and that media sources are responsible in delivering clear, unprejudiced messages about ethnic minorities (NCB Northern Ireland & ARK Young People's Life and Times, 2010).

The University Case

Universities UK International (2018) and The Refugee Support Network (n.d.) state that global figures suggest that only 1% of refugees get to university. In parallel, there appears to be little systematic research on the experience of refugees who enter higher education in the UK and this is coupled with the

TABLE 11.2   School and community recommendations from the Citizen's Panel
(IEF & NICIE, 2010)

School level recommendations

- Projects to counter racism and prejudice should take place at primary school level
- More exposure to positive role models through the sharing of personal stories
- Regular celebrations of difference (e.g. cultural festivals, cultural events, cultural holidays)
- Greater variety of after school clubs for integration of pupils
- Expansion of residential weekend activities to encourage team building and integration
- Continue to host forums such as the Citizen's Panel
- Invite local culturally specific organisations into schools to raise awareness
- Engage in more youth related work and make wider community links

Community level recommendations

- Develop community led programmes and awareness campaigns which facilitate integration
- Eradicate racist graffiti in the local community
- Develop media campaigns which convey positive messages of integration and cultural diversity
- Communicate services and products which reach out to a diverse community audience

practice of refugees' previous qualifications going unrecognized or being dismissed (Houghton & Morrice, 2008; Waddington, 2005). However, in the UK, once individuals have been granted refugee status, they can attend college and university on the same par with UK citizens. Refugees are seen as 'home students' and subject to 'home student fees' and given access to the higher education loans system (Student Finance England, 2018).

Morrice (2009) noted that once refugees enter the UK higher education system, they are not treated as a special group of students with differing needs and are, therefore, not tracked, making their experiences and journey more difficult and complex. In a comprehensive analysis of the refugee experience in higher education, Morrice (2013) established the notion of a series of conflicted subject positions refugee students might hold as they negotiate their university journey. Morrice (2013) points out that refugees who become students should not be treated as a homogenous group but that each individual student refugee will have their own particular cultural capital that they bring to the university setting. This is, firstly, in contrast to the *deficit-exclusion* subject position that refugee students initially experience, and secondly, in contrast to the desirable recruitment of international students who hold a *profit-inclusion* subject position. As a product of such social inequalities and the lack of cohesive social policy initiatives, refugee students are rendered invisible and marginalized in university systems (Fraser, 2007).

To help overcome this, Universities UK International (2018) suggest that higher education institutions audit, plan, set objectives and implement particular strategies for refugee students. These can include issues around access and inclusion; involvement of national and local refugee organisations; offering advice and information to refugees students as part of a more widespread package of support given to vulnerable student groups; being aware of the financial impact of university funded bursaries on refugees students Home Office payments; and delivering access to education through transnational and distance learning modes. In a similar vein, Universities UK International suggest that higher institutions host displaced and 'at-risk' faculty members in UK home institutions.

Extending the Narrative: What Is It Like to Experience Education in a Site of High Intensity Conflict?

The civil war in Syria began in 2011 and Save the Children (2016) carried out 22 focus groups in besieged areas of Syria. The aim was to understand the impact of war had on being a child growing up and being at school in these conditions. At the same time, the UN Office for the Co-ordination of Humanitarian Affairs (UN OCHA) (2016) reported that the number of schools operating in Syria had fallen with, for example, only 1 in 4 schools operating in Moadamiyeh. Textbooks, desks, and stationary were scarce and there were little resources for teaching. School buildings had no heating source and constant power cuts were experienced. There were shortages of teachers with reports of one in five teachers being killed (ibid.). Lessons took place in underground bunkers and were delivered to children who were malnourished and sleep deprived. There were also issues with travel when students wanted to sit official state exams.

Using focus group methodology, Save the Children (2016) interviewed 91 adults (parents and professionals people such as doctors, nurses and teachers) as well as 35 children aged 10–16. Twenty-five in-depth interviews were also conducted with staff that worked in 9 Syrian aid agencies as well as 10 civilians living in the besieged communities. All of the adult group discussions reported that there were significant differences in their children's behaviours during the siege period. This included observations of increased aggression, increased fear, and instances of depression and withdrawal. Local aid agencies also had to provide advice to families about child nocturnal enuresis and children experiencing nightmares.

In half the focus groups, participants reported that children were unable to attend school during the sieges because of the lack of facilities and the lack of secure living conditions during the siege/conflict in Syria. These participants also reported that the children were afraid to go to school because of the widespread bombing and shelling. Furthermore, over a third of the adult participants believed that the quality of schooling had worsened compared to before the siege. Nonetheless, participants emphasized the importance of schooling as it offers children a sense of routine and normality whilst also, more specifically, preventing boys from being recruited into militarised groups and allowing girls to choose options other than marriage.

Save the Children (2016) noted that the school curriculum in besieged Syria has expanded to include psychological support services to help them deal with war trauma as well as providing structured activities (e.g. puppet theatre, singing, painting and sport such as football) to help with the development of social skills. We can conclude that as a result of high intensity warfare, schooling and education are severely disrupted. Despite this, education remains high in terms of people's values. Furthermore, in this case, war has brought children more directly into contact with psychological interventions as a result of the distress and chaos created by political and religious conflicts. These experiences of education in a war site would contrast sharply against experiences of education where conflict is absent.

Extending the Narrative: Do All Child Refugees and Young People Arrive in the UK with Similar Experiences of Education from Their Homelands?

Refugees will have specific educational histories with particular educational needs, some with little experience of schooling and some with an extensive educational history, but all of their schooling will be disrupted as a result of their migrant status. Before the war broke out in Syria in 2011, nearly all Syrian children were enrolled in school and the literacy rates were 95%. Since then, almost a third of school age children have not attended school and in some areas, only 10% of children still attend school (UN OCHA, 2017). When Save the Children asked Syrian children, aged 15–17, how their lives could be improved to make them feel happier and safer, they wanted to attend school regularly and safely (McDonald, 2017).

In contrast, only 2% of children from Southern Sudan have attended a primary school (Victorian Foundation for Survivors of Torture, 2005) and the school infrastructure in Southern Sudan is negligible as a result of one of the worst humanitarian situations in the world (Milner & Khawaja, 2010). The Federal Ministry of Education (2004) stated that universal primary education had not been achieved, primary schools were not adequately resourced and education delivery was biased towards boys. Only 10% of teachers had formal teaching qualifications (ibid.). Educational issues are further compounded for Sudanese refugees as their communication skills are based on an oral culture as opposed to a highly literate print based culture (Burgoyne & Hall, 2005; Sellars & Murphy, 2018).

As outlined above, comparing such differing experiences of education between children from Syria and children from Southern Sudan highlights the complexity of needs that refugee children will have as they arrive in a new country such as the UK. In parallel, local authorities would have to understand and/or appreciate the specific social, cultural, economic, religious and political backgrounds of refugee children and young people in order to appreciate and work with them in a pedagogical manner that brings out an optimal educational endpoint. The Victorian Foundation for the Survivors of Torture (2016) recommends a whole-school approach to support such learners. This involves meshing school policies and practices, the curriculum, teaching and learning, the school's organization, ethos and environment, and establishing partnerships with parents and caregivers and outside agencies.

The Complexities of the Narrative: The Psychological Impact of Conflict on Child Refugees and Young People and How to Ease Trauma in Family and School Settings

Both adult and child refugees may arrive in the UK having already experienced a degree of loss of homeland, culture and family because of the situation they find themselves in. In addition to this, civil disorder, death, torture, rape, destruction of homes and internal displacement are elements of war and civil conflict that contribute to trauma in adult and child refugees (Sousa, Kemp, & El-Zouhairi, 2014). Dejong, Komproe, and Van Ommeron (2003) estimate that between 35–50% of people who are exposed to political violence will become mentally distressed. Trauma suffered in the pre-migration phase often manifests itself in the post-migration phase, especially if individuals have experienced more than three counts of trauma (Steele, Silove, Phan, & Bauman, 2002). This may result in Post-Traumatic Stress Disorder (PTSD) and individuals experiencing intrusive thoughts, flashbacks, a numbing of emotions and/ or hyper-arousal as well as some evidence of cognitive impairment due to the distress they are suffering (National Institute of Mental Health, 2015).

The experience of living in high intensity conflict also usually leads to broken and fragmented family units. Adult refugees may experience a loss in the sense of self, and a lack of purpose and meaning (Schweizter, Melville, Steele, & Lacherez, 2006). This inevitably has a major impact on children and young people as the family unit operates to provide physical, emotional and psychological support to the more vulnerable members and may manifest in the post-migration setting. Refugee children and young people may appear sad, become withdrawn, have difficulties with concentration, be anxious and have trouble sleeping (German & Ehntholt, 2007). In the school setting, refugee children and young people may have difficulty adjusting to a UK school culture, finding it alienating, and they may feel isolated as they attempt to establish peer relationships with individuals from a different culture and background (German, 2004).

Children who are seeking asylum or are refugees tend to be at higher risk in suffering from poorer mental and physical health (Fazel & Stein, 2003). Psychologists in the UK have responded to this by conducting standard clinical interviews as well as using screening measures suitable for children suffering from anxiety and depression (The British Psychological Society, 2018). Psychologists initially help parents support their children but can also work at a school system level by facilitating staff-pupil discussion groups in schools (ibid.). Group interventions follow recommendations by the Children and War Foundation. These concentrate on developing coping strategies to help refugee children and young people deal with daily stressors (Children and War Foundation, 2018). Early and swift entry into schooling systems is also recommended, as this can become a protective factor for child refugees and young people (Crul, Schnieder, & Lelie, 2012; Crul, 2016). Psychologists also clearly noted that 'carers, teachers and others have an important role in helping young people learn the rules of everyday living that they may otherwise take for granted' (The British Psychological Society, 2018, p. 35).

While some theorists and critics have argued that professional psychologists in schools have over-medicalised, over-therapised and over-psychologised vulnerable or at risk children (see, for example, Barker & Mills, 2018; Harwood & Allan, 2014; Kristjánsson, 2009), other charitable organisations have embraced the opportunity to use the school as a setting for recovery work. The Refugee Education Support Program in Victoria, Australia assists schools and community organisations to help meet the educational and psychological needs of refugee children and young people (Victorian Foundation for the Survivors of Torture, 2016). The recovery programme, through establishing specific recovery goals (safety, dignity, value, meaning and purpose) for refugee children and young people works at the individual level and deals with core components of the trauma reaction in a local educational setting. This may lessen the stigmatisation of psychological health issues for child refugees and young people and may lessen the impact of trauma on wellbeing and learning.

However, once settled in school, refugee children and young people experience routine, a sense of security and containment as well as having opportunities for socialisation with their peer group (Taylor & Sidhu, 2012). This does not underplay the importance of the family dynamic in each migration phase. Strong family units can be a buffer in the stressful pre- and post-migration transition for refugee children and young people, providing a source of cultural and social capital through strong attachment and social bonds (Sonderegger, Barrett, & Creed, 2004). Montgomery (1998) comments that strong family cohesion predicts better learning outcomes for child refugees. This is, of course, compromised if offspring do not arrive in the host country with both parents. Nonetheless, resilience can be high in children in the post-migration phase and should not be under-estimated or overlooked (Rutter, 2003).

The Complexities of the Narrative: Legalities of Refugee-Ship as a Child or Young Person

Governments, and specifically the UK government in this case, react and create new laws and policies in line with the demands they see arising within their nation states. The most recent policy development for unaccompanied asylum-seeking children in the UK was the National Transfer Scheme (Part 5 to the Immigration Act, 2016), presented in July 2016 (UK Department of Education and the Home Office, 2018). This allowed for a more flexible allocation of such asylum-seeking children to be placed in local authorities other than the one in which they first presented. Therefore, children could be sent to specific local authorities that had more capacity, funding and resources compared to the source local authority on first registration.

This National Transfer Scheme, of course, is simply one aspect of the legal framework that encases the child refugee (see UK Home Office, 2017). The legal framework draws on both UK and international and European law (see Table 11.3). This includes the primary source of legal protection for refugees, the 1951 United Nations Convention Relating to the Status of Refugees as well as the 1967 Protocol. The 1989 Convention on the Rights of the Child, an international treaty, in force since 1992 is also included. The European Convention on Human Rights (1950) and the Human Rights Act, 1998, ensure that public authorities carry out their duties in relation to human rights legislation.

TABLE 11.3   Laws pertaining to child refugee status in the UK (UK Home Office, 2017)

International Laws
- 1951 United Nations Convention Relating to the Status of Refugees
- 1967 Protocol
- The 1989 Convention on the Rights of the Child
- The European Convention on Human Rights, 1950
- Human Rights Act, 1998

European Legislation
- Dublin Regulation, 1990
- Qualification Directive, 2011

Domestic Laws
- The Immigration Act, 2016
- Section 55 of the Borders, Citizenship and Immigration Act, 2009
- UK Children's Act, 1989 including Social Services and Well-being (Wales) Act, 2014, the Children (Scotland) Act, 1995, and the Children (Northern Ireland) Order, 1995

European legislation encapsulates the Dublin Regulation (the appropriate member state taking appropriate action for looking after unaccompanied children) and the Qualification Directive (harmonization of treatment of refugees across the European Union).

Domestic law directives that involve children include, as mentioned above, Part 5 to the Immigration Act, Section 55 of the Borders, Citizenship and Immigration Act, 2009 which safeguards and aims to promote welfare for asylum-seeking children. This is matched with the Asylum Seekers (Reception Conditions) Regulations 2005 that asserts that the families of unaccompanied children must be traced. The overarching UK Children's Act, 1989, incorporates local authorities in England to be duty bound to safeguard and assess children and provide appropriate service provision. The Welsh equivalent is the Social Services and Well-being (Wales) Act, 2014; in Scotland it is currently the Children (Scotland) Act (1995); and in Northern Ireland, the Children (Northern Ireland) Order, 1995.

However, while the policies exist in law, how do children live out the social policy experience of refugee-ship? And how do we place education in the overall narrative of being a refugee? Children going through the UK asylum process are subject to a number of difficult processes if they apply for asylum either as an independent child or an unaccompanied child (Coram Children's Legal Centre, 2017). Children are photographed and fingerprints of children over the age of 5 are taken. The fingerprints are shared with a European Union database. Children are subject to a welfare interview. A legal representative usually attends the welfare interview and children are asked about their family history and circumstances, how they travelled to the UK, and why they have come to the UK (ibid.).

Alemaychu and Devici (2009 as cited in Devici, 2012) found that some children felt overwhelmed by the questioning from officials, which was described as 'stupid' when officials repeatedly asked them why they came to the UK. Other children felt like they had done 'something wrong' and lived in fear of being returned to their home country. Alemaychu and Devici (2009 as cited in Devici, 2012) also stated that children felt as though they were criminals and felt more vulnerable as a result of UK 'welfare' interviews. In response, Devici (2012) points out that the role of practical and emotional support for refugee children is significant and must be delivered from point of arrival in the UK through to the transition to early adulthood. Furthermore, I argue that understanding refugee-ship as a *holistic* process, vis-à-vis a series of separated experiences such as legal processes, accommodation seeking, job seeking, social service delivery, education and supporting physical and psychological well-being, is more pertinent and useful in appreciating refugee narratives.

Re-framing such narratives underpins the key role education can play in a child refugee's experience. Through its delivery, the process of education can ameliorate loss and displacement amongst the chaos and confusion of resettlement (Rutter & Jones, 1998). Coping with adversity, developing hope, encouraging resilience and meeting ambition are all key facets of an psycho-educational process for refugee children and young people (Lanyado, 1999; Maclean, 2004). The potential of education is in contrast to what Cooper (2005) terms 'surface instruments' – [UK] policies, procedures and processes that children and families are subject to without allowing for a deeper appreciation of context and human suffering. While the education of refugee children and young people can be viewed simply as a responsibility of local government, it can also be thought of as a significant attempt to integrate and care for vulnerable citizens-to-be.

The Complexities of the Narrative: The Relationship between Austerity, Child Poverty and Education in the UK

The World Education Forum (WEF) and the UN have worked together to produce a framework for delivering a unified education agenda (Save the Children, 2015; UN Division for Sustainable Development, 2015). This includes advocating for the most marginalized and poorest groups of children in the world (see also the UN Educational, Scientific, and Cultural Organization, 2009). WEF and the UN advocate that the needs of the most marginalized groups of children must be prioritized and that targets set should ensure equitable progress across the globe (UN Division for Sustainable Development, 2015). Integral to this process is the commitment to narrowing education gaps between the most advantaged and least advantaged groups of children.

Reay (2017) argues that the current class based educational system in England (comprehensive schools, free schools, private schools and academies) disadvantages pupils with less social and economic capital. Children receiving free school meals and pupil premiums are less likely to reach minimum thresholds for academic achievement and immigrant and other disadvantaged children are more likely to be taught alongside working class rather than middle class children (ibid.). Migrant children are also more likely to be (and remain) in poverty compared to other groups of children as a result of the complex and multiple challenges that refugee adults and children face (Allsopp, Sigona, & Phillimore, 2014; Rutter, 2011).

Compared to 2013, almost 400,000 more British children found themselves in poverty in 2017, the first sustained increase in child poverty in the UK for over 20 years (Joseph Rowntree Foundation, 2017). The Institute for Fiscal Studies (2017) also predicted that there will be a 1.2 million rise in children living in poverty from 4 million in 2017 to 5.2 million by 2022. Hood and Waters (2017) stated that this rise in child poverty is a direct result of UK welfare cuts as a result of austerity while Bradshaw, Chzhen, and Main (2017) argued that children and young people in the UK in 2016 have been major losers in the period following the global financial crisis of 2008. It is likely that child refugees and young people will be particularly vulnerable as a group to fare worst in this context of austerity. Davidson and Carr (2010) found that asylum seeking and refugee children were generally both income and asset poor compared to children from the home nation.

The UK class system was only recently acknowledged by the current UK government who set up a social mobility commission to tackle social injustices[4] (see https://www.gov.uk/government/organisations/social-mobility-commission/about). The commission produced a social mobility index that examined the outcomes for disadvantaged children across England. There were wide educational variations in advantage and disadvantage for children in schools. The report found that compared to more materially wealthy groups, children in their early years who came from disadvantaged and poor backgrounds did not substantially progress in terms of school attainment and achievement (Social Mobility and Child Poverty Commission, 2016). Therefore, there must be considerable concern for child refugees and young people and their families who may find themselves in this social stratum. Castles (2003, p. 17) added that '[failing] economies generally also mean weak states, predatory ruling cliques and human rights abuses' and with the imminent exit of the UK from Europe, this will further deepen the resources and sympathies available to a [child] refugee population.

Reflections and Recommendations for Educational Practice Concerning Child Refugees and Young People in the UK

We know that refugees hold education in high regard and education is a priority for all family members. It appears that charities, NGOs, and some schools and community groupings often offer more services and psychosocial support to refugees and their communities compared to governmental policy and practice. Some governmental initiatives fall below the bar and the follow-through is patchy while the legal processes, especially for independent child or unaccompanied child refugees, can be distressing. Having reviewed the academic literature, noting both local and national legislative practices, auditing accounts of the work of charities and NGOs, and being attuned to the findings of specific projects and initiatives, the following recommendations for educational practice are advised:

– As refugee children and young people arrive in the UK from their homelands with diverse experiences of education, the heterogeneity of migrant groups must be acknowledged. This must be reflected in pedagogical practices such as teacher training and classroom management.
– Swift entry into education for refugee children and young people improve their chances of successful psychological and educational outcomes. Local authorities and schools must make school entry and school transitions efficient and smooth for child refugees and young people.
– Schools can create individual pathway plans for their refugee students to support long-term goals and future aspirations.
– Refugee children and young people face prejudice and racism, particularly in the educational system, and more generally, in UK culture. School and community-led initiatives can help ameliorate this reaction and facilitate tolerance and acceptance.
– Targeted support is needed for teachers delivering education to child and youth refugees, and a whole school approach is preferable.
– There must be a consciousness among educational professionals and a targeted policy to deal with the psychological impact of growing up and/ or being educated in a high intensity war zone or conflict situation. This includes the acknowledgement that trauma will be manifested in the post-migration phase for child and adolescent refugees. Supporting systems must be available and accessible.
– Schools and colleges can offer routines, safety, and development of a sense of belonging as the host culture for refugee children and young people.
– Refugee children and young people must have increased opportunities to access higher education in the UK. A specific UK government-university policy should be developed.
– Coupled with an exit from Europe in 2019, specific monitoring of the vulnerable position refugee children and youth find themselves in during a period of austerity should be established by the UK government and measured against international conventions and humanitarian legislation.

Concluding Comments

Kushner (2006) observed that the accounts and experiences of refugees in recent history do not become absorbed into mainstream accounts of nation states and can, therefore, be susceptible to a form of 'academic amnesia.' This, compounded with a deficit model of 'being a refugee' as a result of forced migration, alongside hostile government policies and denigrating public discourses, places the refugee at the very bottom of the social order (Morrice, 2013). Feldman (2012) further comments that while the costs of immigration accrue at the local level, the benefits of an increased labour supply accrue at the national level and so the contribution migrants make to a UK economy is less visible. This will garner strong civic opinion to strengthen borders and oppose migrants' entry.

The content of this chapter tells us that there appears to be a piecemeal approach to refugees and refugee policy in the UK, and that when it comes to UK policy in the European context, we are not as generous as we think we are compared to our European neighbours. In late June 2018, the European Union brokered a new migration plan agreeing on joint processing sites, tightening external borders and increasing funding to Turkey, Morocco and North Africa to lessen migration to Europe (European Commission, 2018). However, the UK is due to leave Europe in March 2019 and the managed ambiguity of Brexit has left migration policy low on the UK political agenda (see Commons Select Committee 'call for written evidence,' 2018).

In contrast, we acknowledged the necessity of a compassionate response aligned with the intensity of psychosocial support needed during transition periods for refugee children and young people, and recommended the 'whole-school' systems approach from Australia that could be adopted for UK schools. Schools, colleges and universities have the potential to be sites for healing and recovery for refugee children, refugee students and their families; and education can act as an agent of care and be a site for compassion for these (and other vulnerable) groups. The question is whether or not the UK can find the resources for schools and for higher education to carry this out, and whether or not teachers and academics have the capacity or willingness to deliver those programmes, and take on, what are essentially, civic duties on behalf of the state.

Notes

1 'Children' are defined as those individuals no older than 16 years of age. 'Young people' are defined as being between 16–18 years of age. This follows the legal age limit of compulsory schooling in the UK up to age 16 and the legal responsibility of social service delivery for young people up to age 18 in the UK. However, we note that recent changes to Children and Adolescent Mental Health Services (CAMHS) in the UK can now deliver psychological support to young adults up to age 25.

2 *Unaccompanied* child refugees up to the age of 18 are the responsibility of local social services in the UK. In terms of educational provision, these separated children differ from other accompanied child refugees and young people in that they will have a specific 'pathway plan' that deals with education, training, employment and career aspirations.

3 Murphy and Vieten (2017) also point out that an integrated refugee strategy that separates out Northern Ireland statistics from Scotland (both are conflated as part of Home Office policy) is also desirable.

4 At time of writing, the members of the Social Mobility and Child Poverty Commission resigned as they felt that the work of the commission was being undermined by larger political concerns. Issues cited include the perceived lack of commitment from the current UK government to social mobility and the over-riding policy challenges of the UK leaving the European Union (The Financial Times, 2017; The Guardian, 2017).

References

Alemauchu, M., & Devici, Y. (2009). *In search of protection: Separated children seeking asylum alone.* Unpublished manuscript.

Allsopp, J., Sigona, N., & Phillimore, J. (2014). *Poverty among refugees and asylum seekers in the UK: An evidence and policy review* (Working Paper Series, No. 1/2014). Birmingham: Institute for Research into Superdiversity (IRiS).

Barker, B., & Mills, C. (2018). The psy-disciplines go to school: Psychiatric, psychological and psychotherapeutic approaches to inclusion in one UK primary school. *International Journal of Inclusive Education, 22*(6), 638–654.

BBC News. (2015, September 24). *Nigel Farage: Britain in grip of immigration crisis.* Retrieved from https://www.bbc.co.uk/news/uk-england-surrey-34348834

BBC News. (2018, May 2). *Ten charts explaining the UK's immigration system.* Retrieved from https://www.bbc.co.uk/news/uk-43960088

Bradshaw, J., Chzhen, Y., & Main, G. (2017). Impact of the recession on children in the United Kingdom. In B. Cantillon, Y. Chzhen, S. Handa, & B. Nolan (Eds.), *Children of austerity: Impact of the great recession on child poverty in rich countries* (pp. 275–296). Oxford: Oxford University Press.

Brownlees, L., & Finch, N. (2010). *Levelling the playing field: A UNICEF UK report into provision of services to unaccompanied or separate migrant children in three local authorities in England.* Retrieved from http://www.childmigration.net/files/levelling-playing-field.pdf

Burgoyne, U., & Hall, O. (2005). *Classroom management strategies to address the needs of Sudanese refugee learners.* Adelaide: National Centre for Vocational Education Research.

Castles, M. (2003). Towards a sociology of forced migration and social transformation. *Sociology, 31*(1), 13–34.

Castles, M., & Miller, M. J. (1998). *The age of migration: International population movements in the modern world.* London: Macmillan.

Chase, E., Knight, A., & Statham, J. (2008). *Promoting the emotional wellbeing and mental health of unaccompanied young people seeking asylum in the UK.* London: British Association for Adoption and Fostering.

Children and War Foundation. (2018). *Teaching recovery techniques.* Retrieved from http://www.childrenandwar.org/resources/teaching-recovery-techniques-trt/

Commons Select Committee. (2018). *Post-Brexit migration policy – Call for written evidence.* Retrieved from https://www.parliament.uk/business/committees/committees-a-z/commons-select/home-affairs-committee/news-parliament-2017/post-brexit-migration-call-for-written-submission-17-19/

Cooper, A. (2005). Surface and depth in the Victoria Climbie inquiry report. *Child and Family Social Work, 10*, 1–9.

Coram Children's Legal Centre. (2017). *Claiming asylum as a child.* Retrieved from https://www.childrenslegalcentre.com/resources/asylum/

Correa-Velez, I., Gifford, S., & Barnett, A. (2010). Longing to belong: Social inclusion and wellbeing among youth with refugee backgrounds in the first three years in Melbourne, Australia. *Social Science and Medicine, 71*(8), 1399–1408.

Crul, M. (2016, 18 September). *Early education is key to helping migrant children thrive.* Retrieved from https://www.theguardian.com/commentisfree/2016/sep/18/early-education-key-migrant-children-thrive-integration

Crul, M., Schneider, J., & Lelie, F. (2012). *The European second generation compared: Does the integration context matter?* Amsterdam: Amsterdam University Press.

Daily Mail Comment. (2016, May 26). *Mass migration and our quality of life.* Retrieved from http://www.dailymail.co.uk/debate/article-3609918/DAILY-MAIL-COMMENT-Mass-migration-quality-life.html

Davidson, G., & Carr, S. C. (2010). Forced migration, social exclusion and poverty: Introduction. *Journal of Pacific Rim Psychology, 4*(1), 1–6.

Dejong, J., Komproe, I. H., & Van Ommeron, M. (2003). Common mental disorders in post-conflict settings. *The Lancet, 361*(9375), 2128–2130.

Dennis, J. (2002). *A case for change: How refugee children in England are missing out: First findings from the monitoring project of the Refugee's Children Consortium.* London: The Children's Society, Save the Children and the Refugee Council.

Department for Communities. (2017). *Syrian vulnerable persons relocation scheme: Briefing document.* Retrieved from https://www.communities-ni.gov.uk/publications/syrian-vulnerable-persons-relocation-scheme

Department for Communities and Local Government. (2015). *Syrian vulnerable person resettlement fact sheet.* Retrieved from https://www.gov.uk/government/publications/syrian-vulnerable-person-resettlement-programme-fact-sheet

Department for Education & the Home Office, UK. (2018). *National transfer scheme protocol for unaccompanied children.* Retrieved from https://www.gov.uk/government/publications/unaccompanied-asylum-seeking-children-interim-national-transfer-scheme

Department of Education, Northern Ireland. (2015). *Integrated schools.* Retrieved from https://www.education-ni.gov.uk/articles/integrated-schools

Devici, Y. (2012). Trying to understand: Promoting the psychosocial well-being of separated refugee children. *Journal of Social Work Practice, 26*(3), 367–383.

Doyle, L., & McCorriston, M. (2008). *Beyond the school gates: Supporting refugees and asylum seekers in secondary school.* London: Refugee Council.

European Commission. (2018). *Migration: Towards an European agenda on migration.* Retrieved from https://ec.europa.eu/commission/priorities/migration_en

Fazel, M., & Stein, A. (2003). Mental health of refugee children. *Archives of Diseases in Childhood, 87,* 366–370.

Federal Ministry of Education. (2004). *The development of education: National report of Sudan.* Retrieved from http://www.ibe.unesco.org/International/ICE47/English/Natreps/reports/sudan_ocr.pdf

Feldman, D. (2012). Migrant London. In P. Cardullo, R. R. Gupta, & J. Hakim (Eds.), *London: City of paradox* (pp. 110–115). London: University of East London.

Financial Times. (2017, July 4). *Local councils to see central funding fall 77% by 2020.* Retrieved from https://www.ft.com/content/9c6b5284-6000-11e7-91a7-502f7ee26895

Fraser, N. (2007). Identity, exclusion and critique: A response to four critics. *European Journal of Political Theory, 6,* 305–338.

Freedman, J. (2007). *Gendering the international asylum and refugee debate.* London: Palgrave Macmillan.

Geraghty, T., McStravick, C., & Mitchell, S. (2010). *New to Northern Ireland: A study of the issues faced by asylum seeking and refugee children in Northern Ireland.* London: National Children's Bureau.

German, M. (2004). Working with Somali boys in a secondary school: An educating experience. In P. Travers & G. Klein (Eds.), *Equal measures: Ethnic minority and bilingual pupils in secondary schools* (pp. 65–77). Stoke-on Trent: Trentham Books.

German, M., & Ehntholt, K. (2007). Working with refugee children and families. *The Psychologist, 20*(30), 152–155.

Gupta, R. (2012). Visible and invisible migrants. In P. Cardullo, R. R. Gupta, & J. Hakim (Eds.), *London: City of paradox* (pp. 116–122). London: University of East London.

Hall, J. C. (2003). *Mentoring and young people: A literature review.* Glasgow: The SCRE Centre, University of Glasgow.

Hart, R. (2009). Child refugees, trauma and education: Interactionist considerations on social and emotional needs and development. *Educational Psychology in Practice, 25*(4), 351–368.

Harwood, V., & Allan, J. (2014). *Psychopathology at school: Theorizing mental disorders in education*. Abingdon: Routledge.

Home Office, UK. (2017). *Children's asylum claims*. Retrieved from https://www.gov.uk/government/publications/processing-an-asylum-application-from-a-child-instruction

Hood, A., & Waters, T. (2017). *Living standards, poverty and inequality in the UK: 2017–18 to 2021–22*. London: Institute of Fiscal Studies.

Houghton, A. M., & Morrice, L. (2008). *Refugees, asylum seekers and migrants: Steps on the education and employment progression journey*. Leicester: National Institute of Adult Continuing Education.

IEF & NICIE. (2010). *Welcoming newcomer and minority ethnic pupils in Northern Ireland: A case study with Hazelwood Integrated College*. Belfast: Integrated Education Fund and Northern Ireland Council for Integrated Education.

Institute for Fiscal Studies. (2017). *Benefit cuts set to increase child poverty, with biggest rises likely in North East and Wales*. Retrieved from https://www.ifs.org.uk/publications/10029

Joseph Rowntree Foundation. (2017). *UK poverty 2017*. New York, NY: Joseph Rowntree Foundation.

Korac-Sanderson, M. (2018). *Refugees in Europe: Production of fear and securitization of migration*. Research and Knowledge Exchange Conference, University of East London.

Kristjánsson, K. (2009). Medicalised pupils: The case of ADD/ADHD. *Oxford Review of Education, 35*(1), 111–127.

Kushner, T. (2006). *Remembering refugees: Then and now*. Manchester: Manchester University Press.

Lanyado, M. (1999). The treatment of traumatization in children. In M. Lanyado & A. Horne (Eds.), *The handbook of child and adolescent psychotherapy* (pp. 275–291). London: Routledge.

Maclean, K. (2004). *Resilience: What is it and how can young people be helped to develop it?* Retrieved from http://www.cyc-net.org/cyc-online/cycol-0304-resilience.html

Marfleet, P. (2012). City of paradox: The refugee experience. In P. Cardullo, R. Gupta, & J. Hakim (Eds.), *London: City of paradox* (pp. 48–52). London: University of East London.

McDonald, A. (2017). *Invisible wounds: The impact of six years of war on the mental health of Syria's children*. London: Save the Children.

Milner, K., & Khawaja, N. G. (2010). Sudanese refugees in Australia: The impact of acculturation stress. *Journal of Pacific Rim Psychology, 4*(1), 19–29.

Montgomery, E. (1998). Refugee children from the Middle East. *Scandinavian Journal of Social Medicine Supplement, 54*, 1–152.

Morrice, L. (2009). Journeys into higher education: The case of refugees in the UK. *Teaching in Higher Education, 14*, 663–674.

Morrice, L. (2013). Refugees in higher education: Boundaries of belonging and recognition, stigma and exclusion. *International Journal of Lifelong Education, 32*(5), 652–668.

Murphy, F., & Vieten, U. M. (2017). *Asylum seekers and refugees' experiences of life in Northern Ireland*. Belfast: The Northern Ireland Executive Office and The Queen's University of Belfast.

National Institute of Mental Health. (2015). *What is post-traumatic stress disorder?* Retrieved from https://www.nimh.nih.gov/health/topics/post-traumatic-stress-disorder-ptsd/index.shtml

NCB Northern Ireland, & ARK Young People's Life and Times. (2010). *Attitudes to difference: Young people's attitudes to and experiences of contact with people from different ethnic minority and migrant communities in Northern Ireland*. London: NCB.

Pinson, H., & Arnot, M. (2010). Local conceptualisation of the education of asylum-seeking and refugee students: From hostile to holistic media. *International Journal of Inclusive Education, 14*(3), 247–267.

Reay, D. (2017). *Miseducation: Inequality, education and the working classes*. Bristol: Policy Press.

Refugee Support Network Higher Education. (n.d.). *Higher education*. Retrieved from https://www.refugeesupportnetwork.org/pages/25-higher-education

Rutter, J. (2003). *Supporting refugee children in 21st Century Britain: A compendium of essential information*. Stoke-on Trent: Trentham Books.

Rutter, J. (2011). Migration, migrants and child poverty. *Child Poverty Action Group Poverty Magazine, 138*, 6–10.

Rutter, J., & Jones, C. (Eds.). (1998). *Refugee education: Mapping the field*. Stoke-on-Trent: Trentham Books.

Ryan, L., D'Angelo, A., Sales, R., & Roddriguez, M. L. (2010). *Newly arrived migrant and refugee children in the British educational system*. Middlesex: Middlesex University. (Action for Social Integration)

Save the Children. (2015). *Fulfilling the promise: Ensuring the post-2015 education agenda delivers on equity and learning*. London: Save the Children.

Save the Children. (2016). *Childhood under siege: Living and dying in besieged areas of Syria*. London: Save the Children.

Schweizter, R., Melville, F., Steele, Z., & Lacherez, P. (2006). Trauma, post-migration difficulties, and social support as predictors of psychological adjustment in resettled Sudanese refugees. *Australian and New Zealand Journal of Psychiatry, 40*, 179–187.

Sellars, M., & Murphy, H. (2018). Becoming Australian: A review of southern Sudanese students' educational experiences. *International Journal of Inclusive Education, 22*(5), 490–509.

Sempowicz, T., Howard, J., Tambyah, M., & Carrington, S. (2017). Identifying obstacles and opportunities for inclusion in the school curriculum for children adopted from overseas: Developmental and social constructionist approaches. *International Journal of Inclusive Education*, 1–16. (Advance online publication) doi:0.1080/13603116.2017.1390004

Social Mobility and Child Poverty Commission. (2016). *The social mobility index*. Retrieved from https://www.gov.uk/government/publications/social-mobility-index

Sonderegger, R., Barrett, P. M., & Creed, P. A. (2004). Models of cultural adjustment for child and adolescent immigrants to Australia: Internal process and situational factors. *Journal of Child and Family Studies, 13*, 357–371.

Sousa, C., Kemp, S., & El-Zouhairi, M. (2014). Dwelling within political violence: Palestinian women's narratives of home, mental health and resilience. *Health and Place, 30*, 205–214.

Stanley, K. (2001). *Cold comfort: Young separated refugees in England*. London: Save the Children.

Steele, Z., Silove, T., Phan, D., & Bauman, A. (2002). Long term effect of psychological trauma on the mental health of Vietnamese refugees settled in Australia: A population based study. *The Lancet, 306*, 1056–1067.

Student Finance England. (2018). *Student loans – A guide to terms and conditions*. Retrieved from https://www.gov.uk/student-finance

Taylor, S., & Sidhu, R. K. (2012). Supporting refugee students in schools: What constitutes good practice? *International Journal of Inclusive Education, 16*(1), 39–56.

The British Psychological Society. (2018). *Guidelines for psychologists working with refugees and asylum seekers*. Leicester: The British Psychological Society.

The Financial Times. (2017, December 3). *Theresa May's social mobility's commission walks out*. Retrieved from https://www.ft.com/content/e4426dce-d808-11e7-a039-c64b1c09b482

The Guardian. (2017, March 1). *Britain is one of the worst places for asylum seekers in Western Europe*. Retrieved from https://www.theguardian.com/uk-news/2017/mar/01/britain-one-of-worst-places-western-europe-asylum-seekers

The Guardian. (2017, December 2). *Theresa May faces new crisis after mass walkout over social policy*. Retrieved from https://www.theguardian.com/politics/2017/dec/02/theresa-may-crisis-mass-walkout-social-policy-alan-milburn

Trades Union Congress. (2007). *The economics of migration*. London: The Trades Union Congress.

UN Committee on the Rights of the Child (UNCRC). (2008). *Concluding observations on the rights of the child of the UNCRC in relation to the UK*. Geneva: UNCRC.

UN Division for Sustainable Development. (2015). *World education forum 2015-equitable and inclusive quality education and lifelong learning for all by 2030*. Retrieved from https://sustainabledevelopment.un.org/index.php?page=view&type=13&nr=1360&menu=35

UN Educational, Scientific, and Cultural Organization. (2009). *Policy guidelines on inclusion in education*. Paris: UN Educational, Scientific, and Cultural Organization.

UN Office for the Co-ordination of Humanitarian Affairs. (2017). *Humanitarian needs overview: Syrian Arab Republic*. Retrieved from https://reliefweb.int/report/syrian-arab-republic/2017-humanitarian-needs-overview-syrian-arab-republic-enar

UN Office for the Co-ordination of Humanitarian Affairs. (2016). *Flash update on Mad-amiyet Elsham*. Retrieved from https://reliefweb.int/report/syrian-arab-republic/syrian-arab-republic-flash-update-madamiyet-elsham-31-january-2016

Universities UK International. (2018). *Higher education and displaced people: A guide for UK universities*. London: UK Universities International.

Victorian Foundation for Survivors of Torture. (2005). *Annual report*. Retrieved from http://www.foundationhouse.org.au/rebuilding-shattered-lives-2/

Victorian Foundation for the Survivors of Torture. (2016). *School's in for refugees: A whole-school approach to supporting refugees and families of refugee background*. Victoria: The Victorian Foundation for the Survivors of Torture.

Waddington, S. (2005). *Valuing skills and supporting integration*. Leicester: National Institute of Adult Continuing Education.

Walker, S. (2011). *Something to smile about: Promoting and supporting the educational and recreational needs of refugee children*. London: The Refugee Council.

CHAPTER 12

Schooling Displaced Syrian Students in Glasgow
Agents of Inclusion

Melanie Baak

Introduction

Since conflict began in Syria in 2011, more than 5 million people have been displaced from their homes. Many of those who have been displaced have begun to rebuild their lives in new countries. Rebuilding lives requires access to key resources including housing, health care, employment and education. This chapter explores the role of schools in supporting Syrian students and their families in rebuilding their lives in Glasgow, Scotland. In Glasgow, all newly arrived students attend their local school and each school is required to respond to these students with language and other support. This chapter reports on interviews and a focus group conducted with 8 Syrian parents and individual interviews conducted with five school staff from different school settings. Building on the emerging body of literature, which describes 'inclusive education' for students with refugee experience (Pugh, Every, & Hattam, 2012; Taylor & Sidhu, 2012), this chapter highlights various factors that shape the degree of inclusivity of schools for Syrian students and families. While the policy contexts in Glasgow prescribe inclusion of all students in mainstream settings, whether or not students and their families actually experience inclusion in its full sense varies from school to school. Through considering the role of people I refer to as 'agents of inclusion' from school leadership, English as Additional Language (EAL)[1] teachers and peers, I argue that the school responses and inclusion of Syrian students in Glasgow are largely dependent on individual 'agents of inclusion.'

This chapter does not specifically examine aspects of pedagogy, curriculum or assessment that have been identified as critical in the inclusion of students from diverse backgrounds. Rather it identifies key moments, as identified by participants, in which particular actors undertook particular actions that facilitated inclusion for displaced Syrian students and their families. By reflecting on these key moments and the actors involved, I argue that the actions of these actors, or 'agents of inclusion' are necessary and important steps in facilitating inclusion, and in order for better inclusion to occur, these actions need to be recognised and replicated. While there was significant discussion by both participant groups of experiences of exclusion as well as inclusion, in this chapter

© KONINKLIJKE BRILL NV, LEIDEN, 2019 | DOI: 10.1163/9789004401891_012

I have chosen to focus on the moments and agents of inclusion as a means to facilitate future conversations of hopeful possibility for inclusion. The chapter begins by introducing the contexts to the resettlement of Syrian families in Glasgow followed by a brief consideration of displacement from Syria. I then introduce the research context and participants before considering the ways in which the educational policy contexts in Scotland facilitate inclusion. Finally I consider some of the key moments, which illustrate the importance of 'agents of inclusion' in facilitating and enabling the inclusion of displaced Syrian students in Glasgow's schools.

Syrian Context and Resettlement

Prior to the outbreak of war in Syria in 2011, education in the country had made significant gains with approximately 97% of primary-school-aged children attending school and youth literacy at approximately 96% (US Department of Health and Human Services, 2016). As a result of the conflict over 5.6 million people have fled Syria, with all demographics and regions being affected, seeking safety in countries around the world through whatever means they have. While a majority of Syrians in the UK have been resettled through the Vulnerable Person Resettlement program (VPR), some have made their way to the UK through other means, sometimes seeking asylum on arrival; or other times able to use their social, economic, and educational capital to secure employment enabling 'skilled migration' to the UK. For example, the Council for Assisting Refugee Academics (CARA) provides an avenue for academics from refugee contexts to seek employment in the UK.

As a result of diverse pre-displacement skills and expertise and the multiple different migration pathways to the UK, the Syrian community in Glasgow is very diverse. Syrians in Glasgow have diverse education levels, English literacy, and prior employment skills in addition to having different visa types, entitlements, work rights, and accommodations. As a result of this, the research reported in this chapter refers to the Syrian community members and students displaced Syrians, rather than specifically as migrants, refugees, or asylum seekers, as the term displaced can capture the diverse migration pathways and labels for this cohort.

Background to Resettlement in the UK and Scotland

The United Kingdom has a relatively recent and small commitment to resettling refugees in comparison to other countries of resettlement such as the

US, Canada and Australia. The UK began its resettlement programs in 2004 (UNHCR, 2014), and in a five-year period to 2014/15 accepted approximately 740 refugees for resettlement each year (International Catholic Migration Commission Europe, 2013). This grew significantly from 2015 following the United Kingdom's Prime Minister's launch of the Syrian Vulnerable Persons Resettlement Scheme (VPR), committing to resettle 20,000 Syrian refugees during the following five years (COSLA Strategic Migration Partnership, 2018). Scotland's First Minister agreed to take a minimum of 10% of the total number of Syrians to be resettled. By the end of 2017, Scotland had received the planned quota and had resettled over 2,000 Syrian refugees in 31 of Scotland's local authority areas (ibid.). These resettled Syrians are granted five years leave to remain, with the Home Office providing per capita funding to local authorities to provide services to support recent arrivals. During the five years leave to remain, resettled Syrians are able to access statutory health care and education services as well as being entitled to work and claim benefits including child benefit and tax credit (ibid.). At the end of the five-year period, individuals may be eligible to apply for indefinite leave to remain in the UK. The VPR resettlement scheme sits in stark contrast to other countries of resettlement, where those who are resettled are given permanent residency. The uncertainty of staying in the UK beyond five years results in continuing uncertainty for those who are resettled, thereby impacting on the resettlement experience of families.

While the Syrian VPR is the largest significant resettlement program in the UK in recent years, services in the UK have significant experience supporting those who arrive seeking asylum. In the five-year period from 2012–2016, the UK received an average of approximately 26,750 asylum seekers per year (Home Office, 2017). Since the introduction of the *Immigration and Asylum Act 1999,* asylum seekers have been 'dispersed' throughout the UK, with Scotland, and particularly Glasgow City Council receiving its first significant numbers of asylum seekers in the early 2000s (Scottish Refugee Council, 2018). As such, school and education systems in Glasgow have been developing and evolving their responses to the needs of students with refugee and asylum seeker backgrounds for almost 20 years.

The responses of schools to refugee and asylum seeker students are shaped by the broader government policies and discourses in Scotland. With regard to social inclusion, Scottish governments since devolution in 1999 have endeavoured to position themselves in distinction to the neoliberalism introduced in England during the Thatcher era (Watson, 2010). Scottish governments have worked to 'present Scotland as a society founded on a deep-seated sense of egalitarianism' (ibid., p. 93). This has been particularly evidenced in policy responses to refugees and asylum seekers. While this has not always translated into the everyday experiences of displaced people living in Scotland, there has been continued government effort to accommodate and provide adequate services for refugees and asylum seekers to make Scotland their new home. The response of a range of Local Authorities to resettle the 2,000 Syrian refugees who arrived in Scotland three years ahead of the 2020 scheduled timeframe (COSLA Strategic Migration Partnership, 2018) indicates the relatively positive and inclusive response to refugees in Scotland.

In addition, Scotland developed an internationally recognised strategy 'New Scots: Integrating Refugees in Scotland's Communities 2014–2017' (Scottish Government, 2013). The purpose of the strategy was to 'co-ordinate the efforts of all organisations involved in supporting refugees and people seeking asylum in Scotland in order to make Scotland a welcoming place to people seeking protection from persecution and human rights abuses' (ibid., p. 6). The first version of the strategy was implemented from 2014–2017 and following a significant review the 'New Scots Refugee Integration Strategy 2018–2022' was implemented in 2018 (Scottish Government, 2018). The 2014–17 strategy contained chapters explicitly considering refugee integration in relation to employment and welfare, housing, education, health and communities and social connection. While the classroom and EAL teachers interviewed as part of this project were not directly aware of the New Scots strategy, the 'New Scots' strategy has been credited for shifting public attitudes towards refugees, with the results of a 2016 survey indicating that 57% of Scots agreed that they were confident that most refugees will successfully integrate into their new community (IPSOS MORI, 2016). This was 17% higher than the responses across the UK and the highest figure amongst all European countries polled in the research (Scottish Government, 2017a). In addition, the final report on the 2014–2017 strategy indicates that the key educational achievements have been particularly focussed at a policy level as well as through targeted professional learning opportunities such as the 'Bilingualism Does Matter workshops' which were not specifically badged as initiatives of the New Scots Strategy (Scottish Government, 2017b), perhaps explaining why the classroom and EAL teachers interviewed were not aware of the strategy.

Literature Review: Inclusive Education for Refugee Students

Research into the educational experiences of refugee background youth has previously typically focussed on individualised problems and barriers to educational success at school, including trauma, low levels of literacy and interrupted schooling (Brown, Miller, & Mitchell, 2006; DeCapua, Smathers, & Tang, 2007; Miller, 2009). Acknowledging this, the focus of recent research has

SCHOOLING DISPLACED SYRIAN STUDENTS IN GLASGOW

shifted to consider the importance of developing inclusive school communities (Block, Cross, Riggs, & Gibbs, 2014; Keddie, 2012; Miller, Ziaian, & Esterman, 2017; Pugh et al., 2012; Taylor & Sidhu, 2012). In this chapter I utilise inclusive education research developed in response to the inclusion of students with disabilities (Slee, 2013, 2018; Slee & Allan, 2001) along with international research that argues for the importance of inclusive education in supporting students from refugee backgrounds.

Understandings of inclusive schooling for students with refugee experience has built on the seminal work of Rutter (2006), whose summary of a number of academic and government texts from the late 1990s identified three main aspects of 'good practice' for supporting refugee students in the UK: a welcoming environment *free of racism*, the need to meet psycho-social needs (particularly for those who have experienced trauma), and ensuring that linguistic needs are met (p. 5). Rutter's work has been further developed in recent years with authors (i.e. Baak, 2018; Block et al., 2014; Keddie, 2012; Miller et al., 2017; Pugh et al., 2012; Taylor & Sidhu, 2012) identifying a range of approaches to creating inclusive school environments for refugee background students such as the following:

– English language support;
– Rejecting deficit views of refugee students;
– Partnership approaches to supporting students;
– Parental engagement;
– Strong school leadership and advocacy;
– Policy and system support; and
– Fostering an 'ethos and environment of inclusion and celebrating cultural diversity' (Block et al., 2014, p. 1349).

This chapter particularly concurs with authors who have argued the need for 'whole school' approaches to including students from refugee backgrounds (de Wal Pastoor, 2016; Pugh et al., 2012). This includes consideration of 'education policy, school structures, classroom practice, curricula, pedagogy and teaching materials, as well as cultural awareness and refugee competence' (de Wal Pastoor, 2016, p. 107).

The school enrolment process has been particularly identified as an important aspect of facilitating inclusion of students and families from the first point of contact (Block et al., 2014; Sale, Sliz, & Pacini-Ketchabaw, 2003). Johnson (2003, p. 20), for example, has argued that by

> establishing culturally responsive admission procedures for enrolling students from diverse backgrounds, schools can provide reliable direction to school staff on matters such as evaluating a student's previous education

and academic ability and assessing special language or learning needs for appropriate placement and service provision decisions.

In addition, the roles of staff, particularly school leaders, have been explored in response to the inclusion of diverse learners. Riehl's (2009) extensive literature review of the role of school leaders in responding to the needs of diverse students indicated three tasks for facilitating inclusion: 'fostering new meanings about diversity, promoting inclusive school cultures and instructional programs, and building relationships between schools and communities' (p. 183).

A majority of the current research on inclusive educational responses to students from refugee backgrounds has come from Australia, where the educational provisions and policy contexts for students with refugee experience are quite different from those in Scotland. As such, it is imperative to explore the policy contexts for educational provision in Scotland for students who have experienced displacement. The Scottish policy contexts are explored below in the section on policies of inclusion for students at schools in Glasgow.

Theoretical Framework: Agents of Inclusion

Beyond the refugee specific literature on inclusive education, a range of academics has explored the roles of different actors or agents in facilitating inclusion. In this chapter, I draw on the ideas of Pantić and Florian (2015) who proposed theories of teacher agency and inclusive pedagogy to interrogate the role of teachers as 'agents of change in the context of inclusion' – or what they refer to as 'teachers as agents of inclusion' (p. 333). They build on the view of teachers as 'agents of change' which they suggest has been aligned with social justice agendas 'concerned with educational inequalities and a desire to raise educational attainments and improve outcomes for all learners' (Pantić & Florian, 2015, p. 333). Through this, they argue that teachers play a role in facilitating and enabling inclusion not only through their classroom practices, pedagogy, and assessment, but also through challenging systemic inequality and some of the institutional features of schooling (Liston & Zeichner, 1990).

I do not endeavour to undertake a review of the concept of agency in this chapter, but my understandings of agency draw on the work of a range of authors, particularly in relation to recent theorising of teacher agency (Biesta & Tedder, 2007; Priestley, Biesta, & Robinson, 2013, 2015). These authors argue for an ecological conception of agency as 'the interplay of individual efforts, available resources and contextual and structural factors' (Biesta & Tedder, 2007, p. 137). In this chapter I develop this ecological conception of agency beyond just teacher agency, to consider other agents of inclusion as well. Pantić and Florian (2015) have argued that to address 'the risks of exclusion and marginalisation in education often requires the collaboration of many actors ... and a capacity of various professionals to align their purposes and actions' (p. 342). However, I argue that while the agency and actions of teachers and 'professionals' are important, it is also necessary to consider the actions and agency of those beyond the 'professional' to observe how the actions of multiple agents facilitate inclusion. As such, in the following sections I explore the roles of multiple 'agents of inclusion' through a consideration of individual efforts of school leaders, teachers, other school staff, students and families and the intersections with resourcing and contextual and structural influences.

Methods

The research for this project was undertaken over a period of four months in 2017. The research process was designed to facilitate an understanding of the diverse experiences of schools and families. As such, the project drew on the experiences of two participant groups: educational staff (i.e. school teachers and educational leaders) and parents of Syrian students. Previous research has identified that schools have very different responses to the needs of students with experiences of displacement (McBrien, 2005; Miller, Mitchell, & Brown, 2005; Roxas, 2010). As such, teachers from across different school settings, including primary and secondary schools, and with differing degrees of student diversity were recruited for participation in this project. The detailing of these participants' positions and schools is intentionally left slightly vague to avoid identification of the participants. While the educator participant group for the project was relatively small (n=5) these participants represented diverse positions, including leadership within the local authority education department, a head teacher, two EAL coordinators and a classroom teacher. The school contexts the educator participants were working in were also very diverse, including a secondary school with approximately 15% students with EAL and 15–20 Syrian students; a primary school with approximately 85% EAL students, including a number of recently arrived Syrian families; and a primary school with approximately 25% EAL students with two recently arrived Syrian families. Authority to conduct research in the schools was gained from the Glasgow City Council, and potential participants and schools were recommended by the EAL department at the Glasgow City Council due to their known enrolment of students from Syria. Approximately 10 possible participants were identified, with individual semi-structured interviews being conducted with four participants from three schools and a fifth participant from a leadership position within the Council. Individual semi-structured interviews were conducted either in the participants' schools or in another suitable location.

In addition to the educator participants, qualitative focus groups and interviews were also conducted with Syrian parents. Previous research with refugee families has identified that students may feel more comfortable discussing their experiences at school when interviewed outside the school setting (Baak, 2016, 2018). As such, the researcher engaged with a Syrian community group who met at a local community centre to identify possible parent participants. Initially the research plan was to conduct one focus group with 8–10 parents at the community centre. However, this approach was unsuccessful. After an initial focus group with three mothers, subsequent participants requested interviews in parent pairs, with just the mother and father present. These interviews and the focus group were all conducted at the community centre. The parents discussed a range of schooling experiences for their children, and it was identified that the individual interviews with parents enabled them to speak more openly about their and their children's negative experiences at school than in a focus group. Three interviews were conducted with pairs of a mother and father. In these three interviews, the English language competency of the mother was limited, so the interviews relied on the fathers to interpret for the mothers. It is acknowledged that this will have influenced the ability of the mothers to articulate their experiences (Murray & Wynne, 2001). In total, eight Syrian parents were interviewed, as one mother was part of the focus group as well as requesting an individual interview with her husband. The parents had between one and seven children. Their children were in education settings ranging from preschool to university. The families had been living in Glasgow for between eight months and three years. A limitation of this study was the inability to interview Syrian children due to the time constraints of the project and ethical processes to gain approval to interview children with refugee experience.

Interviews and focus groups with both participant groups were audio recorded and transcribed. A data-driven inductive thematic coding approach was utilised to identify key themes within the data (Boyatzis, 1998). NVivo was used to code the data once the themes had been identified.

Findings

Policy Contexts in Glasgow: '... Inclusion is Inclusion'

In the past 15 years, there have been significant policy shifts regarding how schools respond to the needs of recently arrived refugee and migrant students

SCHOOLING DISPLACED SYRIAN STUDENTS IN GLASGOW 275

in Glasgow. Prior to 2004, there was a distinct 'Language Centre' with two units: one based in a mainstream primary school and the other in a secondary school. In an interview with Jane, who held a leadership position in the local authority, she reflected that, in 2004, the increase in migrant student numbers in the Language Centre 'reached a point where it was becoming quite unsustainable.' At this time, Jane suggested the new director of the Local Authority 'was asking lots of questions: Is this the way we do it? Should we be educating children in units? Should they not be in the local school?' These questions aligned with shifts in the education of students with disabilities, with the Scottish Executive passing the Standards in Scotland's Schools Act (2000) which, among other things, 'set out the 'presumption of mainstreaming' in relation to pupils with special educational needs' (Watson, 2010, p. 94). The 'presumption of mainstreaming' in this Act 'assumes that schools will be geared to meet a diverse range of 'needs' (Watson, 2010, p. 94). This Act requires that, regardless of ability, language level, visa status, or recency of arrival, all children are included in mainstream schools in Scotland (Allan, 2010). However, as Slee (2011) has argued, policies (and Acts)

> are not detached, neutral or benign but are constituents of and agents for ways of understanding, maintaining or changing our world … it is inevitable that policy is characterized by contest and struggle given the competing views of the world that policy actors will have. (p. 100)

Implementing the 'presumption of mainstreaming' set out in Scotland's Schools Act (2000) has, thereby, been reliant on a range of actors at varying levels with varying views about the how, why, where, and what of including diverse learners in mainstream schools. This was evidenced in the interview responses of the school-based staff to the expectation and practice of including refugee learners in their local school on arrival in Glasgow. Some staff, such as Mary, the head teacher of a primary school, were very supportive of processes of mainstreaming and active agents of facilitating its success. Mary argued that

> anybody that arrives in a country should go to the local school … the teacher's job is to find a way for children to access the learning no matter what … Here we are not changing our kids to fit another agenda; we're changing their agenda to fit our kids … the policy's there because it says respond to the learner … the learner's the learner; inclusion is inclusion, getting it right for every child is every child, not just some children … I mean your right is to have your needs met.

Mary draws on the language used in Scotland's policy documents such as 'Getting it Right for Every Child' (GIRFEC), a national approach to supporting the wellbeing of all Scotland's children and young people through partnerships across a range of services including health, education and early childhood (Scottish Government, 2017c). Mary's emphasis is really that all staff in all school settings should be able to respond to the needs of all students, regardless of their background or abilities. She goes on to emphasise the importance of a range of supports and resourcing to enable staff to meet these aspirations, but is nonetheless strongly committed to the policies and processes of inclusion. Mary's role as an agent of inclusion through her leadership will be further considered in the following section.

While the policy context necessitates 'inclusion' in the mainstream, it is questionable as to how inclusive these processes of mainstreaming actually are. As Graham and Slee (2008) have argued, 'to include is not necessarily to *be* inclusive' (p. 278). With this policy of inclusion in mainstream education came significant challenges for students and teachers. The first three to six months in Scotland were identified by both parents and school staff as a period of significant struggle socially, academically, and linguistically for students. As Adnan, a father of one son in primary school, described:

> well our son has no English before he comes here. He started from the beginning, and I'm sure it was very difficult period for the first two or three months, has no any kind of communication with the pupils, and with the teachers ...

Amena, a mother in the focus group who was in tears at the time of recalling her son's experience, described that:

> My son when he came here the ... My son is alone ... last year he had three months in the school ... [Upset] ... It's hard – [cry] ... You can speak if you like ... but if he can't speak there's a big problem.

Amena further recalled how her son did not want to go to school and this had resulted in conflict between her and her son and a feeling of helplessness for her as a mother, as she felt unable to adequately support her son or to communicate with the school about the challenges they were facing due to her limited English competency.

Further to the observations of the parents, the teachers also expressed concern in their ability to adequately support the newly arrived students. Wider research relating to the inclusion of students with disabilities in Scotland that has found that 'teachers are increasingly talking about inclusion as an impossibility in the current climate ... lacking confidence in their own competence to deliver inclusion with existing resources' (Allan, 2010, p. 200). Like the research relating to the inclusion of students with disabilities, school staff participants identified significant challenges in responding to and meeting the needs of students with refugee experience. For example, a personal testimony received via email from a Glasgow high school student support assistant (writing anonymously) indicated the complex challenges, particularly around language and communication, for teachers:

> In my workplace, there's no framework on how to work best with refugee pupils new to English and so subject teachers are struggling to find ways even to communicate. The only person in school who can advise is the pupils' key teacher who is currently delivering EAL, despite very limited training. I'm kind of astounded that with the weight of policies at national levels and online advice from education departments there isn't more accessible support which teachers can use in the classroom. There's a real need for intensive training in language awareness across mainstream I think. It feels like it's all down to one teacher getting to grips with managing a situation.

The observations from this student support assistant resonate with the reflections of the other school staff. It was up to key people, such as EAL teachers, to develop expertise to enable them and the broader school to respond to the needs of displaced students. Without a systemic approach supporting schools to respond and meet the needs of students with experiences of displacement, school responses are ad hoc and piecemeal. However, despite these identified challenges when 'presumption of mainstreaming' is assumed to facilitate inclusion, there is also evidence from this research project that suggests that students and their families are having experiences of inclusion in Glasgow's schools. As such, this next section turns to consider the roles of particular agents in facilitating inclusion for displaced Syrian students.

Agents of School Inclusion for Displaced Syrian Students in Glasgow
Key agents were necessary to facilitate inclusion in schools for the displaced Syrian students, particularly within the early months after arrival. In the following sub-sections I explore the roles of multiple 'agents of inclusion' through a consideration of individual efforts of school leaders, teachers, school staff, students and families and the intersections with resourcing and contextual and structural influences.

Due to the two perspectives considered as part of this research project, those of school staff and those of parents, very diverse school contexts have also been considered. The school staff participants represented diverse school contexts, with some of the schools having significant experience in working with students from diverse cultural and linguistic backgrounds, whereas for others this was a relatively new experience. In addition, the parents' discussions of their children's experiences also represented diverse school contexts. As such, the approaches of all of the schools in supporting displaced Syrian students were varied. In the sections below I focus on key actions, which demonstrated the role of particular agents of inclusion in an attempt to highlight the critical role that individuals can and do play with particular resources in particular contexts.

School Leadership: 'For a Head Teacher to Go on a Home to Visit Was Such a Big Deal'

Staff at two of the schools particularly noted the importance of school leaders in facilitating inclusion. For example, Elspeth, a primary EAL teacher, described the importance of school leaders 'leading from the front' when it came to inclusion:

> I do think that it should be led from the front in that respect. And I think the families will see that the head teacher has taken on interest and making sure that we're welcome, I think that does speak volumes as well.

This resonates with other research in the UK which found that, particularly in the early stages of a head teacher's time at a school, successful leadership for inclusion was frequently a top-down approach (Muijs et al., 2010). Elspeth indicated that families would see the head teacher's interest and involvement as a sign of welcome within the school community; however, this is only one element of the role of the school leader in facilitating inclusion. The interview conducted with Mary, a head teacher of a primary school, highlights these three key roles of school leaders in responding to the needs of diverse students identified by Riehl (2009, detailed above). This demonstrates how she challenges understandings of diversity through her expectations of teachers and talking back to policy and her work to promote inclusive school cultures and build relationships.

Mary had been the head teacher at John West Primary school for about five years at the time of the interview. John West Primary was a school with approximately 98% British minority ethnic group enrolment. Of these, approximately 85% spoke English as an Additional Language (EAL). This included a number

SCHOOLING DISPLACED SYRIAN STUDENTS IN GLASGOW   279

of recently arrived Syrian families. Mary described her leadership approach, which clearly aligned with the findings of much recent research on the role of school leaders in facilitating school inclusion. Her strong leadership resulted in a clearly articulated vision for inclusion and achievement for all students. Her expectations of staff were that they would respond to the needs of all students, regardless of their backgrounds. As she described:

> ... so if you're a refugee, right, you should be assuming that your teacher, and all our teachers are degree educated, will go and learn what that means, will look at the current research, will find a colleague that's handled it before. If your teacher that you arrive at is tearing their hair out and holding their hands up and saying "I can't do it" then you need to question whether that teacher is able enough, rather than the student ... So if working in a fairly utopian everything's as it should be, then everybody, every child should walk in the door and have her needs met. (Mary, head teacher of a primary school)

Mary held high expectations of teachers and school staff to have or be willing to develop an understanding of the needs and experiences of all of their students. As a result of these expectations, Mary also explained the need to challenge some staff, which resulted in some staff leaving the school:

> I mean we challenge teachers too, and have challenged teachers and some teachers have left because that's the – you know maybe not comfortable with it and loads of teachers have come to us and want to stay.

Mary described a context in which she constantly struggled to challenge deficit understandings of her students, not only within her school and community, but also more broadly including with policy makers. She described the need to challenge broader educational contexts with their focus on 'competitiveness, performativity and measurable outcomes' (Mcglynn & London, 2013, p. 157) which frequently frame students who speak English as an additional language as deficient (Alford, 2014) and lacking. For example, Mary described the following:

> Scotland has introduced a standardised assessment and I've just emailed them; I haven't been engaged with the debate at all but I've now emailed them to ask them what provision they're making for children who don't speak English and it looks like the answer I've got back is they can do a lower level, but they're not lower level ... They just can't tell you in English

and folk can't get their head round that ... So it's like why on earth would you have to do something easier?

In this way, Mary endeavoured to challenge the structural inequities for her students, not only identifying the inequities, but doing all that she can to change them in recognition of the abilities that her students have. As well as the wider structural changes that Mary continued to challenge to facilitate inclusion of all students, she also undertook a range of practical actions in her role as an agent of inclusion. One of these actions, which seemed particularly important for Mary and her school community, was home visits. She described visiting some of the recently arrived Syrian families:

> I also visited our families at home ... My husband and I visited actually so we had a whole big, you know we were there and for fruit and coffee and so I've been to visit quite a few times; aim to visit the kids at home just to see what they have and for them culturally for a head teacher to go on a home to visit was such a big deal.

Mary's home visits indicated a culture of welcome and inclusion, not only for the families she visited with whom she built a strong and trusting relationship, but also for her school staff who observed and also benefited from the work that Mary did in building these relationships. Mary clearly worked in her school and community as an agent for inclusion. She recognised the structural inequalities in the educational context in which she worked, but worked in multiple ways to facilitate everyday inclusion and overcoming systemic exclusions for her students. She also recognised the absolute importance of her staff in striving to create a school community of inclusion. As such, this next section turns to consider the role of school staff as agents of inclusion.

Classroom Teachers

The ways in which teachers can facilitate inclusion of diverse students is multiple and includes approaches to pedagogy, curriculum, and assessment. Many aspects of teachers' practice in relation to including students from refugee backgrounds in schools have been considered in other studies (see, for example, Burgoyne & Hull, 2007; Due, Riggs, & Mandara, 2015; Miller et al., 2005; Nagasa, 2014; Naidoo, 2013; Pinson & Arnot, 2010). This chapter does not specifically focus on teachers' practice. Only one classroom teacher was interviewed as part of this research; as such, in this section, understandings of the importance of classroom teachers as agents of inclusion is predominantly taken from the discussions of the Syrian parents.

Most of the families identified that their children's experiences with teachers had been 'good.' Little depth was gained in these responses, in part due to the language issue, which was a result of limitations in the design of the research, such as lack of access for participants to an interpreter. However, some families had few experiences with teachers to compare; two of the families' children only had one or two teachers in Scotland at the time of their interviews. The parents' responses resonated with other research with students from contexts of displacement, where teachers were recognised as 'good' because they were caring and there was no corporal punishment (Baak, 2016). The responses from two of the mothers in the focus group demonstrate this:

> ... the teacher at school is very nice and important about children very, very good ... Very caring. (Amena, mother's focus group)

> All the teachers are good – they are very kind and here no punishment for the children. (Fatima, mother's focus group)

One mother and father described their five-year-old son's teacher who was particularly noted for her effort to engage with their son. This family had a number of children at primary and secondary school, but their five-year-old's experience was one which particularly focussed on a strategy which enabled this teacher to act as an agent of inclusion. The mother, Amira, described that the "teacher ... was lovely" and Hassan, the father, further identified that:

> ... we couldn't realise from the beginning that is good situation for him, but the teacher was ... very, very, very good teacher ... the teacher I can say was, I mean, very good taking care of him ... And she tried to learn some words Arabic ... Just to talk to him. I mean she made a lot of effort just to keep him, I mean, feel happy in the school.

As an example of one of the ways in which this teacher endeavoured to include their son and make him feel welcome, the father commented on the teacher's efforts to learn Arabic. This was a significant strategy from the teacher that signalled to the student and his family that their background, experience and language capabilities were recognised and important. This strategy was also used by an EAL teacher interviewed in this study to facilitate inclusion and will be further considered in the sub-section below.

Given that students spend a majority of every day with classroom teachers, it was somewhat surprising that there was not more mention of the role of class teachers in facilitating inclusion, but perhaps this is a result of the reliance of staff and students on the support of EAL teachers, which will be considered below.

The EAL Teacher as 'Go To'

Research on classroom teachers' preparedness to teach English language and literacy to EAL students suggests that they may be 'ill-equipped to cope with such learners' or not see a place for themselves in the teaching of EAL (Reeves, 2006; Watkins, Lean, & Noble, 2016; Windle & Miller, 2012). As such, EAL teachers are seen to play an important role not only in supporting the language learning for displaced students, but also for enabling staff understandings of these students and their families and for building connections with students and families. School staff participants strongly recognised the importance of the role of EAL staff, not only for English language teaching, but also in a pastoral care, staff professional development and advocacy roles. Jane (leadership in local authority) and Ian (secondary EAL teacher) both recognised the EAL teacher as a 'go to' for students and families:

> So I think having an EAL teacher and having that person that you can go to and you can talk about things is really important support for young people and their families ... (Jane)

> ... what tends to happen is the pupils latch onto me because they know me and I become the link with pastoral care. So as regards social ... teachers and it probably happens in other schools as well, they gravitate towards the EAL teacher – they see them as the go to person. (Ian)

A number of teachers also recognised the importance of the EAL teacher in guiding school staff to support displaced students. For example, Elspeth (primary EAL teacher) identified that 'as the only EAL teacher in the school, the school kind of does look to me for guidance themselves.' However, she also identified the limits to this approach:

> They do tend to rely on the EAL teacher, so if a school has an EAL teacher who's experienced this before, then yes, they can guide them and lead them. But if it's a school that doesn't have an EAL teacher or hasn't had the experience of having these kinds of families before, then they're just kind of trying to do their best. (Elspeth)

Elspeth identified that the reliance of many schools solely on the EAL teacher to provide them with knowledge and guidance and to act as the main support

SCHOOLING DISPLACED SYRIAN STUDENTS IN GLASGOW 283

for displaced students and families meant that schools who had inexperienced or no EAL staff may find it difficult to appropriately work with displaced students.

The EAL teacher participants identified a number of strategies that they used to facilitate inclusion including home visits, learning the language of students and influencing school processes and policies. Like Mary, Elspeth, the primary EAL teacher who worked across two schools, identified the importance of home visits, particularly with recently arrived Syrian families.

> I made a point of doing a few home visits ... The families really, really appreciated someone just coming in and spending a bit of time with them ... It was probably the most valuable thing I've done in the last few years was to go and do that home visit with the family because I really did feel like – I don't know, I just got the vibe that they were like "Oh, somebody cares."

Elspeth recognised how visiting her students and families at their homes enabled the building of deeper relationships and demonstrated a care for the students beyond the classroom. The importance of home visits for students in contexts of high poverty has demonstrated that these visits can improve teachers' understandings of students and families, improve relationships with parents who may not regularly visit school and minimise the power imbalance between school staff and families (Amatea & West-Olatunji, 2007; Terrill & Mark, 2000; Van Velsor & Orozco, 2007). Elspeth was initially reluctant to visit families at home and suggested that this is not common practice; however, after her first visit, she wished she had done it sooner and committed to home visits with subsequent families if she identified this as appropriate.

Elspeth also identified that she had been learning Arabic to try and improve her engagement with the Syrian students:

> I've been learning a few words and things ... I'm not too bad now, I know my colours and my numbers and my days of the week and a few basic phrases and stuff like that and mainly because I wanted to kind of have that connection with the children, so I tried to kind of learn a bit.

Shared language learning becomes a way for Elspeth to build connection with her students as they see her modelling the language learning process. In addition, it enables the Arabic-speaking students to become the experts and teachers with language while the teacher becomes the learner.

Elspeth also identified the ways in which she had influenced the enrolment processes at the primary school in which she was teaching which had significant numbers of recently arrived Syrian students. She drew on her experiences gained as an EAL teacher at another school with significant EAL enrolments to propose and facilitate a more inclusive and supportive enrolment process for newly arrived students:

> When I first came to this school they hadn't had an EAL teacher for years because they'd never really had that much of an EAL population before ... So one of the things that I've kind of introduced, that I do insist on, is that I'm involved in the enrolment meeting as well ... [previously] I didn't think it was a particularly welcoming process and that wasn't that the school was trying to not be welcoming, it's just that that was the process that was to be followed. So now we do have a proper enrolment meeting and usually the school has a meeting first to do all that kind of getting the paperwork out of the way and getting the interpreters in to help and all of that ... so I definitely think that having that enrolment process and just making the families feel welcome from the outset is really, really important, that kind of first step of establishing a relationship with the school.

A range of scholars have identified the importance of school enrolment processes in facilitating inclusion of students and families (Block et al., 2014; Sale et al., 2003). As identified by Johnson (2003) culturally appropriate enrolment processes can be of benefit to the school. However, Elspeth's observations suggest that inclusive enrolment processes also have significant benefits for students and the families in building a welcoming ethos from the outset.

Office Staff: 'There Is Something about Having Welcoming Staff'

School office staff play a critical role in facilitating inclusion, as they are often the first point of contact for families in a school. A number of school staff participants identified innovative ways in which school office staff acted as agents of inclusion for students and families. Jane (leadership in local authority) identified a school at which the head teacher held expectations that office staff would provide a warm reception for all students, no matter the context.

> I think there is something about having welcoming staff and your office staff and your janitors and so on ... It was a head teacher, she always said to her office staff, "Whenever a child comes in here – whether you know them or not, you must smile at them because you don't know what they come from."

SCHOOLING DISPLACED SYRIAN STUDENTS IN GLASGOW

Office staff can play a crucial role in facilitating schools of inclusion and welcome. While it has been identified that a positive school climate is important for the inclusion of displaced students in schools (West, 2004), little research has been done to identify some of the everyday practice that facilitate this school climate. As well as simply smiling and being welcoming, the office staff at some schools in Glasgow had developed other creative ways to communicate with recently arrived Syrian families. For example, Elspeth explained how the secretary at her school was always seeking new ways to communicate with families:

> the secretary's got an app on her phone, it's like a Google one that you can scan something and it'll translate it … So she was the one that found that, she came in one day and she's like, "Look what I've found, it does this!" … So they do try really hard to find the ways to communicate and I think the families do get that vibe off them and they're more than happy.

When families 'get that vibe' that school staff are willing to try new and different things in order to facilitate communication, it sends a message to families and students that they are wanted and they belong in the school community. The important role of office staff is frequently overlooked in schools, where these 'front-line' staff can be key agents to facilitate inclusion through their actions.

Peers: 'We've Got Arabic Speaking Children'

The key role of peers in either facilitating inclusion or enabling exclusion was identified strongly by parents and school staff participants. Schools spoke of formal and informal buddying programs for recently arrived students. Some schools drew on the language capabilities of existing students by buddying the recently arrived Syrian students with Arabic speaking buddies who could act as interpreters as well as help the Syrian students become familiar with the school setting. Almost all of the parents identified the significant importance and role of other students at the schools who spoke Arabic in supporting their children in their early days and weeks at school. For example, Farid, a father with one son in early primary school described the following:

> He [my son] has a Lebanese friend when he start in the school. I told you he doesn't speak English and he can't understand anything. This, I think this boy born here, he speak English very well and Arabic … If my kids need anything from the teacher or from anybody, just we ask him to help him you know … And he can translate for him and if he want to ask the

teacher for anything we can translate for him or ask the teacher, or told the teacher what my kid needs.

Some students were at schools with significant numbers of Arabic-speaking students who were either born in Glasgow, or had been living there for a number of years. These students were an important resource for staff and for recently arrived Syrian students, particularly in their early days and weeks at school. Some schools formally recognised the role of these students in interpreting and translating for recently arrived students with schemes such as 'young interpreters' or 'language ambassadors' introduced in a number of schools. These schemes facilitated training and enabled formal recognition through certificates for multi-lingual students who played an important role of including the recently arrived Syrian students through language. Ian, a secondary EAL teacher, identified how buddying recently arrived Syrian students with those who have been in Glasgow can be mutually beneficial:

> So what we tend to do is pair them up with somebody who is a recent arrival from Syria with someone who has been here for 3–6 months who has just started to master it and that's great because suddenly that person transforms into the knowing guide and they've been the little quiet lost one and then they suddenly get to be a bit empowered and guide the other person around.

Buddying longer-term Syrian arrivals with new arrivals benefits both students as the longer-term students have recent first-hand experience being new in Glasgow schools as well as being able to support the recent arrival with language and communication. In addition, the longer-term student gains confidence from being the 'expert' guide to the school.

While the role of Arabic-speaking peers was critical, the teachers and parents both identified the importance of not just relying on Arabic students to engage with and facilitate inclusion of the recently arrived Syrian students. Jane, the local authority leader, described how the 'young interpreters scheme' was designed to be an option for monolingual English speakers:

> Young interpreter scheme is actually designed to be used by people who are monolingual English speakers as well and it focuses on using body language and gesture ... how to explain things ... how you can actually help someone to learn what the name of something is and to show things. So we find some of our secondary schools quite a lot of young people who are monolingual English speakers opt to do that.

The parents also recognised the importance of peers, particularly English speaking peers, in facilitating English language learning. Yara, a mother of two, suggested that 'the children learn [English] from a friend, not from teacher, you know.' Fatima, a mother of nine, supported this describing her children's experience:

> When my children came first time they can't speak English – when they walk with a friend or like they make friends they said, "No – no walk with us." One year my children walk with – together. They can't learn English like this. They stay one year without English, like just with teacher … teacher without friends. When they move to another school like the majority are Scots they become better. They can make friends; they can speak; they can go and come with them. Now they are better.

Fatima describes how her children's exclusion from English-speaking peers at their first school limited their conversational language development. When her children moved to a new school, where it would appear that the English-speaking students were more inclusive, Fatima's children were able to make friends, speak and hence better develop their conversational language skills.

Language was the key element identified by teachers and parents in enabling peer inclusion. While Arabic-speaking peers were identified as essential for inclusion for the Syrian students in the early weeks after arrival, English-speaking peers also played an essential role to support the English language development of Syrian students to enable longer-term inclusion.

Conclusion

Glasgow is an interesting context of resettlement in which to consider the educational provisions for recently arrived students who have experienced displacement. Scotland's policy context necessitates the physical inclusion of all students in their local neighbourhood school on arrival. This research, while small in scale, indicates that the ways in which schools respond to this imperative for the physical inclusion of displaced Syrian students is ad hoc and relies on the interests and care of individuals within these schools settings.

In this chapter I have explicitly focussed on experiences and actions of agents which facilitated inclusion. That is not to say that the participants didn't detail experiences of exclusion, but rather this chapter is a considered attempt to focus on the hopeful possibilities and everyday practices that can be undertaken to facilitate inclusion in schools. Where Slee (2018) argues that 'the mobilisation of exclusion through the structures, processes, programmes and ethos; that is, the cultures, of schooling is an embodiment of our social condition' (p. 16), this chapter has endeavoured to highlight the ways in which individual 'agents of inclusion' can challenge and sometimes change these structures, processes, programmes and ethos. For some agents, such as the peers described above, their role as agents is limited to enabling everyday inclusion and connection through language and support to understand the systems and structures of schools.

For other agents, such as the EAL teachers who provide guidance to classroom teachers and act as a 'go to' for students and families, their actions enable broader inclusion of displaced Syrian students and their families within the school. The role of school leaders means that when a head teacher acts as an 'agent of change' their actions shape not only the everyday inclusion of displaced students and families, but the broader structures and resources which shape the ability of others within their school to enable inclusion. It is when all of these elements come together, from the policy, structural, contextual and resource based factors to the everyday actions and agency of individual actors, that it will become possible to really enable the inclusion of displaced students in Glasgow's schools in a way that does not just physically include the students but actually is inclusive.

Acknowledgements

This research was undertaken as part of an Australian Government funded Endeavour Research Fellowship. I am very grateful to the participants from the Syrian community in Glasgow and the community group who facilitated my engagement with the Syrian community. Thank you also to the school staff who offered their time and expertise. Finally, thank you to Professor Alison Phipps and the School of Education at the University of Glasgow for their hospitality and support in undertaking this research.

Note

1   While English as an Additional Language or Dialect (EALD) is the more commonly internationally recognised phrase to recognise those who speak or learn English as an additional language, the commonly used phrase in Glasgow's schools is English as an Additional Language (EAL). As such, in this chapter, to keep coherent language between the quotes and the broader text, the term English as an Additional Language is used.

References

Alford, J. H. (2014). "Well, hang on, they're actually much better than that!": Disrupting dominant discourses of deficit about English language learners in senior high school English. *English Teaching: Practice and Critique, 13*(3), 71–88.

Allan, J. (2010). Questions of inclusion in Scotland and Europe. *European Journal of Special Needs Education, 25*(2), 199–208.

Amatea, E., & West-Olatunji, C. (2007). Joining the conversation about educating our poorest children: Emerging leadership roles for school counselors in high-poverty schools. *Professional School Counseling, 11*(2), 81–89.

Baak, M. (2016). Overcoming the 'hidden injuries' of students from refugee backgrounds: The importance of caring teacher–student relationships. In A. Sullivan, B. Johnson, & B. Lucas (Eds.), *Challenging dominant views on student behaviour at school: Answering back* (pp. 145–161). Singapore: Springer.

Baak, M. (2018). Racism and othering for South Sudanese heritage students in Australian schools: Is inclusion possible? *International Journal of Inclusive Education, 15*(1), 1–17.

Biesta, G., & Tedder, M. (2007). Agency and learning in the lifecourse: Towards an ecological perspective. *Studies in the Education of Adults, 39*(2), 132–149.

Block, K., Cross, S., Riggs, E., & Gibbs, L. (2014). Supporting schools to create an inclusive environment for refugee students. *International Journal of Inclusive Education, 18*(12), 1337–1355.

Boyatzis, R. E. (1998). *Transforming qualitative information: Thematic analysis and code development.* Thousand Oaks, CA: Sage Publications.

Brown, J., Miller, J., & Mitchell, J. (2006). Interrupted schooling and the acquisition of literacy: Experiences of Sudanese refugees in Victorian secondary schools. *Australian Journal of Language & Literacy, 29*(2), 150–162.

Burgoyne, U., & Hull, O. (2007). *Classroom management strategies to address the needs of Sudanese refugee learners: Advice to teachers – ERIC.* Retrieved from https://eric.ed.gov/?id=ED499678

COSLA Strategic Migration Partnership. (2018). *Refugee resettlement.* Retrieved from http://www.migrationscotland.org.uk/our-priorities/current-work/syrian-refugee-resettlement

de Wal Pastoor, L. (2016). Rethinking refugee education: Principles, policies and practice from a European perspective. In A. W. Wiseman (Ed.), *Annual review of comparative and international education 2016* (Vol. 30, pp. 107–116). Sheffield: Emerald Group Publishing Limited.

DeCapua, A., Smathers, W., & Tang, L. F. (2007). Schooling, interrupted. *Educational Leadership, 64*(6), 40–46.

Due, C., Riggs, D. W., & Mandara, M. (2015). Educators' experiences of working in intensive English language programs: The strengths and challenges of specialised

English language classrooms for students with migrant and refugee backgrounds. *Australian Journal of Education, 59*(2), 169–181. doi:10.1177/0004944115587365

Graham, L. J., & Slee, R. (2008). An illusory interiority: Interrogating the discourse/s of inclusion. *Educational Philosophy and Theory, 40*(2), 277–293.

Home Office. (2017, February 23). *National statistics asylum.* Retrieved from https://www.gov.uk/government/publications/immigration-statistics-october-to-december-2016/asylum

International Catholic Migration Commission Europe. (2013). The UK resettlement programme at a glance. In *Welcome to Europe! A comprehensive guide to resettlement* (pp. 263–272).

IPSOS MORI. (2016). *Mixed views on the refugee crisis among Scots.* Retrieved from https://www.ipsos.com/ipsos-mori/en-uk/mixed-views-refugee-crisis-among-scots

Johnson, L. S. (2003). The diversity imperative: Building a culturally responsive school ethos. *Intercultural Education, 14*(1), 17–30.

Keddie, A. (2012). Refugee education and justice issues of representation, redistribution and recognition. *Cambridge Journal of Education, 42*(2), 197–212. doi:10.1080/0 305764X.2012.676624

Liston, D. P., & Zeichner, K. M. (1990). Reflective teaching and action research in pre-service teacher education. *Journal of Education for Teaching, 16*(3), 235–254.

McBrien, J. L. (2005). Educational needs and barriers for refugee students in the United States: A review of the literature. *Review of Educational Research, 75*(3), 329–364.

Mcglynn, C., & London, T. (2013). Leadership for inclusion: Conceptualising and enacting inclusion in integrated schools in a troubled society. *Research Papers in Education, 28*(2), 155–175. doi:10.1080/02671522.2011.600458

Miller, E., Ziaian, T., & Esterman, A. (2017). Australian school practices and the education experiences of students with a refugee background: A review of the literature. *International Journal of Inclusive Education, 22*(3), 1–21.

Miller, J. (2009). Teaching refugee learners with interrupted education in science: Vocabulary, literacy and pedagogy. *International Journal of Science Education, 31*(4), 571–592.

Miller, J., Mitchell, J., & Brown, J. (2005). African refugees with interrupted schooling in the high school mainstream: Dilemmas for teachers. *Prospect, 20*(2), 19–33.

Muijs, D., Ainscow, M., Dyson, A., Raffo, C., Goldrick, S., Kerr, K., ... Miles, S. (2010). Leading under pressure: Leadership for social inclusion. *School Leadership and Management, 30*(2), 143–157.

Murray, C. D., & Wynne, J. (2001). Researching community, work and family with an interpreter. *Community, Work & Family, 4*(2), 157–171.

Nagasa, K. (2014). Perspectives of elementary teachers on refugee parent-teacher relations and the education of their children. *Journal of Educational Research and Innovation, 3*(1), 1–16.

Naidoo, L. (2013). Refugee Action Support: An interventionist pedagogy for supporting refugee students' learning in Greater Western Sydney secondary schools. *International Journal of Inclusive Education, 17*(5), 449–461. doi:10.1080/13603116.2012.683048

Pantić, N., & Florian, L. (2015). Developing teachers as agents of inclusion and social justice. *Education Inquiry, 6*(3), 333–351.

Pinson, H., & Arnot, M. (2010). Local conceptualisations of the education of asylum-seeking and refugee students: From hostile to holistic models. *International Journal of Inclusive Education, 14*(3), 247–267. doi:10.1080/13603110802504523

Priestley, M., Biesta, G., & Robinson, S. (2013). Teachers as agents of change: Teacher agency and emerging models of curriculum. In M. Priestley & G. J. J. Biesta (Eds.), *Reinventing the curriculum: New trends in curriculum policy and practice* (pp. 187–206). London: Bloomsbury Academic.

Priestley, M., Biesta, G., & Robinson, S. (2015). *Teacher agency: An ecological approach.* London: Bloomsbury Publishing.

Pugh, K., Every, D., & Hattam, R. (2012). Inclusive education for students with refugee experience: Whole school reform in a South Australian primary school. *The Australian Educational Researcher, 39*(2), 125–141. doi:10.1007/s13384-011-0048-2

Reeves, J. R. (2006). Secondary teacher attitudes toward including English-language learners in mainstream classrooms. *The Journal of Educational Research, 99*(3), 131–143.

Riehl, C. J. (2009). The principal's role in creating inclusive schools for diverse students: A review of normative, empirical, and critical literature on the practice of educational administration. *Journal of Education, 189*(1–2), 183–197. doi:10.1177/0022057409189001-213

Roxas, K. (2010). Who really wants "the tired, the poor, and the huddled masses" anyway?: Teachers' use of cultural scripts with refugee students in public schools. *Multicultural Perspectives, 12*(2), 65–73.

Rutter, J. (2006). *Refugee children in the UK.* London: McGraw-Hill Education.

Sale, L., Sliz, L., & Pacini-Ketchabaw, V. (2003). Creating an inclusive climate for newly arrived students. In S. R. Schecter & J. Cummins (Eds.), *Multilingual education in practice: Using diversity as a resource* (pp. 17–31). Portsmouth, NH: Heinemann.

Scottish Government. (2013). *New scots: Integrating refugees in scotland's communities 2014–2017.* Retrieved from http://www.gov.scot/Resource/0043/00439604.pdf

Scottish Government. (2017a). *New scots: Integrating refugees in scotland's communities 2014–2017 final report.* Retrieved from http://www.gov.scot/Publications/2017/03/5825/8

Scottish Government. (2017b). *New scots: Integrating refugees in Scotland's communities 2014–2017 final report.* Retrieved from https://beta.gov.scot/publications/new-scots-integrating-refugees-scotlands-communities-2014-2017-final-report-9781786526960/documents/00515713.pdf?inline=true

Scottish Government. (2017c). *Where did GIRFEC come from?* Retrieved from http://www.gov.scot/Topics/People/Young-People/gettingitright/what-is-girfec/where-girfec-came-from

Scottish Government. (2018). *New scots refugee integration strategy 2018–2022.* Retrieved from http://www.gov.scot/Resource/0053/00530097.pdf

Scottish Refugee Council. (2018). *Responding to the challenges of dispersal.* Retrieved from http://www.scottishrefugeecouncil.org.uk/about/history/dispersal

Slee, R. (2011). *The irregular school: Exclusion, schooling and inclusive education.* London & New York, NY: Taylor & Francis.

Slee, R. (2013). How do we make inclusive education happen when exclusion is a political predisposition? *International Journal of Inclusive Education, 17*(8), 895–907. doi:10.1080/13603116.2011.602534

Slee, R. (2018). *Inclusive education isn't dead, it just smells funny.* London: Routledge.

Slee, R., & Allan, J. (2001). Excluding the included: A reconsideration of inclusive education. *International Studies in Sociology of Education, 11*(2), 173–192.

Taylor, S., & Sidhu, R. K. (2012). Supporting refugee students in schools: What constitutes inclusive education? *International Journal of Inclusive Education, 16*(1), 39–56.

Terrill, M. M., & Mark, D. L. (2000). Preservice teachers' expectations for schools with children of color and second-language learners. *Journal of Teacher Education, 51*(2), 149–155.

UNHCR. (2014). *Country chapters – UNHCR resettlement handbook: United Kingdom of Great Britain and Northern Ireland.* Retrieved from http://www.unhcr.org/40ee6fc04.pdf

US Department of Health and Human Services. (2016). *Syrian refugee health profile.* Retrieved from https://www.cdc.gov/immigrantrefugeehealth/pdf/syrian-health-profile.pdf

Van Velsor, P., & Orozco, G. L. (2007). Involving low-income parents in the schools: Communitycentric strategies for school counselors. *Professional School Counseling, 11*(1), 17–24. 2156759X0701100103

Watkins, M., Lean, G., & Noble, G. (2016). Multicultural education: The state of play from an Australian perspective. *Race Ethnicity and Education, 19*(1), 46–66. doi:10.1080/13613324.2015.1013929

Watson, C. (2010). Educational policy in Scotland: Inclusion and the control society. *Discourse: Studies in the Cultural Politics of Education, 31*(1), 93–104.

West, S. (2004). School's in for Australia's refugee students: [How can principals and their schools assist young refugees?]. *Principal Matters, 61*, 30–32.

Windle, J., & Miller, J. (2012). Approaches to teaching low literacy refugee-background students. *The Australian Journal of Language and Literacy, 35*(3), 317–333.

Conclusion

Jody L. McBrien

During the production phase of this volume, the world was at its highest point of forced migration: 68.5 million people (UNHCR, 2018). This is a rate of one person every two seconds. The populations include refugees, asylum seekers, and internally displaced persons. Those fleeing describe hunger that led them to eat weeds and tree leaves (UNHCR, 2018). Major populations recently affected include Congolese, South Sudanese, Rohingya, and Syrians. Contrary to popular opinion, most of the world's displaced people live in developing countries in the global south (85%). They have not been able to flee to industrialised countries.

This volume is concentrated on the small percentage who are able to resettle into wealthy English-speaking countries in the globalised north. Such a placement is considered a great fortune. However, as the chapters detail, such placements are hardly a ready-made journey into prosperity and welcome.

Taken altogether, these chapters provide several highly important themes in the realm of globalisation, education, and refugee resettlement. One: global change is occurring with remarkable speed. The international community is not prepared for it, but it is unstoppable. There are currently no indications that these high numbers of refugees and asylum seekers will reduce in the near future, given the continuation of the Syrian War, and major unrest in other Middle Eastern, African, Asian, and Central/South American countries.

Second, economic and social challenges worldwide are causing countries to reduce their welcome to immigrants, including refugees and asylum seekers. The opposition to immigration is depicted in many chapters contained in this volume. For instance, in the United States, President Trump and his followers have continued to campaign for a physical wall between Mexico and the United States in an attempt to deter asylum seekers from Central and South America. Australia and many European countries continue to demonstrate opposition against hosting refugees and asylum seekers.

The nature of culture and how it is perceived plays a role in how refugees are welcomed or met with hostility. Culture, the socially transmitted beliefs, behaviours, and values of groups, can be seen as static. From this viewpoint, groups with different lifestyles will be seen as outsiders. Without large-scale integration trainings for communities, this sentiment is understandable. Residents of small communities throughout European countries are seeing their towns transformed by practices and traditions that have never been a part of

© KONINKLIJKE BRILL NV, LEIDEN, 2019 | DOI: 10.1163/9789004401891_013

their daily lives, such as a daily call to prayer for Muslims and clothing that they find unfamiliar. These worries have also become prevalent in North America and Australasia. In contrast, there are a number of NGOs that work to provide citizens and newcomers with ways to learn about one another and work together to forge integrated communities (see Welcoming America, n.d.).

Local concerns must be mediated by the concerns of highly diverse people who have fled for their lives into countries in which the culture is vastly different from their own. Much of the culture of the newcomers is bound to their religious and social beliefs. As they flee in search of safety, must their pursuits require them to alter their religious and cultural traditions? Need those traditions cause local residents to fear for their own traditions and their very safety?

Adding to the crisis of cultural clashes is the era of 'fake news.' Frequently the conservative political right uses this term to deny information uncovered by news media with a more liberal perspective. It has been reinforced by rapidly changing media, in which broadcasting (e.g., having few main TV networks) has been replaced by narrowcasting (literally hundreds of channels and websites that cater to the social and political whims of individual citizens). As a result, individuals no longer need to receive their news from a small number of networks that propose to broadcast a 'neutral' version of newsworthy topics. For example, in the United States, citizens know that if they are conservative, they want to get their news from Fox News. If they are liberal, they turn to MSNBC. As such, 'fair and balanced' reporting is not the goal of the most watched new media agencies; Fox dropped that mantra in 2017.

This is a challenging, and a frightening, time for those engaged in social justice and liberation work. The history of such times also indicates that this work has become highly important. Researchers must find a way to overcome political walls to provide information to policy makers on both sides of the liberal and conservative boundaries. Somehow, legitimate research must supplant the personal opinions held and used by politicians in their powerful positions to create national policies.

Certainly, the authors of this book believe in the work of schools and societies to support refugees and asylum seekers, and the chapters provide not only challenges, but also proven methods for welcoming newcomers and helping them to succeed. We hope that our research will be read not only by academics, but also those in positions of determining policy.

In spite of our disparate studies, reflecting diverse country policies and practices from early childhood through higher education, our conclusions are remarkably similar. Were policymakers to heed them, they might support similar policies with regards to practice:

CONCLUSION

1. Language learning (and sufficient time for such) is paramount to gaining necessary skills for higher education and skilful employment.
2. Refugees need to be seen in the light of resilience, and not as victims.
3. Most refugees are eager to learn and want to contribute to their new countries.
4. Educational models that consider not only children, but also families (and, in particular, mothers) provide the greatest support for family learning.
5. Course subject teachers need to consult with English-language teachers to provide appropriate content- and language-rich opportunities for immigrant children.
6. Refugee and asylum-seeking children frequently hold within them stories of terrible trauma. As such, they should be handled with respect and delicacy, and not pushed to tell their stories unless they volunteer to do so.
7. Successful academic resources need to include well-researched methods for language learning, coordinated culturally relevant psychosocial practices and integrated learning opportunities with native students. The arts and sports are often useful opportunities for inclusive practice.
8. Best practices afford refugee families the opportunities for self-sufficiency and their own decision making.
9. Although it begins at the school level for refugee and asylum-seeking children, integration must include community-level awareness and opportunity.

It is understandable that settled communities fear change resulting from the influx of international populations into their regions, especially when those newcomers arrive with different languages, beliefs, and behaviours. It is natural to fear the unknown. When such fear is followed by curiosity rather than anger, positive change can occur. Curiosity and interest result from research and education, and not from propaganda and misinformation.

Welcoming America is one non-profit organisation that has set up sites throughout the United States (and has also created workshops in Germany and New Zealand) for facilitating meetings between community residents and resettled refugees. Participants discover that they have similar fears and similar goals. Long-standing community residents find that refugees fear deportation and violence. Refugees learn that the residents fear violence by the refugees. Goals of both groups involve a happy family life, good education, and jobs that allow them to support their families. As individuals work together on community events, they realise that they are more alike than different. This work follows the pattern of Allport's contact theory (1954).

Similar adjustments must be made in communities worldwide. Citizens may feel initially reticent to acknowledge the changes occurring in their communities, and teachers may be frustrated by the changes they must make to accommodate newcomer students. However, in the long run, such accommodations will not only benefit the newcomer students and families, but also the adapting communities, as they support resettled refugee students and families to receive a quality education. By so doing, the refugees can contribute to the national success and economic portrait of their new country of resettlement. As such, both the nation and the newcomer become winners.

Refugees should be resettled because they are unsafe within their homelands, not because they can provide financial gain to their new country of residence. However, the long-term consequences of providing an appropriate education and social support create the framework for a healthy, safe, and economically secure society.

As has been demonstrated in the chapters of this book, necessary supports are similar throughout the English-speaking nations of resettlement, and perhaps throughout all resettlement countries. Refugees need the time to learn the language and cultural attributes of their host country. They also require time to heal from physical and mental traumas suffered during their years between fleeing their homelands and being resettled. They need to gain social networks. They need support to gain access to skilled jobs, especially when they had credentials in their homelands for such employment.

Teachers require training to understand best practices to support refugee and asylum-seeking children. Many of these best practices are currently in conflict with national policies. As such, it is imperative for nation states to reconsider policies based on research if policy makers are truly interested in creating successful procedures of resettlement and acculturation. This statement is not meant to suggest that such policies would create an easy social transition. Settled communities are understandably concerned about change to their way of life. However, creating opportunities for children to be welcomed into schools and adults to be accommodated and supported is far more likely to create the possibility of co-created and accepted social change rather than increased conflict in nations of resettlement.

References

Allport, G. (1954). *The nature of prejudice.* Cambridge/Reading, MA: Addison-Wesley.
UNHCR. (2018, June 19). *Forced displacement at record 68.5 million.* Retrieved from https://www.unhcr.org/news/stories/2018/6/5b222c494/forced-displacement-record-685-million.html
Welcoming America. (n.d.). Retrieved from https://www.welcomingamerica.org/

Index

academic support 74

access/accessible/accessing 2, 4, 5, 7, 9, 10, 18, 24, 42, 44, 47, 50–54, 60, 61, 64, 76, 78, 79, 81, 89, 91–100, 102, 103, 125–127, 131, 132, 147, 158, 161, 162, 165, 166, 177, 178, 180–183, 185, 187, 188, 200–206, 211, 213–215, 223, 224, 226, 228–231, 241–244, 247, 249, 258, 267, 269, 275, 277, 281, 296

acculturation ix, 4, 24, 58, 98, 115, 144, 146–148, 150, 177, 179, 180–183, 185, 190, 191, 296

achievement 43, 69, 115, 132, 133, 141, 142, 151, 170, 172, 177, 229, 232, 256, 257, 270, 279

agency x, 9, 18, 20, 31–33, 35, 44, 62, 65, 76, 114, 120, 123, 137, 149, 178, 201, 202, 206, 207, 223, 229, 242, 272, 273, 288

assimilation 163

asylum seeker/asylees 1, 5, 9–11, 48, 54, 88, 90–93, 100–104, 133, 148, 178, 199, 200, 203–206, 208, 209, 212–215, 221–224, 227, 229, 230, 233, 234, 240, 241, 247, 255, 268–270, 293, 294

career x, 6, 53, 55, 102, 115, 122, 124, 125, 151, 189, 213, 260

caring 5, 61, 62, 77, 78, 225, 244, 281

case study 58, 63, 150, 245, 246

child soldier 24

collaborate/collaboration/collaborative xv, 5, 31, 33–36, 62, 63, 76, 77, 79–81, 89, 103, 104, 116, 127, 171, 172, 209, 212, 215, 232, 273, 271–273

community 4–7, 18, 20, 22, 23, 25, 26, 33–35, 43, 47, 62, 64, 77–81, 88, 89, 94, 95, 100, 101, 104, 114–122, 124–127, 131, 133, 138, 139, 144–150, 158, 161, 162, 166, 167, 171–173, 178–181, 183, 187, 209, 210, 213, 215, 222, 223, 228, 229, 232, 233, 246–251, 253, 257, 258, 268, 270–272, 274, 278–280, 285, 293–296

conflict 20, 32, 33, 42, 46, 69, 92, 95, 113, 114, 163, 180, 208, 222, 232, 233, 242, 246, 249–252, 258, 267, 268, 276, 296

constructivist 4, 26, 34, 36

convention refugee 9, 54, 200, 201, 203, 213

counselling 20–24, 30

cultural capital 8, 102, 177, 182, 184, 187, 189, 228, 249

culturally appropriate ix, 6, 33, 116, 232, 284

culture 4, 7, 8, 11, 12, 26, 28, 34, 58, 61, 73, 115, 117, 122, 124, 143–146, 148–150, 158, 164, 165, 167, 171, 177, 179, 182–184, 189, 214, 242, 244, 248, 251, 252, 258, 272, 278, 280, 288, 293, 294

Deferred Action for Childhood Arrivals (DACA) 133

dependency 22, 224

Direct Provision 9, 10, 201, 203, 204, 207, 208, 210, 223–226

discrimination x, 8, 101, 115, 148, 226, 245

displaced 89, 113, 133, 136, 157, 158, 162, 168, 178, 240, 241, 249, 267–269, 271, 273, 275, 277–279, 281–283, 285, 287–291

diversity 6–8, 32, 55, 78, 98, 103, 116, 128, 145, 146, 184, 185, 210, 211, 220, 248, 271–273, 278

educational outcomes 35, 46, 53, 247, 258

emigration 8, 26, 46, 199, 221

employment ix, , x, 2, 3, 6, 8, 10, 22, 23, 24, 33, 43, 44, 46, 53, 58, 95, 96, 100–102, 115, 123–126, 138, 177, 179, 180, 189–191, 224, 233, 240, 242, 247, 260, 267, 268, 270, 295, 296

empowered/empowering/empowerment 3, 21, 22, 26, 28, 31, 33, 34, 61, 63, 79, 166, 182, 188, 190, 286

English Language

    English as an Additional Language (EAL) 12, 57–61, 63–65, 68–71, 73, 74, 78, 80, 81, 97–99, 212, 213, 230, 267, 270, 273, 277–279, 281–284, 286, 288

    English as a Second Language (ESL/ESOL) 47, 49, 50, 53, 94, 97, 99, 102, 104, 161, 210, 247

    English Language Learner (ELL) 4, 6–9, 132, 135, 136, 139–143, 147, 150, 151, 156, 158–161, 164, 167, 169, 170, 172

    English Language School (ELS) 4, 5, 57, 58, 60, 61, 63, 65–69, 72–76, 78, 79, 81

298 INDEX

ethnographic/ethnography   4, 58, 63, 64, 158, 167

exclusion   26, 46, 163, 224, 225, 249, 267, 273, 280, 285, 287, 288

family reunification   204

Freire, P.   169

genocide   178

Global Compact on Refugees (GCR)   89

globalisation   149, 163, 221, 240, 293

goal(s)   6, 42, 44–46, 49, 51–55, 89, 96, 132, 158, 180, 182, 186, 190, 192, 212, 223, 243, 253, 258, 294, 295

graduate students   48

healing   18, 22–25, 29, 31, 34–36, 259

higher education   4, 5, 8, 11, 48, 49, 52–54, 88, 89, 91–96, 101, 103, 104, 132, 177, 180, 181, 185, 186, 191, 211, 246, 248, 249, 258, 259, 294, 295

high school students   47–50, 167

housing   ix, x, 2, 3, 12, 22, 23, 42, 115, 181, 223, 224, 233, 240, 247, 267, 270

immigrant   3, 6, 9, 11, 20, 42, 43, 46, 50, 53, 90, 100, 103, 113, 114, 119, 127, 131–133, 135–139, 141–151

inequality   11, 102, 228, 272

Intensive English Centre (IEC)   97–99

integration   2, 8, 9, 11, 17, 31, 35, 36, 42, 46, 80, 95, 97, 102, 118, 120, 125–127, 156, 164, 166, 167, 169, 177–179, 182, 188, 189, 199, 202, 206, 208–210, 223, 227–230, 233, 244, 248, 270, 293, 295

internally displaced   178, 240, 293

intervention   17, 18, 21–23, 28, 33, 45, 113, 116, 121, 214, 229, 250, 253

language learning   4, 5, 10, 12, 88, 94, 96, 171, 212, 231, 282, 283, 287, 295
    language acquisition   3, 12, 23, 32, 146, 159
    language classes   22, 31, 180
    language programmes   31, 35, 101, 136

leadership   76, 81, 94, 116, 146, 147, 216, 267, 271, 273–276, 278, 279, 282, 284

Local Education Authorities (LEA)   10, 227–229, 232

mainstream   4, 9, 32, 57, 58, 60, 61, 63, 74–79, 81, 95, 97–99, 126, 140, 141, 158, 203, 209, 212–215, 230, 231, 258, 267, 275–277

Māori   21, 28, 34, 35

marginalised   34

mediation   232, 233

medical   2, 3, 19–22, 113, 183, 184, 186, 188, 191, 192, 223, 233, 253

mental health   1, 17–23, 25, 31, 36, 116, 138, 144, 150, 203, 213, 223, 224, 247, 252, 259

mental illness   19

mentor   6, 119, 122–124, 189, 191, 212, 243, 244, 245

migrant/migration   23, 26, 31, 66, 88, 89, 91, 95, 100–103, 113–116, 120, 121, 123, 133, 138, 143, 144, 147, 148, 150, 151, 161, 165, 168, 177, 178, 186, 188, 190, 191, 199, 205, 206, 208, 210, 212–216, 229–231, 233, 234, 240, 246, 251–253, 256, 268–270, 274, 275, 293

motivation   21, 50, 52, 89, 104, 171, 205, 242, 243

multicultural/multiculturalism   4, 28, 57, 59, 65, 68, 76, 114, 216

National Certificate of Educational Achievement (NCEA)   43, 47, 49–51, 53, 54

natural disaster   157, 179

neoliberal   5, 88, 95, 97, 100, 103, 269

newcomer   x, 4, 5, 7, 31, 32, 34, 57–60, 65, 81, 138, 140–143, 147, 150, 157, 158, 160, 162, 164–167, 169, 172, 179, 180, 182–184, 186, 188–191, 246, 247, 294–296

New Zealand Refugee Resettlement Strategy   43, 50, 53

normalisation   23, 30

outcomes   2, 12, 18, 22, 33, 35, 43, 46, 53, 62, 78, 80, 81, 89, 94, 95, 124, 125, 142, 148, 158, 172, 201, 205, 209, 213, 247, 248, 253, 257, 258, 272, 279

partnership   5, 58, 61, 116, 118, 119, 127, 181, 210, 212, 252, 271, 276

pathology/pathologising   3, 17–20, 22, 23

pedagogy   5, 26, 45, 267, 271, 272, 280
    pedagogical   17, 62, 170, 172, 203, 251, 258

policy/policymakers   5, 7, 8, 12, 28, 44, 46, 54, 59, 60, 61, 76, 78, 80, 88–91, 94–96,

INDEX 299

98, 100, 102–104, 113, 116, 120, 131, 132,
142, 143, 146, 147, 160, 162–164, 177, 178,
181, 188, 190, 192, 199, 201, 202, 205,
206, 209–211, 216, 224, 227, 229, 230,
242, 249, 254, 255, 257–260, 267–272,
274–276, 278, 279, 287, 288, 294, 296
Post-Traumatic Stress Disorder (PTSD)
17–20, 35, 252
power/powerful   5, 8, 18, 20, 24, 25, 26, 32,
33, 35, 36, 43, 62, 63, 76–80, 123, 151, 156,
165, 227, 247, 250, 283, 294
powhiri   34
prejudice   x, 19, 131, 165, 247, 248, 258
prevention   31
problem-solving   31–33, 35
programme refugees   9, 200, 202, 203, 205,
207, 213–215
psychosocial   ix, 7, 8, 20, 45, 54, 115, 117, 143,
150, 257, 259, 295
psychopharmacology   21
psychotherapy   21
purpose/purposeful   10, 26, 33, 63, 116, 133,
141, 144, 147, 149, 179, 200, 223, 241, 252,
253, 270, 273

quota refugee   17, 42, 43, 47, 48, 54

recertification   8, 180, 186, 188, 191
refugee-background   3, 4, 18, 23, 26, 32, 34,
44, 45, 47, 53, 55, 57, 64
Refugee Education Center (REC)   18, 25–35
religion   7, 157, 205
resettlement   ix, x, 1–6, 9, 11, 12, 19, 23, 24, 33,
35, 42–45, 47, 50, 53–55, 58, 61, 89, 90,
93, 94, 96, 102, 116, 136–138, 140, 144,
164, 177–179, 181, 188, 190–192, 200, 201,
207, 215, 221, 223, 227, 241, 247, 256, 268,
269, 287, 293, 296
resilience   3, 4, 18, 20, 23, 25, 26, 36, 42,
62, 79, 115, 120, 202, 244, 253, 256, 295
resilient   x, 17, 36, 79, 192
resources   19, 20, 23, 28, 36, 52, 54, 60, 79, 80,
97, 99, 100, 102, 120, 126, 132, 140–142, 144,
145, 147, 159, 163, 173, 177, 188, 210–212,
228, 229, 231, 240, 246, 250, 251, 254, 257,
259, 267, 272, 277, 278, 286, 288, 295
rights   1, 7, 10, 18, 25, 26, 28–30, 32, 35, 42,
43, 62, 88, 91, 92, 104, 161, 163, 187, 191,
199, 201, 202, 204, 214, 224, 227, 228,
240–242, 254, 257, 268, 270

safety   x, 4, 18, 24, 25, 28–31, 36, 144, 226, 244,
253, 258, 268, 294
school-based programmes   116
self-sufficiency/self-sufficient   8, 36, 102,
177–180, 189–191, 295
separated children   9, 201, 202, 204, 205, 208,
213, 214, 224, 260
services   4–6, 17, 20–24, 36, 43, 44, 53, 54,
59, 81, 94–96, 100, 102, 113, 114, 116, 117,
119–121, 125–127, 136, 137, 144, 160–162,
178, 181, 182, 192, 202, 205, 208, 212–215,
223, 228, 229, 232, 233, 245–248, 250,
255, 257, 259, 260, 268–270, 272, 276
social capital   23, 182, 183, 186, 253
social justice   79, 88, 91, 103, 272, 294
stigma/stigmatised   18, 20, 101, 204, 253
strength-based   3, 120
support   ix, x, 1–12, 17, 19–21, 23, 25, 26, 29,
31–33, 35, 44–48, 50, 51, 53–55, 57–61,
63, 64, 75–81, 90, 91, 93–100, 102–104,
113, 115–122, 125–128, 132, 133, 136, 137,
140–147, 149, 150, 156, 157, 159, 160, 162,
166, 168, 170–172, 177, 181–183, 187, 191,
200–205, 208–216, 223–225, 228–234,
243–246, 248–253, 255, 257–259,
267, 269–271, 275–278, 282, 284–288,
294–296
specialist support   212
survivor   19, 22, 24, 26, 36, 57, 62, 251, 253
Syria   ix, 10, 11, 17, 90, 131, 178, 242, 246,
247, 249–251, 267–270, 274, 277–280,
283–288, 293

tertiary study   44
therapy   3, 19–22, 24, 30, 31, 35, 228
therapeutic   17, 18, 22, 25, 35
transition   xii, 4, 5, 10, 57–81, 97–99, 121, 140,
157, 160, 162, 171, 204, 205, 214, 241, 242,
253, 255, 258, 259, 296
trauma   2–4, 7, 17–20, 22–26, 29, 31, 35, 36,
45, 58, 91, 93, 95, 100, 115, 120, 138, 144,
146, 148–150, 162, 179, 183, 203, 212, 215,
250, 252–253, 258, 270, 271, 295, 296
trust   11, 17, 18, 24–27, 35, 63–65, 78, 114, 126,
134, 213, 280

unaccompanied minors   9, 166, 200–203,
205, 207, 213, 222, 225, 229, 230
undocumented   131, 132, 138
unemployment   22, 101, 123, 199, 221

United Nationals High Commissioner of Refugees (UNHCR) 2, 9, 19, 42, 44, 89, 90, 92, 93, 113, 114, 131, 178, 200, 202, 208, 231, 269, 293

United Nations Convention on Refugees 17

victim x, 3, 4, 8, 19, 23, 26, 242, 295

welcome x, 7, 17, 18, 24, 26, 27, 28, 30, 34, 36, 73, 77, 90, 136, 160, 164, 180, 228, 278, 280, 289, 281, 284, 285, 293, 296

welcoming 4, 6, 12, 22, 24, 25, 27, 28, 31, 33, 34, 78, 121, 136, 160, 172, 183, 270, 271, 284, 285, 294, 295

wellbeing/well-being 18, 29, 36, 42, 44, 62, 115, 126, 137, 150, 156, 201, 255, 276

women x, 2, 21, 88, 94, 103

World Health Organisation (WHO) 18, 36